ISRAELI JUDAISM

Studies of Israeli Society

VOLUME VII

The Sociology of Religion in Israel

ISRAELI JUDAISM

Publication Series of the Israel Sociological Society

EDITED BY

Shlomo Deshen
Charles S. Liebman
Moshe Shokeid

SERIES EDITOR

Ernest Krausz

Studies of
Israeli Society

VOLUME VII

Transaction Publishers
New Brunswick (U.S.A.) and London (U.K.)

ISSN: 0734-4937
ISBN: 1-56000-178-X (cloth); 1-56000-762-1 (paper)
Printed in the United States of America.

Contents

Acknowledgments   ix

Sources   xi

PART I Introduction

1. Editorial Introduction: The Study of Religion in Israeli Social Science   1
   Shlomo Deshen

2. Sociological Analyses of Religion   19
   Stephen Sharot

3. Dimensions of Jewish Religiosity   33
   Peri Kedem

PART II Political Dimensions of Israeli Judaism

4. Jewish Civilization: Approaches to Problems of Israeli Society   63
   Shmuel N. Eisenstadt

5. State Ceremonies of Israel: Remembrance Day and Independence Day   75
   Don Handelman and Elihu Katz

6. Religious Adherence and Political Attitudes   87
   Yochanan Peres

7. Religion in the Israeli Discourse on the Arab-Jewish Conflict   107
   Shlomo Deshen

PART III Ultra-Orthodoxy

8. Life Tradition and Book Tradition in the Development of Ultraorthodox Judaism   127
   Menachem Friedman

9. Ultraorthodox Jewish Women   149
   Tamar El-Or

PART IV Nationalist Orthodoxy

10. Religious Kibbutzim: Judaism and Modernization   173
     Aryei Fishman

11. A Mystic-Messianic Interpretation of Modern Israeli
     History: The Six-Day War in the Religious Culture
     of Gush Emunim   197
     Gideon Aran

PART V The Sephardic Pattern

12. The Religiosity of Middle Eastern Jews   213
     Moshe Shokeid

13. Secularization and the Diminishing Decline of
     Religion   239
     *Hannah Ayalon, Eliezer Ben-Raphael,
     and Stephen Sharot*

14. Saints' Sanctuaries in Development Towns   255
     Eyal Ben-Ari and Yoram Bilu

15. The Religion of Elderly Oriental Jewish Women   285
     Susan Sered

PART VI Secularism and Reform

16. Hanukkah and the Myth of the Maccabees in Ideology
     and in Society   303
     Eliezer Don-Yehiya

17. Death Customs in a Non-Religious Kibbutz   323
     Nissan Rubin

18. Americans in the Israeli Reform and Conservative
     Denominations   335
     Ephraim Tabory and Bernard Lazerwitz

19. Religion and Democracy in Israel   347
     Charles S. Liebman

Selected Bibliography   367
     Shlomo Deshen with Sigal Goldin

About the Authors   383

Acknowledgments

We are thankful to Ernest Krausz who, in his role on the Editorial Board of the Series, was particularly encouraging and instrumental in obtaining financial support for the volume from the Bar-Ilan University Schnitzer Foundation. Also Yochanan Peres, who at the time we did most of the work was President of the Israel Sociological Society, was very helpful. We share responsibility for the selection of contributions, and entrusted Shlomo Deshen with writing the introduction. Comments on that chapter by Shmuel Eisenstadt, Nissan Rubin, and Stephen Sharot, are gratefully acknowledged.

Shlomo Deshen
Charles S. Liebman
Moshe Shokeid

Sources

We wish to gratefully acknowledge the permission to use copyrighted material granted by journals and publishers.

Chapter 2 is reprinted from *Sociological Analysis* 51 (1990): 63-76.

Ch. 3 is reprinted from *Tradition, Innovation, Conflict: Jewishness and Judaism in Contemporary Israel*, edited by Z. Sobel and B. Beit-Hallahmi, Albany, N.Y.: State University of New York Press, 1991, pp. 251-272. By permission of State University of New York Press. © 1991.

Ch. 4 is reprinted from *Jewish Civilization: the Jewish Historical Experience in a Comparative Perspective*, by S.N. Eisenstadt, Albany, N.Y.: State University of New York Press, 1992, pp. 199-210. By permission of State University of New York Press. © 1992

Ch. 5 is reprinted from *Models and Mirrors: Towards an Anthropology of Public Events*, by D. Handelman, Cambridge: Cambridge University Press, 1990, pp. 191-201.

Ch. 6 is reprinted from *Sociological Papers* (Bar-Ilan University), October 1992.

Ch. 7 is reprinted from *Beyond Boundaries*, edited by G. Palsson, Oxford: Berg Publishers, 1993, pp. 58-74.

Ch. 8 is reprinted from *Judaism Viewed from Within and From Without: Anthropological Studies*, edited by H.E. Goldberg, Albany, N.Y.: State University of New York Press, 1987, pp. 235-255. By permission of State University of New York Press. © 1987.

Ch. 9 is reprinted from *Educated and Ignorant: Ultraorthodox Jewish Women and Their World*, by T. El-Or, Boulder Co.: Lynne Rienner, 1994, pp. 89-133. Copyright © 1994 by Lynne Rienner Publishers, Inc. Used with permission of the Publisher.

Part I

Introduction

Part 1

Introduction

1

Editorial Introduction
The Study of Religion in Israeli Social Science

Shlomo Deshen

Beginning in 1980, the Israel Sociological Society has regularly issued selected collections of its members' research on Israeli topics. The topics covered have been important ones: Israeli politics, kibbutz life, ethnicity, education, the sociology of medicine, women's studies. Still it is remarkable, that only with this, the seventh volume, has the association turned its attention to religion, a topic which for many years now has been highly salient in both Israeli affairs and in the wider Middle Eastern context. The ever-increasing presence of religious extremism and activism has made the relevance of the topic, for an understanding of contemporary Israel—and much of the world generally—inescapable.

The reason for the rather belated concern with religion is rooted in matters that lie at the heart of Israeli culture and society. Modern Israeli society was founded by European immigrant pioneers of the early decades of this century, who mostly had a marked secularist, even anti-religious bias. This disposition had ramifications in many areas of life, and even in Israeli social science. Consideration of the academic background of Israeli sociology and anthropology—the fact that no less a spiritual figure than Martin Buber (1878-1965) filled the chair of sociology at the Hebrew University in Jerusalem for the duration of a decade in the late 1930s and 40s—underlines the strength of the bias. Buber had distinguished students, and was instrumental in raising the first generation of professional sociologists in Israel. One of them in particular, the late Yonina Talmon-Garber (1923-1966), pioneered the teaching of

1

sociology of religion at what was then Israel's sole university. Yonina, as she was known by all, was an outstanding teacher, and it is in fond memory of her that we dedicate this volume. But remarkably, only a few of her numerous students and colleagues developed creatively in the field of sociology of religion. Despite the potential for the development of the field in Israel, nearly all Israeli sociologists of the next generation developed in other directions, along with the conceptions and values of Israelis of their time, of their background and social ambience (the main exception is Aryei Fishman).

Even more remarkable is the history of Israeli social anthropology. Ever since the late 1950s the latter developed vigorously, because the salience of the so-called "Oriental" immigrants fired the imagination of many scholars, who were disposed to delve into the seemingly exotic. Around a dozen anthropologists were active in Israel during the period of the late 1950s to the early 1970s and they produced books and numerous papers. Besides these scholars, many foreign graduate students conducted fieldwork in Israel during those years for their Ph.D. dissertations. Given the strong interest in anthropology generally in issues of culture one would have expected this research effort to lead to a major illumination of religious matters among Israeli Sephardim. But in fact nothing of the sort occurred. Most of the anthropologists of that period were as disinterested in religion as were the sociologists. The main exceptions at the time were the two anthropologists who now figure among the editors of this volume. Although during the 1960s and 1970s the salience of religious extremism, in Israel and elsewhere in the Middle East, became glaring, Israeli social scientists confronted the new reality only rarely in their research and teaching. As late as the mid 1970s most introductory university courses in sociology and anthropology in Israel had highly positivist and functionalist orientations, and to this day they feature only little religio-cultural material. The social scientists of that time were probably uncomfortable personally with religious phenomena.

After the hiatus of the period during which most sociologists and anthropologists in Israel had little interest in religion came a development in Israeli social science that is reflected in the present collection. It is illustrated by Jeffrey Alexander (1992) in a fragment of intellectual biography of the senior Israeli sociologist, Shmuel Eisenstadt (who like Talmon studied with Buber). Most of the twenty-three scholars, creative in sociology of religion, whose papers compose this anthology, matured in the late 1960s and thereafter, eight of them within the past decade. Quite a few were trained outside Israel, in the United States and Britain, and emigrated to Israel as mature scholars. Our collection reflects elements of intellectual and social marginality. While our contributors evince awareness of the centrality of religion, along with the prevailing contemporary theories and intuitions of social scientists of late twentieth-century persuasions, it is notable that only three or four of them specialize in the sociological study of religion. For the majority of our authors the sociology of religion is not their predominant field of research.

The authors are notable on another count: about half of them are practicing orthodox Jews. That is a much higher proportion than the number of people of that category among Israeli social scientists generally. This datum parallels the very high representation of women among scholars in the study of women and gender (as evidenced by Volume Six in this series). It suggests that, like women's studies, sociology of religion attracts scholars whose personal motivations and interests in the field are obvious; religious studies and women's studies do not seem to be fields that attract primarily for rarefied scholarly reasons. The social profiles of sociologists in gender and in religious studies, might be taken as evidence that these fields are based on endeavors that are rooted foremost in personal existential problems of the scholars, that they are fields of scholarship that are highly relevant to ongoing life.

The authors of this collection are marked by heterogeneity in terms of academic subdisciplines. About a third are sociologists of a quantitative bent, another third are anthropologists who engage in observation and ethnography, and the remainder are sociologists and political scientists with a predilection for textual and historical analysis. Again, this heterogeneity can be viewed positively, as such lack of an institutionalized disciplinary center is sometimes the foundation for work of interest and originality. Finally, we note that only four women figure among our authors, underrepresenting the number of women in Israeli sociology and anthropology. While there are particular local factors that account for the marginality of the sociology of religion in Israel, the subdiscipline is in fact somewhat insulated in sociology in general (Beckford 1985).

The profile of scholars that has emerged in our presentation of Israeli sociology of religion is of course an artifact of editorial policy, and that requires explication. First, we were constrained by the general guide-lines of the "Studies in Israeli Society" series, as determined by the edi-torial board of the series. The aim is to make accessible widely scattered material by Israeli sociologists and anthropologists on a particular ma-jor topic, and the volumes aim to be collective "state of the art" state-ments. As a matter of policy the volumes include only materials that have been previously published in English in journals and books issued under academic auspices, and that were peer-reviewed in one way or another for those publications. The series is thus an avenue of collation for work that has already passed a hurdle of academic scrutiny. The claim to originality of the series lies in the presentation of the material in a selective and systematic way. Each of the volumes is intended to serve as a baseline from which to contemplate the future of its particular field.

In this volume on religion, more than in previous ones, the editors felt limited by considerations of space. The volume is slimmer than others in the series, and we eliminated papers that we would have liked to include. For instance, there is a considerable amount of research in the field of Israeli Judaism by educational sociologists and social psycholo-gists. That work seeks mostly to elucidate questions of education and of general behavior, which do not lie at the crux of our present concern with religious belief and practice. We have therefore not included it, but we do take note of it in the bibliography. Further, we aim in this collec-tion to focus on recent material; therefore we only include papers that were published after 1983, a decade prior to the time of editing. The volume aims to represent the state of art in its field, but as the organ of the Israel Sociological Society it is also an outlet for suitable work of as many members of the Society as possible. Certain scholars are more prolific than others, and more of their work warranted inclusion. But in aiming to strike a happy medium between our various editorial guide-lines we limited authors to one contribution only, and we have favored papers by multiple authors.

The main concerns of sociology of religion in Israel, are outlined in the detailed review by Stephen Sharot (chapter 2). The next introductory chap-ter by Peri Kedem (chapter 3) details the basic concepts that pertain to Israeli Judaism, and is aimed at forging methodologically appropriate in-struments for its measurement, following previous attempts of this kind such as Aaron Antonovsky (1963), and Asher Arian (1973), and most re-cently Levy *et al.* (1993). Islam and other non-Jewish religions have hardly been studied by Israeli social scientists, despite the fact that Muslim fundamentalism has assumed a major role in the region ever since the late 1970s. Indeed, until very recently there were virtually no studies dealing with the religious behavior of Israeli Arabs (see now Rekhess 1993). We do have studies of some small and relatively unimportant denominations, on the Christian Armenians of Jerusalem who were studied by Victor Azarya (1984, 1988-9), and on the Bahai's of Acre who were studied by Erik Cohen (1972). The avoidance by scholars of research fields where mainline activities can be observed is remarkable, and we notice it also below in our review of the study of Judaism.

The uneven overall research coverage of religions in Israel does have an advantage. Since the available sociology of religion research is primarily on Judaism it drove us, in the compilation of this collection, to focus onto the particular features of the field as presented in extant research, namely its Jewishness and its Israeliness. This leads to conceptualizing the religious phenomena on hand in a way that highlights the particularity of Israeli Jewish phenomena, through the concept "Israeli Judaism." The concept assumes that Judaism in Israel is different, in various nuanced ways, from Judaism elsewhere. This assumption is founded on a combination of existing information and of hypotheses, and it figures in a recent comparative study of American and Israeli Judaism (Liebman and Cohen 1990, chapters 6-7).

Our focus, Israeli Judaism, leads us away from a related, but distinct field of inquiry, that of the general sociology and anthropology of Judaism. That field has a distinguished history, going back to the late nineteenth century, stemming from dual sources in anthropology and in sociology. Anthropologists, starting with William Robertson-Smith (1889), James Frazer (1918), and later Raphael Patai (1964), Edmund Leach (1969), Mary Douglas (1966, 1993) and others, developed research focused mostly on biblical texts. These studies had strong cultural emphases to them, largely divorced from the social reality of the particular people who created and later related to the texts. The research tradition of anthropology of Judaism is carried on, in the contemporary work of Howard Eilberg-Schwartz (1990), Harvey Goldberg (1987, 1990a, 1990b), Nissan Rubin (1990, 1992, 1993), Joelle Bahloul (1983), Ruth Fredman (1981), Shlomo Deshen (1979b), and many others, whose research has now branched out, beyond biblical studies, to rabbinic texts and to medieval folk custom.

Similarly, sociologists have focused on ancient Judaism, starting with Max Weber (1952), continuing through the work of such scholars as Werner Sombart (1952), Shmuel Eisenstadt (1992), Aryei Fishman (1992), Stephen Sharot (1982), and others. The latter have branched out to later historical periods, but they have the common aim of making sociological statements about Judaism as a whole. The most elaborate and insightful research of the sociology of Judaism school is that of Jacob Katz (1961, 1989) and his numerous followers, whose prolific work, albeit, has strong affinity with that of social historians. Suffice it to state that social science study of both these genres—the anthropological and the sociological—is beyond the purview of this volume, which is devoted exclusively to work on contemporary Israel. However, where possible, we have favored the inclusion of papers that are inspired by the scholarly traditions of the sociology and anthropology of Judaism. Such, particularly are the contributions that comprise chapters four (Eisenstadt), eight (Friedman), ten (Fishman), and seventeen (Rubin).

The value of the concept "Israeli Judaism" lies in its potential for researchers to recognize particular phenomena, which they might otherwise overlook, or to which they might otherwise be insensitive. This value can be tested by the extent to which the concept orders and illuminates various phenomena. Accordingly, the organizing principle of the present anthology is a typology of variants of Israeli Judaism. According to this typology Israeli Judaism is conceived as rooted in disparate historical responses to conditions that developed in nineteenth-century diaspora countries. Immigration brought these responses to pre-state Israel, where local conditions molded them further. Three variants were developed by the Ashkenazic immigrants, ultra-orthodoxy, nationalist-orthodoxy and secular nationalism (so-called Israeli "secularism"). All three religio-cultural patterns are recent, nineteenth-century and early twentieth-century, creations and manifest various symbolic innovations—despite the clamor of the orthodox to the contrary. Similarly, all three patterns manifest traditional symbolic content—despite the clamor of many secular people to the contrary. All are characterized by high, virtually strident, ideological awareness.

The fourth variant of Israeli Judaism is that of immigrants from Muslim countries. The latter are often popularly termed "Sephardim," scions of medieval Spanish Jewry. In fact, the background of contemporary Middle Eastern and Mediterranean Jews is far more complex than the term "Sephardim" implies. Its usage reflects a simplified and superficial view of reality. We nevertheless use the term as the issues involved in the terminology are not crucial to our present concern. The central point from our perspective is that, due again to particular historical circumstances, the Sephardim evince considerable continuity with the past, together with a comparatively low level of ideological articulation. The four variants of Israeli Judaism are characterized by different configurations of symbols and by different ramifications of social and political activities. This typology of Israeli Judaism (for elaboration see Deshen 1978, 1979a, 1982) has the virtue of usefulness in conceptualizing religious phenomena at a relatively low-level of abstraction, down to particular communities, social circles, and even individuals. Parts two to five of the material of this volume are organized accordingly.

But for an understanding of the role of Judaism at the collective societal and state levels more abstract and general conceptualizations are needed. Shmuel Eisenstadt (1992) has written about the principled political anarchism that inheres in Judaism historically, and of its continuation in latter-day Israel. He has analyzed various internal struggles of Israeli society in terms of collective identity, as challenged by the dual forces of anarchic politics rooted in Judaism on the one hand, and the solidarity of small particular social sectors on the other. The selection by Eisenstadt (chapter four) permits a glance at work in "the sociology of Judaism" tradition, and places the contemporary situation in a context of antiquity that is informed by Eisenstadt's theory of "axial age civilizations" (Eisenstadt 1982).

Another general conceptualization of Israeli Judaism, Judaism as "a civil religion," has been formulated by Charles Liebman and Eliezer Don-Yehiya (1983). According to this the crux of religion in Israel is the memory of the Holocaust and the political and existential lessons that people draw from it. Liebman and Don-Yehiya note three stages in the development of Israeli civil religion. At first, in the pre-state period it self-consciously confronted, and to some extent rejected, the tradition, but formulated its symbols in terms of this rejection. The link to the tradition was maintained by the seriousness which it accorded traditional symbols, as it deliberately transformed them in order to adapt them to new needs and values. The second stage characterized the period from the creation of the state in 1948 until the mid-sixties. At this stage the civil religion was composed of a variety of strands reflecting different sets of symbols and values, some of which were affirmed while others were ignored, rather than confronted and rejected as they were in the earlier period. At the third stage which characterized the civil religion from 1967 until the present, the entire tradition is nominally affirmed. The civil religion is penetrated by traditional symbols which are diffused throughout the culture, and reinterpreted so that new values may be imposed upon them. Nominally, the attitude toward tradition is positive. The symbols are reinterpreted without admitting to their reinterpretation. Such an approach is only possible with a decline of secular belief systems on the one hand (systems which might compete with the tradition for the nominal allegiance of the population), and on the other hand, an ignorance of the tradition which allows for its widespread, unselfconscious, reinterpretation.

Part two of the collection concentrates on the discussion of Israeli religion at the level of general beliefs and their political ramifications. The contribution of Handelman and Katz (chapter five) illustrates the most salient manifestation of Israel's civil religion, the complex of state ceremonies that marks the late spring, and which includes Holocaust Day, Remembrance Day (for fallen soldiers), and Independence Day. The contribution of Yochanan Peres (chapter six) reflects the tradition of quantitative research. Peres addresses the issue of the correlation of various levels of religious belief and practice with particular political convictions. His argument implies that the steadily hardening commitment of orthodox voters to right-wing policies entails a weakening of their coalition bargaining position, and hence might lead to important long-term changes in the Israeli political map. In chapter seven Deshen traces broader ramifications of these trends in the crucial area of the Jewish-Arab conflict. The latter has salient religious elements and their analysis leads to practical recommendations. The overall praxis record of sociology and anthropology in Israel is not very impressive, and sociology of religion is no exception. This chapter reflects an attempt to apply sociological insight of the field of religion to what can only be considered as the single most important issue in Israeli life.

Part three is the first of the sections devoted to a particular variant of Israeli Judaism, ultra-orthodoxy. Despite the great salience of Israelis of this stripe to all observers of the Israeli scene, comparatively little sociological work has been devoted to them. The field is dominated by Menachem Friedman, whose work, of a general sociological nature, is strongly informed by historical and textual research. Also an American scholar, Samuel Heilman (1992), has done pertinent fieldwork in Jerusalem. The ultra-orthodox tend to remain aloof of other Israelis and maintain a coherent and highly articulate religio-symbolic system, that is more or less foreign to outsiders. Even to the few social scientists who command the pertinent skills, the field of the ultra-orthodox is not very amenable. These scholars are often personally involved in controversies revolving on ultra-orthodoxy and therefore, they lack the kind of detachment that is a pre-requisite for good sociological research. Hence they usually avoid research in this area.

Friedman's contribution (chapter eight) is one out of a corpus that includes *inter alia* work on religious community structure (1986) and on ultra-orthodox theology (1989). The particular virtue of the present selection is that it concerns concrete religious practice. Charles Liebman (in press) studied ultra-orthodox publications and uncovered the change of attitude that led the ultra-orthodox to join the ruling government coalition in 1977, after decades of principled opposition. He demonstrates how that shift is rooted in religious conceptions about the place of Jews in the world of nations and of the role of divinity in the order of nations. Chapter nine consists of excerpts from an ethnography by Tamar El-Or on the adult education of hassidic women (El-Or 1994, chapter 3). It focuses on the new phenomenon of religious women being highly literate in traditional Jewish learning while at the same time maintaining a religiously motivated radically subordinate stance vis-à-vis their menfolk. Our selection is composed of four sections that were joined in the original chapter by additional material, but because of considerations of space we had to shorten the original. Despite the fact that ultra-orthodoxy is only represented by these two chapters, we have highlighted them as a separate part of the anthology. We underline thereby the importance of the subject, in terms of a "state of the art" summation of our field.

Part four reflects research on another major category of Israeli Jews, the nationalist orthodox. Research here, like in the previous section, is of an ethnographic-historical nature. The two papers of this section are devoted to the most salient and colorful manifestations of nationalist-orthodoxy, "the religious kibbutz" movement and "the Gush Emunim" movement. The former, discussed by Fishman (chapter ten), is a religious variant of the pioneering socialist movement that was dominant in Israeli polity in the early years of the state. Gush Emunim is a right-wing movement, that spearheaded the Jewish settlement movement in the West Bank and Gaza. It was particularly active in the 1960s and 1970s, and has aroused some analytical debate among sociologists: in the contribution to this volume by Gideon Aran (chapter eleven) Gush Emunim is seen primarily as a messianic movement (see also Aviad, 1984), but it has also been viewed with greater emphasis on socio-political elements (Deshen 1982). The two movements, while having much in common in terms of religious practice and overall life style, are radically opposed in their social policies. The people of the Gush Emunim movement and those who follow their ideals, exhibit much religious vitality coupled with highly controversial politics. It is for that reason that Gush Emunim has aroused research interest, and some of the studies are mentioned in the appended bibliography. The kibbutz movement is modern Israel's prime claim for a place in any good list of basic readings in comparative ethnography. In that context the religious kibbutz movement is a particularly interesting phenomenon. Even more than the general kibbutz movement it intersects several basic problems in human organization, some of which Fishman addresses in his contribution. This paper provides some of the socio-intellectual background for the emergence of the religious kibbutz movement, and serves as an overall introduction to nationalist-orthodoxy.

There is a considerable amount of work that pertains to nationalist-orthodoxy, by education researchers and social psychologists, such as Yehuda Amir, Mordechai Bar-Lev, Avraham Leslau, Joseph Schwartzwald, Leonard Weller, and others, to which, for considerations of space, we regretfully draw attention only in the bibliography. The research of Bar-Lev is particularly notable in providing quantitative information on the education and religiosity of nationalist-orthodox Israelis (Krausz and Bar-Lev 1978). The fact that our collection does not include an account of the religiosity of the numerous nationalist-orthodox people, who happen not to adhere to the two particular movements represented here, reflects a lacuna in research coverage.

Part five, devoted to the religiosity of Israelis of Sephardic, Middle-Eastern background, is the relatively richest and most comprehensive of the sections of this collection. Though this section lacks the historical-documentary dimension which we have in the previous ones, it reflects the considerable bulk of material produced by anthropologists in particular, attracted to study the immigrants from Muslim countries. These scholars have included American and European-based researchers besides Israelis, and some of their work also figures in the bibliography. The significance of the contribution of Moshe Shokeid (chapter twelve), the first of three ethnographic chapters in this section, lies in the fact that it deals with an ordinary urban center, lacking any overt spatial or ethnic insulation , in which we see how elements of Sephardic Jewish tradition remain vital. There is also some work of quantitative nature on immigrants from Morocco and Iraq specifically, presented in the contribution by Hannah Ayalon, Eliezer Ben-Rafael, and Stephen Sharot (chapter thirteen). The very different chapters by Ayalon *et al.* and by Shokeid, the one quantitative and the other ethnographic, document the thesis as to continuing religiosity and traditionalism among Middle Eastern Israelis. The data fly in the face of secularization theorists of the past.

The Eyal Ben-Ari and Yoram Bilu contribution (chapter fourteen) reflects a considerable body of work on hagiolatric pilgrimages and saint veneration, particularly of Moroccan immigrants, which anthropologists have studied (such as Shokeid 1974, 1979). Alex Weingrod (1990), and folklorist Issachar Ben-Ami (1981) have contributed to this endeavor, but much of the latter's work is not available in English. The religious innovation of hagiolatric pilgrimage is of a salience and significance on par with the forementioned innovations of the nationalist-orthodox. Finally, in this part of the collection, Susan Sered (chapter fifteen) analyzes the religiosity of aged Sephardic women. This work exposes a variant of Judaism that was never documented prior to the recently developed sensitivity in social science to the lives of women. Sered's research dovetails recent work by feminist historians of Judaism such as Chava Weissler and Marion Kaplan (in Baskin 1991) as well as El-Or on hasidic women. Her attention to a particular segment of Israeli Judaism underlines the overall sketchiness of Israeli sociological work in the field of religion. Indeed, we now have this work on aged Sephardic women, but that arouses awareness to the fact that we lack work on the religion of other women of various social groups and categories, on people of various particular sub-ethnic categories, on people of various residential localities, on particular hasidic sects, and so forth.

In part six we aim to represent the vast and amorphous category of Israelis who term themselves "secular" (*hiloni*), and often, rather incongruously, "traditional" (*masorti*). Many, perhaps most, of the people of the secular category maintain numerous practices of tradition (such as holding the Passover feast, restricting normal activities on Yom Kippur, celebrating rites of passage, and they practice circumcision universally). But at the same time Israelis of this category recoil from much of the culture of orthodoxy, its institutions, and in particular the rabbinate. So-called secular Israelis remain a fascinating and complex phenomenon, which has been explored only superficially, mainly in the context of general surveys. A preliminary approach to "secular religion" was attempted by the late Ilana Shelah (1975) in an in-house Hebrew monograph, and Shokeid, in a study of Israeli emigrants of secular background in New York (1988, ch. 6), has presented a general ethnographic portrait of their culture and beliefs. He revealed their malaise at encountering the majority of American Jews whose ethnic identification is dependent on some sort of engagement with Jewish religious communal life. Secular Israelis constitute a vast category of people and their doings are legion. The ideologies that attracted them in the past, militant socialism and principled secularism, have largely lost their resonance, and there is currently much turmoil in their beliefs and values. The chapters that we have selected for part five are illuminating, but limited in coverage.

The paper by Don-Yehiya (chapter sixteen) analyzes the phenomenon of reinterpretation of the traditional festivals, which was practiced particularly in pre-State times and in the kibbutzim. Vestiges of the phenomenon remain to this day, and they arguably constitute the most colorful and salient feature of Israeli secularism. Nissan Rubin (chapter seventeen) studies the comparable phenomenon in rites of passage of the individual. Elements of traditional mourning rites in particular, are widely practiced among secular people, hence they are important venues for insight into this kind of Israeli Judaism.

One ramification of the turmoil in Israeli secularism is the attraction of many people to cults such as Transcendental Meditation, and the popularity of astrology. Aside from a psychological overview of these phenomena, which dismisses them as "nonsensology" (Beit-Hallahmy 1992), little substantial research is available. Another notable, but quantitatively less important, development is the emergence of innovative religious movements, similar to the Reform and Conservative movements of American Jewry. The movements have indeed taken root in Israel, but contrary to the wishful thinking of many American activists of these movements, their growth has not been impressive. Moreover, some of the growth that has occurred can be attributed to American immigration only. Despite these caveats the Israeli Reform and Conservative movements are a phenomenon of the Israeli religious scene and warrant our attention.

Most Israelis who are attracted to the Reform and Conservative movements are former secularists, hence the movements should be viewed as a response to the religious concerns of people of the secular category. However, some individuals of the Israeli Reform and Conservative movements also come from the kind of Sephardic traditional background we saw earlier. The complexity of the movements thus remains to be explored. Ephraim Tabory and Bernard Lazerwitz (chapter eighteen) examine the nature of Israeli Reform in the context of the sub-ethnic origins of the members. The interface of religion and ethnicity is an important topic in Israeli sociology, and has been studied particularly in the field of Middle Eastern immigrants (Deshen 1970, Ben-Rafael and Sharot 1991, and many others). The topic is also treated in this collection by Shokeid (chapter twelve), and the two selections dovetail. Despite the virtues of existing research, the religious element *per se* of the innovative movements remains to be explored.

The attenuation of ideologies, and the general existential turmoil of the past three decades, have had additional ramifications. One of them is the movement of "return" (*teshuva*) to Judaism, which entails a shift from an irreligious style of life to the life style of the ultra-orthodox enclaves in Jerusalem and Benei-Berak. Relative to the sensational attention that the media have devoted to the phenomenon, I have the impression that quantitatively the movement is not so important. But the Return phenomenon remains an element of the culture and religion of Israeli secularists, and as such it warrants our attention. The Return movement pertains also to the Israeli Sephardim, since many Returnees come out of the particular ambience of the latter. Also, the movement pertains to the nationalist-orthodox variant, since many young people of that background have shifted towards the ultra-orthodox. There are thus three variants of the Return movement which are phenomenologically distinct, despite their superficial similarity. Research on the movement has been done mainly on young American students who come to Israel to explore Judaism, and often return to America (Aviad 1983, Shaffir 1983, 1991). But those students reflect a phenomenon that pertains primarily to American Judaism. Work on them is therefore tangential to our volume with its focus on Israeli Judaism. Also there is work by sociologists of education that addresses itself, to some extent, to the question of the social roots of the Return movement (i.e., Yogev and El-Dor 1987).

The people of the kibbutz, and religious Return and Reform movements, are often ideologically articulate, and therefore they constitute the most accessible parts of the field of secular Israelis. But they represent small-scale phenomena, virtually on the fringes of latter-day Israeli society. In general, secular Israelis are not so overt in their beliefs and commitments. Hence the great difficulties that the main part of the field of secular Israelis presents to social scientists. Therefore that field as a whole constitutes a glaring sociological lacuna, and we hope, by underlining this emphatically, to encourage scholars to expend their curiosity there.

The paper by Charles Liebman (chapter nineteen), on religion and democracy, concludes the collection. It is based on the kind of descriptive materials on the major configurations of Israeli Judaism that compose most of the contributions to this volume, and builds on them. The nature and future of Israeli democracy touches on most facets of Israeli life—material, political, cultural, internal and external—and Israeli Judaism, as the paper shows, is a potent factor in the vicissitudes of democracy. The concluding chapter also reflects on one of the theses that inform the overall conception of this volume, the idea of variety in Israeli Judaism. Liebman argues that the developments of recent years indicate a decrease in the differences between the variants. And, importantly, as Israeli Judaism becomes more homogeneous, it evolves in ways that oppose it in general to American Judaism. The volume ends appropriately with speculations about possible future developments, and it remains to be seen which of these avenues, if any, will be taken by Israeli Jews in the years ahead.

Our overall review of Israeli social research in the field of Judaism reveals a feature that we also noted in regard to the field of non-Jewish religions in Israel. Namely, that much of the research has a tendency to skirt mainline arenas, where lies the action of the majority of the population. Also in terms of problems studied, the overall impression that the research leaves is that there are significant lacuna. While the extant research does enlighten us on the ways that Israeli Jews contend with their collective culture, myths, religio-national beliefs, and communal celebrations, much remains to be explored as to how Israeli Jews confront the great existential questions of their lives, as humans in general and as latter-day Jews in particular. Only on the religious symbolizing of some of the life-cycle transitions, giving birth and dying, is there a little material (represented by Rubin, chapter seventeen; see also Abramovitch 1991, and recently Sered 1993). The research desiderata pertain to the most universal and poignant levels of culture: how people grapple religiously, or ideologically, with problems of the individual, issues of death, pain, fear, yearning, frustration and want.

The collection closes with a list of predominantly English-language publications on the sociology of Israeli Judaism. We include references to material published since 1970, and also references to studies in psychology, history, and political science, that are valuable to sociology of religion. However, we have remained selective here too, and included only references to material that, we feel, might be directly useful for future sociological studies of Israeli Judaism.

References

Abramovitch, H. "The Jerusalem Funeral as a Microcosm of the 'Mismeeting' Between Religious and Secular Israelis." in *Jewishness and Judaism in Contemporary Israel*, 71-101, eds. Z. Sobel and B. Beit-Hallahrni. Albany: State University of N.Y. Press, 1991.

Alexander, J.C. "The Fragility of Progress: the Interpretation of the Turn Toward Meaning in Eisenstadt's Later Work." *Acta Sociologica* 35 (1992): 85-94.

Antonovsky, A. "Social-Political Attitudes in Israel." *Amot 6* (1963): 11-22 (Hebrew).

Arian, A. *The Choosing People: Voting Behavior in Israel.* Cleveland: Case Western Reserve University Press, 1973.

Aviad, J. *Return To Judaism: Religious Renewal in Israel.* Chicago: University of Chicago Press, 1983.

Aviad, J. "The Contemporary Israeli Pursuit of the Millennium." *Religion 14* (1984): 199-222.

Azarya, V. *The Armenian Quarter of Jerusalem: Urban Life Behind Monastery Walls.* Berkeley: University of California Press, 1984.

Azarya, V. "Armenians in Jerusalem: A Look Behind the Walls of the St. James Monastery." *Israel Social Science Research 6* (1988-9): 24-39.

Bahloul, J. *Le Culte de la Table Dressée: Rites et traditions de la table juive algérienne.* Paris: Metailie, 1983.

Baskin, J.R. (ed.) *Jewish Women in Historical Perspective.* Detroit: Wayne State University Press, 1991.

Beckford, J. "The Insulation and Isolation of the Sociology of Religion." *Sociological Analysis 46* (1985): 347-354.

Beit-Hallahmi, B. *Despair and Deliverance: Private Salvation in Contemporary Israel.* Albany: State University of N.Y Press, 1992.

Ben-Ami, I. "The Folk-Veneration of Saints Among Moroccan Jews." In *Studies in Judaism and Islam,* 283–344, eds. S. Morag, I. Ben-Ami and N.A. Stillman. Jerusalem: Magnes Press, 1981.

Ben-Rafael, E. and Sharot, S. *Ethnicity, Religion, and Class in Israeli Society.* Cambridge: Cambridge University Press, 1991.

Cohen, E. "The Baha'i Community of Acre." *Folklore Research Center Studies 3* (1972): 119–141.

Deshen, S. *Immigrant Voters in Israel: Parties and Congregations in an Israeli Election Campaign.* Manchester: Manchester University Press, 1970.

Deshen, S. "Israeli Judaism: Introduction to the Major Patterns." *International Journal of Middle East Studies 9* (1978): 141–169.

Deshen, S. "The Judaism of Middle-Eastern Immigrants." *Judaism Quarterly 13* (1979a): 98–119.

Deshen, S. "The Kol Nidre Enigma: An Anthropological View of the Day of Atonement Liturgy." *Ethnology 18* (1979b): 121–133.

Deshen, S. "Israel: Searching for Identity." In *Religion and Society in Asia and the Middle East,* 85–118, ed. C. Caldarola. Berlin: Mouton, 1982.

Douglas, M. *Purity and Danger.* London: Routledge and Kegan Paul, 1966.

Douglas, M. "The Forbidden Animals in Leviticus." *Journal for the Study of the Old Testament 59* (1993): 3–23

Eilberg-Schwartz, H. *The Savage in Judaism: An Anthropology of Israelite Religion and Ancient Judaism.* Bloomington: Indiana University Press, 1990.

Eisenstadt, S.N. "The Axial Age: The Emergence of Transcendental Visions and the Rise of Clerics." *European Journal of Sociology 23* (1982): 294–314.

Eisenstadt, S.N. *Jewish Civilization: The Jewish Historical Experience in a Comparative Perspective.* Albany, N.Y.: State University of N.Y. Press, 1992.

El-Or, T. *Educated and Ignorant: Ultraorthodox Jewish Women and their World.* Boulder, Co.: Lynne Rienner, 1994.

Fishman, A. *Judaism and Modernization on the Religious Kibbutz.* Cambridge: Cambridge University Press, 1992.

Frazer, J.G. *Folklore in the Old Testament.* London, 1918.

Fredman, R.G. *The Passover Seder: Afikoman in Exile.* Philadelphia: University of Pennsylvania Press, 1981.

Friedman, M. "Haredim Confront the Modern City." *Studies in Contemporary Jewry 2* (1986): 3–18.

Friedman, M. "The State of Israel as a Theological Dilemma." In *The Israeli State and Society: Boundaries and Frontiers,* 165–216, ed. B. Kimmerling. Albany: State University of N.Y Press, 1989.

Goldberg, H. (ed.) *Judaism Viewed from Within and from Without.* Albany: State University of N.Y Press, 1987.

Goldberg, H. "Anthropology and the Study of Traditional Jewish Society." *Association for Jewish Studies Review 15* (1990): 1–22.

Goldberg, H. "The Zohar in Southern Morocco: A Study in the Ethnography of Texts." *History of Religion 29* (1990): 233–258.

Heilman, S.C. *Defenders of the Faith: Inside Ultra-Orthodox Jewry.* N.Y: Schocken, 1992.

Katz, J. *The Shabbes Goy: A Study in Halakhic Flexibility.* Philadelphia: Jewish Publication Society, 1989.

Katz, J. *Tradition and Crisis: Jewish Society at the End of the Middle Ages.* Hanover, N.H.: New England Universities Press, 1993 (1961).

Krausz, E. and Bar-Lev, M. "Varieties of Orthodox Religious Behavior: A Case Study of Yeshiva High School Graduates in Israel." *Jewish Journal of Sociology 20* (1978): 59-74.

Leach, E.R. *Genesis as Myth and Other Essays.* London: Cape, 1969.

Levi, S., Lewinson, H. and Katz, E. *Beliefs, Observances, and Social Interaction Among Israeli Jews.* Jerusalem: Louis Guttman Israel Institute of Applied Social Research, 1993.

Liebman, C.S. "The Haredi Response to the Yom Kippur War." *YIVO Annual* (in press).

Liebman, C.S. and Cohen, S.M. *Two Worlds of Judaism: The Israeli and American Experiences.* New Haven: Yale University Press, 1990.

Liebman, C.S. and Don-Yehiya, E. *Civil Religion in Israel: Traditional Judaism and Political Culture in the Jewish State.* Berkeley: University of California Press, 1983.

Patai, R. and Graves, R. *Hebrew Myths: The Book of Genesis.* N.Y.: McGraw Hill, 1964.

Rekhess, E. "The Resurgence of Palestinian Islamic Fundamentalism in the West Bank and Gaza." In *Jewish Fundamentalism in Comparative Perspective*, ed. L.J.Silberstein. N.Y.: N.Y. University Press, 1993.

Robertson-Smith, W. *Lectures on the Religion of the Semites.* Edinburgh: Black, 1889.

Rubin, N. "The Sages' Conception of Body and Soul." In *Essays in the Social Scientific Study of Judaism and Jewish Society,* 47-103, eds. J. Lightstone and S. Fishbane. Montreal: Concordia University Press, 1990.

Rubin, N. "The Price of Redemption: Jewish First-Born and Social Change." In *Essays in the Social Scientific Study of Judaism and Jewish Society II,* 3-12, eds. S. Fishbane and S. Schoenfeld. N.Y: Ktav, 1992.

Rubin, N. "The Blessing of Mourners: Ritual Aspects of Social Change." In *Approaches to Ancient Judaism,* 119-141, eds. H. Basser and S. Fishbane. Atlanta: Scholars' Press, 1993.

Sered, S. "Religious Rituals and Secular Rituals: Interpenetrating Models of Childbirth in a Modern Israeli Context." *Sociology of Religion 54* (1993): 101-114.

Shaffir, W. "The Recruitment of Baalei Tshuva in a Jerusalem Yeshiva." *Jewish Journal of Sociology 25* (1983): 33-46.

Shaffir, W. "Conversion Experiences: Newcomers to and Defectors from Orthodox Judaism." In *Jewishness and Judaism in Contemporary Israel,* 173-203, eds. Z. Sobel and B. Beit-Hallahmi. Albany: State University of N.Y Press, 1991.

Sharot, S. *Messianism, Mysticism and Magic: A Sociological Analysis of Jewish Religious Movements.* Chapel Hill: University of North Carolina Press, 1982.

Shelah, I. *Indications Towards Secular Religion in Israel.* Papers in Sociology, Dept. of Sociology, Hebrew University of Jerusalem, 1975 (Hebrew).

Shokeid, M. "An Anthropological Perspective on Ascetic Behavior and Religious Change." In *The Predicament of Homecoming,* 64-94, Deshen, S. and Shokeid, M. Ithaca, N.Y.: Cornell University Press, 1974.

Shokeid, M. "The Decline of Personal Endowment of Atlas Mountains Religious Leaders in Israel." *Anthropological Quarterly 52* (1979): 186-197.

Shokeid, M. *Children of Cicumstances: Israeli Emigrants in New York.* Ithaca, N.Y.: Cornell University Press, 1988.

Sombart, W. *The Jews and Modern Capitalism.* Glencoe: Free Press, 1952.

Weber, M. *Ancient Judaism.* Glencoe: Free Press, 1952.

Weingrod, A. *The Saint of Beersheba.* Albany: State University of New York Press, 1990.

Yogev, A. and El-Dor, J. "Attitudes and Tendencies Toward Return to Judaism Among Israeli Adolescents: Seekers or Drifters?" *Jewish Journal of Sociology 29* (1987): 5-17.

2

Sociological Analyses of Religion

Stephen Sharot

The sociology of religion does not have a high profile in Israeli sociology, but the historical circumstances of the Israeli state provide a challenging opportunity for studying the convergence between the religion of a diaspora people and a modern nationalist movement. The picture is complicated by the fact that Judaism is not a state church or a formal state religion and that Israelis display widely differing patterns of religiosity. But research shows that ethnic and generational differences divide Israelis into numerous categories, and instead of becoming more privatized, Judaism has recently been acquiring greater prominence in public life. The power of Orthodox and Ultraorthodox groups has also been growing, but new religious movements have achieved little success. As a result, Judaism in Israel falls into three main currents: the dominant Ashkenazim pattern; a characteristically Asian and North African pattern; and a minority Ashkenazim pattern which tends to be indifferent toward Zionism and the religious meaning of the state.

Despite the fact that religion is of enormous significance in the social and political divisions in Israeli society, the sociology of religion has not been one of the most important subfields of Israeli sociology. In terms of number of publications, the sociology of religion falls far behind the field of ethnicity and ethnic equality among Jewish groups or categories of origin from different countries and continents. However, interest in the sociology of religion has grown in recent years, and although there is no comprehensive book length study of religion in Israeli society from a sociological perspective, there has been an accumulation of books and articles (widely scattered in various journals) that have dealt with a number of important facets of religion in Israel.[1]

At first glance, there might appear little relationship among the sociological works on religion reviewed in this article: the general questionnaire surveys of religiosity, the anthropological studies of religious change among Jews from Asia and North Africa,

---

[1]For earlier short general accounts of religion in Israel see Deshen, 1978, and Yaron, 1976. A collection of previously unpublished articles on religion in Israel, edited by Zvi Sobel and Benjamin Beit-Hallahmi, will be published by SUNY Press. Almost all sociological studies of religion in Israel have been confined to the Jewish population, and because of the confines of space this article will not deal with the Moslem and Christian populations. This does not, of course, detract from the importance of the divisions and conflicts among the different religions in Israel (for a general short account see Webber, 1985).

civil religion, the religious settlement movement in the conquered territories, the Ultraorthodox and converts to Ultraorthodoxy, the Conservative and Reform movements, and the "new religious movements." There is, however, a common thread insofar as most studies relate, in various degrees and from various perspectives, to what might be called the historical meeting between Judaism, a traditional religion that for two thousand years was a religion of a "diaspora people," and a modern nationalist movement, Zionism, in a state that is legitimized by the majority of its Jewish population in terms of Zionist ideology.

HISTORICAL BACKGROUND

Prior to the establishment of the state of Israel in 1948, the Jewish community in Palestine was divided between the "Old Yishuv" and the "New Yishuv" (Settlement). The majority in both sectors had originated from the Jewish communities of Eastern Europe, but they differed radically with respect to religion. The Jews of the Old Yishuv led a life regulated by, and devoted to the study of, the Torah or religious law (halakha). Their immigration had been motivated solely by religious considerations; they sought a way of life that was not threatened by the Haskalah (Jewish Enlightenment) and other secular trends in Europe, and without the worldly pressures of having to make a living. They depended on a system of economic contributions from the diaspora communities, and they saw in their economic inactivity and material dependence on others an expression of the highest Jewish values: an opportunity to devote themselves to prayer and religious study.

The immigration of modern Jewish nationalists whose aliyah (ascent, referring to immigration to the Land of Israel) was not motivated by traditional religious considerations began in the 1880s. The Jews of the first aliyah, or wave of modern immigrants (1882-1902), desired to create a productive and self-supporting community, but they tended to be traditionally inclined in their religious outlook. It was the way of life and ideology of the second (1903-14) and third (1919-1923) aliyot that presented a radical challenge to the Old Yishuv. These immigrants rejected the religious and "petty bourgeois" character of their communities of origin in Eastern Europe, and they aimed to create a new Jewish society built on revolutionary socialist and secularist principles. They saw the Old Yishuv as a deformed and parasitical society, and they were seen in turn by the Old Yishuv as the worst representatives of all that was evil and dangerous in Zionism (Abramov, 1976; M. Friedman, 1977; Knaani, 1975; Azili, 1984).

During the period of the British mandate, changes occurred in the attitude of many Orthodox Jews towards Zionism, and although the majority of the Ultraorthodox remained non-Zionist or anti-Zionist, a modus vivendi developed between the more moderate Orthodox, including an increasing number of religious Zionists, and the secular Zionist leadership. By the time of the establishment of the state, the secularist orientation of the second and third aliyot had already become milder, and on the religious side, the militant Ultraorthodox had become outnumbered by the religious Zionists. The Zionist religious party was included in the government coalitions, and it was supported by many Jews from Asian and North African countries who, until the 1980s, rarely voted for an Ultraorthodox party.

Divisions along religious-secular lines were far less evident among Jews from the Middle East (understood here to include North Africa). At the time of the establishment of the state, Jews of Middle Eastern origin made up from ten to fifteen percent of the total Jewish population of 630,000. This demographic ratio began to change radically with the mass immigration from Middle Eastern countries that started on the eve of independence and continued, with occasional lulls, in the 1950s and early 1960s. Today, Jewish Israelis of Middle Eastern origins constitute about one half of the three and one half million Jewish population in Israel.

In contrast with both the secular Zionists and the non-Zionist Orthodox Jews from Europe, many immigrants from the Middle East saw Zionism and the establishment of the State as affirmations of the religious tradition that they had upheld in their countries of origin. Some interpreted their *aliyah* in traditional messianic terms. There were communities from the Middle East, such as the Yemenite and those from the rural areas of Morocco and Tunisia, whose traditional religious life had remained substantially intact prior to the immigration. Among other communities, secularization had made inroads, but in most cases it was moderate in comparison with the European communities, and this also meant that there was no militant Orthodoxy with a self-conscious task of defending the tradition (Deshen and Zenner, 1982; Eisenstadt, 1985; Friedlander and Goldscheider, 1979; Ayalon, Ben-Rafael, and Sharot, 1985).

INSTITUTIONAL BACKGROUND: RELIGION AND STATE

With the establishment of the state, it was agreed between the political leaders and the rabbinate that the principal arrangements for religion that had been settled before 1948 should continue, and the majority of Israeli Jews accepted, or became reconciled to, the formal institutionalization of Judaism in the institutions of the state. Judaism did not become a state church or formal state religion. The religious authorities and courts of the "recognized communities" of all three religions (Jewish, Islamic, Christian) are financially supported through the Ministry of Religions and are empowered to deal with matters of personal status and family law, such as marriage, divorce, and alimony, that are binding on all members of the communities. However, the influence of the Jewish religion on the character of the state is evident in its symbols, public holidays, restrictions on employment and entertainment on the Sabbath, and regulation of *kashrut* (dietary regulations) and other religious matters in public institutions by rabbinical authorities. The religious authorities of the Conservative and Reform movements are not officially recognized and their institutions are, with some minor exceptions, not financially supported by the state. Orthodox Judaism may, therefore, be considered the "official" religion of the Israeli Jewish population (Liebman and Don-Yehiya, 1984; Samet, 1979; Tabory, 1981; Gutmann, 1981; Elazar and Aviad, 1981).

SURVEYS OF RELIGIOSITY

In the context of talmudic or Orthodox rabbinical Judaism, individual religiosity is measured by the number and strictness of religious observances (*mitzvot* or "commandments"). In the United States some Reform Jews claim that ethical behavior is the core of Jewish religiosity, but the Reform movement is very small in Israel, as is the Conservative movement, and the yardstick of religious *practice* is generally accepted as the measure of religiosity, among observant and non-observant alike. This need not mean that sociologists should confine themselves to a study of practice, but it makes the focus on practice in surveys understandable.

One survey, however, based on a sample of 1,530 adults living in urban areas, has provided data both on the observance of a wide range of specific practices and on beliefs in a number of religious doctrines. Ben-Meir and Kedem (1979), reported that there was no clear cut dichotomy between religious and non-religious Jews in Israel, but a continuum of religiosity. Certain practices were observed by a small minority, such as putting on *tefillin* (phylacteries) every day by men (14%) and going regularly to the *mikveh* (ritual bath) by women (14%). About half the population observed such practices as separation of milk and meat utensils (44%) and lighting candles with a blessing on the Sabbath (53%). Some practices were observed by the majority, such a lighting *Hanukkah* candles (88%) and participating in the *Seder* night Passover meal (99%).

The percentages of respondents who acknowledged belief in central religious doctrines in Judaism demonstrate that observance of the most "popular" *mitzvot* is by no means dependent on religious belief. The distribution of respondents with respect to beliefs was much narrower than the distribution of religious practices. The most widespread belief was belief in God, but even here a substantial minority were disbelievers: 64% said that they believed in God, 56% believed that God gave the Torah to Moses on Mount Sinai, 36% believed in the coming of the messiah, and 29% believed that the spirit continues after death. It would appear that many Israelis observe at least a number of practices, not because of a belief in their divine origins or obligations, but because they are conforming to common practices that express a Jewish-Israeli national identity.

Ben-Meir and Kedem noted significant differences between Israelis of Middle Eastern and European origins in both practices and beliefs. Greater attention was given to these differences by Goldscheider and Friedlander (1983) who found that, according to the measures on their scale of religiosity, 47% of Eastern Europeans and 43% of West Europeans could be classified as secular, compared to 17% of Asians and 13% of North Africans. The ethnic difference remained substantial in the second generation, although it was less than in the first: 53% of Israeli born of European origins and 27% of Israeli born of Asian or North African origins were secular on all measures (similar findings were reported in earlier surveys by Antonovsky, 1963 [summarized in G. Friedman, 1967]; Matras, 1964; Herman, 1970; Bensimon, 1968). From a comparison of the religiosity of marriage cohorts and of female respondents and their parents, Goldscheider and Friedlander concluded that modernization has resulted in the secularization of various dimensions of religiosity, subjective as well as objective, in all Jewish groups of origin. They qualified this statement, however, by noting that secularization does not necessarily mean the total abandonment of all forms of religiosity, at the same pace, by all groups, and that new forms of religious expression, not covered in their survey, may be emerging.

The issues of ethnic differences among Israeli Jews, socioeconomic divisions, and secularization were taken up in a study by Ayalon, Ben-Rafael, and Sharot (1985).

The findings from this research indicated that the categorization in previous studies of "Oriental" Jews from the Middle East and "Western" Jews from Europe had resulted in an oversimplified picture. A comparison of four groups of origin (Moroccan, Iraqi, Romanian, Polish) showed that the Moroccans were the most observant and the Poles the least, but that the Iraqis were significantly less observant than the Moroccans and were only slightly more observant than the Romanians. A regression analysis demonstrated that fathers' religiosity was the most important variable determining respondents' religiosity, but Jews from the Middle East who had been exposed more to Israeli society, either because they had lived there longer or by mobility into the higher socioeconomic strata, in which Europeans are overrepresented, were likely to have lower levels of religiosity (see also, Kedem and Bar-Lev, 1983).

The intergenerational decline in religiosity was greater in the Moroccan and Iraqi groups, especially in the observance of the "stricter" practices such as donning *tefillin*, but there was almost no difference between the generations in any of the groups with respect to the "popular" practice of fasting on Yom Kippur. Once religious practice reaches a low level, as it had done among Poles and Romanians, there is a diminishing decline of religiosity between the generations. It is suggested that one reason for this stabilization at a minimal level is the interpenetration of religion and national identity.

ANTHROPOLOGICAL STUDIES

Anthropologists studying religious change in Israel have focused on Jews from the Middle East, and especially the more "traditional" immigrant groups from Morocco, Tunisia, and Yemen. They have recorded a decline in religious practice among these groups, but they have shown that it would be a gross simplification to describe the changes in terms of a linear secularization process or to argue that "tradition" is being abandoned for "modernity." Not only has the decline in observance been confined to the "stricter" practices, but a number of traditional practices have also increased in importance in recent years.

In his detailed analyses of ritual actions among Jews from North Africa, Shlomo Deshen (1972, 1976, 1980) has pointed to the changing content and meanings of religious action rather than the abandonment of practices. Religious innovations did not involve the rejection of old practices but rather the infusion of traditional symbolic actions with meanings that related to new social contexts and experiences. The new meanings did not necessarily exclude the older meanings that related to the particularity of the specific group of origin, but they associated religious action with more encompassing associations and cultural styles of the larger Israeli society (on changes in religious leadership see Shokeid, 1980).

Deshen (1989) writes that, although the majority of Middle Eastern Israelis have abandoned a strict pattern of religious observance, they do not see themselves as "secular." They retain many practices, especially those related to the family, and accept the basic beliefs in God, divine rewards and punishments, redemption, spirits, the status of the Torah scholar, the sacredness of the Land of Israel, and the Jews as the chosen people. Shokeid (1985) emphasizes that the "partly religious" or *mesoriti* (traditional) pattern is particularly prevalent among Jews of Middle Eastern origin who see themselves as continuing in the tradition of their fathers. The term "tradition" is widely used in a favorable way by Middle Eastern Israelis, but it rarely denotes for them a militant defense of religion or a concern with consistency; for example, many will go to synagogue but also ride to the sea on the Sabbath.

Religion was strongly tied to family and local community in the Middle Eastern communities of origin, and in Israel this symbiosis remains important. Whereas among Israelis from Europe ethnic synagogues (based on country of origin) rarely continue beyond the immigrant generation, among Middle Eastern Israelis they continue in the second generation, especially in the lower strata (Ben Rafael and Sharot, 1987). The close relationship of religion and the ethnic community among Jews from North Africa is clearly indicated in the revival of the veneration of saints and the pilgrimages to the tombs of saints on the anniversary of their deaths. In Morocco the *hillulah* (celebration) at the tomb of the saint was a major event, in some cases attracting large numbers from a large area, but in the first years after immigration to Israel hagiolatry appeared to diminish in importance and the *hillulot* were celebrated in a modest manner in neighborhood synagogues. Public display of religiosity was inhibited by the insecurity and low status of immigrants in a society where they were expected to abandon their "primitive" ways. The revival of the pilgrimages followed a period of immigrant acculturation to the dominant culture and an improvement in their material conditions and social status. Once they felt that they were accepted as Israelis, Jews from Morocco and Tunisia felt less inhibition in demonstrating their ethnic pride and traditions. Thousands come to participate in celebrations that combine spiritual themes, the promise of cures for illnesses, a festive atmosphere in which much food and drink is consumed and traditional dances performed, and a market where both religious and secular items are sold (Deshen and Shokeid, 1974; Bilu, 1987; Ben Ari and Bilu, 1987).

CIVIL RELIGION AND ULTRANATIONALIST RELIGION

In contrast to the often proclaimed "privatization" of religion in Western societies, religion in Israel has become more prominent in the public domain in recent years. This has been shown by Liebman and Don-Yehiya (1983) in their analysis of changes in Israel's civil religion. They write that the primary strategy of the first major civil religion of the new Israeli state, Statism, was a selective affirmation of only some elements of the Jewish religious tradition. Its major exponent, David Ben-Gurion, saw modern Israel as a successor to the Jewish independent state of ancient times, and he tended to denigrate that part of the traditional culture that originated in exile. The "New Civil Religion" that developed after the Six Day War and became even more important after the Yom Kippur War has incorporated traditional religious symbols through a strategy of reinterpretation that "points the symbols away from God and toward the Jewish people, the Jewish state, and the particular needs of the state." There are emphases on the unity of all Jews, Israelis or not, on the sacred writings, on the centrality of the Holocaust, and on the Jews as an isolated nation confronting a hostile world. The "New Civil Religion" has its symbols, such as Masada, its rites, such as Holocaust Day and Memorial Day, and its sacred places, especially the Western Wall.

Among the reasons for the change in the civil religion is that the negative attitude of Statism to much of the traditional religion was not in tune with the culture of Middle Eastern immigrants, but perhaps a more important factor was that Statism was not able to meet the legitimacy crisis that arose out of the conquest of territories and the high demands made by the state on its citizens. The "New Civil Religion" largely overcame these deficiencies by grounding the values of the political system in a transcendental order. An emphasis on the ties of the Jews to the conquered territories, especially "Judea and Samaria" with its biblical associations and holy sites, invoked a penetration of religious symbols (see also Weissbrod, 1981, 1983; on religious ritual in secular kibbutzim see, Lilker, 1982; Rubin, 1986).

Among religious Zionists, the conquests and the Yom Kippur War accelerated an extreme nationalist tendency that was expressed in the formation of *Gush Emunim* (Block of the Faithful) in 1974.[2] The movement represents a fusion of traditional messianism and modern nationalism. Its leaders and spokesmen have proclaimed that the messianic process of redemption of the Jewish people has begun, that the Jews have an essential role to play in this process, and that the most important *mitzvah* at this time is the settlement of the Land of Israel. They have pointed to the actualization of a number of signs of the messianic period that were predicted in the sacred writings: the fertility of the land, the ingathering of the Jews from all parts of the world, the foundation of an independent state, and the conquest of the city of Jerusalem. The Holocaust, the Arab-Israeli wars, the international support for the Arabs, and the internal confusion in Israel following the war in 1973 were seen as "birth pangs of the messiah." They have maintained that the Jewish people are able to reduce the "birth pangs" if they take their part in the process of redemption (Aviad, 1984; Lustick, 1988).

The emergence of *Gush Emunim* has been interpreted as a response to a crisis of values and identity in Israel society, and as an extreme expression of wider changes in Zionism and national culture in Israel (Weissbrod, 1985; Don-Yehiya, 1987). The beginnings are traced at least as far back as the 1950s when the decline of the idealistic, revolutionary vision of the labor Zionist movement became apparent. The crisis became far more acute after the October 1973 war which shook the post-1967 feelings of security, strength, and self-sufficiency. However, although *Gush Emunim* spokesmen presented the movement as a solution to the crisis of values in Israeli society, those in the religious core of the movement have not themselves experienced a crisis of values in the sense of a rejection of previously held values and a search for a new system of meaning. They were already strong adherents of religious Zionism and embedded in its institutions and organization. However, religious Zionism in Israel had been subject to tensions and paradoxes, and *Gush Emunim* can be interpreted as an attempt to overcome them.

From its beginnings in the early years of the twentieth century, the religious Zionist movement attempted to combine two ideological streams in Jewry, Orthodox Judaism

---

[2]*Gush Emunim* and its impact on Israeli society have had extensive coverage (see the collection in Newman, 1985). There has been little analysis from the perspective of the sociology of religion, but see O'Dea, 1976; Sharot, 1982; Aronoff, 1984; and Aran, 1985.

and modern Zionism, that were for a long time fundamentally opposed to each other. The religious Zionists' Orthodox way of life and their belief that a Jewish state should be founded on the *halakha* alienated the secular Zionists, and their desire to create a pre-messianic state was condemned as a violation of the covenant by the anti-Zionist Orthodox. Although the majority of Orthodox Jews came to accept the idea and then the actuality of a Jewish state, the foundation of the state did not remove the tensions within religious Zionism: their goal was a halakhic state, but they cooperated in the role of a junior partner with politicians who adopted Western social and political institutions and norms that were hardly consistent with traditional Judaism.

In *Gush Emunim* ideology the tension between Jewish Orthodoxy and modern nationalism is removed by defining the entire Zionist movement and the Jewish state as sacred phenomena, regardless of the absence of religious observance among the majority. They expect that in the future stage of the process of redemption the whole of the Jewish people will return to the Torah, but the conception that all Jews are part of a sacred collectivity justifies the movement's cooperation with non-religious Jews who support their political aims. Secular Zionists are seen to have played an important role in an early stage of the redemption process, but the religious Zionists see themselves as the new authentic elite who understand the deep meaning of historical events, as the new pioneers of a transformed Zionism that will awaken the dormant forces within the Jewish people and advance the process of redemption (Raanan, 1980; Aran, 1986; Liebman, 1987; Aviad, 1984).

ORTHODOXY AND ULTRAORTHODOXY

Gush Emunim represents what Liebman and Don-Yehiya (1983, 1984) have called the expansionist response of Orthodox Judaism to modernization and secularization, especially as represented by secular Zionism. This response appropriates Zionism and reinterprets it in the spirit of traditional religious symbols and values. Three additional responses are distinguished: the adaptationist, the compartmentalist, and the rejectionist. The adaptationist or reformist response is represented by the religious kibbutz movement that adopted elements from secular Zionism and gave them religious meaning. The religious kibbutzim have been studied extensively within the framework of sociology of religion by Aryei Fishman (1983, 1987). He has demonstrated that the religious kibbutzim have been more successful economically than the far more numerous secular kibbutzim, and by drawing on Weber and Sombart he argues that this is related to the transformative potential within rabbinical Judaism.

The compartmentalist Orthodox accept secular education and modern styles of life but insulate themselves from the nonreligious population by autonomous institutions and concentrating in particular neighborhoods (a general account of the religious-secular division is included in Smooha, 1978). In fact, many religious Jews live in mixed neighborhoods and apartment buildings where the majority of residents are secular, but Tabory (1989) has shown, in a study of a Tel Aviv suburb, that even in such cases religious Jews tend to restrict their friendships to other religious Jews.

The compartmentalist response possibly includes the majority of religious Zionists, but it is not represented by a popular ideology or movement, and this perhaps explains why it has hardly been studied (on the variation in religiosity among Orthodox Israelis see, Krausz and Bar-Lev, 1978). Far more has been written on the *haredim* ("God-fearing") or Ultraorthodox Jews who, in contrast with the compartmentalists, reject the secular world. They also reject, in contrast to the expansionists and adaptationists, the endowment of worldly activity, such as settlement or labor, with religious meaning, interfering as it does with the major religious task: the study of, and full conformity to, the religious law. Most *haredim* deny that Zionism and the state of Israel have any positive religious meaning, and a minority among them, members of the *Satmar hasidim* and the *Neturei Karta* movement, condemn Zionism and the state as blasphemous abominations (M. Friedman, 1989a). The different orientations toward the state are just one of the issues that divide the *haredim* into a number of camps, some of which are violently opposed to each other. In addition to the general historical separation of *hasidim* and *mitnagdim* (opponents), these sectors are divided by loyalties to particular religious leaders and hassidic courts, and in recent years a division has emerged between Ashkenazi *haredim* and *haredim* of Middle Eastern origin (Dan, 1989; M. Friedman, 1989b).

The clothes, Yiddish language, and other cultural characteristics of the *haredim* demonstrate their concern to continue the way of life of traditional Eastern European Jewry, but to describe them as a remnant of traditionalism would be inadequate. In contrast with the interwar period when traditional religious leaders were bemoaning the decline of observance among the younger generation, the leaders today point to the younger *haredim* as not simply emulating their forefathers but superceding them in their religious knowledge and strict conformity to the *halakha*. This tendency can be understood only against the background of the destruction of the traditional communities of Easern Europe, for Ultraorthodoxy had to be reconstructed on the basis of voluntary communities whose conformity to the tradition could be secured only by the tradition of written codes. In the traditional society, the tradition embodied in codes had been softened by the traditions of the local community and the responsibility of rabbis to bear in mind the needs of all its inhabitants who differed widely in their levels of involvement in the material world. In the voluntaristic, neo-traditional community, the young are less constrained in the promotion of the tradition embodied in codes beyond the traditional ways of their fathers, and religious leaders need concern themselves only with committed members.

Vastly improved economic conditions have made stricter interpretations of the law more feasible, and they have also made possible the extensive development of the central institution of the Ultraorthodox community: the *yeshiva*. A large proportion of the male youth and young adults receive economic support to study in the *yeshivot* for a number of years, and as a "cloistered community," unconcerned with making a living and often sheltered from the pressures of families and local communities, they develop a self-image of an elite of Torah scholars who lead the way in their emphasis on the necessity of the most stringent interpretations of the religious law (M. Friedman, 1986, 1987; Liebman, 1983; Liebman and Don-Yehiya, 1984).

The neo-traditional community, by its strict separation from the wider society, succeeds in incorporating the vast majority of those socialized within it, and mainly as a consequence of their high birth rate the *haredim* have spread into an increasing number of towns and neighborhoods, especially in Jerusalem (Shilhav and Friedman,

1985). The number of *baalei teshuvah*, "penitents" from secular backgrounds who become Ultraorthodox Jews, amounts to a few thousand, mainly between the years 1975-87, and is modest compared with the natural growth of the *haredim*; but the phenomenon has generated great interest in Israel, and it invites comparison to work on conversion elsewhere.

Janet Aviad (1983) writes that the pattern of motivation of the *baalei teshuvah*, their rejection of Western culture and the seeking of a compelling knowledge and way of life that would provide meaning and contentment, cannot be distinguished from that of other alienated youth who, in America at least, have been able to choose from a number of countercultural religious options. (Many were young Jews who migrated from the States.) Aviad argues that the particular path chosen by the *baalei teshuvah* can be understood largely in terms of their Jewish consciousness: there is a feeling of return to a heritage in which the individual recovers his "essence" and true past. It is the theme of "homecoming," "returning to the fold," that is the most distinctive Jewish component of the *teshuvah* process and sets it off from other forms of conversion.

Perhaps a larger numerical addition to the Ultraorthodox community has come from the modern Orthodox. Both adaptationists and a sector of the expansionists, associated with *Gush Emunim*, have adopted in increasing numbers the characteristics of neo-traditionalism, abandoning secular studies and emphasizing more stringent rules in such areas as relationships between the sexes (for a case study, see Weingrod, 1981).

SMALL RELIGIOUS MOVEMENTS

In contrast to their dominant position in North American Jewry, Conservative and Reform Judaism, with a combined membership of about two thousand families, have had little success in attracting members in Israel. The Orthodox establishment has succeeded in preventing the movements' incorporation into the institutional framework of public religious services, but the major problem of the movements in Israel has been the indifference of the nonobservant and partly observant majority rather than the opposition of the strictly observant minority. Whereas in the United States affiliation to a synagogue or temple is the most important means of expressing Jewish identity, most Israeli Jews feel little need to affiliate with a synagogue in order to identify ethnically or nationally as Jews. Association with a synagogue is mainly confined, therefore, to highly observant Jews who are mostly Orthodox, and Conservative and Reform synagogues tend to remain "ethnic" congregations of immigrants from English-speaking countries (Tabory, 1983, 1986; Tabory and Lazerwitz, 1983).

New religious movements from outside Judaism, which began to appear in Israel in the early 1970s, never attracted a significant proportion of the population, and the total membership today of the eighteen or so movements is probably no more than two thousand. The fiercest opposition to the movements, often involving violent methods, comes from the Ultraorthodox, but coverage in the secular media has also been almost wholly negative. The high level of opposition to a movement such as ISCKON (which has only about twenty members) is related to the fact that such movements are perceived not only as threats to the family (as in the United States) but also as challenges to the very basis of the Israeli state and society: its Jewish religious and national identity.

CONCLUSION

The traditional Jewish society in which religion was diffused throughout the whole social structure and culture no longer exists, but the religious responses to its breakdown and destruction have been varied and contradictory. One important component distinguishing the various responses in Israel has been the orientation toward modern Jewish nationalism and the state of Israel, and this has been an important focus of the sociology of religion in Israel. Three major patterns may be distinguished.

First, there is the dominant pattern among the Ashkenazim, most of whom originated in recent times from European countries. They demonstrate a mixture of positive and negative orientations to the tradition. The almost wholly negative approach that was typical of the second and third *aliyot*, who were in rebellion against their communities of origin, has almost disappeared, but with the exception of a few, there has been little interest among the secularized majority in a "return" to the traditional religious patterns. Religious observance has declined, and most religious practices that have been retained are those that can be interpreted as statements of national identity. Religious practice is retained at a minimal level because national symbols and myths must necessarily draw upon the religious tradition.

Second, the pattern that has been typical of Jews from Asia and North Africa has been a decline in religious observance but a continued positive orientation toward the "tradition of one's forefathers." In contrast with the Ashkenazim, there was never a clear differentiation made by Middle Eastern Jews between the traditional codes and the meanings of Zionism and Israeli identity. This has meant that certain traditional practices, especially those requiring infrequent observance, have been revived, albeit in somewhat modified fashion. These practices express both the particular heritage of the community of origin and the theme of national unity.

The third pattern, which has been more typical of an Ashkenazi minority but has spread to some Jews of Middle Eastern origins in recent years, has been to emphasize a religiosity based on the tradition of codes that, in its depth and intensity, goes beyond, and even to some extent opposes, the more tolerant forms of religiosity of the traditional society. This pattern has most often involved a denial of any religious meaning to Zionism and the state, but in recent years it has spread to a section of the religious expansionists who incorporate Zionism and the state within their religious world view.

There are other responses to the tradition, such as religious accommodation in an ideologically explicit fashion to modern society, as in the Conservative and Reform movements, but the pressures for such a transformation have been largely confined to the diaspora (Sharot, 1976). In the United States, in particular, such accommodation among Jews has involved a fusion of religion and ethnicity with an emphasis on liberalism and universalistic themes (Liebman, 1973; Cohen, 1983; Furman, 1987). In Israel, small "dovish" religious Zionist movements have emerged in reaction to ultra-nationalist religious Zionism, but universalistic themes have been expressed in recent years mainly by secular sectors of the population. The dominant ideologies among the religious population are highly particularistic, both those that have rejected modern Jewish nationalism and those that have appropriated it.

REFERENCES

Abramov, S. Zalmon. 1976. *Perpetual Dilemma: Jewish Religion in the Jewish State.* Rutherford, NJ: Fairleigh Dickinson University Press.

Aran, Gideon. 1985. *Eretz Israel Between Politics and Religion: The Movement to Stop the Withdrawal from Sinai* [Hebrew]. Jerusalem: Jerusalem Institute for Israel Studies.

———. 1986. "From religious Zionism to Zionist religion: the roots of Gush Emunim." *Studies in Contemporary Jewry* 2:116-43.

Aronoff, Myron J. 1984. "Gush Emunim: the institutionalization of a charismatic, messianic, religious-political revitalization movement in Israel," pp. 63-84 in Myron J. Aronoff (ed.), *Political Anthropology* 3. New Brunswick, NJ: Transaction.

Antonovsky, Aaron. 1963. "Israeli political-social attitudes" [Hebrew]. *Amot* 6:11-22.

Aviad, Janet. 1983. *Return to Judaism: Religious Renewal in Israel.* Chicago: University of Chicago Press.

———. 1984. "The contemporary Israeli pursuit of the millennium." *Religion* 14:199-222.

Ayalon, Hannah, Eliezer Ben-Rafael, and Stephen Sharot. 1985. "Variations in ethnic identification among Israeli Jews." *Ethnic and Racial Studies* 8:389-407.

———. 1986. "Secularization and the diminishing decline of religion." *Review of Religious Research* 27:193-207.

Azili, A. 1984. *The Attitude of HaShomer Hatzair to Religion and Tradition (1920-1948)* [Hebrew]. Givat Haviva: Documentation and Research Center.

Ben-Ari, Eyal and Yoram Bilu. 1987. "Saints' sanctuaries in Israeli development towns: on a mechanism of urban transformation." *Urban Anthropology* 16:244-72.

Ben-Meir, Yehuda and Peri Kedem. 1979. "Index of religiosity of the Jewish population of Israel" [Hebrew]. *Megamot* 4:353-62.

Ben-Rafael, Eliezer and Stephen Sharot. 1987. "Ethnic pluralism and religious congregations: a comparison of neighborhoods in Israel." *Ethnic Groups* 7:65-83.

Bensimon, Doris. 1968. "Pratique religieuse des Juif d'Afrique du Nord en France et en Israel." *Archives de Sociologie des Religions* 26:81-96.

Bilu, Yoram. 1987. "Dreams and the wishes of the saint," pp. 285-313 in Harvey E. Goldberg (ed.), *Judaism Viewed from Within and from Without.* Albany: State University of New York Press.

Cohen, Steven M. 1983. *American Modernity and Jewish Identity.* New York: Tavistock.

Dan, Yosef. 1989. "Dance of R. Elimelech" [Hebrew]. *Politica* 24:10-13.

Deshen, Shlomo. 1972. "Ethnicity and citizenship in the ritual of an Israeli synagogue." *Southwestern Journal of Anthropology* 28:69-82.

———. 1976. "Ethnic boundaries and cultural paradigms: the case of southern Tunisian immigrants in Israel." *Ethos* 4:271-94.

———. 1978. "Israeli Judaism: introduction to the major patterns." *International Journal of Middle East Studies* 9:141-69.

———. 1980. "Religion among oriental immigrants in Israel," pp. 235-46 in Asher Arian (ed.), *Israel: A Developing Society.* Assen, Holland: Van Gorum.

———. 1989. "Understanding the special attraction of the religion of Mizrachim" [Hebrew]. *Politica* 1989:40-43.

Deshen, Shlomo and Moshe Shokeid. 1974. *The Predicament of Homecoming: Cultural and Social Life of North African Immigrants in Israel.* Ithaca, NY: Cornell University Press.

Deshen, Shlomo and Walter P. Zenner (eds.). 1982. *Jewish Societies in the Middle East: Community, Culture, and Authority.* Washington, DC: University Press of America.

Don-Yehiya, Eliezer. 1987. "Jewish messianism, religious Zionism, and Israeli politics: the impact and origins of Gush Emunim." *Middle Eastern Studies* 23:215-34.

Eisenstadt, S. N. 1985. *The Transformation of Israeli Society.* London: Weidenfeld and Nicolson.

Elazar, Daniel J. and Janet Aviad. 1981. "Religion and politics in Israel," pp. 163-196 in Michael Curtis (ed.), *Religion and Politics in the Middle East*. Boulder, CO: Westview Press.

Fishman, Aryei. 1983. "Judaism and modernization: the case of the religious kibbutzim." *Social Forces* 62:9-31.

————. 1987. "Religion and communal life in an evolutionary-functional perspective: the orthodox kibbutzim." *Comparative Studies in Society and History* 29:763-96.

Friedlander, Dov and Calvin Goldscheider. 1979. *The Population of Israel*. New York: Columbia University Press.

Friedman, Menachem. 1977. *Society and Religion: The Non-Zionist Orthodox in Eretz Israel, 1918-1936* [Hebrew]. Jerusalem: Yad Izhak Ben-Zvi Publications.

————. 1986. "Haredim confront the modern city." *Studies in Contemporary Jewry* 2:74-96.

————. 1987. "Life tradition and book tradition in the development of ultraorthodox Judaism," pp. 235-55 in Harvey E. Goldberg (ed.), *Judaism Viewed from Within and from Without*. Albany: State University of New York Press.

————. 1989a. "The state of Israel as a theological dilemma," pp. 165-215 in Baruch Kimmerling (ed.), *The Israeli State and Society: Boundaries and Frontiers*. Albany: State University of New York Press.

————. 1989b. "Their political behavior: complex characteristics" [Hebrew]. *Politica* 24:50-53.

Friedman, Georges. 1967. *The End of the Jewish People*. New York: Doubleday.

Furman, Frida Kerner. 1987. *Beyond Yiddishkeit: The Struggle for Jewish Identity in a Reform Synagogue*. Albany: State University of New York Press.

Goldscheider, Calvin and Dov Friedlander. 1983. "Religiosity patterns in Israel." *American Jewish Year Book* 83:3-39.

Gutmann, Emanuel. 1981. "Religion and its role in national integration in Israel," pp. 197-205 in Michael Curtis (ed.), *Religion and Politics in the Middle East*. Boulder, CO: Westview Press.

Herman, Simon J. 1970. *Israelis and Jews: The Continuity of an Identity*. New York: Random House.

Kedem, Peri and Mordechai Bar-Lev. 1983. "Is giving up traditional religious culture part of the price to be paid for acquiring higher education?: adaptation of academic western culture by Jewish Israeli university students of Middle Eastern origin." *Higher Education* 12:373-88.

Knaani, David. 1975. *The Labor Second Aliyah and Its Attitude toward Religion and Tradition* [Hebrew]. Tel Aviv: Sifriat Po'alim.

Krausz, Ernest and Mordechai Bar-Lev. 1978. "Varieties of orthodox religious behaviour: a case study of yeshiva high school graduates in Israel." *Jewish Journal of Sociology* 20:59-74.

Liebman, Charles S. 1973. *The Ambivalent American Jew: Politics, Religion and Family in American Jewish Life*. Philadelphia: Jewish Publication of America.

————. 1983. "Extremism as a religious norm." *Journal for the Scientific Study of Religion* 22:75-86.

————. 1987. "The religious component in Israeli ultra-nationalism." *Jerusalem Quarterly* 41:127-44.

———— and Eliezer Don-Yehiya. 1983. *Civil Religion in Israel: Traditional Judaism and Political Culture in the Jewish State*. Berkeley: University of California Press.

————. 1984. *Religion and Politics in Israel*. Bloomington: Indiana University Press.

Lilker, Shalom. 1982. *Kibbutz Judaism: A New Tradition in the Making*. New York: Herzl Press.

Lustick, Ian S. 1988. *For the Land and the Lord: Jewish Fundamentalism in Israel*. New York: Council on Foreign Relations.

Matras, Judah. 1964. "Religious observance and family formation in Israel: some intergenerational changes." *American Journal of Sociology* 69:464-75.

Newman, David (ed.). 1985. *The Impact of Gush Emunim*. London: Croom Helm.

O'Dea, Janet. 1976. "Gush Emunim: roots and ambiguities." *Forum* 25:39-50.

Raanan, Tzvi. 1980. *Gush Emunim* [Hebrew]. Tel Aviv: Sifriat Po'alim.

Rubin, Nissan. 1986. "Death customs in a non-religious kibbutz: the use of sacred symbols in a secular society." *Journal for the Scientific Study of Religion* 25:292-303.

Samet, Moshe. 1979. *Religion and State in Israel* [Hebrew]. Papers in Sociology, Hebrew University, Jerusalem.

Sharot, Stephen. 1976. *Judaism: A Sociology*. New York: Holmes and Meier.

————. 1982. *Messianism, Mysticism, and Magic: A Sociological Analysis of Jewish Religious Movements*. Chapel Hill: University of North Carolina Press.

Shilhav, Joseph and Menachem Friedman. 1985. *Growth and Segregation — The Ultra-Orthodox Community of Jerusalem* [Hebrew]. Jerusalem: Jerusalem Institute for Israel Studies.

Shokeid, Moshe. 1980. "From personal endowment to bureaucratic appointment: the transition in Israel of the communal religious leaders of Moroccan Jews." *Journal for the Scientific Study of Religion* 19:105-13.
_____. 1985. "Cultural ethnicity in Israel: the case of Middle-Eastern Jews' religiosity." *AJS Review* 9:247-71.
Smooha, Sammy. 1978. *Israel: Pluralism and Conflict*. London: Routledge & Kegan Paul.
Tabory, Ephraim. 1981. "State and religion: religious conflict among Jews in Israel." *Church and State* 23:275-83.
_____. 1983. "Reform and conservative Judaism in Israel: a social and religious profile." *American Jewish Year Book* 83:41-61.
_____. 1986. "Pluralism in the Jewish state: reform and conservative Judaism in Israel," pp. 170-93 in Stuart A. Cohen and Eliezer Don-Yehiya (eds.), *Conflict and Consensus in Jewish Political Life*. Ramat Aviv: Bar-Ilan University Press.
_____. 1989. "Residential integration and religious segregation in an Israeli neighborhood." *International Journal of Intercultural Relations* 13:19-35.
_____ and Bernard Lazerwitz. 1983. "Americans in the Israeli reform and conservative denominations: religiosity under an ethnic shield?" *Review of Religious Research* 24:177-87.
Webber, Jonathan. 1985. "Religions in the Holy Land: conflicts of interpretation." *Anthropology Today* 1:3-10.
Weingrod, Alex. 1981. "Rashomon in Jerusalem." *European Journal of Sociology* 22:158-69.
Weissbrod, Lilly. 1981. "From labour Zionism to new Zionism: ideological change in Israel." *Theory and Society* 10:77-803.
_____. 1983. "Religion as national identity in a secular society." *Review of Religious Research* 24:188-205.
_____. 1985. "Core values and revolutionary change," pp. 70-90 in David Newman (ed.), *The Impact of Gush Emunim*. London: Croom Helm.
Yaron, Zvi. 1976. "Religion in Israel." *American Jewish Year Book* 76:41-90.

3

Dimensions of Jewish Religiosity

Peri Kedem

Surveys carried out between 1962 and 1985 (Antonovsky 1963; Ben-Meir and Kedem 1979; Liebman and Don-Yehiya 1983) found that about 15 to 25 percent of the population define themselves as Orthodox (*dati*), 40 to 45 percent as traditional (*mesorti*), and another 35 to 45 percent as non-Orthodox (*lo dati*). But what do people mean when they thus define themselves?

How many Jews in Israel are religious?
Who are they?
How does this religiosity express itself?
What role does religion play in the lives of Israelis?

It is with these questions that this chapter is concerned. The approach here is that religion is a multifaceted concept. Four of the five dimensions presented by Glock and Stark (1965) in their model of religion will be separately analyzed in an attempt to answer the questions posed.

*The author wishes to thank the many people who collaborated with her in the various aspects of her studies: Dr. Yehuda Ben-Meir for his initiative in conducting the first survey and for supervising her Ph.D. dissertation; Dr. Mordechai Bar-Lev for his consent to publish the findings of two of our shared studies; by students Naomi Brontvain and Isaac Prilleltensky for their cooperation in the attempt to study religious experience; and Grace Hollander for her assiduous editing.

1. *The ritualistic dimension* deals with religious practices. The Jewish religion has an established ritual that covers every aspect of social and private behavior. These rituals are codified in many books, the *Shulhan Aruch* being the one most referred to.

2. *The ideological dimension* deals with specific religious beliefs. In comparison to the ritual dimension, this dimension is much less defined. Jewish theology stresses actions, including rites, above theoretical belief—quoting *The Encyclopedia of the Jewish Religion* (Werblowsky and Wigoder 1960):

> The absence of a supreme ecclesiastical body authorized to formulate a creed is not the sole reason for the virtual absence of creeds in Judaism, and it was often felt that the very idea of such formulation ran counter to certain fundamental tendencies in Jewish theology, which is concerned not only with beliefs but very largely with commandments. (101–102)

3. *The experiential dimension* deals with emotions related in some way to God or to religion. This has had a strong impact on psychology since the nineteenth century, as seen in William James' classic *The Varieties of Religious Experience* (1902).

In the Bible one is commanded to "love God" and to be in "awe" toward God. There is also a commandment to rejoice in the holidays. The manner of expressing such emotions obviously cannot be codified. Over generations, various schools of thought have emphasized different emotions, the most famous being the Hassidim who emphasize rejoicing, while the *Mitnagdim* emphasize rational thinking and the feeling of awe.

4. *The consequential dimension* deals with attitudes and values that stem from the individual's approach to religion. In Israel, the most direct consequence of a religious stance is the approach to the issue of state and religion. There is a difference of opinion about how much public observance should/must be enforced in order to maintain the Jewish character of the state, without arousing open hostility. This chapter will try to integrate the findings of six studies that the author and coauthors conducted over the years in order to understand how complex religiosity is in Israel.

THE RITUALISTIC DIMENSION

Judaism has a codified law of 613 commandments. In actual practice there is a very specific gradation in the percentage of people observing each commandment: some commandments are observed by almost everyone, while others are kept by hardly anyone.

The Ben-Meir and Kedem Commandments Scale (Table 10-1) shows the gradations of observance (The Guttman Reproducibility coefficient was 0.93 and the scalability, 0.69) as found in a survey of a representative sample of the adult Jewish population of Israel. (See Appendix, Study I)

Table 10-1 Ben-Meir and Kedem's Commandments Scale

	PERCENT OBSERVING THE COMMANDMENT
Participates in a seder	99
Has a mezuzah at the entrance to the house	89
Participates in the ligthing of Hanukah candles	88
Does not eat bread on Passover	82
Buys only kosher meat	79
Fasts on Yom Kippur	74
Koshers the meat (in water and salt)	61
Lights Shabbat candles with a blessing	53
Uses special Passover dishes	54
Separates meat and milk dishes	44
Makes kiddush on Friday night	38
Attends synagogue on Shabbat	23
Does not travel on Shabbat	22
Hears havdalah Saturday night	21

Table 10-1 (Continued)

	PERCENT OBSERVING THE COMMANDMENT
Goes regularly to the ritual bath (wives)	14
Covers hair (wives)	11
Wears skullcap regularly (men)	11
Goes to synagogue every day (men)	6
Does not use any electricity on Shabbat	1

Are these findings still valid today, 20 years later?

An indication of the similarity of ritual behavior over the hears can be found in surveys carried out by the Israel Institute for Applied Social Research. Table 10-2 demonstrates the similarity of responses of representative samples over a 26-year span.

Table 10-2 IIASR Observance of the religious tradition

RESEARCHER YEAR OF SURVEY	ANTONOVSKY 1962	ARIAN 1969	SHYE 1982	LEVINSON* 1988
Complete observance	15%	12%	14%	10%
Observance to a large extent	15%	14%	20%	18%
Some observance	48%	48%	41%	40%
No observance at all	22%	26%	25%	32%

*The survey found that 75% fast on Yom Kippur, and 25% do not travel on Shabbat; this is almost an exact replica of the 74% and 22% found twenty years before.

In studies on different samples of university students in 1977, 1978, 1980 (see Appendix, Studies II, IV, V), the same hierarchical order of observed commandments was found as in the Ben-Meir and Kedem scale. A similar Guttman scale was created by Laslau and Schwarzwald (1985) to study observance among 710 parents of kindergarten children. The results are given in Table 10-3.

Table 10-3 Laslau and Schwarzwald's Commandments Scale

| | PERCENT THAT OBSERVE COMMANDMENTS | |
	Sepharadim	Ashkenazim
Eats kosher meat	95	83
Lights Shabbat candles	85	66
Separates dishes	77	53
Goes to synagogue on Shabbath	59	44
Doesn't travel on Shabbat	39	29
Doesn't watch TV on Shabbat	28	25
Prays daily wearing phylacteries	26	23
Goes to synagogue daily	16	8

Considering the many differences between the Ben-Meir and Kedem study and the Laslau and Schwarzwald study (the 17-year interval between them, the different sample composition, the dissimilar wording of the questions), the similarity in the results is astounding. The results of these studies demonstrate a continuum ranging from the extremely observant, through various degrees of religious and traditional behavior, to the almost completely nonobservant.

Although the continuum indicates that the ritual behavior is unidimensional, the varying degrees of observance and the finding that many of the observant do not define themselves as religious (*dati*), led to an attempt to categorize the commandments into clusters according to their "popularity" among the three types of people. A factor analysis of the ritual behaviors measured in the Ben-Meir and Kedem study yielded three rotated factors that mirrored the theoretical division of different levels of commandments. The first factor included all those behaviors that can be defined as Orthodox: not using electricity on Shabbat, synagogue attendance, wearing a skullcap, women covering their hair, ritual bath, havdalah, not traveling on Shabbat. The second factor can be defined as traditional: praying on Shabbat, kiddush, separate dishes, Passover dishes, blessing candles, koshering meat, and fasting on Yom Kippur. The third, secular factor consisted of those three rituals in the scale that over 88 percent of the population kept: Passover seder, mezuzah, and Hanukah candles. This last factor was found to be correlated with practices not included in the scale, such as setting the table in a festive manner and cooking special food for the Sabbath meals, which also were observed by the vast majority of the sample.

The fact that people who call themselves nonreligious observe quite a few commandments led a few researchers (Liebman and Don-Yehiya 1983; Shelah 1975) to differentiate between Orthodox and secular, or civil religion, the assumption being that the commandments kept by the nonreligious are different conceptually than those kept only by the Orthodox.

As stated above, the belief code is far from a defined dogma. Yet, though there is no official set of beliefs, rabbis through the ages have formulated principles of faith. Closest to a creed are the "Thirteen Principles of Faith" of Maimonides, which served as the basis for the Ben-Meir and Kedem belief scale. As a result, the belief scale in the Ben-Meir/Kedem study (Appendix, Study I) was more limited than the ritual scale. Only 6 items were found to fulfill the demands of a Guttman scale, with a narrower range of answers. Within these constraints it was found that the belief scale is unidimensional, discriminating between people as to their "amount" of belief. The reproducibility coeffieient of the belief scale was found to be 0.92, and the scalability was 0.80 (Table 10-4).

Table 10-4   The Traditional Belief Scale

	PERCENTAGES		
Do you believe...	Believe	Don't Know	Don't Believe
In God?	64	6	31

Table 10-4 (Continued)

| | PERCENTAGES | | |
Do you believe...	Believe	Don't Know	Don't Believe
That the Jews are the chosen people?	57	6	37
That God gave Moses the Torah on Mt. Sinai?	56	14	30
That there is a transcendental power who directs the history of the Jewish people?	47	15	38
In the coming of the Messiah?	36	12	52
That the soul continues to exist after death?	29	20	51

The percentage of "don't know" concerning belief "in God" and "that the Jews are the chosen people," is quite small in comparison to the percent of those that don't know what they believe regarding existence after death.

All other studies (Appendix, Studies III, IV, and VI) led to the same conslusion. Beliefs about God and the Jewish people are the most accepted, while beliefs about life after death are the most doubted. This finding might be a reflection of the lesser emphasis in the Jewish religion on the afterlife (hell and heaven) than in the Christian tradition.

Beliefs appearing in certain theological writings are regarded by some as part of traditional Jewish belief and by others as superstition, or as mysticism. One such question was asked in the Ben-Meir and Kedem study: Do you believe in the evil eye? It was found that 64 percent of the population did not believe, 4 percent didn't know, and 32 percent believed.

In a most recent study (Bar-Lev and Kedem 1988) (Appendix, Study VI), students attending religious high schools answered questions about six such beliefs (Table 10-5).

Table 10-5   Mystical Beliefs Scale

| | PERCENTAGES | | |
Do you believe...	Believe	Don't Know	Don't Believe
That the blessings of a rabbi can help a sick or needy person?	74	14	12
That the righteous men have caused and are still causing miracles	51	30	19
That prayer at the grave of a zaddik has power to help men?	50	29	21
Reincarnation (the soul will be reborn in another Jew's body)?	51	32	17
That amulets can bring luck and prevent injury?	19	28	54
That devils and spirits exist and even interfere in the life of man?	9	20	70

The students' responses to the Traditional Belief Scale is very different than their responses to the Mystical Belief Scale. Factor analysis of the items from the combined belief scales yielded two separate factors, following the theoretical division. The students, on the whole, believed much more in the traditional than the mystical beliefs: 89 percent held traditional beliefs versus only 46 percent who held to the mystical beliefs, the "don't knows" 7 percent versus 22 percent and the "nonbelievers" 4 percent versus 32 percent.

The differences between students of Sepharadi and Ashkenazi origins as far as traditional beliefs were concerned were minimal; when it came to mystical beliefs, there were significantly more Sephardi than Ashkenazi believers.

THE EXPERIENTIAL DIMENSION

In the last few years, interest in the experiential dimension has increased due in part to the large number of conversions to conventional religions or to cults (Lofland and Skonovd 1981; Stark and Bainbridge 1981).

In Israel, research on the experiential aspect of religion has been almost completely neglected. A few studies dealing with converts or penitents investigated this experiential dimension (Glanz and Harrison 1978; Aviad 1980; Kedem et al. 1985), but we limited to a qualitative analysis of yeshiva students "returning" to religious living from their former secular life, which represented a specific group and not the general population.

The lack of quantitative analysis of religious feeling might stem from the absence of emphasis on epiphany in the Jewish religion, which stresses the theological legalistic system and intellectual comprehension rather than emotional experience. However, it might well be that the paucity of work on the experiential dimension is due merely to methodological difficulties, emotion being more subjective and elusive than behavior or attitudes, making its measurement more complex and more problematic.

To conceptualize religion, a consideration and an evaluation of emotional involvement must be made. In this chapter, despite the methodological flaws in the studies under analysis, an attempt will be made to interpret some of the findings in this dimension. The Ben-Meir and Kedem study (Study I) is the most informative because it is based on a representative sample. But the question format was somewhat limited. The Bar-Ilan survey (Study II) is almost a replication of the former study, and it is based on an observant sample. The Brontvain and Prilleltensky study (Study V) delved into the subject in much greater depth than the former studies, but this study suffers from an unrepresentative sample.

The Ben-Meir and Kedem study (Study I) asked the question "Was there ever any incident in your life which led you to feel close to God?" Forty-six percent of the representative sample confirmed that indeed they had such experiences. They were then asked "What was the event that promoted this feeling?" Ten percent claimed that they felt close to God when an event of *national importance* occurred (such as winning the Six-Day War). Twenty-nine percent mentioned that they experienced a feeling of "closeness to God" during a *personal event:* 21 percent referred to personal survival in war, the Holocaust, sickness, and accidents; family events, 2 percent; personal success, 1 percent; and sundry intimate personal happenings 5 percent. Only 1 percent mentioned prayer as an instigator of such feelings. A marginal 1 percent were unable to pinpoint any particular incident, moment, or event because they "always feel close to God."

The question, "In which of the following events do you feel religious emotion?", though similar in spirit to the former question ("Which events led you to feel close to God?"), did not evoke the same reaction. To the question on *religious* emotion, 39 percent answered that they had never had a religious emotion and 18 percent said they always have such a feeling. Eighteen percent have such a feeling when they pray, 15 percent claimed that they feel religious when "something important happens to the state or the nation"; 7 percent mentioned having the feeling when they "do a good or just deed," and 3 percent when there is "happiness in the family." No one revealed a religious feeling about "Shabbat and the holidays," "when alone," "when afraid or worried or when very happy."

In another attempt to study religious emotion, a representative sample of Bar-Ilan students (Study III) were asked a question, similar to the previous one, about events arousing religious feelings. Instead of being required to choose only one situation from a list of situations, they were required to respond to each situation independently. With this changed format, all the events seemed to have equal arousal potential. All events mentioned triggered religious feeling in about to to 70 percent of the students.

In the study specifically dealing with religious experience (Study V), the students were given a list of 20 situations, and they were required to check those situations that arouse spiritual experiences. The situation that aroused the greatest emotion was "watching national events" (70 percent). "Listening to music" was second with 50 percent. Other situations were mentioned by a third of the respondents: prayer; birth, marriage, and death; disaster, fear, and war. Religious feelings provoked by works of art, poetry, or literature were scarcely mentioned.

To a list of 50 emotions that could be felt during a religious-spiritual experience, the division was as following: words used to express the religious-spiritual experience were "a feeling of well-being, pleasure," 56 percent; "calm", 54 percent; "security," 40 percent; "love," 39 percent; "close to God," 28 percent. The feelings mentioned by James (1902) and others (Hood 1975, Margolis 1979) as part of the religious experience and especially during conversion—that is, "transcednance of body," "voices heard," "bodily change," etc.—were not mentioned at all.

To summarize: emotions are varied and it is not possible to create stable factors, or scales. There does, however, seem to be on one hand a strong emphasis on personal or individualized religious feeling and, on the other hand, a feeling of religious emotion stemming from national events.

The consequence of a religious attitude that most strongly affects daily life in Israel is the incorporation of religious law into civil law. Sociologists (Tabory 1981a,b; Smooha 1978) stress the tensions arising from these problems. The Ben-Meir and Kedem (Study I) measured what people thought about the dilemma. The State and Religion Scale (Table 10-6) was a Guttman scale of 17 items (reproducibility 0.89 and scalability 0.67).

Table 10-6   State and Religion Attitude Scale

	PERCENTAGES	
	for	against
Are you for or against a law:		
Prohibiting all traffic on Shabbat	13	87
Prohibiting taxis on Shabbat	18	82
Closing gasoline stations on Shabbat	24	76
Closing cafes and restaurants on Shabbat	31	69
Prohibiting entertainment programs on Shabbat	32	68
Closing the cinemas on Shabbat	44	55
Prohibiting the sale of nonkosher meat	41	59
Obliging pupils in secular schools to wear skullcaps during Bible lessons.	41	59
Prohibiting buses from travelling on Shabbat	43	57
Prohibiting civil marriage?	47	53
Prohibiting the raising of pigs?	54	46
Prohibiting intermarriage with non-Jews?	59	41

Table 10-6 (Continued)

	PERCENTAGES	
	for	against
Closing the streets to traffic on Shabbat in religious neighborhoods	70	30
Closing shops on Shabbat	79	21
That the government supply religious needs like synagogues and ritual baths for interested citizens	80	20
That the government guarantee separate religious education to all who desire it?	83	17
That the general school curriculum should include lessons in Jewish tradition?	86	4

This scale, like the Commandments Scale, is wide-ranging, hierarchical in nature, and consistent over time. Studies on students some years later (Appendix, Studies II, III, IV) showed high correlations with the original scale.

Although the attitudes can be constructed into a unidimensional scale, a factor analysis revealed a subdivision into four factors. The first factor included all the attitudes about Shabbat laws except for the closing of shops. Only a minority of the sample endorsed the items in this factor. The second factor included laws dealing with the selling of nonkosher food, raising pigs, civil marriages and intermarriages, and the ruling about wearing skullcaps. About 50 percent of the population endorsed those laws.

The third factor included items that showed tolerance towards religious people's needs. The vast majority endorse those laws that commit the government to supply synagogues or education for the religious and the right to close a street in a religious neighborhood on Shabbat. The fourth factor included those civil religious laws that the vast majority endorsed for everyone: closing stores on Shabbat, and teaching Jewish tradition in the elementary school. The endorsement of the last two factors by the majority shows that the concept of separation of state and religion is understood differently in Israel than it is in the United States. People see no contradiction in the endorsement of these laws even while many (47 percent) claim to support the separation of state and religion.

THE CONNECTION BETWEEN RELIGIOUS DEFINITION AND THE RELIGIOUS DIMENSIONS

The Relationship between the Dimension and Self-definition

What do people mean when they define themselves as Orthodox, traditional, and non-Orthodox? An answer might be found by relating to the other religious dimensions. In Table 10-7, the correlations of the six studies are presented. (Because the studies varied in the number of dimensions measured, each study includes different correlations).

Table 10-7   Correlations between religious self-definition and ritual, belief, attitude to the state-religion issue and emotion

	STUDY I	STUDY II	STUDY III	STUDY IV	STUDY V	STUDY VI
Ritual	.72	.89	.84	.82	.71	.61
Belief	.65	.77	.71	.67	.45	
State & Religion	.80	.70	.73	.78	.40	
Religious Emotion	.43	.43				

The correlations indicate that all the dimensions are significantly correlated to religious self-definition, the ritual dimension being the most related. In other words, in Israel people define themselves as Orthodox, traditional, or nonreligious on the basis of the observance of religious commandments. The lower correlations in study VI result from the limited range of answers because the sample consisted only of students from religious high schools.

The correlation between self-definition and the attitude toward the state-religion connection attitude was almost as high as that with ritual. The more people define themselves as religious, the more they want the country to have a religious civil code. Belief is less related to definition, and indices of religious experience show the least relationship.

These results lead us back to Jewish tradition in which carrying out the commandments takes the predominant role, while belief and feeling are secondary. This explains the high significant correlation between ritual and self-definition. It would be virtually impossible to find anyone considering himself religious who does not keep the rituals.

Another way of analyzing the results is to compare the three groups of people—religious, traditional, and nonreligious—as to the amount of religiosity professed on the various scales. The Ben-Meir and Kedem study (Study I), as the most representative and the broadest in scope, has been chosen for presentation. As described above, we found that ritual can be subdivided into three factors and the state-religion attitude into four factors. Belief was a single factor, and emotions did not yield stable factors, but we saw that the situations arousing religious feeling can be clustered into national and personal situations. Table 8 will show how the different self-defined groups respond to these various indices of religiosity.

Table 10-8   Religiosity of the three self-defined groups

| | RELIGIOUS SELF-DEFINITION | | |
	Dati Religious	*Mesorti* Traditional	*Lo Dati* Not religious
Religiosity index	n = 258	n = 619	n = 641
Ritual	72.16	> 45.46	> 27.66
orthodox ritual	48.06	> 7.67	> .82
traditional ritual	84.88	> 66.41	> 33.64
secular ritual	99.22	> 93.86	> 86.88
Belief	88.43	> 45.46	> 27.66
State and religion	79.75	> 51.75	> 30.49
orthodox attitude	68.93	> 26.84	> 7.49
traditional attitude	84.88	> 53.50	> 20.44
secular attitude	92.44	= 88.21	> 76.99
tolerance attitude	85.53	> 73.77	> 65.63

Table 10-8   (Continued)

| | RELIGIOUS SELF-DEFINITION | | |
	Dati Religious	*Mesorti* Traditional	*Lo Dati* Not religious
Experience			
close to God	81.39	> 54.60	> 23.56
national	12.40	= 13.57	> .06
personal	33.72	> 25.69	> 10.92
religious feeling	72.16	> 45.46	> 27.66
always	41.86	> 11.15	> .02
never	.78	< 9.85	< 53.51

Note: (a) In order to compare the various indices, all scores were transformed to be expressed 0 to 100 giving the scores a meaning similar to percentage. (b) Significance of p < .0001 is marked by >.

Table 10-8 shows how the amount of religiosity of the three self-defined groups accord with their position on the various religious dimensions. As can be expected, religious people, on the average, observe more ritual than the traditional, and they in turn observe more than the nonreligious. By dividing the observances themselves into factors, we find that the more extreme ones we named Orthodox observances were not observed at all by those that defined themselves as nonreligious. The traditional group also hardly kept those strict rules, and only about 50 percent of the religious group held to all of the Orthodox observances. The traditional rituals were observed not only by the majority of religious people, but also by a majority of those who define themselves as simply traditional. Even those who defined themselves as nonreligious kept about 33 percent of the traditional rituals. The secular rituals were kept by a vast majority of the population no matter how they defined themselves.

The religious group endorsed about 88 percent of the beliefs in the scale, the traditional group about 50 percent, and even the nonreligious people held to about a third of the beliefs. In the study of the religious high school students (Study IV), mystic beliefs were held by 69 percent of those who defined themselves as religious, 66 percent of the traditional group, and 52 percent of the nonreligious students. It is interesting to compare these figures with the beliefs of the same high school students on the Traditional Belief Scale. On that scale, the religious students scored 96 percent, the traditional 91 percent, and the nonreligious 69 percent. The nonreligious students (by self-definition) believed less than the other two groups, but the gap was much greater for the traditional beliefs than for the mystical ones.

The state and religion category shows the same trend as the ritual scale. The majority of the nonreligious group favor enforcing the religious laws affecting the general public. They are also tolerant of the needs of religious people.

The experience category shows, as would be expected, that the less religious by self-definition have less feeling of closeness to God and less religious feeling. Even among the nonreligious, however 47 percent claim that they have had religious feelings at one time or another.

DISCUSSION

Can we explain the descending hierarchy or ritual, belief, and attitude and particularly the religiosity of nonreligious people who define themselves as traditional or nonreligious?

Neuman (1982) tried to theorize that the amount of ritual observed is determined by the amount of effort required to observe the ritual. By applying ingenious mathematical formulas to Ben-Meir and Kedem's data (Study I), she "proved" her hypothesis. Obviously it takes more time and effort to pray daily than to pray once a year. It also has an appeal because it can serve as an explanation for Jews abroad as well as for Israeli Jews. The theory, however, is in error. The amount of effort many nonreligious women put into housecleaning before Passover is cogent disproof. Moreover, the theory does not explain the descending order of attitudes connected with the subject of the state and religion or the belief scale: Neither more nor less effort is required for any given belief than for an alternative one.

Two other theories are more helpful. Shelah(1975) did a study called "Indications towards secular religion in Israel." On the basis of theoretical writings and on an empirical study of women who defined themselves as traditional or secular, she concluded that secular religion is separate from traditional religion. Her indication of secular religion is that rituals observed are based upon free personal choice, while according to her, traditional religion is dictated.

The secular-traditional Jew, according to Shelah, observes the rituals not because of faith in supernatural factors, but from faith in social values derived from Jewish tradition, while others maintain a faith in universal social values such as human life, the family, and the home. She emphasized the dominant role the family has in the secular religion. She considers it to be "a substitute for religion, constituting a focus for ritual activity."

Liebman and Don-Yehiya (1983) developed and documented a theory of civil religion. Their theory is based mainly on writings of politicians, authors, philosophers, and the media and is backed by a small number of surveys.

The theory states that civil religion went through three stages. From 1919–1945 Zionist socialism was predominant and claimed that "there is no inherent relationship between religion and Judaism." They tried to create the "new Jew" and rebelled against their own religious background in the Diaspora. The second stage, "statism" (1948–1956), repeated the "no inherent relationship" theme. At that time, ritual was either discarded or subjected to change, both in interpretation and in behavior. The Shavuot holiday serves as a good example. The new Shavuot emphasised only the agricultural aspect of the holiday, disregarding the religious significance of the day the Torah was given to the Jewish people. The third stage, from 1956 until today is the period of the "new civil religion." In this stage there is a complete reversal: Israel as a Jewish state must recognize the relationship between religion and Judaism. "Some measure of religious observance, of knowledge about and respect for the Jewish tradition are important attributes of the good Israeli. The state itself should incorporate traditional Jewish symbols." Liebman and Don-Yehiva, (p. 219).

Before attempting to integrate the findings of the six studies within a theoretical framework, something must be said about Jewish religious identity of non-Israelis and Jewish identification of Israelis. Studies in the United States on religiosity found a similar descending order of ritual and belief (Lazerwitz 1973, 1978; Liebman 1973; Polasky 1958; Sklare 1958). Percentages are different, as are ways of building samples and representation within the samples, but the trend is similar to what happens in Israel.

As far as Jewish identity of Israelis are concerned, findings of research (Herman 1977, Levy and Guttman 1975, Levy 1986, Etzyoni-Halevy 1969, Bar-Lev and Kedem 1986) at different times, on different types of samples, with differently worded questionnaires, all disclosed some similar trends. In Study IV a representative sample of students were presented with a list of 30 components of Jewish identity. They were required to state how much each component contributed to their identity as a Jew. The 30 components led to six factors.

The most important factor in the students' Jewish identity was Israeli identity: about 90 to 100 percent mentioned living in Israel, being in the army, and speaking Hebrew as important components.

The second most important factor was religious tradition. In this connection about 85 ot 90 percent mentioned marriage to a Jew, marriage in a religious ceremony, circumcision, celebrating a bar mitzvah, religious burial, celebrating Jewish holidays like Passover. Belief in one God belonged to this factor as well, although a smaller percent of students (75 percent) mentioned it as contributing to Jewish identity. Jewish solidarity, Jewish history, and reaction to anti-semitism are important components for about 75 percent of the sample.

The factor that the vast majority of students saw as having no relevance to their Jewish identity was the Jewish ethics factor. They did not perceive that values—honesty, honoring parents, not stealing, good family relations, study, and care for the needy—as part of their specifically Jewish identity, but only as the universal identity.

Integration of the various findings on Jewish religiosity in Israel requires one to accept that much religious behavior can be explained by individual emotions tied to childhood memories and the desire to instill similar memories in children.

Secular religious behavior is related especially to special occasions that have child-centered elements. Much of the seder night ritual is carried out to appeal to the child's interest. Yom Kippur and Rosh Hashanah are filled with symbolic behavior to distinguish those Days of Awe from all others. In Israel, the synagogues are filled with children when it is time for the blowing of the shofar. Certain Shabbat behaviors—lighting candles, saying kiddush, a festive table, and traditional food—all can be related to a holiday atmosphere that children respond to from generation to generation.

On the other hand, the same people might observe the same behaviors out of identification with the Jewish nation as well. The rituals serve as symbols expressing attachment to the Jewish people. All Israeli Jews circumcise their sons as part of the Jewish covenant. The bar mitzvah is also a religious act expressing national identity. All these rituals have existed for generations among Jews all over the world and hence link the Jews in Israel and those in the Diaspora. As the Israelis see it, being Israeli is an integral part of being Jewish. These symbols are perceived as part of their Jewish-Israeli identification.

The state and religion attitudes are another expression of the collectivistic approach of most Jews in Israel. All the population want the state to have a Jewish identity. The difference lies in the amount of laws considered necessary. There is also a difference of opinion on the degree of coercion that can be applied tactically or diplomatically. As we saw, the most accepted civil law related to religion is the one stating that children should be taught something about their Jewish religious tradition. In the political context, too, religious laws are acceptable in relation to children.

Beliefs are also affected by national feeling. Many people believe in Jewish destiny. Mystic beliefs seem related to ethnic group. Those youngsters who grew up in a culture that believes, accept them. But as these beliefs are not universal among Jews, they are not accepted even by all those who define themselves as Orthodox.

Religious experience has a personal-individual aspect and a Jewish-Israeli aspect. In the main survey, 22 percent of the respondents mentioned a personal event, while 10 percent mentioned a national event as causing a religious experience. University and high school students both mentioned personal and national situations that aroused religious feeling.

Another question is whether there is a dictated "religious" religion and a freely chosen "secular" religion, as postulated by Shelah (1975) and previously mentioned. The Orthodox also seem to be making a choice. In the six studies where the religious group was compared to the traditional or even to the nonreligious, we saw that all groups had personal motivation and national associations, and the difference was more in degree than in kind. Religious people, however, see religion as more encompassing, more part of their whole being, and more as emanating from a divine source.

REFERENCES

Antonovsky, A. 1963. Israeli political-social attitudes. *Amot 6:* 11–12 (Hebrew).

Arian, A. 1973. *The choosing people: Voting behavior in Israel.* Cleveland: The Press of Case Western Reserve University.

Aviad, J. 1980. From protest to return: Contemporary teshuva. *The Jerusalem Quarterly, 16:* 71–82.

Bar-Lev, M. 1977. *The graduates of the Yeshiva high-school in Ertz-Yisrael: Between tradition and innovation.* Docroral dissertation, Bar-Ilan University, Ramat Gan, Israel (Hebrew).

Bar-Lev, M., A. Har-Even, and P. Kedem. 1981. *The Jewish world of the Israeli student: His social, national, religious and cultural values.* Ramat Gan & Jerusalem, Bar-Ilan University in cooperation with Van-Leer Institute in Jerusalem (Hebrew).

Bar-Lev, M., and P. Kedem. 1986. Unity and compartmentalization in Israeli students' perceptions of their Jewish-Zionist identity and identification. *Hebetim Bechinuch 1:* 155-77 (Hebrew).

Bar-Lev, M., and P. Kedem. 1988. *Youth Aliya students of Yishivot and Ulpanas.* Ramat Gan: Bar Ilan University. Research report submitted to Youth Aliya.

Ben-Meir, Y., and P. Kedem. 1979. A measure of religiosity for the Jewish population of Israel. *Megamot 24:* 353-62 (Hebrew).

Brontvain, N., and I. Prilleltenski. 1980. *Religious experience: An empirical and conceptual analysis.* Internal report. Bar-Ilan University, Ramat Gan, Israel (Hebrew).

Etzyoni-Halevy, H. 1969. Jewish Identity of Tel-Aviv University students. M.A. Thesis, Tel-Aviv University: Tel-Aviv Israel (Hebrew).

Glanz, D., and M. Harrison. 1978. Varieties of identity transformation: The case study of newly Orthodox Jews. *Jewish Journal of Sociology 20:* 129-41.

Glock, C., and R. Stark. 1965. *Religion and society in tension.* Chicago: Rand McNally.

Herman, S. N. 1977. *Jewish identity a social psychological perspective,* Beverly Hills: Sage.

Hood, R. 1975. The construction and validation of a measure of reported mystical experience. *Journal for the Scientific Study of Religion 14:* 29-41.

James, W. 1902. *The varieties of religious experience: A study of human nature.* New-York: The Modern Library.

Kedem, P. 1979. *Centrality, salience, and ego involvement as measures of the importance of the religious attitude.* Doctoral dissertation, Bar-Ilan University, Ramat Gan, Israel.

Kedem, P., and M. Bar-Lev. 1983. Is giving up traditional religious culture part of the price to be paid for acquiring higher education? *Higher Education 12:* 373-88.

Kedem, P., and I. Birinbaum, I. Kopiz, and R. Siboni. 1985. *The relationship between ego-identity and attraction towards new religious groups.* Abstract Israel Psychological Association. The 20th conference.

Kedem, P., and J. Lewin. 1978. *Change in attitudes on Judaism during studies at Bar-Ilan University.* Ramat Gan: Research Authority of Bar-Ilan University, Ramat Gan, Israel.

Laslau, A., and J. Schwarzwald. 1985. *Parents' considerations in applying for state religious schools for their children*. Jerusalem: Ministry of Education and Culture.

Lazerwitz, B. 1973. Religious identification and its ethnic correlates: A multivariate model *Social Forces 52*: 204-20.

Lazerwitz, B. 1978. An approach to the components and consequences of Jewish identification. *Contemporary Jewry 23*: 57-69.

Levinson, H. 1988. Attitudes and Evaluations of the public on religious and Jewish issues, and towards the institutes responsible for the religious services. Jerusalem: The Israel Institute of Applied Social Research (Hebrew).

Levy, S. 1986. *The structure of social values*. Jerusalem: The Israel Institute of Applied Social Research.

Levy, S. and L. Guttman. 1976. Jewish identity of Israelis in the midst of the war. In M. Davis (Ed.). The identity of the nation with the state following the Yom-Kippur war. Jerusalem: The Zionist Library (Hebrew).

Levy, S., and L. Guttman. 1976b. *Values and attitudes of Israel high school youth*. Jerusalem: The israel Institute of Applied Research (Hebrew).

Liebman, C. 1973. *The ambivalent American Jew: Politics, religion and family in American Jewish life*. Philadelphia: Jewish Publication Society.

Liebman, C. S., and E. Don-Yehiya. 1983. *Civil Religion in Israel. Traditional Judaism and political culture in the Jewish state*. Berkely: University of California Press.

Lofland, J., and N. Skonovd. 1981. Conversion motives. *Journal for the Scientific Study of Religion 20(4)*: 373-85.

Margolis, R. D. 1979. A typology of religious experience, *Journal for the Scientific Study of Religion 18(1)*: 61-72.

Maslow, A. 1964. *Religions, values and peak experience*. Columbus, OH: Ohio State University Press.

Neuman, S. 1982. Cost of time devoted to religious activities. Doctoral dissertation, Bar-Ilan University, Ramat Gan, Israel (Hebrew).

Polasky H. E. 1958. A study of Orthodoxy in Milwaukee: Social characteristics, beliefs and observances. In *The Jews*, ed. M. Sklare. New York, NY: The Free Press.

Samet, M. 1979. *Religion and state in Israel,* Jerusalem: Hebrew University (Hebrew).

Shapiro, J. 1977. *Democracy in Israel.* Ramat Gan: Massada Press.

Shelah, I. 1975. *Indications towards secular religion in Israel* Jerusalem: The Hebrew University Press (Hebrew).

Shye, S. 1983. *Public attitude towards religious literature and religious institutions.* Jerusalem: The Israel Institute of Applied Social Research.

Sklare, M. 1958. *The Jews.* New York, NY: The Free Press.

Smooha, S. 1978. *Israel: Pluralism and conflict,* London: Routledge & Kegan Paul.

Stark, R. and W. Bainbridge. 1981. Secularization and cult formation in the jazz age. *Journal for the Scientific Study of Religion 20:* 360-73.

Tabory, E. 1981a. State and religion: Religious conflict among Jews in Israel. *Church and State 23:* 275-83.

Tabory, E. 1981b. Religious rights as a social problem in Israel. In *Yearbook on Human Rights.* Tel Aviv: Tel Aviv University, Israel, 256-71.

Werblowsky, Z. R. J., and G. Wigoder. 1985. *The Encyclopedia of the Jewish Religion. NY: Holt, Rinehart & Winston, Inc.*

APPENDIX

STUDY I:
INDEX OF RELIGIOSITY OF THE JEWISH POPULATION OF ISRAEL

BEN-MEIR AND KEDEM

The sample consisted of 1,530 subjects chosen by area sampling design from the adutl urban Jewish population. The sampling procedure was done in two stages: the first stage consisted of a stratified random sample of 400 statistically divided areas from the whole of Israel. From this sample, 161 areas were chosen at random. In the second stage, 10 dwellings were chosen at random to represent each of the 161 areas. In each, one subject was interviewed, in the evening, by a female interviewer from the regular pool of a large opinion survey institute. All interviews were based on a standard questionnaire.

The questionnaire consisted of 150 questions, covering many different topics, directly and indirectly relating to religion. The analyses of the questions related to ritual, consequential, and ideological dimensions will be reported here. The choice of the questions was based on the following three conditions:

1. Derivation from established Jewish religious creeds.

2. The questions on ritual were linked to halacha.

3. The attitudes on state and religion were based on proposals for new laws or existing legislation.

Beliefs were taken mostly from Maimonides' "Thirteen Articles of Faith." In order to be readily understood, the questions were simply worded, short and concrete.

All the items stemmed from traditions common to all Jews.

Reference

Ben-Meir, Y., and P. Kedem. 1979. A measure of religiosity for the Jewish population of Israel. *Megamot 24:* 353-62 (Hebrew).

STUDY II:
CENTRALITY, SALIENCE AND EGO-INVOLVEMENT
AS MEASURES OF THE IMPORTANCE OF THE RELIGIOUS ATTITUDE

PERI KEDEM

Four hundred and forty-one students from five universities answered a questionnaire designed specifically to measure intensity of feelings toward keeping commandments and the issue of state and religion.

The sample was constructed so as to have a wide dispersion of positions along the state and religion continuum. About 60 percent the sample were graduates of a nonreligious high school, while the other 40 percent graduated from religious ones.

Reference

Kedem, P. 1979. *Centrality, salience, and ego involvement as measures of the importance of the religious attitude.* Doctoral dissertation, Bar-Ilan University, Ramat Gan, Israel.

STUDY III:
BAR-ILAN STUDENTS' ATTITUDES TOWARD JUDAISM

PERI KEDEM AND ISAAC LEWIN

A questionnaire was mailed to a representative sample of Bar-Ilan students, relating to all six dimensions of religiosity: ritual, belief, experiential, knowledge, and attitude relating the state and religion issue. Questions as to religious and Jewish identification as well as questions about the Jewish studies offered at the university were also put to them.

Bar-Ilan, unique in that it is a religious university, requires some basic Jewish studies for its degree. The student body is divided almost equally between religious and nonreligious students, very differently from other universities in Israel.

This study was executed in 1977, repeated in 1978, and again in 1980. Each study covered a representative sample as verified by comparison with university statistics: sex, percentage in various departments, age, and martial status.

Reference

Kedem, P., and J. Lewin. 1978. *Change in attitudes on Judaism during studies at Bar-Ilan University.* Ramat Gan: Research Authority of Bar-Ilan University, Ramat Gan, Israel.

STUDY IV:
THE JEWISH WORLD OF THE ISRAELI STUDENT

PERI KEDEM AND MORDECAI BAR-LEV

Sample A random sample (N = 1250) was a representative sample of all the Jewish undergraduates studying for their B.A. degrees in the academic year 1979–1980 at the six Israeli universities. The students received a closed questionnaire delivered by the secretary of the university. The questionnaire form bore only the heading of the Van-Leer Institute (a cosponsor of this research project) to disengage the research from the universities where the students studied.

MEASURES

1. *Ritual Dimension:* The questions were based on the Ben-Meir and Kedem Scale and on a scale designed for graduates of yeshiva high schools (Bar-Lev, 1979) dealing with more extreme Orthodox practices.

2. *Belief Dimension:* Five items were taken from the Ben-Meir and Kedem Scale with expanded answer categories. The three original "believe," "don't know," "don't believe" were increased to five with the addition of provision for degrees of doubt.

3. *Consequential Dimension:* The State and Religion Scale was based mainly on the Ben-Meir and Kedem Scale with new questions added to include current issues, that is, legalizing prostitution and abortion.

4. *Jewish Identity and Identification.* A chapter devoted to the question, "What are the components of Jewish identity, and how much does the student feel thus identified? (See Bar-Lev and Kedem 1986)

References

Kedem, P., and M. Bar-Lev. 1983. Is giving up tradition religious culture part of the price to be paid for acquiring higher education? *Higher Education* *12:* 373-88.

Bar-Lev, M., A. Hareven, and P. Kedem. 1981. *The Jewish world of the Israeli student: His social, national, religious and cultural values.* Ramat Gan & Jerusalem, Bar-Ilan University in cooperation with Van-Leer Institute in Jerusalem (Hebrew).

Bar-Lev, M., and P. Kedem. 1986. Unity and compartmentalization in Israeli students' perceptions of their Jewish-Zionist identity and identification. *Hebetim Bchinuch 1:* 155-77 (Hebrew).

STUDY V:
RELIGIOUS EXPERIENCE

KEDEM, BRONTVAIN AND PRILLELTENSKY

Subject and Procedure. The sample consisted of 113 adolescents (16-18 years old), 56 were students in a religious high school and 57 in a nonreligious high school. The structured questionnaire was administered during a regular class session.

In order to measure feelings relating to religious-spiritual experience. The questionnaire was worded not in terms of "religious" experience but in terms of spiritual experience, so that the nonreligious student could feel comfortable with the questionnaire.

The items were derived from Glock and Stark's (1965) measurement of the experiential dimension; Margolis' (1979) typology of religious experience; Hood's (1975) work on mystical experience; Kedem and Lewin's (1978) study on students' religious attitudes; and items based on the theoretical works of James (1902) and Maslow (1964).

After a pilot test on a few students in the university, and a pretest on a class in a nonreligious high school, the items that were misunderstood or caused antagonism were deleted.

Reference

Brontvain, N., and I. Prilleltenski. 1980. *Religious experience: An empirical and conceptual analysis.* (Internal Report) Bar-Ilan University, Ramat Gan, Israel (Hebrew)

STUDY VI:
DIMENSIONS OF RELIGIOSITY OF HIGH SCHOOL STUDENTS

MORDECAI BAR LEV AND PERI KEDEM

In 1984, 2,580 students in religious high schools answered a questionnaire on various aspects of their lives. One chapter was dedicated to religiosity and contained many detailed questions not asked in the aforementioned studies about ritual. The belief questions included six from the Ben-Meir and Kedem scale as well as questions pertaining to mystical belief. Attitude and Jewish identity was measured similarly to Study V.

Reference

Bar-Lev, M., and P. Kedem. 1988. *Youth Aliya students of Yeshivot and Ulpanas.* Ramat Gan: Bar Ilan University. Research report submitted to Youth Aliya.

Part II

Political Dimensions of Israeli Judaism

4

Jewish Civilization: Approaches to Problems of Israeli Society

Shmuel N. Eisenstadt

The Major Approaches to the Problems of Israeli Society

Inward and Outward Looking. All the processes leading to the disintegration of the original institutional mold of Israeli society—changes in the ethos and the relative importance of the original ideological visions, the transformation of elite groups into the ruling class, the growing dissociation among elite groups, the weakening of solidary frameworks, as well as their repercussions—evinced several characteristics common to other postrevolutionary and other small modern societies. Israeli society shared with these the tendencies to routinize and demystify the original revolutionary vision and showed a similar stagnation in its postrevolutionary ethos. The processes leading to this disintegration highlighted, in Israel perhaps even more than in other such societies, some of the conflicting and the cross-cutting choices inherent in the very institutionalization and dynamic development of such a mold. Above it all was a choice between commitment to a monolithic ideology as against pluralism; between elitism as against populism; between the stress on duty and obligations as against rights and entitlements; between active participation in societal and cultural creativity as against the more passive or privatized ones. Finally, there was the great challenge of finding new ways to combine these various orientations without entirely giving up any of them. The ways in which these processes and their repercussions crystallized in Israeli society evinced some specific characteristics, closely related to its being a small state with aspirations exceeding its actual scope.

Two distinct approaches developed within Israeli society to cope with the dilemmas arising out of this situation. One approach assumed that these aspirations would be realized through the existing social structure and its attachment to Jewish or socialist traditions. This approach often was combined with strong extremist religious and nationalist movements and slogans, characterized by a growing intolerance. An opposing approach stressed that Israel's aspirations could not be realized through its mere existence or upholding the symbols of its identity; direct participation in social and cultural frameworks beyond its borders, close relations with various Jewish and international communities, and with other civilizations was required to forge its own identity. Such orientations tended to strengthen the pluralism of Israeli society against the monolithic tendencies of the former approach. Although these different approaches cut to some extent across the different political camps, the first was (and became even more so in the last two decades) characteristic of the right, and the second was more prevalent at the center and to the left of it.

These different approaches were manifested in the contradictory attitudes toward all the preceding problems. They became especially visible after the Six-Day War and continued to be so throughout the following periods: punctuated by the Yom Kippur War, the Lebanon War, and the Intifada. From then on the door was opened toward the Arab world and toward various movements in both Jewish and non-Jewish communities. These developments, on the one hand, strengthened the reshaping of Israeli identity toward broader and more flexible contacts. On the other hand, however, currents of sometimes extreme chauvinism appeared, combining religious and secular nationalism nourished by feelings of superiority and isolation from the outside world, extreme xenophobia toward Arabs, cultural provincialism, and increased rigidity in the construction of the Israeli collective identity.

The Resurgence of Major Themes of Jewish Political Traditions.   The appearance of these tendencies was due largely to the fact that the institutionalization of the initial Zionist labor mold and its disintegration were closely connected with, and intensified by, the problems of implementing the Jewish civilizational vision in the setting of a small, beleaguered society. And in these ways, it also highlighted the problems and dilemmas of the Jewish re-entry into history.

Therefore, the growing dissociation among different elite groups and the weakening framework of solidarity gave rise to the resurgence of different themes of Jewish civilization and the Zionist vision: the Messianic, territorial, solidary, primordial components of the collective identity. These emerged, each claiming its autonomy from the others, challenging the validity of the opposition, and claiming total predominance in the institutional formation of the society.

The resurgence of these themes was facilitated by the weakening institutional framework and ideological symbols that brought together in the initial institutional mold of Israeli society the various themes of Jewish political culture. It was easy for tendencies to develop combining the anarchic politics of the higher law and the solidarity of small sectors. Paradoxically, because of the existence of the Jewish state, such a combination could become connected with relinquishing the responsibility (quite strong in Medieval times) for the entire community and for the maintenance of some order within its framework.

Indeed, many indications suggested that these political tendencies, when transposed into the setting of a territorial state, and a modern democratic one in particular, might undermine the very viability of its institutional framework, as they probably did in the period of the Second Commonwealth.

The Struggles about the Basic Contours of Israeli Society

Collective Identity. The major efforts at reconstruction of the Zionist ethos of Israeli collective identity moved toward strengthening the political-territorial components, in tandem with the weakening of the revolutionary components of Zionist ideology and intensive promulgation of ethnic themes and symbols, as well as of the anti-Zionist or at least a-Zionist religious ones.

The most important change in the Zionist themes, one inherent in the old Revisionist vision, was the emphasis on and partial sanctification of military might and struggle. Closely related to this was the new emphasis on the territorial dimension of Zionism. Many attempts were made at the sanctification or semisanctification of this component in historical and religious terms, a sanctification that was not a very strong component of the original Revisionist vision.

The conception of territoriality changed from the perception of territory as a means for realizing the national reconstruction, as an expression of the special relationship of the nation to its land, or as a basis for national security to the almost total secular or religous sanctification of territory and settlement as an end in itself, as the very epitome of the Zionist vision.[17] The secular version of this sanctification was found among many of the supporters of "Eretz Israel Hashlema," in the labor sector, in many kibbutzim and moshavim, as well as among broad urban sectors. It combined a secular primordial orientation with a strong emphasis on settlement and security. The religious-nationalist version, which developed among Gush Emunim and those close to them, stressed the religious, historical, and sometimes almost mystical dimensions of territory, often conflating the territorial dimension with political-mystical Messianism.

Among the general Jewish and Zionist themes, those of Jewish solidarity and the religious dimension of the Jewish tradition and historical experience were stressed. This often was related to a strong emphasis on particularism, on closing oneself off from the outside world, on the inherent superiority and morality of the Jewish or Israeli collectivity, and on the weakening of the civilizational and hence also universalistic—as opposed to national and particularistic—dimensions of the Zionist or Israeli identity, as well as of the "revolutionary" institution building dimensions.

The second major change with respect to Zionist symbols, connected with the exhaustion of the older labor-Zionist ethos, was the dilution of the elitist components of this vision. Such dilution was manifest first of all in a weakening of the elitist emphasis on duty and obligation, as against the more distributive emphasis on rights and entitlements—and best illustrated in the saying "Leheitiv Im Haam" (doing right by the people)—often used by the Prime Minister Begin, but inherent in the earlier distributive policies. This tendency became a part of a much wider one: the dilution of the revolutionary, reconstructive components of Zionist ideology, those components which emphasized the recontruction of the major dimension of Jewish life.

One of the most important manifestations of this dilution was in the attitude to the exilic history, traditions, and life in the Diaspora. The original negative attitude gave way to a much more tolerant, even affirmative one. One reason for this was connected with one of the major impacts of the Holocaust, the difficulty of continuing rebellion against communities and ways of life that were wiped away in such catastrophic circumstances. As against the earlier negating, a rebellious attitude to the ways of life embodied by these communities, a more positive, commemorative one developed.

An even more positive attitude developed to the religious tradition and Diaspora in the wake of the "ethnic" tensions and revival in Israel, and with the process that probably was among the most constructive aspects of this era; namely with the incorporation of new sectors into the center. Such incorporation was closely connected with the growing inclusion of ethnic and religious themes in the central symbols of collective identity. These themes were initially promulgated in a rather divisive way. Only later did some of them, especially the ethnic and "milder" religious ones, become less divisive, forming part of a wider pluralistic spectrum of themes of collective identity.

Moreover, within some of the older sectors of Israeli society, including some kibbutzim, there developed a greater interest in various aspects of Jewish tradition: history and religion. The development of this interest was to no small degree rooted in the disintegration of the labor-Zionist ideological and institutional mold and the feeling that this mold did not do justice to the richness of Jewish tradition.

In extreme, highly publicized cases, this feeling gave rise to the phenomenon of "Hozrim Biteshuva" (those who "return to the fold"), who became as it were converted to extreme orthodoxy. Beyond these cases such growing interest did not signal any such "return," but rather a quest to find ways of incorporating some aspects of these traditions into the "nonreligious" ways of life of these sectors. Such quest could take the form of study groups, inclusion of some religious rituals such as lighting of candles on Sabbath-eve, and the like. It could also find expression in exploration of Reform and Conservative branches of Judaism brought over from the United States, thus providing yet another signal of changing attitudes to the traditions of the Diaspora.

This changing attitude toward the traditions of the Diaspora and Jewish existence within it was reinforced by new developments in the different communities of the Jewish Diaspora and by changing relations between Israel and the Diaspora. After the Second World War, the Jewish community in the United States became the leading Diaspora community. The majority of its members, or their parents, came from Eastern Europe, as did the pioneers of the Yishuv. The incorporation of Jews in the United States took place (see Chapter 5) in a different mode from that in Europe, the background against which the Zionist movement developed. This new mold entailed, as we have seen, a different reconstitution of Jewish collective life from the one envisaged by the Zionist vision. Accordingly, as we have seen among American Jews, the strong identification with the state of Israel that developed was based on feelings of solidarity, collective pride, but not on the denial of its own way of life, thus seemingly going against the basic Zionist attitude to Jewish existence in the Diaspora.

At the same time, the internal changes in Israeli society, the great surge to modernization and economic development, the intensification of the problems of a small society, especially of maintaining high economic, professional, and cultural standards, have de facto greatly changed the attitude of large sectors of Israeli society to the Diaspora. That many Jews in the Diaspora, especially but not only in the United States, were very successful in these arenas, intensified this orientation to the Diaspora. Growing contacts with different sectors of America, both academic and economic institutions, to use T. Friedman's phrase, made "America very central in the mind of Israel"; and the growing emigration from Israel, called *descent* or yeridah (as against ascent or aliyah), also seemed to threaten many of the classical Zionist premises. All these have considerably weakened and eroded the "negation of the Diaspora" attitude.

There was yet another, rather paradoxical, side to this development. The growing orientation of large parts of the "older" sectors of Israeli society toward the United States, and later also toward Europe, intensified the feelings among large sectors of the Oriental groups that what they confronted among the older sectors of Israeli society was not the pioneering spirit but rather Western patterns of life. Many Oriental sectors began to orient themselves to the Diaspora where, especially in France and North America, many members of their own communities from Iraq and North Africa have settled, often attracting many of the relatives from Israel. But this only increased their feelings of dissociation from the older mold of Israeli society and its westernizeed Ashkenazi sector.

Zionist and Religious Themes.   The emphasis on the reconstruction of various Zionist themes, the incorporation of symbols of ethnic identity, came from within the mainstream of Israeli society. However much they changed the symbolic repertoire of Israeli society, deemphasizing its universalistic components, the changes all took place within its basic, Zionist, symbolic framework. The situation differed with respect to the various anti-Zionist, or at least non-Zionist, religious orientations, as articulated by Agudat Israel and other extreme Orthodox groups. At best these groups accepted the state of Israel as a de facto given, or stressed "settlement of the Land of Israel" as against the Zionist vision of reconstructing Jewish society. Paradoxically, during this period in which the nationalist Zionist themes predominated, their stance gained at least partial legitimacy.

The importance of the religious groups generally was facilitated by their key positions as potential partners in the government coalition; but this was not the whole story. Sensing the ideological vacuum or turbulence that developed within the major sectors of Israeli society with the disintegration of the labor-Zionist mold, the religious groups launched a continuous series of attacks on the Zionist premises and symbols and presented themselves as the bearers of the true Jewish tradition and heritage distorted by the Zionist quest for the reconstruction of this tradition in a modern vein.

Here, a very interesting transformation of the original negative attitude of the ultraorthodox groups to the Zionist movement took place, which we discussed in the preceding chapter. The basic negative attitude to the "revolutionary" dimensions of Zionist ideology, those dimensions concerned with the reconstruction of Jewish tradition, continued and even intensified in some of the more extreme groups among the ultraorthodox. But at the same time most sectors of the ultraorthodox accepted de facto the state of Israel, legitimizing it as indicated, in terms of settlement in Eretz Israel or as a viable existing Jewish community that has to be guarded. They participated more and more in the political life of Israel, making more demands not only for allocations for their institutions but also, as we have seen, for imposing their own conceptions of public life in Israel.

At the same time, as indicated earlier, the tensions between these extreme Orthodox groups and the other sectors of Israeli society became intensified. Such tensions grew, paradoxically, but naturally enough, with many of those in these sectors who joined Reform or Conservative congregations and evinced strong interest in Jewish historical and religious traditions.

This continuous struggle around the construction of the symbolic, as well as territorial, boundaries of the community was related not only to the problems of the place of Jewish tradition or traditions in the construction of Israeli society. Relations to the Middle-Eastern environment constituted another focus of ideological and political struggle around the construction of such boundaries, far beyond the direct or even indirect security problems. The return to the new-old land in the Middle East was seen as an act of great historical significance—as was the attempt at integration into the Middle East. The nature of this integration constituted a focus of potential ideological and political struggle, which was to erupt in periods of intensive confrontation with the neighboring states and the Arabs on the West Bank.

The continuous Israeli occupation of the West Bank and Gaza, the seeming unwillingness of the Israeli governments since 1977 (with the partial exception of the Governments of National Unity in 1984 and in 1988 when the Labor Party tried, unsuccessfully, to push the government in such direction) to enter into serious far-reaching negotiations with the Palestinians), the policies of settlement on the West Bank, the Palestinian uprising (the Intifada) from 1988 on have not only exacerbated the tensions between Israel and the Palestinians but also fueled wider Arab and Islamic resentment against Israel and facilitated the growing importance of Islamic fundamentalism, especially in Gaza as well as among the Israeli-Arabs.

If the peace between Israel and Egypt and the de facto truce long-standing with Jordan indicated the possibility that the confrontation between Jews and Arabs, which started as a confrontation between national movements, might develop in the more pragmatic direction of interstate relations, these latter developments seem to indicate a regression to the former situation, with an intensification and possible widening of the confrontation. Ongoing struggles and confrontations around the collective boundaries and symbols of Israeli society were intensified by the volatility of the international security situation, which emphasized the problems of the place of Israel in the Middle East and by the demands of the Israeli-Arabs for attention not only to their growing aspirations for civil equality, but also to some of their cultural and political aspirations. All these developments intensified with the Intifada, the Arab uprising in the territories in 1987.

Thus, indeed, one of the most important repercussions of this combination of the political-ecological condition of a small society and the primordial-national and historical revolutionary-ideologic orientations of Zionism was that the problems related to the construction of symbols and boundaries of the emerging collectivity have constituted a focus of potential ideological and political contention. The potential for such struggle existed, as we have seen, from the very beginning of the Zionist movement, especially in its relationship to the Jewish historical and religious heritage and the relative importance of the different historical religious, territorial components of that heritage.

The same was true, in varying degrees in different historical periods, in the relations between the universalistic and particularistic orientations of the collectivity. The problems related to the place of these components in the construction of Israeli collective identity surfaced anew, as we have seen, after the Six-Day War and have continued to be in the forefront of political struggles in Israel.[18] All these developments and struggles very sharply posed the basic questions of the major components of the Israeli political-social format, especially with respect to upholding civil rights, civility and the rule of law.[19]

New Policy Directions: The Shift to the Right

The increased promulgation of these themes was connected with the development of new policies under the Likud government and, less sharply, under the Governments of National Unity which were formed in 1984 and 1988. The general political trend was continuously to the right, in the specific sense this term acquired in Israel: a hawkish attitude on security problems, especially with respect to the West Bank; strong emphasis on nationalistic and to some extent religious themes; and weakening of the major Zionist vision of the more universalistic or "liberal" emphases or orientations.

The shift to the right also was manifest in the fact that, throughout this period, the Likud led most of the political agenda, emphasizing security and nationalistic themes, with the Labor Party usually responding to it. But this agenda was not just political in the specific narrow sense of the word. It extended to all the major institutional arenas of Israeli society. The new orientations and their institutional implications were visible most fully in the realms of security, defense, and foreign policy, as well as in the religious arena and in more general cultural ambience.

With respect to security-military-foreign policy, the first new development, and one of great historical significance, was the conclusion of a peace treaty with Egypt in 1979 and the subsequent withdrawal from the Sinai in spring 1982. Whereas this achievement was not necessarily connected with the Revisionist or Likud ideology, it could be—and was—portrayed as demonstrating the basic correctness of this ideology, leading, after a show of strength, to peace with the Arabs.

The second development was the expansion of settlement in Judea, Samaria, and the Golan Heights. Although there was no alteration of the legal status of the West Bank—of Judea and Samaria (a term taken from Mandatory times and officially adopted to replace *West Bank* or *the territories*)—despite vocal demands by extreme right-wing groups for the imposition of Israeli law in those areas or their outright annexation, settlement in Judea and Samaria took new directions after the Likud came to power and became a focus of national controversy. This was an outcome of the Likud government's ideological and political legitimation of settling all parts of Eretz Israel, abolishing the Green Line (the armistice lines established at the end of the War of Independence), and allowing—in fact, encouraging by far-reaching subsidies—a large number of Jews to live in these areas, thus diminishing the chances of withdrawal from Judea and Samaria and the Gaza district.

This policy of settlement was closely connected with a new and more active stance in security matters, an ideology of active struggle against terrorism in general and the PLO in particular. The implementation of this conception culminated in "Operation Peace for Galilee," in June 1982, which developed within a few days into the Lebanon War. This adventure had far-reaching repercussions on the structure of Israeli society, as well as on its foreign relations and international standing. It was the first war not based on a wide national consensus—in fact it tore apart the hitherto strong consensus on security matters.

One of the most important watersheds on the international and domestic fronts was the Intifada, the Arab uprising in the West Bank and Gaza that started in late 1987 and has continued since. It caught the Israeli intelligence and security forces by surprise, and it drastically changed the entire situation in the relations between Israel and the Palestinians. The period of "benign" conquest of the West Bank ended and the West Bank was plunged, along with the Israeli security forces, into a situation of a combined civil uprising and war. In many ways the uprising was a continuation of the Arab-Israeli confict that developed from the beginning of the Zionist settlement. But it was also a civil uprising against Israel as an occupying power, and it was waged by the Arabs in rather unconventional ways. Almost no weapons were used: demonstrations, stone throwing (to a very large extent by children and women), tire burning, insults at Israeli soldiers—these were the most common means of protest. This combination of war and civil uprising undertaken in these rather unconventional ways was extremely serious for Israel on many fronts. The media, especially the international media, continuously reported the seeming brutality of Israeli soldiers who, although abstaining from use of armed weapons, used sticks or plastic bullets against women and children. The portrayal of such brutality made "hot" news, of course, and the media on the whole refrained from emphasizing the overt political use of women and children in these demonstrations, the endurance by Israeli soldiers of insults, their great restraint, on the whole, and the punishment by the courts of many of the instances of brutality—even if not always adequate in the view of wide sectors of Israeli society—often after outrage from the Israeli public.

The continuous military rule that had to face growing resistance on the part of the Palestinians gave rise, especially with the outbreak of the Intifada, to growing repressive measures by the army, generating far-reaching potentialities of brutalization in many aspects of Israei life, as well as a situation in which rule of law was not applied equally in Israel and in the West Bank and Gaza. The Intifada had other far-reaching impacts on Israeli society, intensifying the division between "hawks" and "doves," many of the latter concerned with the inevitable brutalization of large parts of the Israeli public and those soldiers assigned to maintain peace and order in the territories, as well as with the erosion of full rule of law, adherence to proper "normal" legal procedure, and the upholding of civil rights in the territories.

Far-reaching changes also occurred with respect to policies in the religious arena, specifically with respect to the place of religious groups and symbols in Israeli society and the regulation of many aspects of life by religious authorities. First of all, in accordance with their traditional strategy, the religious parties made effective use of their crucial position in the coalition to extend their influence beyond anything previously imaginable. These parties received much larger allocations for their institutions, frequently arranged in ways that contravened standard budgetary procedures, even during periods of drastic budgetary cutbacks in education, security and social services. They also became very influential in setting the general tone concerning the place of religious observance in public life, extending its scope, in fact, to change the constellation of state-religion relations and the role of religion in Israeli society. New religious-inspired legislation included, for instance, the "pathology law," which placed severe restrictions on the performance of autopsies; revocation of the relatively liberal abortion law; broader exemptions for military service by women; and the cessation of flights by El Al on the Sabbath and Jewish holidays. Attempts also were made to limit archaeological excavations (as regards digs in ancient Jewish cemeteries) and to pass the so-called "Who Is a Jew" law that would recognize the validity of conversion to Judaism only if performed in accordance with the Halakhah; that is, only by those recognized by the orthodox rabbinate.

In late 1990, when Agudat Israel joined the right-wing government headed by the Likud and Mr. Shamir, on the condition that the government would promulgate several religious laws: such as prohibition against raising pigs and selling pork, except in Christian sectors; further limitations on public transport on the Sabbath, as well as against what was defined by them as "pornographic" advertising. At the same time the amount of financial allocation to the religious sectors grew, in a period of budgetary restraints, giving rise to strong outcries by many, on the whole helpless "secular" or nontraditional sectors.

In many of the cases the rabbinate has claimed to be the arbiter of conduct, at least in the public sector, for the whole population, implicitly setting itself up as higher than the secular authorities. As a result the level of tensions between religious and nonreligious "secular" sectors was rising continuously, even if intermittently. Religious and ethnic emphases have had an increasing impact on education. An ever-larger segment of the curriculum is devoted to these themes, which tend to sanctify the past, in contrast to the largely future orientations of pioneering Zionists.

A very interesting development combining religious and ethnic elements in a new distinct way crystallized before the 1984 elections in the form of a new religious party, Shas. This party split from the Agudat Israel and was led mostly by rabbis and political entrepreneurs from various Oriental groups who rebelled against the Ashkenazi domination of the Agudat Israel. Its spiritual leader is Rabbi Ovadia Yosef, the former Sephardic chief rabbi, who worked in cooperation with the Ashkenazi rabbi E. Schach, the leader of one of the orthodox groups related to the Agudat Israel and who became the head of its Supreme Religious (and Political) Council.

The new party proved very successful in the 1984 elections and even more so in those of 1988, both on the municipal and countrywide levels. Its success was due both to the combination of ethnic and religious themes and symbols in its appeals and to its very high organizational capacity, which in many ways resembled those of the various labor groups in the Yishuv in the early stages of the state of Israel. The organizational bases were synagogues, religious schools and yeshivoth, and strong family networks.

In the religious area its leadership exhibited a militant tendency that differed greatly from the previous relative toleration predominant among the Oriental communities. This militancy, which probably was not shared, at least in its extreme forms, by the party's broad supporters, developed from within the schools and yeshivoth of the Agudat Israel, in which many of the Shas leaders were educated, as well as through encounters with the "secular Ashkenazi" sectors and centers of Israeli society.

Unlike most of the Agudat Israel, Shas was not isolated from the mainstream of Israeli life, at least initially; rather, it developed from within it. And its general orientation to Israeli society tended to be more open. Although it certainly could not be called a Zionist party in the sense of accepting the revolutionary premises of Zionism—indeed, many of its leaders often expressed ideological opposition to those premises and even declared their bankruptcy—its overall attitude to the state and its institutions was more open and positive than that of the Agudat Israel. Shas was strongly oriented to active participation in the central framework, not only of the state, but also of Israeli society. In matters of security and relations with the Arabs, at least, its leadership seemed to be ready to exhibit rather dovish attitudes.

The Shas leadership lost some of its influence in the second quarter of 1990, when its leaders first joined the Labor Party in toppling the Government of National Unity. Then, under the pressure of the leadership of one sector of the Ashkenazi ultraorthodox group, in June Shas joined Likud in the formation of the right-wing Likud government. From 1990 on, the leadership of Shas became entangled in a series of accusations by the state Comptroller and of police investigations about improper use of public funds. And in 1991 the Shas parliamentary faction was fined twice by the State Controller for disorder in its finances. But whatever the vicissitudes of its political fate, all in all it seemed to constitute one of the most original, even if possibly transient, Israeli developments attendant on the disintegration of the original labor-Zionist mold.

5

State Ceremonies of Israel: Remembrance Day and Independence Day

Don Handelman and Elihu Katz

Daughter:	Why did Herzl write *The Jewish State?*
Mother:	Because he thought the Jews should have a state of their own.
Daughter:	Why is it [Mount Herzl] next to the soldiers' cemetery?
Mother:	Because many people were killed in order to get our state, and here [she points to the cemetery] is where the ceremony for Remembrance Day takes place.
Daughter:	So why, Holocaust Day?
Mother:	That is there [she gestures towards Yad Vashem, over the rise], and the remembrance of Holocaust Day takes place there.

(Mount Herzl, Saturday, 21 March 1987)

Like many nation-states of the modern era, Israel designated a particular date to remember those who sacrificed their lives for the existence of the state, and another to commemorate its coming into being. The first is named Remembrance Day (*Yom Hazikaron*), and the second, Independence Day (*Yom Ha'atzma'ut*). Each is opened by a central state occasion, referred to as a 'ceremony', that is televised in its entirety.

Each ceremony is one in which this nation-state, through official agencies, intentionally presents something of its self-understood purposes, and their foundations, aspirations, and apprehensions. Each ceremony presents a version of moral and social order that contrasts with the other. Each version, suitable to its occasion, stands on its own, valid in and of itself. However, as we will discuss in detail further on, these two ceremonies deliberately are articulated with one another. Taken together, through the sequence of their scheduling, these versions of this nation-state become segments in a dramatic narrative that encodes temporality, and therefore, history. In turn, it is this history, or more accurately, these versions of history, that inform and infuse the overall story with deeper significance.

Although these ceremonies have undergone changes since their inception, their basic formats have remained quite stable for over a decade. However, our purpose is neither to do a historical account of such changes, nor to summarize in detail the histories of these ceremonies. Such aims are beyond the scope of this chapter, and must await future attention. Here our purpose is more structural, and is addressed to the interpretation of state ceremonial in the modern era.

We first address why it is that these two opening ceremonies demand discussion in common. We then show, in a preliminary manner, how their respective Days came to be scheduled as they are. This forms the basis for our thesis that these ceremonies together come to constitute a narrative structure. This is followed, first by an interpretation of the ceremony that opens Remembrance Day, and then of that which opens Independence Day, in order to delineate their respective versions of moral and social order. The concluding section returns to the kind of narrative structure that we think is found through the sequence of these versions, and to the encoding of a rhythm of temporality that, in a broad, cultural sense, is formative and informative of this.

The unit of comparison: sirens and fireworks

From its inception the State adopted as its own the rhythm of the Jewish cycle of holy days and holidays (in distinct contrast to the efforts of certain other revolutionary states to radicalize the cultural ordering of temporality: see Zerubavel 1985: 27–43). Only one new holiday, in the full sense of a 'day of rest' (*shabbaton*), was instituted. This was Independence Day. Moreover the period of observance of State Days became that of all Jewish holy days and holidays: all begin with darkness, as the stars appear, and end with darkness.

The few studies there are on Israel's Independence Day (including references to its opening ceremony) treat it as a separate and wholly autonomous occasion. The sorts of questions asked in these works highlight the sparse attention given by scholars to state ceremonial in Israel, especially in relation to its logic of composition. Kamen's (1977) analysis of survey data asked about the degrees of enjoyment experienced on Independence Day by different social categories of Israelis. More recently, Virginia Dominguez argues that Israelis do not seem to ask themselves what it is that they are celebrating. That is, which aspects of the 'collective self' are marked, expressed, and perhaps formulated through this holiday. Don-Yehiya (1984) discusses how early Independence Day celebrations expressed the impress of a 'statist' polity during that period (see Liebman and Don-Yehiya 1983, on this variety of 'civil religion' in Israel).

Israel is unusual among modern nation-states in that its Remembrance Day is scheduled for the twenty-four hour period that immediately precedes Independence Day. This articulation is intentional; and official announcements of the program of Remembrance Day, published in the daily newspapers, list the last occasion of this Day as, 'Conclusion of Remembrance Day and opening of Independence Day celebrations by Knesset Speaker at Mount Herzl'. That is, the official ceremony that opens Independence Day includes, as its initial segment, the closing of Remembrance Day. However, unlike Independence Day, Remembrance Day is not a 'day of rest.' Still, during the eve of Remembrance Day all public places of entertainment and fun are shut.

Unlike Independence Day, Remembrance Day begins with a singular and shocking sound that penetrates and simultaneously synchronizes the different worlds of everyone in the country. On the appointed minute, and for one minute's duration, siren blasts shriek in every village, town, and city in the land. Human life stands still: people stop in their tracks, vehicles stop in mid-intersection; all is silent, yet all silent space is pervaded by the fullness of the same wail. These sirens also announce crisis and the activation of emergency procedures. The sole difference is not of intensity nor pitch of sound, but of modulation: to announce crisis, the wails rise and fall; to declare bereavement their note is steady and uniform. On the morning of the morrow, again simultaneously throughout the country, the same enactment is repeated, this time for two minutes. The sound synthesizes mourning and action, absence and presence.

The opening ceremony of Remembrance Day has something of the singular and monotonic qualities of the siren's keen, and of the stillness of the land. The next morning, the siren's wail signals the beginning of memorial services at military cemeteries and memorial sites throughout the country, in memory of the fallen of different corps, regiments, and other units of the armed forces, and of geographical localities, sometimes down to the neighborhood level. By contrast, Independence Day expands out of its opening ceremony into a variegated and colorful multitude of activities, planned and informal. On the eve of Independence Day there are open-air stages where popular entertainers perform, dancing in the streets, games of chance (otherwise illegal) in city centres, and bonfires and singing, as well as private house-parties. On the morrow there are special services in synagogues, the opening of selected military bases to the public, and official receptions. If the weather is good, as it usually is in the late spring, Independence Day is marked by a host of family outings and picnics. As the opening ceremony of this Day ends there are sustained bursts of fireworks in the dark sky. Their expansion in space, brilliantly lighting the night in diverse shapes and brightly-colored hues, is an apt metaphor for the meaning of this Day. Each ceremony provides a key to the tenor of activities that constitute the bulk of each Day.

As Dominguez remarks, these two Days form a 'neat conceptual set' of comparison and contrast. But this set is not a construct of the scholar (as is, for example, Da Matta's [1977] interesting comparison of Brazilian carnival and Independence Day). As noted, it is an artifact of deliberate design. This design is seen with the greatest clarity in the articulation of the opening ceremonies, and in the implicit narrative structure that is invoked by their sequencing. Therefore any symbolic analysis that does not relate to these ceremonies as a unified set, and then that does not treat this set as diachronically encoded, simply will miss much of their significance. These ceremonies are a semiotic set: they make meaning together.

The dating of days, the shaping of space: aspects of Zionist cosmologic

That these events make meaning together should tell us immediately that their calendrical scheduling, and so their sequential ordering, are neither 'natural' nor inevitable. As Eviatar Zerubavel (1982: 288) comments, 'Temporal arrangements are closely related to group formation, since a temporal order that is commonly shared by a group of people and is unique to them functions both as a unifier and as a separator'. Moreover, the chronological coding of temporality, as 'before' and 'after', is the production of history (Lévi-Strauss 1966: 257–60). Time and the temporal vision are essential to Zionist cosmology, as they are to that of Judaism (Yerushalmi 1982). So too is the temporal rhythm implicit in this, as well as the rhetoric and sentiments of a unique people, beleaguered in the world (cf. Gertz 1984).

In fact, Israeli Jews accept the contiguity and continuity of these dates as morally correct, even though the immediacy of transition from mourning to celebration is felt as especially heartrending. Thus, a bereaved father, interviewed on television before Remembrance Day 1986, remarked on the lack of any intervening period between the two Days. But he insisted on the justness of this intimate linkage, stating: 'This is the price [bereavement], and this is what you have [independence]'. One may well contend that this suddenness of transition is felt as morally just, precisely because it is so difficult. The transition should be hard, for its abruptness encodes temporally the minute differences in chronological time between the establishment of the State and its War of Independence. This war was well under way before independence was declared, but intensified greatly with that declaration. For Israeli Jews the two were identified indelibly, and perhaps still are. The difficult experience of abrupt transition between the two Days mirrors the reality of experience in the establishment of the State.

However fitting this temporal flow is felt to be, it exists only because decisions were taken as to which dates to mark, and in which order.

Nation-states choose their significant dates according to different semiotic and temporal codes; moreover they may experiment with different calendrical arrangements (Zerubavel 1985). Thus the French promulgated Bastille Day as their 'founding day' only in 1880, following the formation of the Third Republic; while French governments shifted the public focus given to prominent calendrical markers in accordance with prevailing political conditions. So, in 1920, the government combined the fiftieth anniversary of the Third Republic together with the solemnities for the fallen of the Great War – and chose a date other than Bastille Day for this (Rearick 1977: 456). In the instance of Australia, its memorial date, Anzac Day (the date the Anzacs landed at Gallipoli in 1915), has developed as the major marker of Australian nationhood, rather than Australia Day, which commemorates the landing of the first convict settlers from England in the eighteenth century. According to Kapferer (1988), the reasons for the different valencies given to these two dates are intimately related to the formation of Australian national cosmology.

In the Israeli case, a number of dates hypothetically could have been chosen to mark the autonomy of independence, but then each would have given its own thrust of meaning to the new state. So 29 November, the date in 1947 when the United Nations decided on the partition of Palestine, a decision that gave international legitimation to the founding of a Jewish state, would have emphasized the role of foreigners (and gentiles) in the creation of the state. Or, an arbitrary date to mark the end of the War of Independence (that, formally, produced only armistice agreements) would have highlighted the decisive role of armed struggle in achieving independence. Or, the date that marked the election of the first Knesset, the parliament of Israel, would have stressed the values of parliamentary democracy, and so forth.

The date chosen for Independence Day in 1949, apparently with no disagreement, was 15 May. In 1948 independence was declared on 14 May, that then became the eve of Independence Day. A further decision, over which there was some argument, adopted the date in the Hebrew calendar, the 5th of *Iyar*, that corresponded to 15 May of that year. The Hebrew and Gregorian calendrical cycles are independent of one another. Although the date of Independence Day has a fixed and stable location in the annual Jewish ceremonial cycle, it varies from year to year by a matter of weeks in the Gregorian calendar. This was no small matter, since according to the Hebrew calendar, Independence Day falls permanently only thirteen days after the end of Passover. In Judaism, Passover is perhaps the quintessential 'festival of freedom', celebrating the exodus of the Israelites from Egypt. The festive family meal, the *Seder*, on the eve of the holiday, 'is a symbolic enactment of an historical scenario whose three great acts structure the

Haggada that is read aloud: slavery – deliverance – ultimate redemption'
(Yerushalmi 1982: 44; see also Fredman 1981). The metaphysics of the text
of the *Seder*, the *Haggada*, insist on the annual 'fusion of past and present'
(Yerushalmi 1982: 44), and on the identification of each and every Jew with
that ancient attainment of freedom. 'In each and every generation let each
person regard himself as though he had emerged from Egypt', reads the
Haggada. Passover is a holiday beloved of Israeli Jews, secular and religious
alike; and one may say that the great majority celebrate the occasion.

The identification of Independence Day with Passover was speedy. Just
as Independence Day was referred to as the onset of a new period in the
history of the nation, the People of Israel (*Am Yisrael*), so it was perceived in
continuity with holidays of national freedom, but especially with Passover.
And just as Independence Day was seen to sign the rebirth and redemption
of the Jewish nation-state, so too it was compared to the exodus from Egypt
(Don-Yehiya 1984: 10–11). Of all Jewish holidays, Passover had the greatest
influence on the perception of this Day.

Like the scheduling of Independence Day, that of Remembrance Day
required an arbitrary decision, since there was no traditional date to
commemorate the fallen in war. The need to memorialize the war dead was
felt early on. Thus during the Knesset debate in 1949 on the law to
promulgate Independence Day, Shmuel Dayan of the centrist Mapai party
stated: 'Happiness is a universal human matter. Still, there is a special Jewish
tone to happiness. Once it was customary that at the time of the happiness
of a wedding, people would go to the cemetery to invite the dead to
participate in the festivity . . . we have to remember those who with their
blood bestowed upon us arisal and independence'. At the outset, memorial
ceremonies were part of Independence Day, but were decentralized, the
initiative for their observance taken locally (Levinsky 1957: 495ff.). By
1951, the Ministry of Defense began to experiment with a separate
Remembrance Day, the day prior to Independence Day. In 1954, the
Ministry stated that this linkage and sequencing had not aroused controversy; and the Minister of Defense commented that he viewed as 'organic'
this attachment of Remembrance Day to Independence Day. The law that
formalized this schedule was passed in 1963. Unlike Independence Day,
Remembrance Day was not opened by a central ceremony until 1967.

During the period between the end of Passover and Independence Day,
the State scheduled a third date as a national day – Martyrs and Heroes
Remembrance Day, (usually referred to as Holocaust Day) – again according to the Hebrew calendar. Holocaust Day (*Yom Hasho'a*) is discussed in
this section because it is integral to the calendrical sequence of Days
scheduled by the State. Holocaust Day precedes Remembrance Day and
Independence Day in this sequence. Therefore, its timing is integral also to

the kinds of narrative that this sequence evokes. Nevertheless, Holocaust Day and its opening ceremony are beyond the purview of much of this chapter. Instead, the positioning of this Day will be glossed here, to be retrieved again in the concluding section, when the relationships between these Days and national cosmology are discussed.

The eve of Holocaust Day falls on the 26th of the Hebrew month of *Nissan*, five days after the last day of Passover. As its name indicates, this Day commemorates the catastrophe of the Holocaust, the murder of 6,000,000 Jews by the Nazis, the destruction of Jewish culture and community in Europe, and the heroism of Jews who rose in armed struggle against their Nazi oppressors. Like Remembrance Day, Holocaust Day is not a day of rest, but again all public venues of entertainment and fun are shut during its eve. The opening ceremony of this Day is held at Yad Vashem, the memorial and archival centre of the Holocaust in Jerusalem, and is televised live. In its identification with the tragic destruction of Jews in the diaspora (one that is fated, to no small degree, in the Zionist vision), Holocaust Day in most years is perceived generally as of less immediate relevance to the founding, the commemoration, and the celebration of the State, than is Remembrance Day. Indeed, the scale of this Day, and usually of public response to it, is more modest than that of Remembrance Day. So, synchronized sirens do sound throughout the land on Holocaust Day, but only once. Nonetheless, our concern here is not with the manner of meaning made at the interface of the event and wider social order, but with the emergence of a legislated cosmology that has direct bearing on the relationship between Remembrance Day and Independence Day.

The scheduling of Holocaust Day once more is not fortuitous. This Day is identified explicitly with the anniversary of the uprising of the Warsaw Ghetto in 1943, that became the exemplary instance of Jewish armed struggle against impossible odds during World War II. On 19 April of that year, German troops came to strip the Ghetto of its remaining Jews, to ship them to the death camps, and armed resistance began in earnest. 19 April 1943 was the eve of Passover in that year. It was not possible in Israel, for various reasons, to schedule a remembrance day for the Holocaust on Passover eve. Judaism interdicts mourning during Passover. Instead, the commemoration date was made to coincide with the extinction of the Uprising, on 2 May, the 27th of *Nissan* in that year, according to the Hebrew calendar. The German command itself dated the end of armed resistance to 16 May when the great synagogue was blown up: 'This act of destruction was meant to symbolize the end of the ghetto' (Krakowski 1984: 211). (In fact, fighting continued into July.) However, the acceptance of such a date, which actually extended and enhanced the duration of Jewish armed struggle, would have scheduled Holocaust Day almost a week after Independence Day, according to the Hebrew calendar. Whether by design or not, the eve of Holocaust Day, the 26th of *Nissan*, falls seven days before the eve of Remembrance Day, the 3rd of *Iyar*. This period of seven days corresponds to the traditional period of Jewish mourning following death, the *shiva* (literally, 'seven'). We note the implicitness of this association, since it is not marked – nonetheless, it is embedded in this temporal sequence. On the one hand, Holocaust Day, the catastrophe of diaspora Jewry, is distanced from Remembrance Day and Independence Day, occasions of the arisal of nation-statehood. On the other, Holocaust Day is scheduled near to and prior to these occasions, and so is linked intimately to them. This scheduling of what may be termed 'close distance' is itself an apt metaphor for the often ambivalent relationship between diaspora Jewry and the Zionist State.

On the basis of the calendrical sequence of these three Days, we offer here a preliminary reading of its temporal design, to be honed in the conclusion to this chapter. The destruction of European Jewry was followed by the War of Independence, during which the State of Israel was created, and through which the state kept its freedom, as it has ever since through the mortal sacrifices of its citizenry. Given the utter tragedy of the Holocaust, it is appropriate that its Day be followed by a period of separation (or 'mourning', as it were) from the subsequent Days. However the sacrifice memorialized on Remembrance Day led to the revival of the Jewish state and the redemption of the Jewish people. Therefore the celebration of Independence Day is an immediate and fitting response to the commemoration of Remembrance Day.

This semiotic sequence also conveys the following. The utter degradation and despair of the Holocaust finally harvested the inevitably bitter sowing of Jewish seed in the lands of the gentiles. The diaspora was the dead end of Jewish existence. Even so, the Holocaust also kindled sparks of resistance among this downtrodden and humiliated people. The snuffing of these heroic sparks (the Jewish partisans, the ghetto and camp uprisings) are mourned, but also are celebrated on Holocaust Day. For in Palestine, amongst independent and proud Jews returned to their own land and once more battling against seemingly insurmountable odds, these sparks flamed into ramified armed struggle. The outcome was the Jewish State. In Zionist visions, these developments became the only creative response to the Holocaust. In these readings, the sequence of the three Days recapitulates a theme of 'death and the regeneration of life' on a grand scale (cf. Bloch and Parry 1982).

The scheduling of these three Days is a construct of the nation-state, but one that is neither haphazard nor merely instrumental, in any simple way. This sequencing is accepted as natural and appropriate by Israeli Jews, however it is interpreted. It is a statist version of modern Jewish history, but one of cosmological, temporal harmonics that are embedded in Zionist ideology. These relationships were enunciated with clarity by Prime Minister Levi Eshkol, in his address on Holocaust Day, 1964: 'The Martyrs' and Heroes' Memorial Day falls between the ancient Festival of Freedom [i.e. Passover] and the modern Day of Independence. The annals of our people are enfolded between these two events. With our exodus from the Egyptian bondage, we won our ancient freedom; now, with our ascent from the depths of the Holocaust, we live once again as an independent nation.' In its modern, nationalist interpretations, the narrative structure of the sequence of Days is easily identifiable with certain of the overt, processual motifs of Passover: of slavery and oppression, of exodus and arisal. Passover itself corresponds to that which Yael Zerubavel (1986: 5) calls the 'basic conflict formula' of the present-day celebration of many Jewish holidays. In turn, this facilitates the identification of the sequence with the Jewish struggle against oppression that is embedded in other Jewish holidays.

Yet, in one important respect the scheduling of the three Days is more in keeping with the romantic and rationalist reckonings of modern European nationalism than it is with the annual ceremonial cycle of Judaism. In the traditional cycle there is only a limited correspondence between the order of occurrence of holidays and their location in a chronology of historical reckoning (Y. Zerubavel 1986). The ordering principles of the traditional, annual cycle are cosmic and mythic, and not those of chronological history. However, these three Days of national reckoning synthesize their order of sequence and the chronological order of temporal occurrence that this sequence indexes. In other words, the sequence of Days is one of modern history; but one that is harmonized with the rhythms of time in traditional cosmology.

We surmise that it is this synthesis of ontological rhythms of time, the traditional narratives that these enable, and their encoding of modern chronological history that makes the sequence of Days so experientially acceptable to Israeli Jews. These themes are addressed more substantially in the concluding section.

The temporal articulations among these three Days are produced and reproduced topologically. In August 1949, the remains of Theodore Herzl, the visionary of modern Zionism and the founder of the World Zionist Organization, were brought from Vienna and reinterred in Jerusalem, on the summit of the mountain named in his memory. Mount Herzl, perhaps the highest location within the city, affords a vista of 360 degrees of Jerusalem and its environs. Previously, during the War of Independence, the lower reaches of this mountain had become the military cemetery of

Jerusalem. His black, polished basalt tombstone bore the simple inscription, HERZL. Without contextual qualifiers his presence was made more eternal and less historical. Encircled by flower beds, Herzl's tomb stands alone at the apex, separated by broad, open spaces from the graves of others. Mount Herzl is a cemetery wherein Zionist history is encoded topologically, through the spatial locations of ancestors and their descendants.

The spatial layout of gravesites on Mount Herzl is as close as secular Zionism has come to inscribing itself topographically as a pantheon. Radiating outwards from Herzl's tomb, at different levels and in different quadrants of the downslope gradient of the mountainside, are clusters of graves. At a distance from, and lower than, Herzl's tomb, is that of another Zionist visionary, Vladimir Jabotinsky, the founder of the revisionist movement, and those of members of his immediate family. At the same level, in another quadrant, is the cluster of graves of members of Herzl's immediate family and of the presidents, the inheritors, of the World Zionist Organization, and their wives. These widely distanced clusters are themselves set apart from the rest of the cemetery by a horizontal border that follows the contours of the mountainside and that intersects its downslope gradient. Thus, on the highest reaches of the mountain are the graves of modern prophets of Zionism who created the movement in its aims of returning all Jews to the land of Israel, and the graves of those who nurtured and sustained this vision. At their pinnacle and centre lies Herzl. With the passage of time, the visionary figure of Herzl (and to a lesser extent, that of Jabotinsky) has become the depoliticized representation of Zionism as the encompassing ideology of Jewish national resurrection and renewal.

Returning to the border, it is traversed by a gateway that leads further downslope to a cluster of gravesites reserved for the 'Greats of the Nation' (*Gedolei Ha'uma*) and their spouses. These are the presidents and prime ministers of the State of Israel, and speakers of the Knesset, the first citizens and political leaders of the nation-state itself. Without any further demarcation, these graves are close to and virtually continuous with those of the military cemetery which continues downslope and covers the bulk of the mountainside.

The upper slopes of the mountain are carpeted with lawns, shrubs, and flower beds; and resemble most a park dotted here and there by groves of trees and clusters of graves. The military cemetery, although dense with graves, is heavily forested. The overall composition likely derives in part from nineteenth-century European romanticism (see Mosse 1979).

Thus the highest reaches of the mountainside signify the source, genesis, and deeds of the Zionist movement, which culminated in the creation of the nation-state. Further downslope are buried the elected leaders of the State, whose graves are higher than, but continuous with those of the citizen-soldiery who gave their lives to buttress the zionist mountain. On the morning of Remembrance Day, a memorial service is held in the military cemetery. That evening, as it has since 1950, the opening ceremony of Independence Day is held on the summit of this mountain of Zionism, with Herzl's tomb as its spatial centrepiece.

In 1953, a lower spur of Mount Herzl, at some distance from the main massif, but still high above the valley floor, was named the Mount of Remembrance (*Har Hazikaron*). There Yad Vashem was built. As noted, the opening ceremony of Holocaust Day takes place there. Unlike the gateway that internally connects the upper reaches of Mount Herzl to the 'Greats of the Nation' and to the military cemetery, one must leave this Mount to enter Yad Vashem.

In the terms introduced by Erwin Straus (1966: 34), the articulation between the sites of Yad Vashem, the military cemetery, and the summit of Mount Herzl is that of 'historical space', whose direction acquires a 'dynamic momentum'. For the temporal sequence of ceremonialism is matched with, moves through, and infuses space with meaning. Holocaust Day and the tragedy and heroism of diaspora Jewry, are marked on a lower and more distant spur of the Zionist mountain, just as this Day is distanced temporally from those that commemorate and celebrate the nation-state. On the morning of Remembrance Day, the heroism and sacrifice of the citizen-soldiers of the nation-state are commemorated in the military cemetery, on the lower reaches of the main massif itself. That evening the venue climbs to the summit of the mountain, to the tomb of the Zionist visionary and ancestor, to celebrate Independence Day. The heights are scaled spatially in the temporal order of Days, from destruction, through the struggle for renewal, to the pinnacle of triumph, that also is the source of the vision and the annual enactment of its viability. The practice of this ceremonialism integrates axes of space and time in Zionist cosmology and history. This integration of time and space is evident again in Levi Eshkol's speech, from which we quoted above: 'The very struggle against the adversary [the heroism and sacrifice of the Holocaust] and the victory which followed [the War of Independence] laid the foundations for the revival of our national independence [the creation of the state]. Seen in this light, the Jewish fight against the Nazis and the War of Independence were, in fact, a single protracted battle. The geographical proximity between Yad Vashem and Mount Herzl thus expresses far more than mere physical closeness'.

This sequence of ceremonialism is enacted to the present day. However, the addition of a central ceremony at the Western Wall to open Remembrance Day has interposed refractions, likely radical ones, within this vision of the progression of secular Zionism from its antecedents to the present.

6

Religious Adherence and Political Attitudes

Yochanan Peres

The contemporary era has seen an intensification of democracy and greater support for democratic values. At the same time, however, some states have witnessed increasing adherence to religious life styles. Since the earliest days of modern democracy, observers and statesmen have reflected about the extent to which a democratic regime can coexist with a politically oriented organized religion. Democracy is based on public debate and majority rule. In many cases, decisions adopted by the majority are formulated as laws. These laws are enacted by human beings and can be changed or overridden as a result of subsequent discussion and decisions. Religion, however, is founded on belief in absolute, eternal truths whose origin is divine and which can only be interpreted by a limited group of believers or sages.

In the more specific case of Jewish religiosity in Israel, some additional attributes should be considered.

1. Jews in the Diaspora were an eternal minority; thus, while developing appreciation for human rights, they were often less than enthusiastic about majority rule.
2. The national revival of Judaism in modern Israel has a religious interpretation. It is legitimated by the divine promise (of the holy land to the chosen people) and closely linked to strict observance of religious obligations (mitzvot). Religious principles are perceived as the foundation of Israel's revival and a prerequisite for her survival (Deshen 1978a, pp. 157-158; Liebman and Don Yehiya 1984, p. 100).
3. Orthodox communities developed a network of institutions (schools, stores, welfare arrangements, etc.) as well as an elaborate system of social control (Friedman 1991, pp. 114-135; Levy 1989, pp. 31-47).

Lately, national religious circles (specifically those residing in new settlements in the occupied territories) also established closely controlled communities (Lustick 1988, pp. 42-71; Deshen 1978b, pp. 400-408). The total and social

87

nature of religiosity curbed the passing of voters from religious to secular parties (or vice versa). The political function of public debate between religious and secular parties is, therefore, rather limited.

From this brief description of the situation, it might seem that a choice has to be made between removing religion from the public domain and abolishing democratic values (e.g., equality before the law, human rights, freedom of speech). The fact that democracy has survived and even advanced in Israel, where the Jewish religion plays a salient, influential role, shows that a strict, demanding religion can be integrated into a stable democratic system (see Peres and Yuchtman-Ya'ar 1992: 27-30).

The aim of this article is to deal with points of congruence and friction between the perspectives of religious people and the principles of democracy. The tool used to study the issue is a public opinion survey. Although this method has numerous drawbacks, it also has important advantages (some deriving from the drawbacks themselves).

- Public opinion surveys are current and up-to-date. Conclusions drawn from such surveys generally do not rely on "facts" and assumptions that may have been true in the past and may be still accepted by historians and philosophers as self evident.
- Public opinion surveys examine samples of populations. Hence attributes, attitudes and behavior are considered according to their prevalence among the masses rather than in terms of how they relate to an official ideology, to "Holy Scriptures" or to views of leaders and spokesmen. (An opposite view is to be found in Deshen 1978a pp. 141-142.)

Based on a survey conducted among a representative sample of the Jewish population in Israel (with the exception of kibbutzim, army bases, non-Hebrew speaking immigrants and settlements in the territories), we will address the following questions:

1. Which is more characteristic of contemporary Israeli religiosity: observance or faith?
2. To what extent does the religious sector seek to enforce laws obligating the entire population to a religious life style?
3. Is religiosity negatively correlated with commitment to democratic principles?
4. To what extent do the religious and ultra-Orthodox parties determine the balance of power in the Israeli political system?

Faith versus Religious Observance

This issue will be addressed, following the study conducted by Y. Ben-Meir and P. Kedem (1979), by means of responses to a public opinion survey organized along two scales: the scale of "observance" and the scale of "faith". This systematic study enables us to focus on a few key items (particularly in the area of religious observance), taking into account their location on the scales. All our 1287 respondents were categorized according to the following self definitions: Ultra-Orthodox (10%); Religious (10%); Traditional (29%); and Secular (51%). Table 1 shows the percentage of respondents who observe religious obligations (e.g., praying in synagogue; refraining from travel on the Sabbath) and maintain some fundamental Jewish beliefs.

Researchers who deal primarily with the topic of religion tend to question the validity of self definition (religious, traditional, etc.). They contend that different respondents may attribute completely different meanings to terms such as "religious" and "traditional" (see Deshen, 1978a, p. 142). However, these arguments do not take the potential of quantitative research into account. One question may be used to validate another one. The findings of Ben-Meir and Kedem, as well as Table 1, indicate that religious (and traditional or secular) self definition is highly correlated with adherence to religious norms and values. (For example, 84% of the ultra-Orthodox respondents attend synagogue frequently; 90% of the religious respondents believe in reward and punishment in the world to come, compared to 2% and 17% respectively among secular respondents). The reactions of the traditional respondents are particularly surprising. It is commonly believed that the main difference between religious and traditional Jews lies in the intensity of their faith. The latter supposedly have a more routine approach towards religious observance and are more skeptical. Thus, for example, Deshen suggested that the term "observant", which is accepted in Israeli research, be revised to "partially observant". The results of our survey point in the opposite direction: only 18% of the traditional Jews refrain from travelling on the Sabbath, while a majority (57%) believe in reward and punishment in the world to come; and even though 98% of the secular respondents are not observant, approximately 25% believe that the universe was created by God.

Religious literature and attitudes of the religious elite may contradict the above conclusions. However, analysis of the attitudes of the general population indicates that religious beliefs are more commonly maintained than religious observance. In order to confirm our findings we examined how many observant Jews (i.e., those who attend synagogue almost every day and refrain from travelling on the Sabbath) also believe in reward and punishment in the world to come. The result was 99%. Conversely, however, the percentage of believers (in the Creation and in reward and punishment) who also refrain from travelling on the Sabbath amounted to only 56%.

Finally, regarding the question of whether the Israeli population has become more or less religious, it is interesting to compare our findings with those obtained by Ben Meir and Kedem 12 years ago. In the former study 22% of the population stated that they refrain from travelling on the Sabbath, while our finding for the same question was 23%. In Ben Meir and Kedem's study 56% of the population stated that they believe "God gave the Torah to Moses on Mount Sinai", while 50% of our respondents believed that "the Torah derives from a divine source".

The results obtained for "extent of belief in God" were somewhat different in each of the studies. In the 1979 survey 46% of the respondents indicated that they believe God created the universe, whereas 52% expressed the same belief in the 1991 survey. On the whole, the studies seem to corroborate one another, and both support the conclusion that respondents as a whole tend to maintain religious beliefs to a greater extent than they observe religious obligations.

To What Extent are Religious Jews in Favor of Enforcing Religious Observance by Law?

The continuing debate between religious and secular Jews in Israel has largely focused on the question: should a secular body (such as the Knesset or the government) be authorized to enforce religious codes of behavior among the entire population? Each side may rest his case on values that are considered valid by the opposite side as well: the Jewish image of the State of Israel on the one hand, and civil rights on the other (Liebman and Don-Yehiye 1983, pp. 81-122).

These symmetrical perspectives have caused the conflict regarding the need for religious legislitation to become an unresolvable dilemma. A liberal regime without the national-Jewish element would seem to contradict some of the fundamental principles of Zionism. A theocratic regime, however, may impose limitations that most secular (as well as some traditional and even some religious) Jews would not be able to live with. Hence it seems that both parties have to aim towards a viable compromise rather than towards an "all-or-nothing victory".

Table 2 presents the distribution of support among ultra-Orthodox, religious, traditional and secular respondents to various solutions to the dilemma of religious coercion - on a continuum from "turning Israel into a theocratic state" to "abolishing almost all of the religious laws".

The table indicates, as expected, that the more respondents define themselves as religious, the more they advocate enforcement of religious legislation. This correspondence between religious self definition and attitudes is expressed by a high, statistically significant correlation listed at the bottom of the table (tau = 0.55). Closer examination shows that only the ultra-Orthodox expressed a clear preference (93%) for enactment of stricter religious legislation. Conversely, only half of the religious respondents (52%) are in favor of stricter religious legislation.

The attitudes of traditional respondents are particularly interesting: 47% were in favor of maintaining the status quo. Howevever, one cannot argue that "traditional" Jews are, in this respect, halfway between religious and secular. A very large percentage (40%) of these respondents was in favor of reducing or abolishing religious legislation as opposed to a small percentage (13%) in favor of increasing such legislation. Similarly, attitudes expressed by the secular respondents corresponded with our expectations: 78% were in favor of reducing or abolishing religious legislation while only 21% preferred the status quo. On the whole, the findings show that there is a stable balance, and that any change in the status quo is liable to generate more opposition (and subsequent counter-pressure) than support. Traditional Jews constitute a force that maintains that balance.

Table 3 shows that the exemption of Yeshiva students from military service constitutes a special case among the "religious laws"; it generates more opposition and less support than any other religious law.

Table 3 shows almost total opposition among the entire non-Orthodox sample to exemption of *Yeshiva* students from military service. The summation of categories 1 and 2 (regular service and service with provisions for continuous study) shows that 78% of the religious, 80% of the traditional and 97% of the secular respondents are opposed to maintaining the status quo with regard to this issue. The only respondents in favor of maintaining the status quo were the ultra-Orthodox, and even among this group a noteworthy percentage (29%) did not agree that *Yeshiva* students should be totally exempted from the army. Hence the almost inevitable conclusion that this practice, which the vast majority (89%) of the population opposes, is maintained because of coalition commitments.

Religiosity and Commitment to Democracy

Democratic regimes are more dependent than any other regime on public support for their precepts. If these premises are imposed by force, their very essence is lost. Nevertheless, it would be unrealistic to expect everyone to express wholehearted support for democratic principles *all of the time*. Some citizens may not interpret democracy as a set of ideals, but rather as fair and acceptable "rules of the game". These rules are viewed as a *means* through which other ends such as peace, social justice, and even a religious way of life may be achieved. When the attachment to such goals is powerful and intensive, a relative weakening of commitment to democracy should be expected. To the extent that a democratic regime seeks to accommodate extreme ideologies, it must reconcile itself to the existence of substantial minorities whose perspective of democracy is primarily instrumental. In this context, commitment to democracy will be measured among groups of respondents with different degrees of religiosity.

First, we will distinguish between adherence to "abstract" principles of democracy (deriving from Israel's Declaration of Independence), and democratic positions when an actual contradiction arises (e.g., limitation of democracy when national security is at stake).

The data presented in Table 4 do not corroborate the argument that religious and ultra-Orthodox Jews are "anti-democratic"; a substantial minority (about 40%) supports basic democratic values. However, the data does show consistent differences between religious and secular Jews regarding this issue, i.e., the less religious one is, the stronger one's commitment to democratic values. One should note, again, the balanced position of traditional Jews: about 50% of them emphasize democratic values, while 50% are opposed (or indifferent). A majority of religious (and, of course, ultra-Orthodox) Jews reject democratic principles, while a majority of secular Jews support them.

The crucial test of democracy does not occur in the realm of abstract values but in times of crisis, when democratic principles conflict with other essential aims. Such crises occur, for example, when national security is at stake. In such situations many people believe that democratic rights should be suspended until the threat passes. Democratic priorities may also be questioned when elected leaders (who are limited by "checks and balances") seem too "weak" to lead the country successfully. Finally, people are likely to question democracy when the policies of the elected government are diametrically opposed to their own views.

Based on these considerations, the following three questions were formulated:

1. "The slightest threat to national security justifies substantial limitation of democratic rights." (strongly agree... strongly disagree).

2. "Under the present conditions, the country needs a strong leadership that

can 'restore order' without being subject to elections or parliamentary votes".
3. Which government would you prefer?
   a) A democratic government whose policies you oppose.
   b) A non-democratic government whose policies you support.

Before we begin comparing various groups of respondents (see Table 5), it should be noted that only one-third of the sample was strongly opposed to revoking democratic rights, even when national security is in danger; similarly, only one-third of the sample strongly opposed the rise of a "strong leadership" that would restore order while ignoring certain parliamentary restrictions. Most of the respondents at all levels of religiosity were willing to at least consider giving up democracy in such situations. In other words, when national security or the capacity of government are at stake, Israeli democracy faces problems that are not necessarily connected with religiosity.

Examination of the differences between the groups shows, however, that the continuum "Ultra-Orthodox-Religious-Traditional-Secular" is generally maintained in that order (with the exception of the view of traditional Jews on the question of "strong leadership", which is less democratic than that of religious Jews). The largest discrepancy in responses to the first two questions was found between traditional and secular Jews; however, with regard to the last question the main gap was between ultra-Orthodox and religious Jews. A substantial share of ultra-Orthodox Jews indicated that they would prefer a government that imposes a religious way of life, even if it was not elected democratically; the rest of the respondents, however, would not support an undemocratic government, even if they agreed with its policies.

This finding illuminates a major aspect of the democratic perspective. Sincere democrats appreciate procedure as much as outcomes. Even divine ends will not justify undemocratic means. A majority of the ultra-Orthodox seem to believe otherwise: imposed religiosity is preferred to voluntary secularity.

Finally, a different dimension of democratic attitudes - the extent of tolerance towards Israeli Arabs - was examined (see Table 6). Attitudes on this issue constitute a touchstone of democracy. Israel is defined as a Jewish state and has an official ideology - Zionism. These two elements of Israeli life make it difficult to accept Arab citizens as equals deserving equal rights. However, democratic values demand social, political and religious equality for Arab citizens. Of the questions dealing with attitudes towards Arabs, we focused on the right of Arab citizens to be elected to parliament.

Again, only a minority of the sample was strongly opposed to revoking a substantial share of Arab citizens' rights; but that minority is negligible (5%) among the ultra-Orthodox respondents, and increases gradually to a third (33%) among the secular respondents.

Religiosity and Hawkish Attitudes

Israel's social and political problems, including the relationship between religion and state, have been overshadowed for the past 24 years by the dispute over war, peace and the future of the territories. In surveys conducted prior to the elections for the 12th Knesset, 90% of the respondents indicated that foreign policy and national security are the issues that determine how they are going to vote. Hence it is important to address the relationship between religiosity and attitudes towards these issues, which are at the top of the national agenda.

In this connection, the first task is to devise a relatively concise and simple criterion for measuring "hawkishness" (or, to the contrary, "dovishness"). Numerous researchers (including this author) have attempted to measure this variable according to the amount of territory the respondent would be willing to "give up" in exchange for peace.

In recent years, new factors have entered the picture: settlements in the territories, the extent of recognition for Palestinian leadership and the level of autonomy it is accorded, the severity of punishments rendered for perpetrating the Intifada, etc. In light of the increasing complexity of the situation, we found it necessary to indicate one or two key factors that might represent or reflect the multitude of recurring issues. One such factor is the distribution of rights among Jews and Arabs in Israel. Do both nationalities have equal rights? Does one nationality have preferential or even exclusive rights? If we know an individual's location on this basic dimension, we can infer his attitude on almost every relevant issue from freezing settlements in the territories to the Intifada.

A second factor is based on current political jargon: today, "right" and "left" are synonymous with "hawkishness" and "dovishness" respectively. In order to verify this assumption, we calculated the correlation between how respondents placed themselves on the "right-left" continuum and how they placed themselves on the "capitalism-socialism" continuum. The low, statistically insignificant correlation (tau = 0.05), shows that today there is no correspondence between the terms "right-left" and their "classic" usage. However a high, statistically significant, correlation was found (tau = 0.58) between the "right-left" and the "hawkish-dovish" continuum.

Table 7 examines the interrelationship between religious self-definition (=

religiosity) and distribution of territorial rights   among the two predominant nationalities. Table 8 shows the correspondence between degree of religiosity and location on the "right-left" continuum.

The two tables indicate that on the whole, the Jewish-Israeli population tends to be hawkish. Thirty-eight per cent of the respondents in the sample feel that Jews have an exclusive right to Eretz Israel, as opposed to 26% who are willing to accord individual and national rights to members of both nationalities. Forty-three per cent   define themselves as right-wing or moderate right, while only 20% define themselves as left-wingers. This inclination towards right-wing, hawkish attitudes can be attributed to the views of ultra-Orthodox, religious and traditional Jews, since the secular half of the population shows a slight inclination towards the left (23 < 31). The same inclination is reflected by the fact that an approximately equal percentage of respondents supports the extreme and moderate right, whereas a relatively low percentage supports the extreme left.

If the secular respondents are examined separately, or if the sample is examined as a whole, the phenomenon of the "dominant center" is evident: respondents who place themselves in the "center" can tip the scales in either direction by adopting more extreme views. This phenomenon does not occur, however, among the ultra-Orthodox and religious respondents as a separate group. Since the majority of this population is on the right end of the political spectrum, small movements are not likely to change the position of the whole sector.

The most recent, surprising change reflected in both of the tables is the fact that respondents who define themselves as "ultra-Orthodox" are definitely no less hawkish and possibly even a bit more right-wing than their religious counterparts. Hence we submit that contrary to the prevailing stereotype, the ultra-Orthodox population is not politically moderate. Although the leaders of the ultra-Orthodox parties (*Shas, Agudat Israel* and *Degel Hatorah*) tend to espouse more dovish views than the leaders of the National Religious Party, the ultra-Orthodox population itself is not dovish. In fact, they espouse even more hawkish, right-wing views than National Religious Party supporters.

Discussion: A Political Profile of the Ultra-Orthodox and Religious Groups

The religious and the ultra-Orthodox parties have played a key role in the Israeli political system. In the past, these parties have had the capacity to tip the   balance of power in favor of either of the two major political blocs, which were almost evenly divided. They have been able to determine which of the two blocs will form a government and lead the country. However, based on the findings presented above, we submit that the ultra-Orthodox are no longer in this position.

The capacity of a small political party to tip the balance of power between two larger blocs is determined by two factors:

a. The electoral power of the small party must be greater than the gap between the two rival blocs.

b. The small party must be able to align with either of the larger blocs, both in political and emotional terms.

It can be assumed that the ultra-Orthodox parties, which have a total of 13 representatives (6 Shas, 5 Agudat Yisrael, 2 Degel Hatora), fulfil the first criterion. However, their capacity to fulfil the second criterion is doubtful. The National Religious Party, for example, declared that it would only join a right-wing coalition, i.e., a coalition headed by the Likud. Hence the question arises: what caused the National Religious Party to willingly give up the flexibility it enjoyed when it maintained a neutral position?

We maintain that the answer to this question lies in the right-wing/hawkish attitudes of religious voters. Any hesitation on the part of the NRP may cause voters to "escape" to the Likud and/or to other right-wing parties.

For similar reasons, the ultra-Orthodox parties also have cause to be concerned about the attitudes of their supporters, whose views on foreign policy and security are as hard-line as those of NRP supporters. Supporters of the Shas party are just as likely as NRP supporters to shift to the Likud if they are disappointed by the political indecisiveness of Shas. Although supporters of other ultra-Orthodox parties are less inclined to change their affiliation, by expressing strong opposition they may force their leaders to suspend or even break any agreement to support a government with dovish views.

This process was evident after the fall of the Likud government in the spring of 1990. Ultra-Orthodox leaders who had agreed to support a Labor government began to hesitate and ultimately returned to a coalition with the Likud. This enabled the Likud to form a new government without the Labor Party. It can be assumed that some of the ultra-Orthodox party members were influenced more by grass-roots pressure from their own supporters than they were by their rabbis and sages.

If the ultra-Orthodox parties follow the other religious parties and align themselves with the right-wing, they will tip the scales in favor of that bloc. If and when such a change takes root among the political community (and subsequently among the overall population), a new electoral map will emerge: a left-wing camp that begins with the Labor Party, incorporating the Zionist left-wing parties and reaching as far as the Arab parties; and a parallel right-wing camp that begins with the Likud, incorporating the religious parties and reaching extreme right parties such as Tsomet, Hatehiya and Moledet.

A large number of voters may find themselves in the "middle of the road", without actively supporting the platform of either bloc. Immigrants to Israel from the "Russian Commonwealth", for example, are not committed to a hawkish or dovish platform. However, they have viable interests of their own which they seek to pursue. Paradoxically, the bargaining power, once enjoyed by the ultra-Orthodox parties, may shift to a sector of the Israeli population that is least involved in religious-Jewish tradition.

The previous pages were published (in a special supplement to the Hebrew daily, *Ma'ariv*) six months prior to the June 1992 elections to the 13th Knesset. It seems worthwhile to assess, at this point in time (July 1992) to what extent the predictions and evaluations proposed in the earlier version were realized.

During the election campaign all the religious parties pledged to prefer a coalition with the Likud over a coalition with the Labor Party. This pledge seemed to draw the religious sector into the right-wing. The concept of *preference* in this context was, however, based on an assumption that failed to materialize. The results were assumed to allow the religious parties (jointly or even separately) to determine who shall head the next coalition. As we stated earlier, the power to decide between the two major camps can be maintained only if the religious parties exceed the difference between these camps. In the recent (June 1992) elections, the religious parties fell short (by *one* mandate in the Knesset!) of fulfilling their traditional decisive role.

They must now deal with a new reality in which the major party in power is determined during the election, and their own leverage is limited to giving or withholding support and legitimation. A few days after the election, it became quite clear that the commitment of the ultra-Orthodox to the right-wing was a partial and conditional one. The Orthodox parties left no doubt that they wished to join the coalition and that their preconditions would not be in the realm of foreign affairs or national security. The National Religious Party, being somewhat less dependent on financial support for religious organizations and much more committed to the idea of a "greater Israel" (Lustick, 1988, pp. 72-90), exhibited a more reserved position. But even the NRP did not altogether reject the idea of joining the Labor-dominated government.

Where do these new developments leave us, considering the relationship between Jewish religiosity and democracy? The overriding impression is one of appreciable adaptability and flexibility on the part of the religious political sector. Whatever the contradictions between religion and democratic principles might be, the religious leaders seem to have no difficulty in adjusting to the realities of democratic life.

Finally, a general reflection about the relationship between dogmatism and opportunism seems unavoidable. The more a political group is committed to specific principles, the greater this group's flexibility and adaptability in all areas which are not directly associated with those principles. If the principles to which the group adheres are located low in the order of preference of the general public, the "dogmatic" (but somewhat eccentric) group may reap an appreciable advantage: it may exchange consent to policies on issues like national security, economic planning and management of natural resources (which are, after all, only "secular concerns") for concessions to their specific interests and commitments. This pragmatic (or even opportunistic) conduct seems to currently fulfil a vital function for the Israeli democratic system: it transforms a scarce majority into a more stable and operative one.

T A B L E S

Table 1: The Relationship between Religious Self Definition and Observance of Traditions, and Religious Belief

Group of Respondents	Ultra-Orthodox	Religious	Traditional	Secular	Total Sample	N
	10% (126)	10% (133)	29% (375)	51% (653)	100%	1287
A. Religious Observance Do you and your family...						
Go to synagogue every day (or almost every day)	84%	76%	20%	2%	21%	1287
Refrain from travelling on the Sabbath	98%	92%	18%	2%	23%	1265
Mean	91% >	82% >	19% >	2%	22%	
B. Beliefs Do you believe that/in						
The Torah comes from a divine source	99%	98%	66%	23%	50%	1269
Reward and punishment in the world to come	97%	90%	57%	17%	43%	1286
God created the universe	99%	98%	71%	25%	52%	1286
Mean	98% >	95% >	75% >	22%	48%	

Table 2: Support for Religious Legislation

Group of Respondents	Ultra-Orthodox	Religious	Traditional	Secular	Total Sample	N
	10% (126)	10% (133)	29% (375)	51% (653)	100%	1287
Attitude The State of Israel should be theocratic	<u>64%</u>	19%	4%	1%	8%	105
There should be more religious laws	29%	<u>33%</u>	9%	-	8%	108
The status quo should be maintained	5%	<u>39%</u>	<u>47%</u>	21%	30%	386
There should be less religious laws	2%	5%	30%	<u>45%</u>	<u>33%</u>	424
Religious legislation should be abolished	-	4%	10%	33%	21%	264
Total	100%	100%	100%	100%	100%	1287

Correlation: Kendall's tau = 0.55

Table 3: Attitudes Towards Exemption of Yeshiva Students from Army Service.

Group of Respondents	Ultra-Orthodox	Religious	Traditional	Secular	Total Sample
	10%	10%	29%	51%	100%
	(126)	(133)	(375)	(653)	1287
Attitude					
Yeshiva students should be drafted into the army like everyone else	9%	29%	54%	73%	60%
Provisions should be made for continuation of religious education during army service	20%	49%	34%	24%	29%
Yeshiva students should be obligated to undergo a brief period of basic training	8%	9%	9%	2%	3%
The status quo should be maintained (total exemption for Yeshiva students)	63%	13%	3%	1%	8%
Total	100%	100%	100%	100%	100%

Correlation: Kendall's tau = 0.37

Table 4: Relationship between Religious Self-Definition
and Democratic Guarantees (% in favor)

Group of Respondents	Ultra-Orthodox	Religious	Traditional	Secular	Total Sample	N
	10% (126)	10% (133)	29% (375)	51% (653)	100%	1287
Attitude						
The State of Israel should guarantee all of its citizens...						
Equal social and political rights	37%	44%	46%	61%	51%	1284
Freedom of religion and conscience	45%	47%	56%	68%	60%	1278
Mean:	41% <	46% <	52% <	65%	55%	

Table 5: Commitment to Democratic Attitudes by Religious Self-Definition

(% of pro-democratic attitudes)

Group of Respondents	Ultra-Orthodox	Religious	Traditional	Secular	Total Sample	N
Attitude						
"The slightest threat" justifies limitations	24% <	27% <	29% <	40%	34%	1263
Oppose "strong leadership"	31%<	34% >	24% <	42%	35%	1275
Prefer a democratic government even if I disagree with its platform	39% <	59% <	67% <	73%	67%	1239
Mean	35% <	42% <	44% <	57% <	49%	

Table 6: Arab Citizens should not be Eligible to Parliament

(% of strong disagreement)

Ultra-Orthodox	Religious	Traditional	Secular	Total	N
5% <	19% =	18% <	33%	25%	1282

Table 7: Religiosity and Attitudes Regarding the Rights of Jews and Arabs in Eretz Israel

Group of Respondents	Ultra-Orthodox	Religious	Traditional	Secular Sample	Total
	10% (126)	10% (133)	29% (375)	51% (653)	100% (1287)
Attitude					
The Land of Israel belongs exclusively to the Jews; only Jews have rights there	76% >	56% >	43% >	28%	38%
Only Jews have national rights in the Land of Israel but Arabs are entitled to individual rights	16% <	31% <	40% ~	36%	36%
Both people have individual and national rights in the Land of Israel	8% <	13% <	17% <	36%	26%
Total	100%	100%	100%	100%	100%

Correlation: Kendall's tau = 0.27

Table 8: The Relationship between Religious Self-Definition and Inclinations Towards the Right or Left

Group of Respondents	Ultra-Orthodox	Religious	Traditional	Secular	Total Sample
	10%	10%	29%	51%	100%
	(126)	(133)	(375)	(653)	(1287)
Attitude					
Right	(42%	(35%	(27%	(13%	(22%
	70%(	68%(	52%(	28%(	43%(
Moderate Right	(28%	(33%	(25%	(15%	(21%
Center	24%	26%	37%	41%	37%
Moderate Left	(2%	(5%	(8%	(23%	(14%
	6%(	6%(	11%(	31%(	20%(
Left	(4%	(1%	(3%	(8%	(6%
Total	100%	100%	100%	100%	100%

Correlation: Kendall's tau = 0.28

References

Ben-Meir, Y. and P. Kedem 1979. "An Index of Religiosity for the Jewish
Population in Israel", *Megamot* 24(3) (Hebrew), 353-362.

Deshen, S. 1978a. "Israeli Judaism - Introduction to the Major Patterns",
International Journal of Middle East Studies, 9(2), 141-169.

Deshen, S. 1978b. "Two Trends in Israeli Orthodoxy", *Judaism: A Quarterly
of Jewish Life and Thought*, 27(4), 397-409.

Levy, A. 1989. *The Orthodox*, Tel-Aviv, Keter, (Hebrew).

Liebman, C. and E. Don-Yehiye 1984. *Religion and Politics in Israel*.
Bloomington, Indianna University Press.

Liebman, C. and E. Don-Yehiye 1983. *Civil Religion in Israel,* Berkeley,
University of California Press.

Lustick, I.S. 1988. *For the Land and the Lord,* New York, Council on
Foreign Relations.

Peres, Y. and E. Yuchtman-Ya'ar 1992. *Trends in Israeli Democracy,*
Boulder and London, L. Riener.

Acknowledgements

The study was carried out in the framework of the Israel Democracy Institute
(I.D.I.), Jerusalem.

I would like to express my thanks to my colleague Prof. Eppie Ya'ar. Some of
the thoughts expressed in this article derive from our numerous conversations.

I would also like to thank Daphna Goldberg for her help in analyzing the data,
and the Modiin Ezrachi Research Institute for collecting the data.

7

Religion in the Israeli Discourse on the Arab-Jewish Conflict

Shlomo Deshen

In recent decades, social and cultural anthropology has proved to be of value in many fields of social practice. The achievements of applied anthropology are particularly salient in medical training and practice, in agricultural and community development, and in education. But in many other fields the application of anthropology has hardly begun. Astonishingly, this is so in the area of business and industrial administration, where after very promising beginnings with Edward Hall's work (see, for instance, Hall and White 1960), little has happened.

Even more remarkable is the near sterility of anthropology in the practice of international and inter-cultural relations, a field that lies close to the essence of a discipline that claims to be focused on culture (cf. Hannerz and Ingold, both in this volume). In a century that has been troubled on an unprecedented scale with hot and cold wars, nuclear and near-nuclear wars, Holocaust and genocides, anthropology has addressed itself little to urgent issues, which have led to immeasurable bloodshed. Specialists in the study of knowledge and the professions may concern themselves with understanding this feature of twentieth-century anthropology, but for all anthropologists, the irrelevance, for all practical purposes, of the discipline to peace and war, the major anguish of humanity, should at least be a source of malaise.

The year 1989 was thrilling and uplifting to people in many parts of the world directly involved in the confrontation of the West and Communism. Even where a renaissance was aborted, in China, the ugly events of June 1989 there have at least raised hopes for another revolutionary attempt, which might yet succeed. There are even rumbles in Africa. But many other parts of the world seem to have remained untouched by 1989. Protagonists of the Jewish-Arab conflict, for instance, have maintained essentially unchanged stances.

My aim in this article is to contribute to an exploration of the potential of anthropological insight in the field of international relations, war and peace. Mercifully the Cold War has ended – without the benefit of efforts on the part of anthropological practitioners. But where, as in the Middle East, people gaze wistfully upon epoch-making and favourable events, which have not yet impinged on them significantly, there remains a role for applied anthropology.

The current confrontations between Jewish Israelis and Arab Palestinians, as well as many Arab and Muslim states, embed the resolutions of prior internal confrontations of moderates and extremists, 'doves and hawks', of the various adversaries. These separate internal political discourses of Jews and Arabs are crucially important in determining the outcome of the confrontations between the adversaries. I seek here to shed light on the kind of debate that Israelis maintain among themselves, leading on to a practical recommendation, which will flow from the analysis. This recommendation might prove constructive in the quest for a settlement of the tragedy. A comparable analysis of the internal Arab discourse, with a parallel concluding recommendation in terms of a settlement, would be desirable. But that is both beyond my competence and the scope of this article (for pertinent analyses, see Abraham 1983; Harkabi 1988; Steinberg 1988, 1989).

The political and historical context

Uncovering the nature of the Israeli debate on an Arab-Jewish settlement requires summarising some of the salient features of

Israeli politics and society.[1] One of the most remarkable of these is the affinity of hawkish views and orthodox religious practice. Judging by their overall performance in Israeli government coalition-building ever since 1977, orthodox people and their political representatives are evidently comfortable with positions that tend towards the extreme right wing. The movement for establishing Jewish settlements in territories beyond the 1967 borders, the Gush Emunim movement, is very popular among young orthodox people. Moreover, extreme positions such as those of the underground cell of the early 1980s, 'The Faithful of the Temple Mount' group, not to mention the parliamentary extreme right-wing parties, have an aura of fascination. Although most orthodox people stop short of actually joining these movements, they do constitute viable alternatives that people do not reject out of hand. Even the group of Meir Kahana, which voices aggressive racism, and once managed to get elected to the Knesset before it was outlawed, is a serious proposition that is considered and deliberated by young people in particular.

This feature of the Israeli socio-political scene is a matter of crucial significance in the overall context of the Middle Eastern conflict, and in the debates concerning its resolution. My reason for this evaluation is the following: the hawkish position in Israel is fuelled from three distinct intellectual sources. One is that of religious orthodoxy (particularly as currently interpreted by followers of the school of Rabbi Z. Y. Kook, d. 1982); another is that of secular right-wing étatism (stemming originally from the ideology of Ze'ev Jabotinsky, d. 1940, and the Revisionist Party). This second school of thought was maintained by old-time associates of former Prime Minister Begin in the underground movements of pre-Independence times, and by a small number of writers (such as Y. Z. Greenberg, d. 1981, and Yisrael Eldad). The third source is that of pragmatic politicians and soldiers, such as Moshe Arens, Yuval Ne'eman and Ariel Sharon, for whom considerations of secular *realpolitik*, free of

---

1. Different version of this article appeared in *The Jewish Quarterly* (1990) and in *Human Organization* (1992). The analysis presented here is based on a synthesis of copious materials. Short of attempting to offer all the references, I mention some basic publications: Lustick (1988) provides a useful bibliographic introduction; Liebman and Don-Yehiya (1984) give a basic overview from a political science perspective; Krausz (1985) and Kimmerling (1989) contain collections of fine sociological studies; Deshen (1982) provides an anthropologically-oriented overview that leads to the present analysis.

sentimental religious or moral trappings, are operative in preferring hawkish alternatives.

Of the three sources, the second is moribund, and for all practical purposes is no more active. The reason for this is that secular rightist ideologies lack attraction among rank-and-file Israelis, and particularly so among younger people. The ideologists of old Revisionist stripe have departed the scene and have not been replaced. (Of them all there remains primarily Eldad, who is still a vigorous and attractive speaker, but has no political following.) As a result of this, orthodoxy, in the guise of the Rabbi Kook school, is the main ideological bolster of the hawkish position. No other force competes with it in supplying spiritual vitality and depth to the position of the pragmatists, which in itself is ideologically sterile. The orthodox thus fill a crucial position in the Israeli right wing, and consequently in the overall Israeli political spectrum. This importance is distinct from the pivotal position of the orthodox in coalition arithmetics; even if the religious parties were to falter at the polls their ideological importance, as the essential powerhouse of the right wing, would remain unchanged.

The present position of orthodoxy in the Israeli political spectrum is startling when viewed in the context of the not very distant past. When Zionism emerged in Central and Eastern Europe about a century ago, leading rabbis were anything but enthusiastic about it. Despite the activities of a small number of nineteenth- and early twentieth-century rabbis, in favour of Zionism and the pioneering settlement movement, the majority of rabbis and their flocks were apathetic, and a large and vocal minority were stridently opposed. The reason for this was that most rabbis conceived traditional Messianic beliefs in terms that were incompatible with secular Zionist nationalism, and viewed the latter as essentially a heresy. Moreover, the Zionist movement increasingly came to be dominated by non-practising Jews, and this coloured the pioneering effort in Palestine in secular hues, which were additionally objectionable. The main rabbinical position was altogether inimical to emigration from Eastern Europe anywhere, be it to Palestine or to the West, because of the well-founded fear that migration would erode the old style of life. Consequently, the role of observant Jews in the pioneering movement, through the Turkish (until 1917) and Mandate periods (until 1948) was secondary at best, and often insignificant.

Present-day orthodox hawkishness is all the more startling when the political record of the recent past is considered. A fair number of orthodox people did immigrate to Palestine in pre-State years (before 1948), in defiance of rabbinical leadership. Remarkably, these people organised themselves mainly in two sets of political parties. Predominantly they joined the religious workers' party; to a smaller extent they joined ultra-orthodox parties which were stridently anti-Zionist. The religious workers' party in Mandate times elected not merely to be a junior partner of the leading (and presently much-discredited) Labour-Mapai Party, but itself actually had some attributes of socialism. Thus groups of religious workers followed the lead of secular pioneers and established their own kibbutz (pl. kibbutzim) communes, which differed from most kibbutzim only in the fact that the members observed religious orthodoxy. The standing of these religious kibbutzim among religious people was generally high, a model for emulation (at least in theory), just as was the case among the secular socialists.

In the 1920s the religious workers' party seriously considered disbanding and actually joining the federation of socialist workers, and in fact did so for the duration of two years. Through the Mandate period orthodox workers were suffered among their socialist colleagues only as subordinates. Economically, those were often hard years. At times there was unemployment, and orthodox workers were openly discriminated against in the allocation of work. This sometimes led to incidents of violence. Yet the political partnership of religious and secular workers held for nearly fifty years, from the 1920s to the 1970s. The height was in 1937 when the British recommended partition of the country, granting the Jews only a small slice of territory. Labour accepted the proposal over the objections of the right-wing Revisionist Party – and most of the orthodox sided with the former or remained neutral.

By the 1970s the orthodox position had changed dramatically, and attained the present contours. The reasons for this shift are essentially rooted in the turmoil engendered by the Holocaust. The events of the times clearly vindicated the classical Zionist position in the eyes of all survivors, including the orthodox, who had previously been apathetic. Even where the anti-Zionist position remained, it lost its élan. Instead of the pre-Holocaust position there developed among those who remained aloof from

Zionism a pragmatic attitude toward the Israeli state. They accepted it on condition that it extend aid toward rebuilding orthodox communities and institutions in Israel, to replace those that had been annihilated (for a sensitive and full exposition of the mutation of orthodox views about Zionism, in the context of the Holocaust, see Friedman 1990). Actual opposition to the state remained only in insignificant fringe groups. By and large, as long as the orthodox obtained material government support for their talmudic educational institutions (*yeshivot*), and the students of those institutions were exempted from military conscription, the orthodox could be relied upon to support the government.

Among religious workers another factor operated: In Mandate times the religious workers' circles had not, for reasons that are beyond our present scope, been very successful in raising their children as observant Jews; many of the younger generation left the fold of orthodoxy. However, in the 1950s the balance of educational success changed dramatically, and there arose a stratum of youth that were markedly more careful in religious observance, than their older siblings. On the other hand, secular socialism had begun to flounder, under the impact of reaction to late-Stalinism, such as the anti-Semitic Moscow 'doctors' trials'. This dual development heightened the self-confidence of the orthodox, just as it systematically eroded that of the secular socialists. At a time when orthodox people of all shades were establishing yeshivas for their youth who clamoured to enter them, the socialist school system shed its unique ideological character. There developed among the orthodox a view of the socialists as decadent and failing, and this latched on to the old bitterness at having been, for many years, treated shabbily as second-class citizens, by the dominant Labour establishment.

The late 1950s and 1960s was a period when orthodox people felt themselves becoming emancipated and equal, and they began to flaunt proudly their particular identity. In the 1950s, for instance, there began the fashion of orthodox youths walking about in public with knitted skull-caps, whereas previously they wore innocuous berets and other caps.[2] In the 1950s there also

---

2. It is a traditional orthodox Jewish practice for males to cover their heads with hats or at least small skull-caps at all times.

began to emerge the phenomenon of young orthodox people linked with the youth movement of the religious workers' party, who sought to make their political mark in a new way, not like their elders, who were just satisfied with matters of specific practice (such as securing public Sabbath observance and state religious education). Rather, these youths sought to develop, in the context of their religious resurgence, religious policies in areas of general public interest, such as in social welfare and, most crucially and ominously, in external and security affairs.

These incipient developments came to a dramatic head after 1967. The defeat of the coalition of Arab states in the June 1967 war led to major territorial changes. The youth generation came to dominate the religious workers' party and imposed upon it a hawkish agenda. Further, these same circles of young people spearheaded the Gush Emunim movement for Jewish settlement in the newly conquered West Bank and Gaza territories. This movement had a powerful religio-mystical source, that came to be newly formulated, but it also had a source, rooted in the vicissitudes of mundane relations between the orthodox and the secular-socialist strata. Because of the latter's ideological troubles the orthodox felt that the major role-model of Israeli society, that of the pioneer, was slipping out of the hands of the socialists, whereas in the past it was precisely the latter who had produced the major exemplars of pioneering, in terms of both numbers and excellence.

After 1967 and through the following decades, the orthodox developed a view of themselves as having picked up the mantle of self-sacrificing, devoted pioneering, which the socialists had discarded. One of the motives for the settlement élan of Gush Emunim, aside from the religio-mystical factor, was the urge to make the statement that the orthodox had indeed replaced the discredited socialists, who in the past had proudly dominated Israeli society. The settlement drive was an emphatic statement that the orthodox had finally arrived, and were now first-class citizens. The drive actually to settle the territories is unique to only a segment of orthodox people; it is not shared by the ultra-orthodox, nor by Israelis of Middle Eastern background, the Sephardim. However, it is crucial to note that virtually all sectors of orthodoxy favour activism and settlement in the territories. They are sympathetic bystanders. The differences between the various sectors of orthodoxy pertain to personal commitment to activism, but in principle there is accord with and admiration for the new pioneers. This view of the Israeli scene requires emphasis, for the surface developments often lead observers to mistaken conclusions.[3]

Among the ultra-orthodox there operate processes that are basically similar to those operating among other orthodox people, such as the religious workers' party. Among all of them there is a sensation of heightened self-worth, of moving into what they consider their rights as citizens. The orthodox conceive of their styles of life and viewpoints as increasingly vindicated by the erosion of secular socialism. Whereas many young people have left kibbutz life and embraced materialism (not to mention that kibbutz life itself has become much more bourgeois than it ever was), the ranks of the ultra-orthodox are bursting. The rate of self-reproduction is high, with families of eight and more children quite common. More, there is a very small but vocal segment of ultra-orthodoxy, composed of people who have shifted there from a style of secular living, and this phenomenon is another cause of high morale and pride for all orthodox people.

One expression of this morale is the increasing phenomenon of self-help organisations, in ultra-orthodox circles in particular. People innovate imaginatively so as to be able to offer philanthropic service. A multitude of tiny volunteer organisations provide for a great variety of needs: loans of bedding and cutlery for people hosting and celebrating, loans of loaves of bread and cartons of milk and baby's dummies for

3. Thus it is incorrect to interpret the ongoing bickering between the hassidic ultra-orthodox and their 'Lithuanian' opponents (specifically, Rabbi Schneersohn, the head of Habad hassidim, and Rabbi Schach, the head of 'the Lithuanians') as implying significant foreign policy differences, with the hassidim being hawkish and their opponents moderate. In fact, all major factions of ultra-orthodoxy are highly pragmatic in the terms outlined. The infighting is focused on internal matters of religious nature (such as the role of the hassidic leader in society and in respect to Messianism), and on most mundane matters connected with resources of funds and followers. Rabbinical infighting, and social and intellectual discourse generally in Eastern European Jewry in the eighteenth and nineteenth centuries, gained an increasingly abrasive character, and this is carried over also to contemporary life. Thus, infighting among the ultra-orthodox is maintained in strident tones. Insiders do not take the colourful abusive idioms and metaphors literally, but outsiders (as most political commentators are) often do so. This observation about the nature of debate among the ultra-orthodox applies also to the topics that are chosen for dispute. Thus, to return to the analysis of positions over the Jewish-Arab conflict, shades and nuances of different positions of ultra-orthodox faction-leaders are conflated and brought to extremes. In confronting his rival, Rabbi Schach minimises all points of agreement and emphasises points of disagreement. Therefore, he and his followers present him as a dove of kinds, to contrast Rabbi Schneersohn's articulated hawkishness.

people who suddenly find themselves in a predicament at a time when stores are closed, not to mention loans of interest-free cash, and many others. It is remarkable that these ventures do not cater exclusively to the particular in-group of the orthodox activists. On the contrary, activists often pride themselves in providing service to one and all.

There is an element of patronizing here: orthodox people see themselves as superior *vis-à-vis* others whom they consider decadent, and being in a position to assist those aliens bolsters their sense of religio-cultural status. This phenomenon dovetails with the pioneering drive in the West Bank settlement effort. Both activities are, *inter alia*, expressions of the enhanced self-image of the orthodox as well as means to sustain that image. In contemporary anthropological parlance, these doings are both models of and models for the new existential reality of inverted statuses, as experienced by the orthodox. The overall effect of all this is a significant, salient and general shift of the orthodox strategy, away from isolation, centrism and leftism – towards the right-wing pole.

The discussion so far has been focused on the orthodox of Ashkenazi (Northern European) background. Pertinent developments among Sephardim are different from those we have followed in matters of detail only. However, these differences are sufficiently salient to warrant separate discussion of the two social strata. Moreover, the nature of Sephardic religiosity is somewhat different from that of the orthodox Ashkenazim. Therefore, I now reserve usage of the term 'orthodox' for people of Ashkenazi background, and when referring to people of Middle Eastern background, even when clearly observant, I use the general term 'Sephardim', although that term encompasses people of vastly different levels of observance.[4]

The Sephardim appeared massively on the Israeli scene only with the onset of unrestricted immigration, after 1948. In Israel they found themselves in a setting that was clearly dominated by Ashkenazim, and in particular by those of secular-socialist persuasion, the Labour-Mapai establishment. The nature of ensuing relationships between the latter and the immigrants has been recounted many times, and need not be repeated (see, for instance, Smooha 1978; Ben-Rafael 1982; Weingrod 1985). The

---

4. I cannot, in the present context, elaborate on the considerations that underlie these statements. This is offered in my article cited in note 1.

point to be emphasised in the present context is that the orthodox experience had much in common with that of the Sephardim, in terms of subordination to and sometimes discrimination by the socialists. The major difference between the orthodox and the Sephardim lay in the fact that the former came to assert themselves in the mid-1950s, one generation in time before the Sephardim, in the course of the process that I have outlined. The Sephardim, on the other hand, remained dominated by Labour-Mapai institutions, and largely quiescent, until the mid-1970s. In terms of both culture and politics the Sephardim long remained passive, content to be junior partners in socialist-run institutions, much like the old religious workers' party. Because of details unique to the situation of the Sephardim, the change, when it came in the late 1970s, was dramatic. Sephardic personalities were propelled to prominent positions, instead of the socialists who were then replaced by a right-wing government led by the Likud Party.

Crucially, in common with the orthodox, the Sephardim to this day nurture bitterness toward the socialists. There is also a parallel between the development of pragmatism *vis-à-vis* the State among the ultra-orthodox, upon which I remarked earlier, and developments among the Sephardim. In the course of the 1980s there emerged a politically articulate group of ultra-orthodox Sephardim, the Shas Party, that has become a significant political factor. The agenda of Shas is to establish schools and yeshivot which would revive old Sephardic traditions and lead people to heightened ethnic-orthodox observance. In a fashion parallel with that of other ultra-orthodox groups Shas maintains a pragmatic attitude towards the State, as is exemplified in its tactics for coalition formation. Matters of state, security, economy, and so forth, are of relatively minor consideration for Shas politicians.[5]

The dialogue of the deaf

This review of religious and social developments affords us a fresh perspective on Israeli positions concerning Arab–Jewish

---

5. The phenomenon of Sephardic religious resurgence is described in Weingrod (1990), Ben-Ari and Bilu (1987) and Goldberg (1987). For the beginnings of the phenomena, see Deshen and Shokeid (1974). On the Shas phenomenon in particular, there is a Hebrew article (Deshen 1989).

settlement proposals. Israelis holding hawkish positions, whom I introduced at the beginning of this paper, view their opponents who maintain dovish positions in a particular way. As an outcome of the developments that I have traced, right-wing Israelis of many shades – orthodox, ultra-orthodox, Sephardim – view the doves negatively. In the eyes of right-wing Israelis the latter are morally tainted. Most of the doves are of Ashkenazi secular background, and this implies that they will tend to be of middle-class standing materially. Since they have relatively few children, the doves are conceived as being relatively secure in terms of standard of living, income and social status. At the same time, the doves make claims of a humane and social nature, in the context of the international conflict, on behalf of the Arabs. This complex combination causes the hawks to view the doves as hypocrites. They are conceived as mouthing leftist slogans while personally remote from, and insensitive to, the needy in their immediate environment. They are seen to agitate about injuries done to Palestinians, but apathetic when their fellow Jews are hurt.

The doves are seen to nurture alien values, because they present their positions as founded on considerations of human rights, civil rights, minority rights, academic freedom, democracy. In the eyes of contemporary popular interpreters of Judaism in Israel, such as most rabbis, all these values are seen as foreign and clashing with orthodox religion.[6] To take a concrete instance. Two private radio stations in Israel, Kol Ha'shalom and 'Arutz Sheva, propagate the left and right wings' positions respectively. Both stations are similar in mostly featuring light music and songs, thinly interspersed with explicitly ideological rhetoric. There is, however, a glaring difference in the style and covert atmosphere that the two stations convey. Kol Ha'shalom offers a diet of American peace

---

6. These statements are consistent with findings of the American Jewish scene. The following summarises a recent synthesis of research: 'In many ways, non-Orthodox American Jews have deservedly acquired a reputation for adopting social, political and sexual attitudes more liberal than their non-Jewish contemporaries . . . In contrast, the most traditionalist Orthodox generally espouse the most conservative orientations in these areas . . . they are typically more nonliberal on public policy questions for reasons having to do with religious law, institutional concerns, and private morality . . . Between these two poles stand the modern Orthodox who express views between the liberalism of the non-Orthodox and the conservatism of the traditionalists' (Heilman and Cohen 1989: 178–9). To this I would add that the Israeli parallels of the American 'modern Orthodox' are in retreat. In terms of both numbers and moral salience, they have become weaker over the years.

songs and much of the verbiage is hence in English. The rival station offers an exclusive diet of Israeli songs, in particular those with themes of patriotism and attachment to land and nature. 'Arutz Sheva also offers popular religious songs and Sephardic songs, both of religious and of pop nature. This selection leads to an exclusively Hebrew language programme. The covert message that the stations convey is therefore that dovishness is associated with alienness and lack of roots, while hawkishness is associated with the opposite. Clearly, the effect of this image of the dovish station, in terms of moving public opinion, is one of unmitigated self-imposed defeat.

Being popularly seen as both distant from Jewish yearnings and beliefs, and as actual hypocrites, the doves and their agenda altogether lack credibility. In effect, the different positions over the Arab-Jewish conflict become vastly ramified and heavy with symbolic meaning. In the eyes of the orthodox the positions of the doves and the hawks are associated with diffuse cultural differences. It is part of the great clash between those faithful to the heritage of Jewry on the one hand, and the rootless on the other hand, between 'Guardians of the Torah' and detractors of the Torah, between goodness and corruption. This magnification by right-wing partisans of a particular political stand, on an issue that is essentially political, is an important social fact. Though the magnification may be unfounded in terms of reality beyond that of orthodox-hawkish beholders, the fact that they view the situation in this way is itself a crucial element of the social reality. This has important ramifications for internal Israeli foreign policy debates, and ultimately also for overall chances of a non-violent Arab-Jewish settlement. To these we now proceed.

In the prevailing political debate, both outside Israel and within the country, moderate-dovish positions are promoted primarily by left-wing moral and ideological considerations. Thus, for instance, the management of the intifada, the Israeli handling of West Bank schools and universities, the policy towards the establishment of a Palestinian state, are all faulted as being brutal, injurious of human dignity and national rights, violating freedom, and so forth. These criticisms may or may not be valid. But the crucial point, which flows from the foregoing analysis, is that these criticisms do not engage the minds of precisely those protagonists to whom they are addressed, right-wing Israelis. Moral arguments are resonant primarily to Israeli protagonists of dovish convictions. But the latter do not require convincing. Among hawkish people who are secular such arguments might indeed be effective. However, I argued earlier that the hard-core of the right wing does not lie among them.

Hawkish positions are currently not founded on any secular étatist-type ideology. Secular hawkish people maintain an ideological partnership with the orthodox, and it is from the latter that they obtain moral and symbolic support for their positions. The core of the right wing is among the orthodox, who offer to the pragmatic hawks ideological grounding for their positions, primordial images and visions of history. This grounding is combined with pragmatic considerations, such as the risks entailed in permitting or forbidding the operation of West Bank schools, of retaining or retreating from territories, of a Palestinian state – in short, the tragically realistic dangers of compromise.

An attempt to influence Israeli public opinion to move beyond the present tie and deadlock of political views, must be tailored to reach the hawkish position at its crux. Namely, it must be articulated in terms that are reasonable to orthodox people, and not in terms that are obnoxious to them. Paradoxically, it is precisely the richness of dovish positions, in terms of liberal ideology, that causes these positions to be repugnant to orthodox people. On the other hand, it is the shallowness of hawkish positions, in terms of lacking an étatist and fascist ideology, which enables them to be accepted by the orthodox. The debate of doves and hawks in Israel may be summarised as follows. Much of contemporary dovish rhetoric consists essentially of sermons to the converted, and fails to engage (not to mention convince) those whom it most crucially ought to address.

My aim is to formulate a dovish mode of discourse which would overcome this problem. The formulation of such a discourse entails consideration of the various costs of a non-violent settlement to the relevant categories of protagonists. The first such category I proceed to consider is that of the orthodox right wing. Among them the premium on a non-violent settlement is not high, because of the extreme valuation of the actualisation of the ancient dream, the recovery of the entire ancestral Land of Israel. For that any price is tolerable, including armed conflict within the foreseeable future.

The second pertinent category of people is that of the principled left wing, namely people of liberal and socialist background whose secular convictions – humanism, equality, minority rights, self-determination, and so forth – lead them to a willingness to pay the costs of a non-violent settlement. Namely, to undertake the risks of compromise, such as exposed borders, the hazards of a Palestinian state, the threat of armed hostile neighbours. Crucially, however, for this dovish category of people there is a particular cost that they are not called upon to pay. Since they are remote from traditional Jewish beliefs and myths, the dream of a regained Temple Mount, Judea and Samaria (not to mention the Gilead and Bashan regions in present-day Jordan) are not meaningful. Resigning these territories to Arab domination is not very painful to them. The gulf between such left-wing people of principle and the first category of people is therefore very great.

For both these categories of Israelis, the attainment of a non-violent settlement entails accepting the risks of peace, but only for the orthodox right wing does it entail forgoing some of the great yearnings and passions of their religion. Seen from this perspective the clamour of the doves for concessions on the part of the hawks is cheap; it requires relatively little from them and much from their opponents. It is no wonder then that in over two decades of intensive and articulate debate between these protagonists the doves have not advanced their viewpoint in any significant way among the orthodox. One might indeed marvel at the fact that this dialogue of the deaf has been maintained for so many years, without realisation of its futility. This leads us to consider the position of a third category of people over the Arab-Jewish conflict, that of moderates not out of ideological conviction, but out of pragmatic considerations.

These people, pragmatic doves, are not moved by secular ideological commitments of the kind that motivate the ideological left wing. Due to their lack of secular ideological commitment the pragmatic doves may in fact be attuned to the traditional national and mythical values, that propel the orthodox in connection with the Land of Israel and the Temple Mount. The pragmatic doves, however, contrary to the orthodox, are resigned to forgo their yearnings as a part of the price to be paid for a non-violent settlement. The particular price that these moderates are willing to pay is higher than that of their dogmatic left-wing colleagues, because for them the value of liberating the whole ancestral territory is a serious issue, not an inherently repelling position. We have now arrived at an important point in the analysis. There is more affinity between the pragmatic dovish and the orthodox positions than there is between the latter and the ideological dovish position. Before finally proceeding to the important practical recommendation that flows from this analysis, and which is the main point of the discussion, an aside must be made to introduce a pertinent facet of rabbinical Judaism. Ever since its formation in antiquity, and into our times, Judaism as a religio-legal system has been positively receptive of pragmatic considerations.[7] Thus, rabbinical principles of decision-taking include considerations, that a particular course of action might lead to 'mortal danger', 'enmity', or 'great material loss'. Such considerations are religiously and legally legitimate in various particular contexts. It is important to note that those are not considerations that the rabbinical system incorporates out of external overpowering duress; rather, they are internal to the system.

Thus to cite a classical example, when a person is permitted, upon rabbinical discretion based on considerations such as the aforementioned, to perform an action that is normally prohibited on the Sabbath, that person is viewed as having nevertheless sanctified the Sabbath. Moreover, refraining from engaging in an action on the Sabbath under such conditions is considered sinful. Transposing this facet of traditional Judaism onto the political problem at hand we are led to a second important point. Namely, the pragmatic dovish position is more attuned to the orthodox one, not only because the cost of a non-violent settlement is broadly similar for both, but also because pragmatic considerations are considered in the rabbinical tradition as inherently reasonable and legitimate.

We arrive at the following conclusion. The prevailing debate between doves and hawks in Israel is bound to be inconclusive, because the discourse is formulated in the strident terms of contrasting world-views. The orthodox consider their opponents

---

7. The literature on Jewish religion in general is voluminous. For an excellent balanced account that spells out the role of pragmatic considerations in a particular area of Jewish practice, see Katz (1989).

depraved, their positions equally so, and they have no reason to wish to be convinced otherwise. However, if the doves were to present their position in exclusively pragmatic terms, the orthodox, in terms of their own world-view, could not easily lend them a deaf ear. There would at least be a serious engagement of views. From the perspective of people of left-wing ideological persuasion, the forgoing of ideological and moral pathos, and the presentation of their position in pragmatic terms, would entail a significant price. Namely, disregarding some of their deep ideological commitments in the area of human rights. It would, of course, not require acting against these commitments, but it would require realisation that the ideology is irrelevant, worse – self-defeating, in the social reality of contemporary Israel. That is indeed a price to pay, but it is not greater than the parallel ideological price that is paid by pragmatic doves who forgo mythic visions (not to mention the few orthodox people who maintain a dovish position).

Two decades of injurious self-presentation on the part of the left, ever since the 1967 war, are one of the causes for the current frightening ossification in the position of the Israeli right wing. The blame for this falls not only on Israelis of dovish ideological persuasion, but also on foreign friends of Israel among the left. The damage of the prevailing self-presentation of the left *vis-à-vis* its opponents requires to be repaired. This may indeed be ideologically distressing to maintainers of dovish positions, whose convictions are fuelled by leftist and liberal values. However, moving Israeli public opinion is of such strategic importance in the quest for a resolution of the Jewish-Arab conflict, that the matter warrants that price. In short, the pursuit of peace requires a price from one and all, not only from the rightwing hawks, but also from the doves.

This analysis of Israeli doves and hawks uncovers some of the potentiality of contemporary anthropology. We have moved far from the dispassion and detachment of earlier generations of anthropologists, in the heyday of evolutionism and functionalism. The present analysis is the product of a complex commitment, both to one's home society and to anthropology, as a discipline of social commitment and critical insight. The outcome is a fresh view of mainline social positions that leads to the formulation of a new agenda.

In one sense this kind of anthropological discourse is novel. Indeed, ever since the 1960s, anthropologists have not always been satisfied to serve the establishment and to remain disengaged from the people they studied. They have often adopted committed stances in the field, in favour of the disinherited and discriminated. But in taking that option, those anthropologists acted as moral humans; their choice was not commonly fuelled by insight that was particular and unique to the discipline. In contrast, the point of the present analysis is that the practice of the discipline, in a rigorous, methodological sense of the term, can lead to committed conclusions. Chances are that such conclusions, informed with insight that is marked by conventions of methodology, and not just by moral passion and high-mindedness, will be detailed and specific. As the present Israeli example demonstrates, the recommendations are addressed to particular categories of people and take into account individual configurations of social circumstances. Such conclusions, one may reasonably hope, will be of greater applicability than others, that are fired primarily by moral passion, and formulated in generality.

Acknowledgement

I am thankful to friends and colleagues who criticised the thesis of this paper and commented in writing, particularly Aviezer Ravitzky, Ya'aqov Shavit, Moshe Shokeid and Dafna Yizraeli.

Part III
Ultra-Orthodoxy

8

Life Tradition and Book Tradition in the Development of Ultraorthodox Judaism

Menachem Friedman

Rabbbi Simha Elberg is the editor of *Ha-Pardes*, the oldest established orthodox rabbinic journal in America. In the course of the mid-1960s, Rabbi Elberg twice called to his readers' attention a new religious phenomenon which he at first called *Bnei Braqism*.[1] The initial discussion appeared in a 1963 issue of *Ha-Pardes*; the second was in a 1965 issue of *Digleinu*,[2] the organ of the ultraorthodox Ze'irei (Young) Agudat Israel. He defined the phenomenon of Bnei Braqism as "the world of ḥumrot," that is, stringent interpretations.

"The Bnei Braq concept," wrote Rabbi Elberg, "embodies a *major revolution* (emphasis added) in the very structure of religious life. Bnei Braq is looking for increased rather than decreased stringency. Generally speaking, everyone, even within the religious world, is leaning toward greater permissiveness and lesser restrictivenes . . . not so Bnei Braq. A young yeshiva student under the spiritual influence of the Hazon Ish will, when approaching the Shulḥan Arukh [Caro's code of *halakhah*], search out that opinion which forbids, which restricts, which is more stringent. He will not look for the phrase, 'and there are those who are more lenient' nor will he abide by that sort of decision, but will be on the watch for the words: 'there are those who are stricter.'"

Elberg, a very perceptive observer, thus graphically describes the new religious type who makes an all-out effort to discover whether one of the commentators tends toward greater stringency, and when he succeeds in finding one who does, it fills his being with delight (mehayeh et nafsho). He then adopts this stringent interpretation, putting it into practice in his home and in his daily life. This testimony fits in well with other evidence attesting to a major revolution in the total system of religious life. What characterizes this revolution is the readiness of the young to criticize the standards generally accepted within the religious community, in the realms of both custom and halakhah, and to institutionalize within their own lives precisely those alternatives which reflect a more stringent approach.

Elberg attributes this phenomenon specifically to those avreikhim (young yeshiva students) who live "under the spiritual influence of the Hazon Ish,"[3] Rabbi Avraham Yeshayahu Karlitz, who had died approximately ten years earlier (1953)—a designation which, as shall be shown, is essentially correct. Elberg's description of the strictness-oriented avreikh (sing.), as one who "makes an all-out effort toward stringency," is undoubtedly highly ironic, especially when he says that "[the student's] very soul is refreshed" when he succeeds in finding a new humrah (sing.). Elberg, whose mother tongue is Yiddish, makes use here of a familiar expression taken from the folk idiom, "er iz zekh mekhaye neifesh," (he refreshes his own soul). The use of this phrase, normally appropriate to physical satisfaction (for example, after a hungry person has been satiated) is not only ironic but also suggestive of an amused bystander. It is clear that Elberg could allow himself to relate to the world of humrot in this manner as it was then only in the first stages of its development. Since then, however, it has become one of the foremost phenomena at work in shaping the life style of all of orthodox Jewry. The tendency to criticize accepted halakhic standards and to prefer, for the most part, the more stringent alternatives is not limited to the modern religious camp. This development within the haredi camp, however, arouses special interest from the sociological point of view.

Later on in this paper haredi will be defined, but it is clear that one of the outstanding characteristics of that society is its greater commitment to the traditional, Eastern European Jewish way of life. This being the case, it would seem that significant self-conscious changes in halakhah and tradition, even if in the direction of greater stringency, would create tension, since such changes must in some way reflect a certain criticism of the religious leadership of one's forebears.[4] The rhetorical question: "Should we find fault with our predecessors?"[5] is typically used by the watchdogs of the tradition when faced with change and innovation, even when it is in the direction of greater stringency. But this protest is not being voiced as the world of humrot, with its far-reaching changes in central areas of life, expands and conquers by the establishment of halakhic norms consciously different from those prevalent within the homes and the communal world of the previous generation.

Elberg believes that this is due to the influence of the Hazon Ish, and there is much truth in this assertion. As a case study, one halakhic area has been chosen for study—the shi'urim (standard measurements minimally required in the performance of a religious commandment)—in which the Hazon Ish developed norms which, while distinctly different from those generally accepted in the traditional camp, have nonetheless been adopted by almost all sectors of the haredi community in a relatively short time. Briefly, a number of the halakhot (pl.) involve size, weight, volume, and the like. The most obvious example relates to the consumption of matzah (unleavened bread) at the Passover seder meal. Halakhically speaking, at the seder, one must eat a quantity of matzah at least "equivalent to an olive" in order to have fulfilled the religious obligation of eating matzah on Passover. But what is the exact size of an olive, technically speaking? According to the Shulhan Arukh, an olive is slightly less than half an egg.[6] At first glance, these are two measurable items, the average size of which is unmistakable, being as they are both things found in nature. However, as early as the eighteenth century, one of the foremost halakhic sages, Rabbi Ezekiel ben Judah Landau, raises the possibility that "the nature of things has changed" (nishtanu ha-teva'im) that is, the sizes of olives eggs have actually changed over the centuries and are not the same today as they had been in the past.[7] When these ideas were first put forth, these legalistic ruminations had virtually no practical impact on the Jewish community.[8] However, once the possibility of natural things changing was raised and granted legitimacy, it created a potential for change. The Hazon Ish utilized this concept as a basis for a reevaluation of the major shi'urim in the halakhah,[9] and his conclusions represent a revolution in certain basic areas of religious life. He concluded, for example, that the present-day olive and egg are in fact significantly smaller in size than their counterparts in the mishnaic and talmudic periods. Therefore, in order to fulfill the commandment (mitzvah) of eating an olive's worth of matzah at the seder, one must actually eat significantly more than the generally accepted amount.[10] The fact is that the shi'urim of the Hazon Ish have become an accepted halakhic concept, these new measurements having become normative for a large segment of the ḥaredi community.

This particular example has been chosen because it has more critical religious-halakhic significance than the ordinary humrot, for two reasons:

1. The change is a conspicuous one, relating to visible and enduring objects in ceremonies which are central to Jewish life. The strict interpretation generally requires the replacement of a ceremonial object (the *kiddush* cup, that is, the wine goblet used in inaugurating the Sabbath or festivals), or ceremonial clothing (*tallit qatan*),[11] in order to meet the new standards of the shi'urim.

2. The change is not seen in the framework of a preferred alternative, in which the previously accepted norm retains its legitimacy, but as an absolute norm implying negation of other alternatives.

It is not normally expected that such a change would take place within the framework of a conservative society in which the living tradition, including ceremonial objects, is passed on from father to son in an orderly fashion. The fact that the shi'urim of the Hazon Ish became the established norm within such a short period, and with regard to such a broad segment of the ḥaredi community, shows that the latter is indeed different in a number of respects from the traditional religious community as it had developed in Eastern Europe up until the late eighteenth and early nineteenth centuries.

The Concept of Haredi (Ultraorthodox)

The term *haredi* Jewry denotes a Jewish religious community with certain defining characteristics. It has occasionally been described as "traditionalist," committed to halakhah in its traditional interpretation, and also committed to a living, vital tradition (specifically that of Eastern Europe), expressed in dress, language, and the like.[12] This definition is only partially satisfactory because the Eastern European commitment is not equally strong in all areas, nor on the part of all segments of the community. For example, even the most casual observation will reveal, that in those circles known as "Lithuanian" and connected with the *yeshivot gedolot* (advanced yeshivot), there is relatively greater flexibility with regard to the commitment to traditional garb and external appearance. In fact, it could well be argued that within these circles there is a conspicuous, self-conscious trend toward adopting Western European dress and outer appearance. Even if these differences are ignored, however, describing ḥaredi Jewry solely in terms of its traditionalism is inadequate because it overlooks the dynamic element of ongoing change so characteristic of this particular society in the last generation.

A statement, made in the name of Rabbi Israel Meir Ha-Cohen (the Hafetz Haim), provides a starting point for the understanding of the ḥaredi approach: "'Happy is the man who fears the Lord, who delights greatly in his commandments. His seed shall be mighty upon earth: the generation of the upright shall be blessed' (Ps. 112:1–2). The man who truly and completely fears God and greatly desires his 'mitzvot' *does not look for ways to free himself from the mitzvot nor does he seek out* 'qulot' [leniencies, the opposite of humrot] and 'heteirim' [relaxations of restrictions], *but rather fulfills the halakhah as it is, without consideration,* and because of this he is assured that his seed shall be mighty upon earth."[13] This statement must be viewed against the reality of Jewish life in Eastern Europe from the second half of the nineteeth century onward. It was characterized by (1) the increasing erosion of religion and tradition which in turn created a rift between the religious and those who no longer considered themselves bound by religious law (secularists); and (2) a schism within the very community desirous of remaining faithful to halakhah, which developed against a background of growing modernization and secularization, leading to a gradual disintegration of traditional religiosity.

The situation can be described generally, if somewhat simplistically, where, on the one hand, there is a group which consciously aspires to adapt itself in one way or another to the technical, social, and political changes taking place around it (within the context of an overall process of secularization and modernization), while maintaining an essential loyalty to halakhah. This results in tension between the accepted halakhic norms and traditional practices, and the changing social, political, and technological reality; this tension is frequently resolved by means of a compromise granting legitimacy to the modern, up to the limits of halakhic possibility. Concurrently, a second group develops which denies the legitimacy of this trend, not only because it deviates by definition from the established norms, but also because the very capitulation to changing reality, regardless of its formal legitimacy from the halakhic point of view, is seen as a first step in the erosion process which will undoubtedly end (so it is claimed) in the complete abandonment of halakhah as an obligatory norm.

It is in this context that we must relate to the words of the Hafetz Haim, one of the protagonists of the latter group, who accuses the opposite camp of looking for gimmicks by which to free itself from the mitzvot and for *qulot* and *heteirim*. His group is seen as aspiring to fulfill the halakhah as it stands, without consideration, that is, without taking the changing reality into consideration. By definition, this is a select group, an elite, whose heroic ideal is to carry out the mitzvot without consideration. It is paradoxical indeed that this ultraorthodox trend is able to develop and to establish itself precisely against the background of the disintegration of the traditional community as an organic society, bound together by a life style based on halakhah and the traditional practices of the community.

As a community which considers itself responsible for the provision of religious leadership to its members, seeing in this the primary expression of its independent identity, traditional society finds it difficult to cope with uncontrolled organization on the basis of the institutionalization of more stringent halakhic norms, as such organization is a threat to its own cohesion.[14] The formation of an elite based on the delegitimization of those who seek qulot and heteirim on the one hand, and the aspiration to fulfill the halakhah without consideration, on the other hand, leads to the creation of a new religious framework, which may be described as a "voluntary community," insofar as it cannot indiscriminately encompass within its bounds everyone living within a defined geographic area as does the traditional community.

Let us return to the statement of the Hafetz Haim. The religious type described as "one who fears God truly and completely" stands above the usual commonplace religious type. The term *yare'* (fearing), when used to denote this special religious type, is synonymous with the more widespread current term—*ḥaredi*, implying "precision without compromise."[15] The concept of ḥaredi is in fact a dynamic rather than a static one; it also has a psychological dimension, for it is precisely within these religious circles that emphasis is laid on the basic weaknesses of man as a human creature in constant struggle with his basic inclinations, a struggle which only ends with death. Thus, fulfilling the halakhah without considerations should be understood as a goal to which one constantly aspires, but whose attainment on a day-to-day basis is extremely difficult. Nevertheless, it is the obligation of the haredi Jew to view this ultimate goal as the legitimate expression of Judaism in its entirety and to attempt to put it into practice.

Having said this, it must also be noted that haredi Jewry considers itself by definition as bound to tradition. This means that there is an inherent tension between the obligatory attachment to tradition and its own inherent dynamism that encourages the breaching of the framework of tradition in the name of fulfillment of the halakhah without considerations and without qulot and heteirim.

Traditionalism in Eastern Europe, as carried within the family and the community, did not disappear but rather disintegrated, more quickly in the cities and less quickly in the small towns where change was relatively gradual. The living tradition, expressed in relationships and common memories extending back for several generations, and embodied in (1) the lives of individuals whose very existence testified to the validity of that tradition; (2) written testimony; and (3) the actual objects (both apparel and ritual artifacts), which were passed on from generation to generation, inhibited the dynamic potential for religious change inherent in the haredi approach. However, against a background of the erosion of traditional life and of existential crisis within part of the Jewish community, haredi organizational frameworks did develop in Eastern Europe, especially in Poland/Lithuania. These then formed the base for the future development of haredi Judaism.

The Yeshiva Gedolah

The yeshiva gedolah of the kind typified by the Volozhin Yeshiva,[16] has long been recognized as one of the most important internal developments to take place within the traditional Jewish framework. From the standpoint of the present discussion, this organizational/cultural structure provides the type of voluntary community ideally suited to the needs of ultraorthodoxy. Organizationally speaking, this type of yeshiva incorporates two innovations relative to the traditional Ashkenazi yeshivot:

1. It is not an institution of the community, but rather an economically independent organization supported by the contributions of individuals from many regions.

2. The vast majority of the yeshiva students are not from the community but come from near and far for the purpose of studying there.

This has two further implications.

1. The yeshiva is a total-like institution whose students are, for the most part, alienated from their surroundings and cut off from their families for most of the year, as a result of which they are united amongst themselves, especially around the figure of the *rosh yeshiva* (head of the yeshiva) and his family. (It is not surprising that the relationships created within this framework are often quasifamiliar.)[17]

2. The students are for the most part young bachelors, economically marginal, who devote most of their time to the study of Torah.

In this sense, the yeshiva is a moratorium institution, and can be defined as a quasimonastic community. Its members are, as has been noted, young men cut off from their families and from direct contact with the halakhic norms and customs which crystallized and became formalized within the local, familial tradition. They spend most of their time in the study of halakhic texts and codes.[18] The system of study employed in the yeshiva tends to develop the students' critical sense; the customs and traditions which they bring with them from home are also exposed to criticism. The seclusion of the yeshiva and the religious tension fostered within it combine to create a situation conducive to the systematic re-examination of family and community traditions through a confrontation with what might be referred to as the "tradition as it finds expression in the codes." The clash between the latter and the tradition anchored in the daily life of a traditional community is, as has been noted, a recognized phenomenon in Jewish history.[19] At times the rabbis succeeded in rooting out a practice which they considered to be misguided; at other times, they were forced to give in to reality and to sanctify that very practice.

Within the quasimonastic community, however, the confrontation was a totally different one. From the outset, the tradition embodied in the codes had the advantage: in the face of the truth emanating from the codes, there was simply no social framework that could be marshalled to come to the support of the ancestral tradition. In the traditional community, if a young man reached the conclusion that this custom or that halakhic norm did not measure up to the standard set by the codes, or if he wished to adopt the more stringent alternative, he would have immediately found himself in conflict with other members of his family and with his surroundings. Within the confines of the yeshiva, however, both the familial framework and the community experience became insignificant and unreal. The yeshiva, as a quasimonastic community alienated from its environment and from economic and social reality, knowingly nurtured the ongoing reexamination of behavior on the basis of a confrontation with the codes and supported the choice of the more stringent alternative.

As has been said, haredi Judaism is consciously committed to the formulation of an elitist self-image. It is relatively simple to develop such an image within the closed groups of students devoted to the study of Torah. Indeed, one of the blatant characteristics of the world of the yeshiva students immersed in Torah learning is the image which they have of themselves as an elite with respect to everyone else, the masses, the *balebatim*.[20] A clear example of this is the saying that "the opinion of the *balebatim* is the reverse of the opinion of the Torah,"[21] which reflects an intellectually elitist self-image, contemptuous of all who are not a part of it. This is also the source of the inverted conception of *merkaz* (center) and *s'vivah* (surroundings, or periphery), which places the yeshivot at the *merkaz*, the true center of existence, in contrast to everything else, which is seen as simply the *s'vivah* in which everything is imaginary, and whose sole raison d'etre is to make possible the existence of the center.[22] The refrain of a Yiddish song,[23] popular among yeshiva students, expresses this clearly and unequivocally:

When the world will be
full of yeshivot
Many centers
and few peripheries
They will learn Torah then
without limit.
Lord of the Universe, when will it be granted to us?

In such an atmosphere, no importance is assigned to practices and traditions that are seen to oppose the halakhic norms of the learned elite. The ḥaredi ideal of "fearing God truly and completely, without searching for gimmicks by which to avoid fulfilling the mitzvot," thus finds a fertile soil, well suited to its development, in the quasimonastic community exemplified by the Volozhin-type yeshiva.

Within the Jewish world of Eastern Europe, faced with extreme economic hardship, and with the very basis of Jewish existence being challenged and the erosion of religion and tradition on the increase, the world of the yeshivot was in a defensive position. Whereas such yeshivot had been open to general currents within the Jewish world at the beginning of the nineteenth century, by the end of the century they had become strongholds of the ḥaredi outlook, reinforced by the Musar movement.[24] Haredism was concentrated in one part of the Jewish world (the Lithuanian/Polish sector), alongside the traditional community found in Hasidic Poland and in other areas with heavy Jewish populations. Paradoxically, it was the destruction of Eastern European Jewry in the twentieth century that created the conditions which enabled the spread of ultraorthodoxy.

New Social Bases of the Growth of Ultraorthodoxy

World War II and the Holocaust created new conditions conducive to the further development of the ḥaredi ideal. First was the changing geographic base or the transition to the West. World War II was the tragic climax to the process of migration, which had already started in the 1880s, in which the center of life and creative religious Judaism was transferred from Eastern Europe to the metropolitan centers of the West. This process, which enhanced the erosion of traditional society, eventually created a situation which was conducive as well to the development of ḥaredi society.

The geographic change caused a break in the direct personal relationships which had characterized the traditional community. In the western countries to which the migrants came, voluntary communities developed. The conditions for membership in voluntary communities are determined by the members themselves, thus replacing the traditional, geographically determined community.[25] The process of migration to the West, at least until World War II, was accompanied by secularization and the weakening of tradition, which naturally had an affect on the character of the vast majority of voluntary communities, including those which consider themselves Orthodox. The latter have been pressured to adopt an attitude of tolerance toward deviation from religion and tradition, and even to find halakhic legitmacy for these trends. They aspired to create a harmonious relationship between halakhah and the values and norms of modern western society, and to minimize the points of conflict between them, based on the assumption that there is no essential contradiction between halakhah and modernity. At the same time, a similar process was under way in Eretz Yisrael; the development of the Zionist Yishuv (community) was also affected by the processes of modernization and secularization. Religious Zionism was also involved in this process, not only in that it had to grant legitimacy to the actions and omissions of militantly secular groups, but primarily in creating experimental social frameworks within which they sought to harmonize, in some way, halakhah and modernity. This experiment entailed what can only be called "concessions" relative to various elements of both tradition and halakhah. This author has previously defined this religious approach as "diminished religiosity" (Friedman 1984). Due to the fact that the process was realized within the framework of the creation of a new Zionist Jewish society in Eretz Yisrael, and in conjunction with the autonomous community groupings of the Yishuv under the authority of a local chief rabbinate, it led to an identification and overlapping between this diminished religiosity and religious Zionism.

Paradoxically, these very same processes formed the background for the development of stringency, that is, haredism. Migration broke the direct connection with the traditional community and this was followed by the Holocaust which involved tremendous human loss and the destruction of the sociocultural milieu in which traditional religion had developed. Practically speaking, it also entailed a loss of household items and religious artifacts that had been passed down through the generations, and in which tradition and custom were embodied. When the tradition-minded groups who had survived the Holocaust came together in the sociocultural reality of the West and of Eretz Yisrael, they found that the living tradition, which they had cherished, had been totally broken; their aim was therefore to rebuild the society which had been and to enlist new members, given the existence of a diminished orthodox Jewish community in the background. Three main factors determined the direction which the renewal was to take:

1. The rupture of the living tradition, which had been transmitted directly from generation to generation, naturally created a sense of a lack of confidence, the remedy for which was found in the strengthening of the attachment to the tradition of the book, written halakhah.

2. With the disappearance of the traditional Jewish world of Eastern Europe in the smoke of the concentration camp furnaces, there developed within the general Jewish world a romantic nostalgic attitude toward the culture which had been. Within the confines of the Jewish society which remained faithful to halakhah, and especially among those elements desirous of reconstructing that which had been, this expressed itself in a clearcut tendency to see the society that was as having been composed of righteous people, a society in which daily life and the tradition of the book were in full harmony with each other.

3. The experience of diminished religiosity constituted a negative reference norm to those attempting to reconstruct the society that had been. The primary basis for the delegitimization of diminished religiosity was its deviation from the norms of halakhah and tradition as found in halakhic literature, based on an unequivocal commitment to the latter as the determinant of life's norms.[26]

These developments found expression within the framework of the voluntary community, an associational framework based on individual choice and not related in any essential way to a geographic determinant. The voluntary community reflects what Berger (1969, 137–49) calls "the market situation," which is characterized by the believer who is free to choose for himself the form of ritual to espouse within a community of believers that he chooses to join. Clearly, in a market situation, great importance is attached to the recruitment of new members to a given community, both for ideological and for straightforward economic reasons. It is this need to grow numerically that underlies the relative pluralism within the Jewish community, even that part of the community which considers itself bound to halakhah in its traditional sense (orthodoxy), and accepts the establishment of communities on the basis of the lowest common denominator in respect to halakhic obligation. At the same time, this situation also allows for the creation of an exclusive voluntary community, based on an elite which tries to fufill the halakhah by choosing the more stringent alternatives. Moreover, the existence of diminished communities, characterized among other things by deviation from tradition and organized on a voluntary basis, frees the more strictly oriented community from its obligation to those who do not want, or are not able, to meet the criteria of a stringent ḥaredi religious approach.

It can therefore be said that it is precisely against the background of the disintegration of the traditional geographically defined community, and the development of voluntary communities, that the way was opened for an institutionalized expression of stringency as reflected in halakhic and Musar literature. Actually, this opened the way for individuals and groups to compete, as it were, among themselves on the degree of stringency and intransigency, within the range of alternatives found in the halakhic literature.

The stringent voluntary communities are in fact selective communities reflecting an elitist approach and are reminiscent of the quasimonastic communities described; the development of the former (ḥaredi) is surely related to the renewal and development of the quasimonastic yeshivot in the West.

The history of the yeshivot gedolot in the West and in Eretz Yisrael is both interesting and important, but cannot be discussed here. Briefly, it should be noted that, until World War II, these institutions were part of the Jewish religious culture of Poland/Lithuania, and, to some extent, of Hungary as well. In the West, they were seen as an essential antidote to the life style of the lands of immigration. A few attempts were made to establish institutions of this sort in Germany and Eretz Yisrael but their influence was at first marginal in the extreme. It was only after World War II that Volozhin-type yeshivot began to flourish there.

Several reasons can be given for this development. Among these are the development of the modern welfare state, economic growth, and the adaptation of traditional religious Judaism to the contemporary metropolis, allowing the recruitment of young people to the yeshivot communities for the entire period of socialization, until marriage and even afterward (in *kollel*-s).[27] Whatever the reasons for the growth of the Volozhin-type yeshiva in the West after World War II, there is no doubt that this development signals one of the most decisive changes within orthodox Jewry in the West and in Eretz Yisrael. The fact that, since the second half of the 1950s, the vast majority of the young men who identify with the ḥaredi camp spent the most important part of their formative years—as human beings and as Jews—in a total-like institution has decisive implications for the image of present-day ḥaredi society.

A number of the relevant consequences of experiencing life within these quasimonastic communities have been discussed. To summarize, the removal of young people from their family circle during a period so crucial to the formation of their world view, and their placement in a totalizing framework in which they come face-to-face with the rich book tradition of the Jewish people, coupled with the crystallization of an elitist self-image and the concept of a center, are experiences which must lead to criticism of the parental religious tradition.

The fact that, beginning with the 1950s, the vast majority of ḥaredi young men spent all their time learning Torah within a Volozhin-type yeshiva (the dominant prototype today among Hasidic groups as well), reflects a most significant social change. The voluntary communities established by the graduates of these yeshivot, or in which they are the dominant element, are known as *kehillot lomdim* (communities of scholars). They are communities whose members are able to come to grips with halakhic questions by means of direct confrontation with the multifaceted legal literature of the codes, whether they continue to immerse themselves in the study of Torah or whether they direct their energies toward making a living. In the majority of cases the level of Torah knowledge of these young men is much greater that that of their parents.[28] This situation lays the foundation for the delegitimization of the traditions and practices of the families from which they came, the latter generally being put in the category of *'amei ha-aretz* (ignoramuses of the Torah).[29] If that same family is in any way identified with diminished religiosity, then the process of family rejection is greatly enhanced, since the only basis on which to recreate a completely religious/halakhic world is the corpus of legal decisions embodied in the codes.

Legal literature, like the rest of halakhic literature, is to be found throughout the ḥaredi community. There is hardly a ḥaredi family today that does not possess an extensive Torah halakhah library. This is particularly true of the middle generation which was educated in the yeshivot. In addition to the classics, one also finds more recent summaries of the codes, adapted to the strict approach. These are composed by *talmidei hakhamim* (scholars), primarily from the kollels; they relate to actual issues, are understood easily, and can be put into practice directly. Most instructive is the fact that, prior to every holiday or out-of-the-ordinary halakhic/religious event, the book market is flooded with legal-type literature intended to guide the reader through the thicket of halakhot related specifically to the festival or event. The streets of ultraorthodox neighborhoods, such as Me'a She'arim in Jerusalem, or Bnei Braq, are covered with posters advertising the availability of this literature. Under these circumstances, the triumph of the legal tradition over the life tradition, as represented by the natural families, is assured.

One must not disassociate these changes from the reality of economics and technology. The rise in the standard of living of haredi families living in the metropolitan centers of the West and of Eretz Yisrael, makes possible, for the first time in Jewish history, a Jewish existence in which one can live by the Torah and carry out the mitzvot in comfort; it is now economically feasible to meet the demands imposed by the stricter interpretation. The increased standard of living, combined with the modern welfare state, allows the vast majority of young men growing up in the haredi community to achieve an advanced halakhic education. Technological changes also create new realities which make it possible to choose a stringent alternative, without that choice creating insurmountable difficulties. All of this undoubtedly influences the world of humrot.

Summary

This analysis has emphasized the background processes of secularization and modernization on the one hand, and the uprooting of Eastern European Jewry and its migration to the West on the other. The disintegration of the traditional Jewish community, the rise of the monastic community and a voluntarily based haredi society are the factors which make the dialectic process of rebellion and continuity—as represented in the world of humrot—possible.

The importance of these factors in preparing the ground for the growth of ultraorthodoxy is highlighted by reference to the shi'urim of the Hazon Ish. The ability of Rabbi Karlitz to institutionalize these significant changes in ritual expresses, more than anything else, the rupture within the living tradition. Is it conceivable that within a geographically and historically continuous society, characterized by direct contacts between several generations, in which ritual objects are handed down from generation to generation, that one person (as great a scholar as he might be) could arise and state that the accepted practices, relating to central ceremonies, must be significantly changed, without causing a reaction that would rock the society? The establishment of revised norms can only be understood against the background of a breakdown in tradition, on the one hand, and the emergence of a new generation, educated in total-like institutions and directly involved with halakhic literature, on the other. This almost complete commitment to halakhic literature, as the sole foundation for a fully religious way of life, makes it possible to create a religious experience and a new reality linked to past generations not through direct contact with their life style but through their books.

Notes

1. Bnei Braq is a city near Tel Aviv in which there is a concentration of ultraorthodox groups.

2. *Ha-Pardes* (The Orchard), Kislev 5724 (New York), and *Digleinu* (Our Banner), Kislev-Tevet 5725 (Tel Aviv).

3. It is common practice to refer to famous rabbis by the name of one of their major works. The Hazon Ish immigrated to Palestine from Vilna, settling in Bnei Braq in 1935.

4. This problem has dogged traditional halakhic literature whenever halakhists have attempted to question a local custom which, while having been in practice for generations, has appeared to go against the halakhah. The technical phrase used by those who try to protect the tradition against the innovators is that the change would imply *la'az al ha-'avot* (slander of the progenitors). One well-known example took place in Perpignan, in the Provence, as the result of the arrival of disciples of Nachmanides, from Gerona, in the middle of the thirteenth century, and their questioning of local practice. In his treatise, *Magen Aboth* (1909), R. Menahem Meiri strongly resisted this attack, attempting to protect the honor and religious status of previous generations which had been indirectly undermined by the disciples of Nachmanides: "It behooves all those who would challenge, to consider the fact that the practices of our ancient forebears and the early sages, whose fingernails were superior to our bellies, were not devoid of reason. It is preferable to attribute it to one's own lack of knowledge than to the lack of knowledge on the part of our forefathers and the ancient sages."

5. This phrase is taken from a letter written in 1784 by R. Abraham Katzenelbogen to R. Isaac Levi of Berdichev in which he speaks out against changes in the ancestral tradition introduced by the Hasidim, changes expressing a pietistic trend toward greater stringency (see Dubnow 1962, 31).

6. *Shulhan Arukh, Orah Haim,* cap. 486. Another example is that of the size of the *revi'it* which, in regard to the wine drunk for *kiddush* (the blessing sanctifying the Sabbath) on Friday night, is "an egg and a half."

7. This has been discussed in the book on Tractate *Pesahim* by R. Y. Landau (1876, 109). The concept that "nature has changed" since talmudic times is already found in early halakhic literature. In every case, the concept is used to explain away contradictions between medical remedies or physiological knowledge in the Talmud, and the practical, everyday experience of the halakhists of a later period. For example: (a) The Talmud (BT *'Avodah Zarah* 24b) states that a cow less than three years of age is incapable of calving, which contradicted the experience of the Tosafists (twelfth to fourteenth centuries) who knew that a two-year-old cow could already do so. Therefore, the latter determined that "it is certain that the time period is different now from what it was in former times;" and (b) The Talmud (BT *Mo'ed Qatan* 11a) recommends the eating of fish close to the time when it begins to stink. To this the Tosafists commented that "in our time, those who [go to] the [fish] barrel near the time when it begins to stink are in danger." They explain away the contradiction between that which was medically accepted in their time and in talmudic times with the possibility that "it may have changed, like the medical remedies found in the Mishnah which are not appropriate to our time." However, the comments of R. Landau are essentially different as the reference is not to a contradiction between daily experience and the early sources, but to a new idea relating to central areas of religious life.

8. This arises out of the text itself which is exegetical rather than legal, as well as from the words of R. Landau's most distinguished disciple, R. Eleazer Flekeles (1809, *Yoreh De'ah,* cap. 324).

9. See *Kuntras ha-Shi'urim* in the commentary of the Hazon Ish on the *Shulhan Arukh, Orah Haim, Hilkhot Shabbat* (Bnei Braq, 1957). R. Karlitz was indeed preceded in this respect by the *Hafetz Haim,* R. Yisrael Meir Ha-Cohen (1896–197, *Hilkhot Shabbat,* cap. 271c), but he does not reach a definitive decision (like Karlitz), and his opinion is only a matter of good advice. See Ha-Cohen's commentary *Be'ur Halakhah,* there, to sub-cap. 13.

10. From the very beginning, the conclusions drawn by the Hazon Ish created a halakhic controversy. See Avraham Hai Noeh (1943) and Yaakov Kanevsky (1948). Kanevsky (Steipler), who was the brother-in-law of the Hazon Ish, attempts to come to grips with two issues: (1) the problem of changing that which had been accepted in the past; and (2) the extent to which the acceptance of the basic principle that the measures set by the Torah are relative rather than absolute ("when the shi'urim were given at Sinai, they were given in approximation"), would adversely affect the structure of traditional orthodox society.

This notwithstanding, he claims, it does not reflect any attempt to ascribe either truth or error to the views of various authorities. The legal decisions of the great sages of the generation, such as R. Landau, and those who came after him, are binding on all because these sages have been given the right to determine halakhah. See Kanevsky (1966, 15–17).

11. Many orthodox Jews of Eastern Europe provenance will wear a garment (usually between their undergarments and outer clothing), with ritual fringes attached. This is considered a fuller observance of the law (Num. 15:38) than just wearing the prayer shawl (*talllit*) during morning prayers. This special garment is known as the *tallit qatan*.

12. In my opinion the Eastern European, Ashkenazi character of haredi Jewry remains unquestionable to this day. There are recent signs of similar developments within some segments of Middle Eastern Jewry but this is largely a self-conscious imitation of the haredi (Ashkenazi) structure. The vast majority of the Middle Eastern haredi Jews have studied either in Ashkenazi haredi institutions or in those modeled after them.

13. Meir Hai Yoshor (1959, 2:481n). See also "Hafetz Haim" (1838–1933), in *EJ*, 9:1068–70.

14. A good example of this is the incident cited by R. Jacob Reischer (1719, *Yoreh De'ah*, cap. 58). In one of the communities, the rabbis ruled that meat brought from the smaller communities of the surrounding villages was not kosher because the slaughterers in those places were thought not to know enough and/or not to be careful enough, by the stricter standards of the Jewish community in the large city. R. Reischer unequivocally rejects this approach, but not because he considered those slaughterers to be outstanding scholars. He admits that his position might be considered "lenient," but he defends it on the basis of the principle of the cohesion of the traditionally religious community, which might be adversely affected by the disqualification of village slaughterers. "It is proper for all Israel to be as one man in matters of eating and drinking, and not to distinguish, as Israel is distinguished from them (the nations); we should not multiply separate groups." There is no doubt that R. Reischer's approach represents a deeply rooted Jewish tradition.

15. See Avraham Wolf, one of the major ideologists of haredi Jewry in the present generation, in the local periodical *Le-Hoshvei Shemo* (Bnei Braq), Tammuz 1979,21), wherein he describes the haredi woman as "one who does not eat anything regarding which a scholar has made a ruling," that is, she is stricter for herself even with regard to something which a rabbi ruled as permissible for consumption because some doubt had been raised concerning it.

16. Volozhin, a town in Lithuania, was the site of a major yeshiva, founded at the beginning of the nineteenth century, which attracted students from many countries. Like other yeshivot gedolot, it emphasized the study of Talmud. See Stampfer (1981).

17. Almost every description of the rosh yeshiva (head of the yeshiva) by students emphasizes the fatherly image and the fact that his relations with them were oftentimes at the expense of his family. See, for example, Rabiner (1968, 37, 55).

18. Rabbinic literature which codified the halakhah in a brief, understandable, fashion, as opposed to the literature which discussed the various sides of halakhic questions.

19. See above, note 4.

20. Literally: home-owners. Those who (successfully) spend their time making a living rather than studying Torah.

21. See Meir Hai Yoshor (1958, 1:165n). Another example comes from the exegetic commentary of R. Elhanan Wasserman, one of the outstanding personalities of haredi Jewry of the generation preceding World War II, on Hosea 4:12: "Anyone who rules (leniently) receives the support of the masses." See Aharon Sorsky (1970, 300n). This approach is the keystone of the overall attitude of the Hazon Ish and his disciples. Another example: "Most of the masses follow their base desires and, in any case, we know that the truth is the opposite of what is believed by the masses." See Shlomo Cohen (1966-1973, part 4, 242).

22. Moshe Sheinfeld, an outstanding ideologist of haredi Jewry, wrote in the name of the Hazon Ish: "The Maharam from Lublin [sixteenth century] uses the expression the world asks very frequently and yet, if we go out into the streets of the city we will discover that 'the world' does not ask such questions at all. But we should learn from this that only those who are deeply engrossed in the questions and problems of the Holy Torah are called "the *true* world." See A. Rater (1978).

In haredi legends, the following story, which also reflects this attitude, is told in the name of R. Yehezkiel Loewenstein. "The Soviet authorities laid a long rail line in a remote district which was not economically viable (the Trans-Siberian Railroad), and no one could explain why the line had been laid and why it continued to operate. Only during World War II, when the line was used for the transfer of the Yeshiva of Mir from Lithuania to Japan, thus saving its students from annihilation, did the matter become clear. The railroad had been built and operated in order that, when the time came, it could be used to save the yeshiva." See *Kol be-Ramah,* local newspaper of the Ramat Aharon neighborhood of Bnei Braq, no 49, 1984.

23. Based on a song I learned in my youth as a yeshiva student. Its authenticity is vouched for by the rhyming which accords with Lithuanian Yiddish pronunciation.

24. The Musar movement developed in the latter part of the nineteenth century and stressed moral self-criticism. Musar literature became influential in yeshiva circles after it was viewed as a defense against secular influence.

25. Certain aspects of this process have been dealt with in Friedman (1982).

26. The following description of the changes which took place within the community of Gur Hasidim under the influence of R. Yisrael Alter, when their center moved from Poland to Jerusalem, is a typical reflection of this process: "On new/old foundations did R. Alter build his new house, the Building of the old House of Gur . . . to adapt the ways of Hasidism to the halakhah and to every letter in the halakhah" (Levine 1977, 150).

27. An institution of advanced talmudic study in which married men spend their time when not engaged in making a livelihood. The Kollel in late nineteenth century Eastern Europe was associated with the Musar movement (note 24).

28. Moshe Sheinfeld attempts to explain this change as follows: "Only in the environment of the Jewish villages [in Europe], which was steeped in Torah and the fear of God, could one find simple Jewish folk who, despite their ignorance, were respectful of their rabbis and truly believed in God and in his Torah. Within the secular environment of the Yishuv [in Israel] there is no possibility of an exception to the rule: 'an ignorant person is not fearful of sin.'" *Digleinu*, Iyyar 5715 (1955).

29. This reality often creates tension within haredi society. For example, the American R. Haim Poupko has stated: "Those who continue the tradition of their ancestors, and live by the rules of halakhah and behave according to what they have seen at home, are not sufficiently haredi; there are even those who are ashamed of the splendid past of their forebears," *Tsohar* (Jerusalem), Nisan 1983. A graphic reflection of this situation can be found in the following vignette which appeared in *Ha-Modi'a*, January 29, 1982, the newspaper of Agudat Yisrael, the main haredi political party. A group of haredi children, whose appearance testified to this fact (clothing, sidelocks, and the like) is deep in argument. Suddenly, one of the debaters turns to another and says something which is obviously intended to decide the argument: "My grandmother saw it on TV." His companions are silent for a moment and then one says in amazement: "What! Your grandmother looks at TV?" (There is a generally accepted prohibition on watching TV among haredi Jews.) The first child is confused for a minute but quickly composes himself and says: "My grandmother is from the previous generation."

References Cited

Berger, P. (1969). *The Social Reality of Religion.* London: Faber.

Cohen, S. (1966-1973). *Peer ha-Dor* (on Rabbi A. Y. Karlitz). 4 vols. Bnei Braq. Nezah.

Dubnow, S. (1962). *Chassidiana* (Oppositional Writings to Hasidism). Jerusalem: Akademon, Hebrew University of Jerusalem (in Hebrew).

Flekeles, E. (1809). *Teshuva me-Ahavah.* Prague: Franz Gommer.

Friedman, M. (1982). "The Changing Role of the Community Rabbinate." *The Jerusalem Quarterly* 25:79-99.

_____. (1984). "The NRP in Transition-Behind the Party's Electoral Decline." In D. Caspi, A. Diskin, E. Gutman, eds. *The Roots of Begin's Success.* London: Croom Helm, 141-68.

Ha-Cohen, Y. M. (1896-1907). *Mishnah Berurah.* Warsaw.

Kanevsky, Y. (1948). *Shi'urim de-Oraytah.* Bnei Braq.

_____. (1966). *Yesodot Ne'emanim.* Bnei Braq.

Landau, Y. (1876). *Ziyyun le-Nefesh Hayyah.* Lemberg.

Levine, Y.L. (1977). *The Admors of Gur.* Jerusalem. Hebrew.

Meiri, M. (1909). *Magen Aboth.* I. Last, ed. London: I. Narodiczky (in Hebrew).

Noeh, A. H. (1943). *Shi'urei Torah.* Jerusalem.

Rabiner, A. Z. (1968). *Ha-Gaon Rabbi Eliezer Gordon . . .* Tel Aviv (in Hebrew).

Rater, A. (1978). *Hashqafatenu* (Bnei Braq) 2:95.

Reischer, J. (1719). *Shevut Ya'aqov.* Halle: Bar Avraham.

Stampfer, S. (1981). *Three Lithuanian Yeshivot in the Nineteenth Century.* Ph.D. diss. Hebrew University of Jerusalem (in Hebrew, English summary).

Sorsky, A. (1970). *Ahiezer, A Collection of Letters: Selected Memoirs* (on Rabbi Hayyim Ozer Grodzinski). vol. 1. Bnei Braq: Nezah (in Hebrew).

Yoshor, M. H. (1958 - 1961). *The Hafetz Haim: His Life and Work.* 3 vols. Tel Aviv: Nezah (in Hebrew).

9

Ultraorthodox Jewish Women

Tamar El-Or

Women's education is the outcome of the tension between the changes taking place outside the orthodox community and its internal durability. The "learning men's society" applied a double standard to its own development. It is essential to put the paradox of women's education, as well as the other paradoxes described below, into this perspective. I believe that entering and escaping social paradoxical cycles are a pattern of behavior characteristic of Israeli orthodoxy, an existential strategy, and a means of creating social boundaries. But to do this, I must first describe the paradoxical component of women's education—both its nature and its dynamic.

The study of the social significance of scholarship among orthodox men shows that scholarship is the most significant expression of their Judaism.[1] The situation among women is similar. Women once learned to be kosher Jewish wives and mothers within the ghetto walls, in their mother's houses, and alongside their grandmothers. Today they must learn this in school. When the cultural market around them offers educational alternatives, orthodoxy constructs an educational framework that is, in its external form, a school, but its goal—at least, its declared goal—is to duplicate the Jewish mother's home in Poland.

How is that done, and does it succeed?

In attempting to answer the "how" question, anthropology has a certain advantage. The unmediated observations it conducts of social processes allow a close tracking of the "how."

During my period in the Development, I took part in several study groups, all intended for married women (sometimes the older daughters of one of the women would take part, but these exceptional cases were not accepted sympathetically). Unfortunately, I was unable to conduct observations in the schools, so the literacy under discussion here is that of married women alone.

One framework was a class in Jewish law. These lessons were taught by women from the Development on a voluntary basis.[2] The second framework was a year-long course on the book of Psalms, taught by teachers from

Bene Brak. The third (Rabbi Wolf's class on Maimonides) was held in the home of one of the teachers from Bene Brak. In addition to attending these classes, I also sat in on a broad spectrum of women's study groups held inside and outside the Development, but these were single events rather than regular frameworks.

On the basis of these observations, and in light of the insights collected by the social study of literacy, it seems to me that the women's education I observed strives to pragmatize the social reality and emphasize its material side. Women's education generates an ongoing translation of complex problems into simple actions. It levels questions of morality, faith, and justice into instructions for action in daily life.

Women's education simultaneously creates a social meaning of the world and confirms it. Studies of literacy among underprivileged classes have shown that there is inconsistency between the practical daily reality and the curriculum based in part on abstract thinking. This inconsistency has led to student failure, to aggression, and to withdrawal from the educational system.[3]

In an experiment, Paulo Freire, who has conducted research on literacy and who served as Brazil's minister of education, tried to create, from a practical framework, abstract thinking somewhat detached from the world of action. Through this, he wished to provide a foundation for radical and critical literacy. He based his curriculum for the disadvantaged and the ignorant on the reality that was familiar to them, such as the lives of fishermen or agricultural laborers. Out of the experiences of this reality, he built a set of abstract concepts through which he was able to achieve two important things: students could decipher realities that were foreign to them, and they could leave their familiar reality and move toward a broader consciousness. This is how he claimed to resolve the inconsistency between the reality that is familiar to people and the curriculum they study.[4]

Among haredi women, the situation is reversed. In order to create consistency between the social situation (in which men wish to see women "ignorant") and the actual condition of these women (which is not at all one of ignorance), the axis of learning becomes a pragmatic one.

Fifteen women are seated in Bina's living room. On the table are glasses and bottles of cold water, relief for the hot summer evening. My eyes wander around the circle. All the living rooms in the Development seem to be similar. Here also is the large book case with its religious books and tableware. On the wall across from the book case hangs a needlework landscape, and next to it a photograph of the previous Gur rebbe, Rabbi Yisrael Alter. In an Israeli living room one generally expects to see house plants, family pictures, and various trinkets, but here there are none.

This class, devoted to the requirement that foods be inspected for worms and insects, was supposed to have started five minutes previously, and Nava, the teacher, is usually punctual. The women carry on quiet conversations as they wait. One tells of a successful matchmaking enterprise, another relates news from the Gur development in Hatzor Hagelilit, while another compliments her neighbor's new sandals.

Suddenly Sheindi and Sari burst into the room, out of breath. Both of them had just been married at the end of the Sefira period (the seven weeks between the holidays of Passover and Shavuot).

Nava sends her regrets, but she thought that the class is every two weeks. She didn't prepare herself for today.

The room stirs. The women are disappointed. One of them addresses Bina, the hostess.

"So Bina, why don't you say something, otherwise this will have just been an 'assembly of scorners' [*moshav letsim*, a gathering in which no words of Torah have been spoken]. Convey us something from the college, a lesson you gave the girls. We're counting on you."

Bina is taken by surprise and is unprepared. She is a serious young woman, one of the few hired by the college as a part-time teacher after completing her studies. After a minute of thought she turns to those present and asks:

"Okay, what do you prefer, something substantive or something practical?"

This was the first class I had attended, and I wanted to learn. Something with substance, I wished to myself, let them ask for something with substance.

"Practical!" the women all shouted. "Practical!"

Hannah smiled at me from across the room. She must have guessed what I had been hoping.

Bina, a large woman, rose. She was haphazardly dressed and perspiring. In a characteristic gesture, she straightened her wig in front and began.

This was how I became acquainted with a most significant dichotomy in the lives of these women: the substantive versus the practical.

The two sides of this dichotomy will serve as a basis for surveying the progress and content of the classes, as well as the way they were taught and the social reality created by and reflected in them. The "substantive" and "practical" lessons also bore on the success of education for ignorance.

While Bina's lesson was "practical," I would soon find "substance" as well. During one of the classes on the Psalms, the teacher (a woman of high Gur Hasidic lineage) mentioned that Rabbi Wolf conducted a class at her house. Hannah said that she remembered him from the college, and that if I wanted substance, she was prepared to take me there. We went.

"Substance" Classes

The Class on Maimonides' Eight Chapters

For the past ten years Rabbi Wolf has given a class at the home of Nehama Wachter (who taught the class on the Psalms at the Development). On the first Monday of every month a group of women gathers to hear a man of close to eighty teach. Rabbi Wolf was the brother of the founder and principal of the Wolf Beit Ya'akov college in Bene Brak, and in his youth in Germany he had kept company with educated secularists, Zionists, Reform Jews, and the like. Upon arriving in Israel he had drawn closer to Hasidic circles, and while he did not consider himself a part of them, he felt spiritually close to Hasidism. Before retiring, Rabbi Wolf served as the college's "foreign minister," charged with liaison with local government authorities and the Ministry of Education.

The rabbi entered the Wachter house at 9:00 P.M. sharp, circling the audience of women in the living room via the balcony before taking his place at the head of the table. His wife sat to his right, and the rest of the places close to him were filled by older women, the most senior participants in the class. The average age of those in attendance was much higher than that of the Development's women.

When Hannah and I came for the first time, we were welcomed warmly and commended for our initiative and effort. Hannah saw familiar faces among the women. One was a friend of her mother's, another the mother of a former college classmate, and a third the sister of a friend. All belonged to Gur, whether by birth or by marriage.

The Wachter home in Bene Brak was actually two apartments joined together. The living room was large and different from all the others I had seen. While the basic organization was the same, there were innovations. A large dining table occupied the center of the room, and by it stood another table (which, during meals where there were many guests, could serve as a women's table). A corner of the room had been set off by a screen and contained a writing table, telephone, and office equipment. The part of the room close to the balcony was the actual salon, and contained a few armchairs and a large couch. The room's longer wall was covered by an overloaded book case that also held a small number of silver implements. All the available seats in the room had been occupied, and several more chairs were brought in from the kitchen.

Rabbi Wolf, in a short "German" jacket (as opposed to a long Hasidic coat), was tall and had a wrinkled face, a white beard, and blue eyes with a soft expression. He surveyed those before him, opened a small book he held in his hand, and plunged immediately into the lesson. His Hebrew was fluent, modern, and had a slight German accent.

The structure of the lesson. Rabbi Wolf read a passage from the fifth chapter of Maimonides' *Eight Chapters.* Most of the women had copies of the book in their hands and followed him as he read. When he finished reading, the women laid the books down and did not refer to them thereafter. Two or three of them jotted down comments in notebooks; I later discovered that they were teachers at the college. After reading the selection, he focused on a subject that he believed was the central point of the selection, explained it, adding comments of his own and examining its significance for the present day.

There was no dialogue between him and the women during the lesson. He did not ask them questions (except for rhetorical ones), and did not, during the course of the lesson, ask for their reactions. The women sat in absolute silence, a few closing their eyes, other staring straight ahead, a few directing their gaze at him and listening intently. The lesson lasted for about forty-five minutes. He concluded it without any special closing or comment about the next meeting, rose from his chair, and returned as he had come, with the women rising in a show of respect.

A sample lesson

> And when he is engaged in the acquisition of wealth—the end purpose of his intention should be its acquisition, such that he produce it with virtues and that he use it for his bodily needs and to keep himself alive, until he realizes and knows from God what he may know. (*Eight Chapters,* Chapter 5)

Rabbi Wolf: Maimonides is known as an opponent of luxury. How can he say this when the Gemara says, "A beautiful wife, beautiful furnishings, and a beautiful house broaden a man's knowledge?"
For this it is necessary to understand what "broaden" means. This is what the selection we have read addresses. Even a man who occupies himself with Torah study must interrupt his studies to see to material matters. Going out into the material is a deviation for the purpose of broadening the knowledge of study, spirituality. This break allows a person to return to his study with renewed energy. A doctor working hard and with responsibility must also rest from his work to occupy himself with something material, to restore his power and return to his difficult work. Sometimes this pause even brings about a breakthrough. Both in study and in action. But all this is true only if the intention is to do God's will. If the occupation with the material becomes the main thing, it does not broaden knowledge. The goal is to separate the body and the spirit, and this is a task that only a select few can achieve, the prophets among them. Others must aspire

to it, and they need to take breaks from their study. The same with luxuries. By "broadening a man's knowledge," the Gemara meant not only in the material sense, but also that the material broadens the spiritual.

In our generation there are no prophets. Today, if a man were to say he is a prophet, others would conduct an inspection—what fringes does he wear, what prayer book does he pray from, who are his friends [the rabbi chuckles to himself, and the women smile], and that is why we have no prophets.

There never was and never will be another prophet like Moses, since if there were to be a greater prophet he would be able to demand a change in the Torah. There have been those who have not sinned and were not prophets, while Moses sinned and was the greatest of the prophets. A prophet's sin is subjective. Others can not even reach the place from which Moses sinned. The sin of great men is the sensitive decision between two possibilities, both of which seem at first to be desirable. How can one know which is the truly desirable?

What does a man need in order to be a prophet? First he needs the expressive virtues, which are mind, comprehension, wisdom, and so on. Afterwards he needs the values: character, morality, etc. Prophecy infuses the wise man who understands God's word, the hero—the man who conquers his passions, and the wealthy man— the man who is content with his portion.

On the matter of conquering one's passions and on the matter of the virtues, the Gemara suggests that those born under the sign of Mars (who are hot-tempered) become butchers or circumcisers, and then their bloodletting will be for good. David, for instance, sinned in that he did not conquer his passion for wars, and waged elective wars [wars of conquest] before completing his mandatory wars [wars of self-defense and of conquering the Holy Land]. His bloody hands kept him from being allowed to build the Temple.

This reminds me a bit of Ernest Yefet [the recently retired director-general of Israel's Bank Le'umi, whose extravagant benefits and pension package had generated much controversy]. What happens to a Jew who imitates the customs of the non-Jews, and who takes money for his judgment? [The room awakens, and the silence is broken with laughter.]

Even Moses, who overcame all the barriers between himself and the creator, was not privileged to see God's face. Why? God has said, "A man cannot see me and live." That is, you, too, are a soul [mind] in

matter. The mind is not separate from the matter, that is, it is
not possible for just the soul or the consciousness [the mind], which
are worthy of encountering the creator, to be privileged to see it.
With the mind comes matter, and the material being who sees the
creator dies.

ॐ

At the end of the lesson, Rabbi Wolf's wife waited for him by the door, and
they left together. After the women had eased themselves out of their
silent attention, Rabbanit Wachter rose and said:

As we are accustomed to do, at the end of the lesson one of us
conveys something. Today it will be Shifra.

Shifra rose. She was a part-time teacher at the Scharansky Beit
Ya'akov College in Tel Aviv. Younger than the rest of the participants, her
clothing was especially modest—a simple wig and outdated clothes. She
wore glasses and stooped as she stood, gripping a handful of tissues and
speaking in a nasal voice.

I read in *Hamodia* [the Agudat Yisrael daily newspaper] on Friday
about our whole thing in Iran, how the government got mixed up
there with the weapons. I thought to myself that that's the price we
pay when we're dependent on someone. We, thank God, go our own
way, and don't have to depend on others. But despite that we don't
always act independently. First of all, the way we dress. Women say
to themselves: "What will other people say?" Who decided for them,
who are they worrying about? They should dress their own way,
modestly. Also education. Once we educated in the traditional way
and today there are innovations. Some of the innovations, well,
okay. But a lot of them are superfluous, the way of ancient Israel is
the right way, and we don't have to look to see what others are
doing. Certainly not what the gentiles are doing. What that means
is that we're being enslaved to ways that aren't ours. For instance,
there's a fashion about names. Everyone's giving new names. At first
that sounds wonderful, but after a while it gets ridiculous, the names
get old and there's no point to them. I heard that there are people
who give names like Ron, Shahar, Lihi. A few years later it becomes
funny. We have our own names. They've always been good and they'll
always be good, because the truth does not go out of date, it is eternal.

It looked as if the women in the room were very much affected by the
young woman's words. They congratulated her and went up to her with

broad smiles on their faces, seconding the importance of what she had said.

"You spoke well, good for you, we really needed that, we have to hear that from time to time."

"You don't even know how right you are, if you could see what's going on in the stores in Bene Brak."

It sounded as if Rabbi Wolf's comments on the barriers between man and the creator, on the power of consciousness and the mind, and on the limitations the material places on the soul had all vanished. The authentic, troubling, immediate reality returned to the room. All the women understood Shifra. Not one had drowsed off. It sounded as if each one of them was personally affected by what she had said. Rabbanit Wachter shook the young woman's hand warmly and said:

> Yishar ko'ah, good for you, congratulations, you are so right. I remember that in my time the non-religious gave the name Yoram a lot, it was in fashion. A few days ago someone at the college told me that today the name means something like "dolt." Like schlemiel or schlimazel. But with us, Sarah is Sarah, Rivka is Rivka, Moishe is Moishe.

After rummaging through the pile of coats on the kitchen table, we went out into the cold street. On the way to the bus stop, after a few moments of silence, Hannah said to me:

> I have a horrible headache. I haven't made such an effort for a long time. I'm not used to learning the yekke [German, i.e., rationalist] way. When I was at college I was more used to it, he taught us a class or two there. Now it's different, I go only to classes taught by women.

"Did you enjoy it?" I asked.

> It's hard to say whether I enjoyed it. I know that you must have liked it, but I prefer traditional study. It's too much over my head. Hurry up so we don't miss the last bus to the Development.

Rabbi Wolf's class is a classic "substance lesson." His level of knowledge and his way of thinking shape his style of teaching. The choice of Maimonides as a text is, in and of itself, unconventional. The Hasidim, like most other Ashkenazi Jews, do not base their legal rulings on Maimonides. While parts of his compendium of Jewish law, the Mishna Torah, are studied in the women's college, it does not have the authoritative, unchallengeable status that the Shukhan Arukh has. Maimonides' major philosophical work, Moreh Nevuhim (The Guide for the Perplexed) is not studied by women at all, nor is it a book that people keep at home or refer to. The *Eight Chapters* is notable for its concision and clarity. It is an early work by Maimonides, containing most of the ideas he expressed more fully later. It is written in simpler language than his other works, and is a good introduction to his philosophy for the uninitiated.

Rabbi Wolf's class was entirely different from the other classes I will describe. Even in comparison to the "substance" classes given by Rabbanit Wachter and her sister on the book of Psalms, it was exceptional. Here the teacher was a man, and he was not part of the Gur community. The teachers of the other classes were Gur women, some from the Development itself, and two who came from Bene Brak, but all central figures in the Gur community. Rabbi Wolf stands outside. The school where his brother was once principal, and whose current principal is his nephew, serves women from different haredi groups. When a special Beit Ya'akov college for Gur women was established in Bene Brak in the mid-1970s, Gur women stopped enrolling at the Wolf college. Rabbi Wolf is nevertheless respected and appreciated, as the site of the lesson—the home of a high-placed Hasid—shows.

The scope of this teacher's knowledge was not like that of the women teachers, or even like that of other male haredi teachers. Rabbi Wolf's rich and unconventional past affected the character, content, and form of his lessons.

Rabbi Wolf touched also on psychology and Aristotelian and Platonic philosophy, and applied Maimonides to immediate problems in haredi life (the fear of accepting the standards of the non-Jews) and of the Jewish people as a whole (in the implicit suggestion that deviation from religion is liable to lead to economic predicaments like that of Bank Le'umi's Ernest Yefet). Rabbi Wolf did not choose passages from Maimonides' book that would make it easy for him to comment on subjects the women would consider relevant. There is no lack of such passages in Maimonides, who wrote of medicine, property, art, law, and many other subjects. Rabbi Wolf spoke of faith, reverence, the barriers between God and his creation, and the attributes of the prophets. The connections the rabbi made between study and practice were slight; practically the only reference to practical matters was the mention of Ernest Yefet and the example (itself taken from Maimonides) of the doctor's need for a break from his medical work. Rabbi Wolf lectured, rather than sermonized, telling no stories and offering no instruction in proper behavior. He spoke in a low, even voice, without pathos.

In light of what he said, it is reasonable to assume that the rabbi's intention was not to emphasize the practical and behavioral. The women, who told Bina they wanted to hear a "practical" lesson, would certainly have classified Rabbi Wolf's lesson as "substance." Hannah complained of a headache, and said that she was no longer used to this kind of class. Rabbi Wolf's class, by this data, is exceptional—but so are the women who come to hear him.

Malka Shamir, the ba'alat teshuva, had been present when I first heard of Rabbi Wolf's class. She turned to Rabbanit Wachter and asked if it would be possible for Rabbi Wolf to come to the Development every two or three months. An awkward silence fell over the women present, and Rabbanit Wachter explained to Malka, as if she were an obtuse little girl, that Rabbi Wolf was an elderly and venerable man and that it would not be possible. On the way out Malka mumbled under her breath that she didn't understand what the problem was; the women around her did not bother to explain her error to her.

The women attending the classes at the rabbanit's house were, on the average, about twenty years older than the women of the Development. They had coalesced over close to a decade, and attended the class devotedly. It was a self-selected group. The class was not appropriate for all women, like the women's classes in the Development, nor was it open to all Gur women in Bene Brak. The rabbanit had invited several acquaintances, and these in turn had brought others. The group's welcome of the newcomer determined whether the new participant was to be accepted or rejected. Hannah and I were well-received. Hannah's outwardly evident strictness of observance, the effort she had made to get from the Development to Bene Brak especially for the class, and her husband's standing in the Gur community had paved the way for us.

Rabbi Wolf's class was not meant for the public at large, and was thus held in a private home rather than a synagogue or school, as classes by other rabbis are. But even such a "substance" lesson for older women whose "harediness" is not open to doubt cannot be left at that. At the end of each meeting, they hear "a few words." One of the women gives an educational homily. Apparently, this talk has become the most meaningful part of the class for most of the women. Shifra's lesson, not the rabbi's, was in the air as the women left. It had touched the audience on an emotional level and brought them back to familiar events in their lives. The practical, in this case, was the substance that the young woman presented to the others. It was relevant to their social situation, and was therefore absorbed easily and pleasurably, even though it was critical. To the non-haredi outside observer, it is difficult to understand why the women went to such lengths to congratulate Shifra so warmly. What wisdom had she imparted? And why did they not discuss the rabbi's lesson? But a minute's thought supplied an answer: Shifra's lesson conveyed a message consistent with the women's worldview. It portrayed a world that was not congenial for them (by attacking their consumerism), but it also validated and confirmed that world. Her very brief remarks had the power to validate the formal lesson and at the same time call its realism into question. She took the women from the heights of abstraction and planted them on familiar ground. From the prophetic virtues Rabbi Wolf had spoken of, Shifra had distilled the haredi housewife's shopping list.

What seems to be an absurd juxtaposition of events seems entirely rea-sonable to the women involved. The ancient world of faith, the spirit of Judaism, and Jewish philosophy are diverted into the vessels of reality that they know first-hand. This type of education, which offers substance in a container firmly planted in the foundations of reality, is effective. Such education fashions a view of the world and, simultaneously, confirms it. This is the case with regard to men's study as well, except that the two views of the world—the male and the female—are different. This will become clear as we proceed.

"Practical" Classes

Women define as "practical" classes those that touch directly on their daily lives as women, wives, and mothers. Any information that helps them to perform these roles is considered practical. By definition, then, a "practi-cal" educational framework is compatible with social reality. Such a frame-work, which applies Jewish law to real situations in the lives of the women, is always concrete (that is, it portrays pictures that may be seen from the classroom window) and is directly connected with the lives of the students. It is, for this reason, effective.

The social reality in which the women live is not one-dimensional. They do not just wash dishes, change diapers, and prepare food for their husbands and children. Some of these women work as school and kinder-garten teachers; others help out in family businesses. There are those who run small businesses in their homes, selling school supplies, sewing sup-plies, and the like. Some give private lessons to girls at the college, or work in the evenings at bookkeeping or typing. These account for about a quar-ter of the women. Others are housewives, but they also read books, mostly books on Jewish ethics, the lives of righteous men, and other religious mat-ters. A minority reads fiction, largely in English, because the cultural dis-tance makes it less threatening; they also read Hebrew literature that does not slander religion. They read *Hamodia*, and may read non-haredi news-papers as well. They walk through the streets around the Development and in the big cities, and encounter men and women who are not from their community.

Literacy helps one decipher extreme and complex situations, but it also provides a new paradox. The knowledge that women ask for and receive is supposed to help them construct their world as Jewish women (at the conservative pole) but as Jewish women in Israel at the beginning of the 1990s (at the dynamic pole). As a result, the "practical" classes recon-struct the image of the ignorant woman, and at the same time (paradoxi-cally) help the educated woman who lives in Israel to shoulder all her responsibilities.

It took a long time before I was able to understand this phenomenon. I saw women who could express themselves astutely in certain situations, who demonstrated scholarly expertise, who were sharp-minded—and here they were asking their teachers to discuss yet again the same laws, to repeat the same familiar admonitions and interpretations at the classes they attended.

One evening, after I already had a first draft of my dissertation ready, I went to Bene Brak to meet with four women who did not live in the Development. I presented them with my conclusions about the lessons, especially with regard to the "practical" lessons, and I reiterated my bewilderment. These women, all of whom held senior positions in the Gur community (some economic and some collegiate), laughed. Bracha said:

"Look, *from your point of view* you are right. It really is strange that smart adult women seek out such classes and say they came out of them 'strengthened.' *From our point of view* there is no other way."

That is, my point of view is that of my picture of the world, of the responsibilities and ideologies that I must confront. My point of view is perhaps the point of view of academic or male literacy, which has become *the* literacy for me. Their point of view is that of women who live in a world they have chosen to accept without questioning. They cannot resolve, confront, or liberate themselves from the problems, contradictions, and paradoxes it contains. These are facts for which an appropriate meaning must be found, one that will help the women live with them. In this way, just as they are overcoming the paradox of education for women in this age, they fall into a new paradox of education for ignorance. Educated women are taught to be ignorant, so that they may succeed in living as educated and ignorant.

When the educational arena is emptied of teachers and rabbis, the women remain alone. They initiate classes of their own on subjects that contain nothing new for them. When the women of the Development began to organize classes again (after 200 new young families came to live in the Development in its second stage), they did not look for courses in flower arrangement, French cooking, or sewing (among the courses available at the nearby community center, open to any interested woman). When the women "have a class," they "have Judaism." When women describe a good place to live, they specify that there be "a lot of classes for women" there. Like the Jewish town in Poland that had many study halls, the women's class is proof that the Jewish situation has been reproduced. Like the men described by sociologist Shmuel Heilman, the women also seek in their classes support for the complex situation in which they live.

Without guides, they choose the "practical" type of lesson. If the women's world of public literacy were a pharmacy, the women could take "substance" only with a doctor's (i.e., a rabbi's or teacher's) prescription. Over the counter, on their own responsibility, they take only the practical —but even that is not so simple, as will be shown by the three "practical" lessons that follow.

The Lessons on the Laws of the Sabbath

At the end of summer vacation, after a short break needed by the women
to return their homes to a school footing, the class on the laws of the Sabbath began. This time seventeen women gathered at the home of Devorit,
a Sepharadi ba'alat teshuva. Devorit came from a traditional family in the
adjacent neighborhood. After her marriage, she and her husband decided
to become more observant, so they moved into the Development. For the
time being they lived in a rented apartment. Three young Sepharadi
women had attended Hannah's classes on the laws of dining, as a result of
their personal ties with Hannah. Sensing that they had been welcomed
into the Gur women's framework, Devorit felt herself ready to invite the
group to her home. The invitation was accepted warmly.

Tsipi was noticeably pregnant. A year ago she had married, she was
teaching at the Gur Beit Ya'akov college in Bene Brak, and she was considered to be "a serious young woman." She spoke rapidly and tended to swal-
low her words. Enthusiastic and cheerful, she was always surrounded by her
married friends from the college, who had come to live in the Development.

> As you know, we have decided to learn the laws of the Sabbath.
> Most of the girls here have graduated from the Beit Ya'akov college
> and have grown up, thank God, in good homes. Everyone knows
> the laws of the Sabbath. So why study them anyway? It is said that
> whoever does not study can be sure that the Sabbath will not pass
> without a violation. But we do not study in order to make rulings,
> that's for men, and I want that to be clear, because it came up during
> Nava's class on worms and also during Hannah's class on the laws of
> dining. We are learning so that we will know what to ask.

> Today we will talk about the basic actions forbidden on Shabbat.
> These were derived from the thirty-nine types of action described in
> the construction of the Ark of the Covenant. This derivation was
> made because in the Torah the description of how the Ark was built
> comes right next to the laws of the Sabbath. These labors were done
> in honor of the *Shekhina* [God's presence] and on Shabbat, when the
> Shekhina is with us, pervades us, there is no reason to do them. Each
> of these basic actions includes several other actions, that are borne
> from them.

> *Shoshi:* What do you mean "borne"? Excuse me for interrupting, I've
> never heard that expression before, excuse me, what do you mean
> "borne from"?

Tsipi: I said that we're learning so that we can ask, so you can ask questions. You're correct. It is what comes out of the action, what is borne from it, connected to and similar to it. We'll begin with one of the basic acts: sorting. I'm teaching from my notebook on the laws of the Sabbath from college. Just as it was conveyed to me, I'm conveying it to you.

Minda: And if we saw differently at home?

Tsipi: In Hasidism, what you see at home is what you do. They say there's a little synagogue in Bene Brak where, when the avrechim enter, they bend over a bit. No one asks why, they just bend over. They think it's the custom of those Hasidim. What does it turn out to be? In Poland, in the synagogue they had there, there was a low entrance and they would bend over, so they continue to bend over here, too. That's the way it is.

The act of sorting is to separate food from refuse. If I want to take oranges out of a bowl and there are grapefruit there, too, the oranges are the food and the grapefruit are the refuse. You are permitted to take the oranges out of the bowl if you meet three conditions: food, by hand, immediately. That means that you take out what you want to eat, with your hand and not with an implement, and you eat it now and not later.

There was an uproar in the room. The women began talking among themselves, some quietly and some loudly. The point of contention was the word "refuse."

Rachel: What do you mean, "refuse"? Grapefruit aren't refuse, they're food, too. If you want to eat the grapefruit afterwards, and they're already refuse, how can you eat it?

Tsipi: If you want the grapefruit, then it's food, and whatever else is in the bowl is the refuse.

Rachel: I don't understand, how can it be food one time and refuse the next time. Why call it refuse?

The women try to solve the puzzle among themselves; the discussion takes place in an unorganized way between each woman and her neighbor, with those who think they have understood trying to explain.

Hannah: It's like the primary and the secondary. It's not hard to understand. Sometimes the primary thing can be the oranges, and other times it's the grapefruit.

Varda: So it can be, for instance, if you're eating fish, you take the meat off with your hands and leave the bones in your plate. I've seen people put the whole fish in their mouth and take the bones out of their mouth, what do you say about that?

Tsipi: Varda, what do you want from me, to give you an answer I have to think, and I don't want to think. Ask your husband what to do. I'm telling you what I learned, what they told me at college and what I wrote here in my notebook.

Malka, the ba'alat teshuva, throws me a little smile, as if to say, "Just look at them!" She says: "What's there to understand, what's so complicated about it? They're not saying that the grapefruit is refuse, and your example, Varda, isn't a good one, because the bones really are refuse that you throw away. Tsipi is talking about sorting, when you sort what you want from what you don't want. It's only *as if* at that moment that you want the oranges that the grapefruit are *like* refuse. It's not for real, it's as if."

The lesson was halted for ten minutes and the women continued to struggle with the practical definition of refuse and food, explaining, giving examples, trying to portray refuse in a positive context. It was very difficult for them to take in. They could not accept the word "refuse." When Tsipi finally managed to take control again, she went on to a different type of sorting.

When you eat watermelon, for instance, you really are taking refuse out of the food, and there it's like what Varda said, you put it all in your mouth and spit out the seeds.

Nava: On Friday, before Shabbat, if you have time, you can take out the seeds and cut it up and put it in a closed container, or you can buy the kind without seeds.

"Sure, take the seeds out for a family of ten," laughed Rivka.
Nava, who had been married for a year and was still not pregnant, blushed and fell silent.

Tsipi: Remember the main thing. In Hasidism we don't want to exhaust ourselves while we're eating. You have to obey the law but not go overboard. If you eat and enjoy, that's more to God's liking than if you lose your appetite over the laws.

Nehama: Why get yourself into trouble, you can have a Shabbat without watermelon.

Hannah: That's what you think? Then maybe we shouldn't study at all, so we won't get into trouble. Is that better?

Devorit rose and signaled Tsipi that it was 10:00 P.M. Tsipi promised to pick up where she left off next time. The next Tuesday, same time, same place.

In the two following lessons Tsipi insisted on order and the meetings went smoothly. In the middle of the last meeting the discussion centered on actions carried out by others (non-Jews or secular Jews). Tsipi emphasized that even if someone else performed the forbidden action, the action had been done and that was in and of itself contempt for the holiness of the Sabbath.

> *Varda:* That brings us back again to the debate over the private generator and the battery and timer. I don't have the patience for that argument again. [Varda is referring to the dispute over whether religious Jews may use electricity from the electric company, which employs Jews on the Sabbath.]

> *Tsipi:* That's not the argument, everyone acts according to their custom and both sides can cite authorities in their favor. We have our limitations, and we should get as little as possible into those things.

> *Yochi:* Things you know there's a dispute about shouldn't be brought up. We're one group and there are enough things that are the same for all of us.

> *Tsipi:* I don't want to cause a dispute. I said at the beginning that we're studying to know what to ask, not to make rulings for ourselves.

The lesson on the laws of the Sabbath led me to study women's literacy in the Gur community. I knew that the laws and precepts of the Sabbath were not an unfamiliar or marginal subject in their world. On the average, each of the women present had lived through 1,400 Sabbaths. Just as with the laws of dining and even the class on worms, the Sabbath was a familiar matter that they had already studied in other educational frameworks. Although questions had been raised during the lessons on other subjects, those voiced in this class were so insistent that they signalled the researcher that this was where the treasure was to be found.

At first it seemed to me that the women were unable to engage in pure cognitive thinking—that they could not draw parallels, think in the abstract, reach conclusions. When Tsipi asked that they think of fruit as refuse, there was an uproar. Even Malka thought that their ability to think was limited, and clarified the matter for them in a way that expressed a certain sense of superiority or scorn. But in fact the discussion in the room was about the issue of validity, about the need for and implications of abstract thinking, "substantial" thinking about the life of women.

Tsipi says: "I said at the beginning that we're studying to know what to ask, not to make rulings for ourselves."

"I'm teaching from my notebook on the laws of the Sabbath from the college. Just as it was conveyed to me, I'm conveying it to you."

"In Hasidism, what you see at home is what you do."

"What do you want from me, to give you an answer I have to think, and I don't want to think."

"Ask your husband what to do. I'm telling you what I learned, what they told me at college and what I wrote here in my notebook."

"I don't want to cause a dispute. I said at the beginning that we're studying to know what to ask, not to make rulings for ourselves."

She says this, and teaches, while the women say:

Nehama: Why get yourself into trouble.

Varda: That brings us back again to the debate over the private generator and the battery and timer. I don't have the patience for that argument again.

Hannah: Then maybe we shouldn't study at all, so we won't get into trouble. Is that better?

They say this, yet come to the class.

Women may now study "substance," but they are unsure whether to do so. This uncertainty is a product of the reality in which they live, and that they accept as a part of a package deal. The education that the women have received, and that they reproduce in the little free time that they have, is avowedly directed towards action and not towards thought. Kindergarten and school are supposed to teach girls how to behave. The best curriculum (quoted above from *Marveh Latsameh*) is one focused on behavioral instructions. The ideal woman is portrayed as being of good values, of simple faith, an exemplary mother and wife, benevolent. In the official educational frameworks, study for the purpose of inquiry and speculation, of understanding the source of the law, of delving into the various interpretations of the Bible, is considered negative and dangerous. Tsipi's answer to Varda during the class on the Sabbath sums this up: "Varda, what do you want from me? To give you an answer I have to think, and I don't want to think. Ask your husband."

Does Tsipi not want to think, or is she unable to think? Or maybe she thinks that she certainly can think, but if she thinks, she will change her perspective, will find her worldview challenged, will find herself questioning the social situation that she has accepted as axiomatic. If that is what Tsipi thinks, why in fact should she think? But the real question is, Is she capable of not thinking?

In all three of the classes described, the woman conveying the lesson declared that the class was not intended to make the women into arbiters of Jewish law. Not a single one of the women thinks to herself that after the lesson on the laws of the Sabbath she will be able to make decisions for herself. Even males who study do not presume to hand down rulings on legal issues; for that purpose there are rabbis and scholars. There are two other reasons for opening the meeting with the sentence "We are learning in order to know what to ask and not to know what to answer": (1) to emphasize to the audience that in this place, in this class, everyone sub-scribes to the reality in which it is not women's role to think, and (2) to approach the world of thinking and inquiry, notwithstanding reason 1.

The women's public pledge (to each other, and collectively to their community) is a ritual that upholds their community's definition of their status, yet simultaneously gives them the opportunity to refashion this def-inition. It is important to emphasize that this is not a pro forma statement that in fact allows them to do the forbidden. Declaring their intellectual limitations is not a cynical or conscious act meant to release them from their public obligations and to allow them to engage in forbidden activity. By emphasizing the limitations of their thinking and action, and by attempting to approach the boundaries that define these limitations, they give expression to the complexity of their existential state. The central axis of this existential state is a paradox, and it is the thread that winds through every segment of their lives. These haredi women, perhaps like all haredi women, live their lives in complete accord with their station, yet engage in unceasing attempts to comprehend this situation anew. The great current of Jewish tradition, the structure of the Jewish religious com-munity, and their conservative education sweep them along. Alongside roars the river of modern times, of this place, and of the people around them. And they try to keep their heads above water.

Through ethnography, anthropology attempts to describe the "how," i.e., how women try to correlate the system of study to a social state through pragmatization, and how they use the curriculum to simultaneously create and validate their worldview. It may be that the lessons described here an-swer this question. To clarify it further I will sum up the essence of the social process that occurs during study, and its implications for the status of the haredi woman.

Dual Literacy

The curriculum for women's study has been described as fitting the social reality in which the women live. Status-wise, women who study are seen as a group whose access to the society's important resources, such as decision-making, political influence, and socioeconomic representation, is limited. Unlike other similar groups, such as minorities, the lower classes, and eth-nic groups, the social reality in which these women live does not nullify their social status. Orthodoxy does not present the status of women as inferior, as in need of change or improvement. It is, rather, a "separate" status, different and complementary to that of the men. The women, for their part, accept this status a priori. As a result there is correlation between the curriculum, which culturally describes and reproduces this status, and the social reality.

I have already noted that studies of education and literacy made among socially disadvantaged groups have found a large gap between the curriculum and the social state of the students. This gap created tension and alienation between the students and the curriculum, the teachers representing it, and the culture on which it is founded. In the case of study among haredi women, there is integrated and coordinated action. The women identify with the material under study and with the teachers (who become objects of admiration and models to be imitated), and retroactively reinforce their a priori acceptance of their social state. This, without a doubt, is the ideal model for their education.

But this is complicated by the fact that they live within a Jewish society where the majority is not orthodox, and in a democratic country with an open and competitive cultural market. It presents a challenge to the ideal model.

The sense of strength and gratification that they receive from the sermonizing lessons on Jewish law grows out of routine and a longing for guidance. But the interesting thing is that in the lessons on laws that they organize on their own, there is a discussion of substance in matters that go beyond the program they have determined for themselves. In fact, the discussion of these laws is not new to them. The teacher does not intend to "attack the law from a new direction," because this is not an acceptable program in haredi education; nor does she intend to lead an in-depth, disputational study of the law, in the style of Gemara study, because such study is forbidden for her and she is not to be trusted with it. In going over laws they know, the women seem to be conducting study on two levels. The first level is one that reproduces their social situation, a situation that they accept a priori, and gives it deeper meaning. They reproduce their culture in the same way that men at study do, but unlike them, when women are asked to think they drowse off, waking only for the section considered appropriate for them as Hasidic women. When the teacher speaks of the essence of faith, they do not follow the text. There is no discussion, no discourse, no raising of conflicting contents; the women accept their position in the community completely and passively.

On another level they are carrying out negotiations over their very existence. They examine themselves from outside. At the Psalms class there were some women who did not remain passive—they tested the boundary between the abstract and the practical. Nava asked up to what point they were allowed to stretch this boundary of inquiry and abstraction, in order to know how to teach others. Ita presented watching one's tongue as a form of divine worship by practical behavior. The borders of the substantial and the practical were raised for a contained and controlled discussion, but I could sense that the women in the room were experiencing a troubling complexity touching on their view of themselves. Whether or not it was comfortable for them to present themselves as ignorant, as "conveyers," as those who heard at home and so reported, they were confused, they thought, and sometimes they doubted.

When they remained among themselves, in lessons that took place in the Development, this other level came to the fore. The lesson on worms was at times a parody of the laws under study. The women stretched the confines of obeying the law to an extreme that revealed it as ridiculous. True, they were quick to relate how they solved various problems and showed off their talents as housewives, but the hysterical laughter at the description of the various kinds of worms, the comments about "so we'll stop eating strawberries" and "who needs cauliflower" sometimes overrode their ability to get the worms out of the onion or the maggots out of a package of flour. During the class on the laws of dining, the women conducted a penetrating discussion of the boundaries of the permitted and forbidden in women's literacy. The regular opening presented at all of the lessons, seeking legitimacy for women's studies in general, was broadened in this case into a real discussion. The dialogue between Hannah and Nava, the defenses each of them raised for their learning, and the slide into a debate over the value of tradition in Hasidism added a significant element of flexibility to this knowledge. Instead of knowledge presented as "objective" and "true," there was knowledge subjected to social interpretation and negotiation.

The lesson on the laws of the Sabbath could be stripped of the practical level to reveal that it really contained a discussion of the meaning of women's literacy. On the face of it, the discussion was about the major categories of actions forbidden on the Sabbath, but it included questions like: Why should I think? How do I know what I know? What kind of logic am I permitted to use, and what kind am I capable of using? What is the connection between what I know and what I can do? Such a discussion is not part of what the haredi woman accepts a priori. It is as close as this framework allows to confusion and doubt—close to academic literacy, male literacy, secular literacy.

The women maintain, therefore, a dual literacy. "Know-how literacy" is relevant to their existence as haredi women in what would seem to be a total and authoritative framework. This literacy supplies them with the information and tools they need to live in their world. "Knowledge literacy" is relevant to their lives as highly literate women, aware of what is going on around them inside their community and outside it as well, and partial partners in the social reality of Israel and the world. This literacy allows them, from time to time, to look at themselves and their society from a certain distance.

The constant movement between these two levels of literacy takes place in every educational event. It aids the integration of the meaningful but diverse realities they consistently confront, and allows them to decipher these realities and live within them in relative tranquility.

Women's literacy was promoted and institutionalized in the face of a threat to orthodoxy's very existence. Women study from the age of five to the age of twenty in institutional frameworks, and continue to be educated in informal frameworks from that age onward. They are literate. With the strengthening of orthodoxy and the fostering of the "learning society," their scholarship constitutes a threat to the desire to recreate the "isolationist" or "separatist" community that will be described below. This is a community that separates itself from others similar to it (such as other religious groups) and shapes itself to be the opposite of the secular Jewish community.

Women's education has become an irrevocable fact, so it is presented on an ideological level as "education for ignorance." But the ethnography reveals that the women use their literate ignorance as a conscious, emotional, and social means of living as educated Jewish women. In this way, this two-layered literacy allows women to live with the contradictions inherent in being educated and ignorant.

Notes

1. Sociologists who have written about the emphasis on study among Jewish men argue that the phenomenon should be understood as "making Judaism." Study is more important as a social construction of Judaism than as an activity for the attainment of knowledge. See Heilman 1976, 1983, 1984; Helmreich 1982; Boyarin 1989.

2. It should be noted that the women of the Development spoke of "conveying" (*limsor*) a lesson rather than "giving" (*le'ha'avir*) a lesson. The use of "conveying" is significant—the teacher is seen as passing on the lesson, without making any changes in it. Just as the Avot tractate of the Mishna says that Moses conveyed the Torah to Joshua, who conveyed it on in a chain of succession until it reached the sages, so the teacher presents herself (and is accepted by her audience as someone who is) conveying knowledge rather than creating, improvising, or innovating it.

3. Many sociological and anthropological studies of education describe this phenomenon. Three examples are Dumont and Was 1967; Backs 1972; Mclaren 1989.

4. Freire and Macedo 1987; Heilman 1983.

Part IV

Nationalist Orthodoxy

10

Religious Kibbutzim: Judaism and Modernization

Aryei Fishman

Abstract

This is a study in the sociology of Judaism as a religious culture. The analyses of historic Judaism by Werner Sombart and Max Weber imply that this religion bears a strong modernization potential, but this has not been substantiated by empirical examination. This paper seeks to demonstrate the actualization of this potential, as suggested directly by Sombart and broadly and obliquely by Weber, through modernizing movements that arose within rabbinic Judaism. The orthodox kibbutz federation in Israel is singled out as a case study for demonstrating such actualization, by virtue of the socialist structure of its settlements and its outstanding economic success. It is contended that it is primarily the political ethic of Judaism that impels this religion toward modernization.

The past several decades have witnessed a growing interest in the modernization potential of traditional religious cultures (Bellah, a,b,c; Eisenstadt, b,c). As a point of departure, these analyses have used Max Weber's comparative studies of the major world religions (a,b,c,d,e,f), which focus on the Protestant ethic. But while Weber's studies, centering on the economic institutional sphere, were concerned with the religious *propellant* of modernization, current investigation seeks out the functional equivalents of the Protestant ethic in other religions—factors which could account for their ability to accommodate to rational, especially economic, institutions by systematic and sustained activity (see Eisenstadt, c).

In the case of historic Judaism, this study has been uneven and indeterminate. As we shall see, the writings of Weber and Werner Sombart suggest that Judaism bears a strong modernization potential; but this sup-

Abbreviated versions of this paper were read at the 1978 meeting of the Israel Sociological Association and the 1982 meeting of the Society for the Scientific Study of Religion. I thank Eric Cohen, Akiva Deutsch, Eliezer Goldman, Michael Harrison, anonymous referees, and especially Bernard Lazerwitz, for helpful comments on earlier drafts of this paper, and Priscilla B. Fishman for editorial advice. I am grateful to the Secretariat of HaKibbutz HaDati and to the Department of Calculations and Statistics of Ihud HaKvutzot VehaKibbutzim and HaKibbutz HaDati for permission to use the financial summaries of the department.

position has been no more than tenuously corroborated at the empirical level.

Various Protestant ethic studies note the socioeconomic achievements of Jews in the United States (Featherman; Glenn and Hyland; Glockel; Goldstein, Lazerwitz, a; Lenski; Mayer and Sharp), and thus appear to corroborate the theoretical perspective. In seeking to explain Jewish worldly success, some of these studies draw on the structural analysis of rabbinic Judaism, as developed either by Sombart and Weber (Lenski, 101–2), or by Sombart alone (Mayer and Sharp, 277). Jews in the United States, however, tend to have a lower level of institutionalized religious observance than adherents of other religions (Lazerwitz, b; Lenski; Mueller and Johnson), suggesting that the Jews in these studies represent, for the most part, a break with rabbinic Judaism. One may, therefore, question whether the Jewish religion fashioned their personality traits and played a part in their socioeconomic achievements. Some of these studies do, in fact, raise possible cultural and situational intervening variables linking historic Judaism to modern worldly success (Featherman; Goldstein; Lenski; Mayer and Sharp) and thereby suggest that other social characteristics of Jews are no less relevant to their success than religion (see Glazer; Hurvitz). In short, the above-mentioned empirical studies do not demonstrate the ability of historic Judaism to accommodate to modern life.

Perhaps the most serious shortcoming in the examination of historic Judaism's modernizing potential has been the almost total neglect of orthodox Judaism (see Mayer). For it is orthodox Judaism, with its commitment to *halakha* (Torah law), that is the contemporary expression of the rabbinic Judaism studied by Weber and Sombart (Sombart, 197, 205). But the few relevant sociological studies bearing on the modernization potential of orthodox Jewry have been inconsistent. The stringent ritualism and supposedly inherent traditionalistic orientation of Jewry suggest that it is not conducive to modernization (Parsons, b). And yet, in recent years, a "modern orthodoxy"—as distinct from traditionalistic orthodoxy (Heilman; Liebman)—has emerged in the United States. Its adherents have a positive orientation toward the contemporary world and include professionals, scientists, and academics. The emergence of modern orthodoxy suggests that rabbinic Judaism can come to terms with modernization. This surmise, however, has not been examined.

The Religious Kibbutzim as the Focus of Our Study

In this article, we will attempt to demonstrate the ability of rabbinic Judaism to accommodate to modern political and economic institutions, and, what is more, to serve as a stimulus to them. The focus of our study will be the smallest of the four major kibbutz federations in Israel, HaKibbutz

HaDati, the religious Zionist federation[1] (henceforth, the RKF), whose six-teen settlements constituted about 5 percent of the total kibbutzim in Israel in 1982.[2] The RKF developed a religious subculture which incorporated the central values and norms of Jewish nationalism and of socialism within the orthodox framework. In the process of building a viable, self-contained community patterned after the secular kibbutz, it actualized this subculture and thereby created what is probably the most far-reaching synthesis of modern and orthodox Jewish cultures at the community level. Given the uniqueness of the RKF subculture, the religious kibbutz may be qualitatively different from other orthodox communities in Israel or elsewhere. Never-theless, the RKF can serve as a significant case study to test whether rabbinic Judaism can legitimate and motivate modern social action.

Let us state at the outset that the orthodox kibbutz members have demonstrated that ability simply by adopting a rigorous socialist pattern of living within a traditionally grounded religious framework. It is, however, the economic achievement of the orthodox kibbutzim that most clearly attests the modernization potential of rabbinic Judaism. Recent studies suggest that the religious settlements may be the most economically effi-cient federation in the kibbutz movement. This fact gains added signifi-cance when one considers that kibbutzim are among the most productive sectors within Israeli society (Barkai), and excel by international standards as well (Goldschmidt and Shashua).

We shall attribute the successful performance of the RKF to a rational-izing ethic embedded in rabbinic Judaism, an ethic that reinforces the national and socialist values shared by the RKF and the secular kibbutzim. Using the ideal typological method of inquiry developed and employed by Weber, we shall abstract this religious ethic from the phenomenological world of the RKF members, as reflected in their ideological literature; cor-roborate its cogency by empirical evidence; and connect it causally to the institutionalized action of the RKF members in the political and economic spheres. While our study analyzes a relationship between religious com-mitment and modern institutional performance within a specific Jewish framework, the issue is a generic one in the sociology of religion.

Weber and Sombart on Judaism

In his seminal study of the ancient Jewish religion, Weber (e) identified motivational and structural traits in biblical Judaism that had a significant influence on the formation of the Protestant ethic. Biblical Judaism was an innerworldly religion that conceived the world as a historical product given to transformation. It placed mundane activities in a religious context, and created a world-rationalizing perspective centered on a legalistic ethic. This ethic was broadly focused on the political sphere. The Sinaitic covenant succinctly expressed this ethic, defining the national role of the Jewish people as being to serve God as "a kingdom of priests and a holy people" through the fulfillment of Torah law. From this, the prophets developed a universalistic world view that called for a systematic ethical pattern of conduct, applying to all worldly activities. They thereby created the world-rationalizing mode of salvation. (For a comprehensive evaluation of *Ancient Judaism*, see Schluchter.)

More immediately relevant to our study, however, is Weber's analysis of rabbinic Judaism, which succeeded biblical Judaism and structured Jewish life until emancipation in the early nineteenth century. Weber formulated this analysis as a rebuttal to Sombart's study of the role of the Jews in the creation of modern capitalism. Sombart (205–51) had denoted intellectual rationalism, innerworldliness, self-awareness and asceticism as traits of rabbinic Judaism consonant with capitalism—and, we might add, with modernization in general. He thus conceived the spirit of Judaism as identical with the spirit of capitalism. According to Sombart (222 ff.), the rationalization of life at the religious–legal level encouraged the rationalization of life at the economic level. From that premise, he proceeded to designate Judaism as the religion that directly induced the creation of rational capitalism.

Weber (e, 396 ff.), who perceived that the rationalizing ethic of rabbinic Judaism had been strongly influenced by the biblical ethic, agreed with Sombart that the structural traits of rabbinic Judaism could foster a methodically controlled mode of life consonant with capitalism. He denied, however (f, 256–9), that rabbinic Judaism is systematically ascetic and therefore capable of cultivating a religious ethic that could lead to the creation of capitalism.

"Above all" (f, 257), Weber rejected Sombart's thesis because of the marginal stance that rabbinic Judaism assumed towards the world order. Ever since the Babylonian exile, claimed Weber, the Jews were a pariah people. Accordingly, rabbinic Judaism deflected the universalistic prophetic mode of salvation into a ritual–legal framework (see Eisenstadt, d). This development led to a dualistic relationship to the world. It thus blocked any tendency towards a comprehensive and methodical world-rationalizing ethic that could invest the rabbinic Jew, through his religious culture, with control over all areas of life, thereby ensuring his salvation. Instead, he attempted to attain salvation through observance of the law which, in turn, was connected irrationally to the true medium of salvation —the transformation of the world by divine intervention (f, 256, 259). As a result, the rabbinic Jew could not regard the world as amenable to methodical organization and control by human endeavor, e.g., by religiously motivated economic activity. The capitalism of the rabbinic Jew, according to Weber, was "pariah capitalism."

In Weber's writings the term, pariah, has a number of connotations, not all of which are clear (Momigliano). From one standpoint, "pariah" may have a voluntary connotation, in that Jews segregated themselves from the world by their own choosing. Then again, the term may allude to the legal segregation and occupational restrictions imposed on the Jews by their host nations in the Diaspora. In any case, Judaism's national ethic of world-perfection was relegated in practice to the locally self-governing community (Werblowsky). This community was envisaged as the Jewish people writ small (Golding) and, through its ordering by halakha, as the carrier of the Torah (Katz, a). The community constituted the political mold for organizing the largely segregated life of the Jew in the preemancipation era (Baron). At the same time, it served as the focus of an intensive religious political ethic. Jews were halakhically charged with mutual responsibility for the formation and support of their community (Elazar). Indeed, the political norms necessary for sustaining community life received the sanction of religious law (Golding; Katz, a).

Thus, there were two distinct aspects to rabbinic Judaism's national ethic of world-perfection (Werblowsky). On one level, it was nurtured by a constrained transformative ethos, expressed in the rationalization of daily life in the segregated community through the observance of the law here-and-now. With regard to the world at large, however, the ethic was guided by a transcendental vision of a world which would be created in the messianic era by the miraculous intervention of God. As a result, the ethic induced "a life lived in deferment" (Scholem, 35).

Transformation in the Traditional Religious Outlook

It follows from Weber's diagnosis of the mentality of rabbinic Judaism that the world-rationalizing ethic existed in potential in this mode of Judaism. If he was correct—as we believe he was—then this potential might be energized by a transformation in the world view that would dissolve the "pariah" state of the Jewish people and vitalize its universalistic orientation to the world. Such a transformation would reopen the world-rationalizing road to salvation. It would foster a perception that the messianic process could be accelerated by directed rational activities. As a result, it might well intensify the active drive of this religious ethic.

This radical shift in religious outlook actually occurred, and became a central component in the ideologies of the two major modernizing movements that emerged from traditionalistic rabbinic Judaism in the nineteenth century. The first of these movements was Torah-im-Derekh Eretz —literally Torah and civic life (Breuer)—which arose in Germany in response to emancipation. The second was Religious Zionism (Waxman), which was a response to both emancipation and nineteenth-century nationalism; it was the major expression of traditional Eastern European

Jewry's religious thrust toward accommodation to modernization. Both movements sought to foster a new religious identity for the traditional Jew that would be compatible with his new sense of membership in society at large.

On one level, these two movements reflected a rational desire to ensure the survival of traditional Judaism both as a religious culture and as a social group. But on a second, more basic, level, they sprang from the activation of inner mechanisms of change within the traditional Jewish religious culture. Both movements viewed emancipation as heralding a new cosmic phase in the messianic process, as setting the world on its correct course toward the messianic era (Hirsch, a: see Katz, b). They impugned the legitimacy of the traditionalistic orientation and hailed the present as a distinct and meaningful time—one which could serve as a rational springboard to the messianic era. Such world views represented charismatic breakthroughs, and led to the creation of religious subcultures within orthodox Judaism by both movements.[3] These subcultures contained traditional *and* modern elements, all the while retaining the primary commitment to halakha. Thus, while these modernizing movements repudiated the immediate past, they did not break with it, but continued to recognize the binding force of halakhic norms as the core of their religious subcultures.

Most important, both movements reopened the world-rationalizing path of salvation. The Jewish people was enjoined to become an active partner of God in the messianic process and to partake in the reshaping of the world through sustained economic and political activity within the modern national polity (Hirsch, c; Katz, b). The two movements, however, differed in their choice of polity. Torah-im-Derekh Eretz was oriented to the *universal* dimension of the Jewish messianic ideal; it conceived this polity to be the modern European state. On the other hand, Religious Zionism was oriented to the *particular* dimension of the messianic ideal (for these two dimensions, see Scholem) and saw the modern Jewish state as this polity. In each case, however, the movement combined a rational–active orientation to the world with the traditional messianic vision. The effect was to legitimate a world-rationalizing perspective which made possible modern orthodox accommodation to the contemporary secular perspective.

The RKF later drew heavily from both movements. It transferred the universal messianic orientation of Torah-im-Derekh Eretz to the socialist component of kibbutz life, and the particular messianic orientation of Religious Zionism to the national component. The RKF was thereby able to relate to the world in an integrated fashion, motivated by an encompassing rationalizing ethic.

We do not have space here to dwell on the religious ideologies of Torah-im-Derekh Eretz and Religious Zionism. We note, however, that

Torah-im-Derekh Eretz regarded the world at large as an object for active religious rationalization (Fishman, b) and thus constituted the direct source of the rationalizing ethic of the RKF. Torah-im-Derekh Eretz enjoined the orthodox Jew to rationalize his personality and his conduct so as to partake in transforming the world into the Kingdom of God, working thereby for his own salvation.[4] In short, the movement was able to cast the asceticism of traditional rabbinic Judaism into a systematic design of world-rationalization. Its ability to do this appears to vindicate Weber's analysis that the dualistic world view of the premodern rabbinical Jew was primarily responsible for curtailing his rationality and precluding his salvation through worldly activities.

Emergence of the RKF

It is also beyond the scope of this article to dwell on the formation of the orthodox Zionist pioneering movement in Germany in the 1920s (see Walk), from which the RKF emerged in the early 1930s. Nevertheless, we should note that the orthodox pioneering movement was founded by people who had grown up in the religious culture of Torah-im-Derekh Eretz, and who were repudiating the parent movement because of its limitations in rationalizing religious culture normatively at a political–communal level (see Leibowitz, a, b).

According to Torah-im-Derekh Eretz, the modern orthodox Jew was a member of two non-integrated polities: the universal polity, encompassing most of the institutional (including the economic) spheres in which he participated; and the Jewish religious polity, which emancipation had limited mainly to ritualistic institutions (Wilhelm), but which nevertheless continued to be conceived as a microcosm of the Jewish people (Hirsch, b). Thus it was not possible for the orthodox Jew to order his universal civic life in accordance with halakha. Furthermore, Torah-im-Derekh Eretz explicitly regarded the universal polity as the social vehicle that operated in history to transform the world, while it viewed the halakhically ordered community in an ahistorical, static, perspective. This sharp division between the universal civic life and the particular religious life spurred orthodox Jewish youth to seek a new form of polity, in which it would be possible to integrate the two modes of life in a modern, self-contained Jewish community.

Religious Zionism and Religious Socialism

Zionism, formally created at the end of the nineteenth century, offered youth the rationalization they sought. It advocated the establishment of a national Jewish polity that could integrate traditional religious and modern culture at the operational level. *Religious* Zionism legitimated this polity as the vehicle for world rationalization, by justifying the concerted rational political action of the Jewish people in history, in the context of the messianic process.[5] In the early 1930s, when the orthodox pioneering youth from Germany opted for the kibbutz form of living, they transferred this religious legitimation from a Jewish national macro-polity to the national micro-polity of the kibbutz. Thus, through identification with Religious Zionism, German orthodox youth was able to add a nationalist dimension to Torah-im-Derekh Eretz, and to extend the post-emancipation halakhically ordered community to all areas of life (Fishman, f).

When the RKF was formed in 1935, there was no clear plan for reviving the broad scope of the halakhically ordered community (Unna). The kibbutz had already proven itself as the vanguard of Zionist colonization;[6] this fact, as well as the socialist outlook of the orthodox pioneers, led them to adopt the social structure of the kibbutz. Moreover, the systems of religious socialism that prevailed in Germany in the 1920s and the early 1930s had demonstrated the feasibility of combining socialism and religion in a meaningful fashion (see Laqueur, 118).

The acid test for the successful rationalization of orthodox religious culture at the level of a modern economic and political community, was the ability of the orthodox settlers to absorb the active ascetic ethic and rational life patterns that the secular kibbutz had developed and institutionalized (Cohen; Talmon)[7] and then cast them into a religious mold. The secular kibbutz had fused analytic national and socialist collectivities into one community, and had fostered a vigorous work ethic. The kibbutz thus constituted a singularly potent modernizing agent motivating directed social change (Cohen; cf. Bellah, d). This was most evident in economic production. The kibbutz became an efficient production unit thanks to the high degree of political rationalization of its socialist collectivity—to wit, a strong centralized authority controlling the means of production, the economic roles of the members, and their organization into highly rational patterns.

The RKF Rationalizing Ethic

Similarly, the orthodox pioneer was called on to foster a rationalizing ethic by disciplining his life and systematizing his behavior, channeling it towards rational patterns of conduct focused on the community. Toward this end, he was able to draw on the personality traits of the rabbinic Jew (as specified by Weber and Sombart), augmented by the traditional collective orientation of the religious community. Charged, moreover, with the mission of reshaping world reality, he was able to draw on the vitalized biblical ethic of world transformation and focus it on the socialistic collectivity inherent in the kibbutz. The kibbutz was conceived as an intrinsic religious value, the materialization of the biblical ethic as transmitted to rabbinic Judaism and embodied in the halakhically ordered community, but within a universalistic frame of reference (Admanit).

To demonstrate this rationalizing ethic, we can tap the ideological literature of the RKF. Most of these quotations come from the late 1930s and the 1940s, the heroic period of RKF settlement, in which its religious ethic became institutionalized. This period defined the religious underpinnings for economic action which prevail to this day.

At the center of this ethic is the religious community, patterned by the law and serving as the select theater for the realization of the law. In one formulation:

Jewish religion is revealed to us not in the satisfaction of the psychic needs of the individual, but as law given to us by a supreme Lawgiver to rule the community and to mold the life of the individual therein . . . Man, following the rule of law in nature, is enjoined to institute moral law in the social and individual spheres . . . According to Judaism, only by creating a certain type of person living and educated within the framework of such a society, could man approach God (HaKibbutz HaDati, b, 4).[8]

This type of person is enjoined to develop rationally so as to foster methodical self-discipline, and direct his entire existence toward a principled religious life. In this respect, Judaism is conceived as a religion that promotes rationalization (Goldman). More specifically, the observance of halakha is viewed as conducive to an ethically rationalized life, one that is methodically controlled and governed by conscious ideas. Accordingly, kibbutz life is appraised as "religious life . . . conducted according to a supreme command, rather than according to man's free and changing will . . . It is not natural feeling that rules man's life, but reason" (Kibbutz Rodges, 2).

In the context of the religious kibbutz, the rationalized person emerges as one who self-consciously and voluntarily accepts the rigor of community life; one who maintains his autonomy yet, at the same time, "accepts the yoke of society and responsibility for the group enterprise" (Bar-Giora, 66), and channels his religious impulses toward action in and on the world, within the framework of the community. As stated by one member who was comparing the RKF ethic to the Hasidic ethic: "We cannot rest content with uplifting [religious] experiences. It is to the act of the individual that we attribute significance, within his community, for his community, and together with his community, in the drabness of everyday life" (HaKibbutz HaDati, c, 8). In the last analysis, the ethic is directed towards world transformation, inspired efficiently by the Sinaitic covenant and teleologically by the messianic vision.

It is evident that we have effected a change in the interpretation of the religious value of the precepts of the Torah . . . Traditional religion regarded them as a means to a final end, to refine man. This approach was oriented to the individual and not to the world. But we cannot accept this view. We aim not at man alone . . . but at the world. For man is 'me,' and the world is . . . all that is external to me, the other person and the community as well . . . 'Fill the earth and subdue it' is the mission of man . . . 'To perfect the world in the Kingdom of God' is the deep and sincere wish of our religious outlook . . . There is no perfection in the heavens above . . . until we perfect and renew below. This theocratic view expresses nomocracy. For our King rules by His Torah, as was made clear at the revelation: 'You shall be unto Me a kingdom of priests and a holy people' (HaKibbutz HaDati, b, 8).

Thus, the halakhically ordered community, cast in the socialist mold, is conceived as the specific religious agent for the biblical world transforming ethic; as the true contemporary manifestation of "the reality-perfecting and social aspiration of the Jewish religion [which] was most pronouncedly expressed in the words of the prophets [and which] halakha in its entirety aims to validate and actualize . . . in daily life" (HaKibbutz HaDati, a, 2).

Economic Performance of the Religious Kibbutzim

Studies indicate that the economic success of the RKF farms, as a group, is higher than those of the secular kibbutz federations.[9] In discussing this success, we should make clear that we are concerned with the economic performance of the secular kibbutz only as a point of reference. We will not attempt to answer why the economic performance of the religious kibbutzim surpasses that of the secular kibbutzim. That question requires, and deserves, extensive separate treatment.

The first study we will consider was conducted by Goldschmidt and Shashua. Their mathematical–economic model employs an index based on three profitability indicators (profit margin, capital margin, and returns to owner), and three financial indicators (equity ratio, working capital, and activity ratio) for evaluating the economic performance of a kibbutz. The authors then applied this model to all kibbutzim in Israel for the 1957–68 period, grading economic performance from 0 to 100—100 indicating the highest economic success for a particular year—and using 1968 as a base year in which the average ratings of all kibbutzim were set at 50. They discovered (218–9) that, in each of these years, the average rating of the RKF farms was higher than that of the kibbutz movement as a whole. The differential grew from 6 points in 1957 to 13 points in 1968.

To flesh out these findings, we refer to another study (Department of Calculations and Statistics, a), in which it is possible to compare the farms of the RKF with those of one of the secular kibbutz federations, Ihud HaKvutzot VehaKibbutzim (hereafter referred to as the Ihud), consisting of 83 kibbutzim in 1972. The economic state of the Ihud may be taken as representing the other secular kibbutz federations (Barkai), and so the findings of this study may provide a general picture of the relative economic standing of the RKF in the kibbutz movement. We adduce our data from a sample year of 1972.

Table 1 compares the economic performance of the RKF and Ihud farms in 1972, according to the Shashua–Goldschmidt economic performance index.

Table 1 indicates that in 1972 almost 70 percent of the RKF farms were graded 71 or more, as compared to 25 percent of the Ihud farms. Furthermore, only 8 percent (one of the RKF farms) was graded below 50, as compared to 46 percent (45 farms) of the Ihud. In short, almost all RKF farms were economically successful.

These findings are confirmed by the 1972 summary of the Department of Calculations and Statistics (b) sponsored jointly by the Ihud and the RKF. This summary processed the data on the Ihud and the RKF farms according to profitability and financial indicators per *worker–member*. (Membership population of the Ihud in 1972 was approximately 17,000; that of the RKF about 2,100.) The profitability indicators include gross income, net income, savings, interest, and maintenance expenditure for a person (including children). The financial indicators include total capital and liabilities, and net worth. Tables 2 and 3 present the findings.

We draw the following conclusions from Tables 2 and 3. Gross income of the RKF farms in 1972 roughly equaled that of the Ihud farms, suggesting that the two groups had similar levels of production. On the other

Table 1. ESTIMATES OF ECONOMIC PERFORMANCE, RKF AND IHUD FARMS, ACCORDING TO THE SHASHUA-GOLDSCHMIDT PERFORMANCE INDEX, 1972

Grade of Economic Performance	RKF Farms		Ihud Farms	
	Number	% of Total	Number	% of Total
1-50	1	(8)	38	(46)
51-60	2	(15)	7	(8)
61-70	1	(9)	17	(21)
71-80	5	(39)	9	(11)
81-90	2	(15)	7	(8)
91-100	2	(15)	5	(6)
Total farms	13	(100)	83	(100)

Source: Department of Calculations and Statistics, a.

Table 2. INCOME, INTEREST, AND SAVINGS PER MEMBER, AND MAINTENANCE EXPENDITURE OF A
PERSON PER MEMBER (IN ISRAEL POUNDS), IN ALL THE RKF AND IHUD FARMS, 1972

	1 Gross Income	2 Interest	3 Net Income	4 3 as % of 1	5 Maintenance Expenditure	6 Savings
All RKF farms	38,878	1,625	10,302	26.5	5,039	3,372
All Ihud farms	38,016	2,558	7,890	20.8	5,541	1,050
Ratio of RKF to Ihud	1.02	.63	1.30	1.27	.91	3.21

Net income = gross income--purchased inputs--outside (including hired)
    labor--interest--depreciation of capital productive stock.

Savings = net income--income tax--maintenance expenditure--depreciation
    of durable consumer stock + special income.

Source: Department of Calculations and Statistics, b.

hand, the data on net income and savings per member (the profitability
level) and on net worth per member (the financial level) indicate that the
RKF excelled in economic efficiency and in savings. The relatively low maintenance expenditure emphasizes the ascetic element in the RKF ethic, while
the RKFs relatively high ratio of net to gross income points to a greater
efficiency in resource utilization in the RKF than in the Ihud. Especially
significant is the relatively high ratio of net worth to total capital and liabilities, pointing directly to the accumulated savings of previous years.
Generally speaking, the findings indicate that investment policy is more
efficient in the RKF farms than in those of the Ihud.

    These findings seem all the more impressive inasmuch as there are a
number of significant factors operating against the economic success of the
RKF farms. First, observance of halakhic norms impedes the employment of
rational economic norms. For example, no work will be performed in the
religious kibbutz on the Sabbath and on religious holidays, even in the face
of threatening weather or seasonal farming demands; the orthodox pioneers will incur economic losses rather than violate the holy days.

    Second, the average number of children per member is higher in the
RKF than in the secular kibbutzim (Goldschmidt and Shashua), thus increasing the burden of productivity borne by each worker–member. (In
1972 there were 0.8 children per member in the RKF as against 0.6 per
member in the Ihud, according to the Department of Calculations and Statistics, b.) The greater number of children not only increases the costs of

Table 3. CAPITAL AND LIABILITIES AND NET WORTH PER MEMBER (IN ISRAEL POUNDS) IN THE RKF
AND IHUD FARMS, 1972

	1	2	3
	Total Capital and Liabilities	Net Worth	2 as % of 1
All RKF farms	56,981	14,897	26.1
All Ihud farms	57,934	5,773	10.0
Ratio of RKF to Ihud	.98	2.58	2.61

Source: Department of Calculations and Statistics, b.

consumption and education (Barkai; Kanovsky) but also lowers the proportion of workers in the income-producing labor forces (Kanovsky).

Third, the RKF kibbutzim on the whole were settled considerably
later than those of the secular kibbutz federation. Since the economic performance of a kibbutz is in general directly correlated to its age (Barkai),
one would expect the economic performance of the RKF farms to be lower
than that of the Ihud.

Finally, the RKF is less industrialized than the Ihud. Since the early
1960s, the profitability of agriculture has been decreasing in the kibbutzim,
leading to a greater emphasis on industrial production (Barkai). Industry
provided only 16.7 percent of the gross income of the RKF kibbutzim in
1972; in the Ihud kibbutzim, it provided 26.8 percent.

Eight of the thirteen religious kibbutzim in the 1972 study had a significant component of members of German background. These members
contributed decisively to the establishment of the RKF and to the evolution
of its life patterns. One might reasonably ask whether the strong self-
discipline and universalistic and collective orientations characterizing German culture (Parsons, a) might have affected the economic success of the
RKF settlements. Indeed, Nordhoff, observing nineteenth-century communes in the United States, intimates that individuals of German origin
took more readily than others to communal life. There are also eight kibbutzim of German background in the Ihud.[10] In order to test the German
culture variable in accounting for economic success of the RKF, we decided
to compare the economic performance of the two groups of German background.

This comparison is enhanced by the fact that the groups are similar in two variables that have been singled out as significant to production efficiency in the kibbutz: age and size of the membership (Barkai). The settlements of the RKF and the Ihud were established during the same period of years (1936–37–49), and the mean and median number of worker-members in the two groups in 1972 were almost the same: 226 and 213 respectively in the Ihud group, and 222 and 205 in the RKF. Nor are there geographic factors that might affect the relative economic performance of the two groups.[11]

On the other hand, the ratio of children per worker–member was lower in the Ihud group than in the RKF group (.49 vs. .79); and the percentage of industrial income in total gross income was three times greater for the Ihud group (48 percent vs. 16 percent) (Department of Calculations and Statistics, b).

Tables 4 and 5 compare the economic achievements of the RKF and Ihud kibbutzim of German background in 1972. They indicate that the former attained higher ratings in all of the profitability and financial categories that were used. Again, the maintenance expenditure per worker–member is lower, and the efficiency of resource utilization is higher, in the RKF kibbutzim of German background than in their Ihud counterparts.

It appears then that two factors—the relative individual asceticism and enhanced efficiency—account for the more successful economic performance of the RKF, both factors stemming from a seemingly higher degree of rationality in the conduct of collective life.

Rationale for Economic Success

Students of the kibbutz economy tend to seek extra-economic factors in explaining the successful performance of the RKF. Thus Goldschmidt and

Table 4. INCOME, INTEREST, AND SAVINGS PER MEMBER, AND MAINTENANCE EXPENDITURE OF A PERSON PER MEMBER (IN ISRAEL POUNDS), IN THE GROUPS OF KIBBUTZIM OF GERMAN BACKGROUND IN THE RKF AND THE IHUD, 1972

	1 Gross Income	2 Interest	3 Net Income	4 3 as % of 1	5 Maintenance Expenditure	6 Savings
Eight RKF farms	36,408	1,479	10,292	28.3	4,928	3,380
Eight Ihud farms	40,233	2,377	9,551	23.7	5,636	3.062
Ratio of RKF to Ihud	.90	.62	1.07	1.19	.87	1.10

Source: Department of Calculations and Statistics, b.

Table 5. CAPITAL AND LIABILITIES AND NET WORTH PER MEMBER (IN ISRAEL POUNDS) IN THE
GROUPS OF KIBBUTZIM OF GERMAN BACKGROUND IN THE RKF AND THE IHUD, 1972

	1 Total Capital and Liabilities	2 Net Worth	3 2 as % of 1
Eight RKF farms	51,134	15,940	31.2
Eight Ihud farms	57,635	13,259	23.0
Ratio of RKF to Ihud	.89	1.20	1.35

Source: Department of Calculations and Statistics, b.

Shashua hypothesized that the small size of the RKF might account for its economic success. But after examining the economic performance of another small federation, consisting of five kibbutzim, distinct in ideology and organization, they concluded that group size has no bearing on economic success.

We submit that the success of the RKF is rooted in religious factors. Traditional Judaism lies at the heart of the religious kibbutz life, and religion is what distinguishes the religious from the secular kibbutzim. It is therefore in this sphere that we should seek the ethic explaining the unusual economic performance of the RKF. Our analysis suggests that this performance can best be explained by a religious–political ethic acting as the carrier of the world-transformative ethos.

The keystone of our argument is the relatively low rate of consumption in the religious kibbutzim. If religion serves as a lever for economic activity, then the asceticism derived from the religious ethic is the empirical fulcrum for this lever. Goldschmidt and Shashua found that the maintenance expenditures of the RKF in 1968 were 92 percent of the average in the kibbutz movement as a whole. As we have seen, the maintenance expenditures of a person (adults *and* children) per worker–member in the RKF in 1972 were 91 percent those of the Ihud. In the kibbutzim of German background, RKF maintenance expenditures were only 87 percent those of the Ihud.

A study conducted by Rosner et al. in 1977–78 further showed that the RKF has the strongest ascetic orientation in the kibbutz movement as a whole. The study examined each of the four kibbutz federations, focusing on the relative importance and actual fulfillment of various personal needs in the framework of kibbutz life.[12] In the Artzi, Ihud, and Meuhad federations, consumption was graded lowest among the various needs indicated —3.24, 3.42, and 3.45, respectively (on a scale of 1 to 5). In the RKF, however, it was graded much lower, 2.85. On the other hand, the RKF's *satisfaction* from the consumption standard (3.90) did not differ significantly from that of the other three federations (3.97, 3.91 and 3.87 in the Artzi, Ihud, and Meuhad). Furthermore, individuals appear to have more influence over the consumption budget in the RKF than in the other federations. Respondents were requested to indicate which of four possible factors were important in determining the consumption budget; "member demand" was graded 1.28 in the RKF, as compared with 1.07, 1.08, and 1.09 in the Artzi, Ihud, and Meuhad Federations (2 high and 1 low).

We can again turn to RKF literature to show that the "ascetic" orientation of the RKF is grounded in its religious ethic, and to examine the possible effect of this orientation on the political ethic and its economic results. This time, we quote from the published proceedings of four seminars held between 1961–70—roughly the period covered by the Goldschmidt–Shashua study. These seminars were devoted to the broad relationship between the social group, the farm economy, the polity, and the general value system in the RKF (HaKibbutz HaData, d,e,f,g). The proceedings reveal a strong and unequivocal awareness of the religious ground for moderation, especially in a period of relative affluence. The link between a religious life based on moderation and kibbutz life was explicitly spelled out in a seminar devoted to self-imposed austerity (HaKibbutz HaDati, f), and also appeared in discussions about the farm economy and the religious polity (e.g., HaKibbutz HaDati, d).

The seminar proceedings reveal that in the 1960s, just as twenty or thirty years earlier, the kibbutz member was directed to practice restraint so as to regulate his life and behavior methodically, in order to realize his ultimate values. Thus, the seminar on self-imposed austerity urged self-awareness in consumption, as a means for self-rationalization in the service of an ultimate religious value.

We may apply to [the question of the consumption standard] that which Maimonides stated many generations ago in a comprehensive and calculated form. Man builds his life according to his task in life . . . The general rule determines the secondary rules, and these determine the details. It is not the quantity of consumption that is important, but the designation of consumption. It is not the individual [act of] consumption that is important, but its designation within the context of man's role in general (HaKibbutz HaDati, f, 55).

In the framework of kibbutz life "man's role in general" is conceived as divine worship within the context of the community.

We all agree that asceticism is not an intrinsic value of the kibbutz movement. However, we hold for restraint, self-control, moderation, modesty in demands, not because we cannot consume . . . nor because we do not have something to consume, but because the satisfaction of needs is only a means for the realization of what is essential. What are our essential goals? As religious Jews we emphasize the religious principle [of] the cultivation of society as against the cultivation of the individual. We must add immediately that this stands in opposition to an orientation towards consumption. The moment that one establishes society as a preferred value, the individual must forego [his private demands]. (HaKibbutz HaDati, f, 51).

In the same vein, the economic norms of the kibbutz are specifically related to religion: "In our viewpoint, religion is a broad concept, covering precepts between man and his fellow-man, between man and God, and devotion to the farm-economy" (HaKibbutz HaDati, g, 72). This is spelled out more specifically in the communal context: "With us everything is religion . . . work and farm-economy and society. It is all [part of] community" (HaKibbutz HaDati, g, 90). Again and again, the proceedings stressed the normative mutual responsibility of the members to the community as an ontological religious entity (HaKibbutz HaDati, g). The expression of the Sinaitic mission may be somewhat less intense today than it was in the thirties and early forties, but the concept of the morally perfected community, as expressed in socialist institutions, continues to serve as the basic rationale for religious kibbutz life. Thus the kibbutz is conceived as the subject for realizing "a miniature model of a kingdom of priests and a holy people. That should be the central theme of our existence" (HaKibbutz HaDati, g, 76).

Having focused our discussion on the religious–political ethic of the RKF, we might ask whether a purely religious–economic ethic exists that might account for its economic success. The answer seems to be negative. There is a vigorous economic ethic in the RKF, but it is basically the national economic ethic common to the entire kibbutz movement. We note that in the ideological literature of the RKF there is hardly any reference to a religious–economic ethic of world transformation.[13] On the other hand, we have found dozens of references to a religious–political ethic explicitly focused on world transformation as the religious motivation for worldly activity.[14]

What element in the religious–political ethic of the RKF might influence its economic performance? In the traditional Jewish community, as we have noted, the political norms which systematically sustained community life were legitimated by halakha. In this respect, there is an awareness in the RKF of the potential halakhic significance of all norms regulating the relationship between the socialist community and its individual members (Fishman, c). While these norms have not been formally sanctioned by religious law, the basic halakhic structure of kibbutz life appears to reinforce the self-discipline that conditions commitment to these norms and infuses them with religious cogency.

The religious–legal aspect of the orthodox kibbutz's normative structure constitutes the operational edge of the religious transformative ethos of the RKF. That is to say, kibbutz norms are focused on, as well as derived from, a religious polity whose dynamics are nourished by the biblical charge of reshaping the world. Inasmuch as all economic norms in the kibbutz are community oriented, they are harnessed to the political ethic and focused on religious–political goals.[15] It follows that the socialist collective, serving as the organizational basis of the RKF life, constitutes the intervening agent (cf. S. Berger) connecting the religious ideology of world transformation to the RKF economic achievements.

In sum, religion appears to stimulate and tighten the functioning of the socialist organization of the RKF kibbutzim. Within the conceptual context of this rationally organized community, religion enhances self-discipline; strengthens the collective aspect of daily life; reinforces kibbutz norms—including those involved in production and consumption—with the cogency of its legal norms; and augments the shared responsibility towards a transcendent Being (see Lang).

Discussion

This has been a study of the modernization potential of traditional rabbinic Judaism as actualized in the life of the RKF settlements. It has corroborated the analyses of both Sombart and Weber as to this potential. Sombart's analysis stressed the structural traits of rabbinic Judaism; the economic performance of the RKF bears out Sombart's view (in contrast to Weber's) that these traits can sustain a systematic ascetic ethic directed toward world change. But in a broader perspective, our study has substantiated Weber's unwitting and oblique appraisal of the modernization potential of pre-modern rabbinic Judaism at the motivational level. By dissolving rabbinic Judaism's pariah relationship to the world, emancipation reopened the world-rationalizing road to salvation of biblical Judaism.

In effect, the cessation of the pariah state enhanced the dialectic between Judaism and Protestantism with regard to modernization. The biblical ethic created the breakthrough toward world transformation and constituted a principal source, if not the very matrix, of the Protestant ethic; the latter, in turn, added impetus and scope to the biblical ethic, thereby shaping the modern world (P. Berger). The modernizing movements of rabbinic Judaism, especially Torah-im-Derekh Eretz and the RKF, sought integration into the institutional settings of the Protestant-shaped world, and were thus stimulated to activate basic transformative potentialities embedded in rabbinic Judaism. By tapping the original biblical ethic with regard to the world-at-large, these modernizing movements were able to promote the rationalization of traditional religion in the post-emancipation period. The restricted rabbinic legal ethic was universalized in the spirit of the prophets, seeking ethical control over the world in order to reshape it.

Within orthodox Judaism, with its thrust towards modernization, the RKF is unique in having established an organizational basis for the realization of the religious world-rationalizing ethic. Indeed, the ability of the RKF to adapt the highly rational socialist structure of the kibbutz to the framework of the halakhically ordered community—and to use this structure to achieve outstanding economic results—indicates that the modernization potential of Judaism is high. Our study strongly suggests that the Jewish religious ethic is expressed more in the political than in the economic sphere (cf. Katz, a). In other words, it is the political ethic of Judaism that appears to impel this religion towards modernization. Judaism's political ethic thus appears to serve as the functional equivalent of the Protestant economic ethic (cf. Bellah, a).

Notes

1. In 1978 the total population of the RKF settlements was about 6,200. The largest settlement had a population of approximately 850 and the smallest, recently established, about 60. The mean and the median figures of the RKF settlements population were almost identical, about 450.
2. There are three orthodox non-Zionist kibbutzim, affiliated with the Poalei Agudat Israel movement. Our study does not cover them.
3. The process of the development of the two movements and the crystallization of the charismatic dimension in their subcultures sharply varied. In the case of Torah-im-Derekh Eretz it was largely one person, Rabbi Samson R. Hirsch (1808–1888), the father of this movement and of modern orthodoxy in general, who charismatically revoked the legitimacy of the traditional order (a, 98–101, 195–209), and created the new orthodox subculture.
   The evolution of Religious Zionism was more complex. While the charismatic breakthrough was precipitated in the second third of the nineteenth century by rabbinical figures, a new religious subculture crystallized only in the 1920s in the guise of HaPoel HaMizrahi, the labor wing of Religious Zionism, which under the slogan of "the Holy Rebellion" revoked the legitimacy of the traditional order (Fishman, d). The link between the nineteenth-century originators of Religious Zionism and HaPoel HaMizrahi was the middle-class oriented Mizrahi party, founded at the turn of the century.
4. It is of interest to note that S. R. Hirsch's writings constitute one of the sources used by Sombart (notes 444, 450, 458, 474, 477, 480) to substantiate his argument that the Jewish religious ethic was the generator of modern capitalism.
5. Religious Zionism, emerging for the most part from the preemancipation setting of Eastern Europe, did not, generally speaking, develop an articulate and coherent modernizing ideology, as did Torah-im-Derekh Eretz in Germany. While seeking to overcome the dualism between the universal modern values fostered by East European enlightenment and the particular values of Judaism, as epitomized in the slogan, "Be a Jew at home and a man in the street" (Sachar, 208), Relgious Zionism barely outlined a structure for rationalizing traditional religion in the framework of a modern national state.
6. When the first religious kibbutz settled on the land in 1937, more than a quarter of a century after the very first kibbutz had been established, nearly fifty secular collective settlements existed.
7. For analogies between kibbutz and Protestant values and orientations, see Eisenstadt (a, 421); Talmon (204–6).
8. The ideological literature from which we quote was published principally in the central organs of the RKF, which have appeared since 1938. The articles in English referred to in Fishman (a), were also written by members of the RKF.

9. At the time of these studies the RKF comprised thirteen settlements.

10. I am grateful to Yaakov Glick of the Institute for Research of the Kibbutz and the Cooperative Idea at the University of Haifa for having identified for me those Ihud kibbutzim having a considerable membership of German background.

11. While no index exists for rating geographic conditions, Dr. Yosef Shelhav of the Geography Department of Bar-Ilan University informs me that he has examined regional factors in the two groups of settlements (temperature, precipitation, soil type, topography, and accessibility to the marketing center of the country), and concludes that the RKF group does not enjoy any geographic advantages over the Ihud group. I am grateful to Dr. Shelhav for having made this examination.

12. I am grateful to the authors, especially to Alexander Avnat, for placing the data at my disposal.

13. In one reference to such an ethic, a kibbutz member, after seeing a film on the Tennessee Valley Authority, expressed his wonderment in his local bulletin, on "the spirit that overcomes all the afflictions of nature and subdues them for the sake of society," by quoting Isaiah 45: 18: "He did not create it chaos; He formed it to be inhabited."

14. For a similar inference, that the polity constitutes the institutional locus of the transformative ethos of Judaism, by a nineteenth-century figure, Moses Hess, see Fishman (e). Hess anticipated the RKF by delineating the structural and motivational elements in rabbinic Judaism that render it highly congruous with socialism.

15. Other religious factors may contribute to the economic success of the RKF settlements, in addition to the direct religious–political ethic. For example, the Torah study circles, and especially the daily prayer services, may nourish social solidarity, and this, in turn, may affect collective economic performance. But even taking this and other possible religious factors into consideration, we reiterate that the basic ideological rationale for the religious kibbutz, which pervades and integrates all aspects of collective life, is anchored in the religious political ethic.

References

Admanit, T. 1957. "On the Religious Significance of the Community." In A. Fishman (ed.), *The Religious Kibbutz Movement*. Jerusalem: Youth and HeHalutz Department of the Zionist Organization.

Bar-Giora, N. 1957. *Sdei Eliyahu*. Jersualem: Youth and HeHalutz Department of the Zionist Organization (Hebrew).

Barkai, H. 1977. *Growth Patterns of the Kibbutz Economy*. Oxford: North Holland.

Baron, S. W. 1942. *The Jewish Community*. 3 volumes. Philadelphia: Jewish Publication Society.

Bellah, R.N. a:1957. *Tokugawa Religion*. Glencoe: Free Press.

———. b:1963. "Reflections on the Protestant Ethic Analogy in Asia." *Journal of Social Issues* 19:52–60.

———. c:1965. (ed.), *Religion and Progress in Modern Asia*. New York: Free Press.

———. d:1970. *Beyond Belief*. New York: Harper & Row.

Berger, P. 1969. *The Sacred Canopy*. New York: Anchor Books.

Berger, S. D. 1971. "The Sects and the Breakthrough into the Modern World: On the Centrality of the Sects in Weber's Protestant Ethic Thesis." *The Sociological Quarterly* 12:486–99.

Breuer, M. 1970. *The 'Torah-Im-Derekh Eretz' of Samson Raphael Hirsch*. New York: Feldheim.

Cohen, E. 1966. "Progress and Communality: Value Dilemmas in the Collective Movement." *International Review of Community Development* 15–16: 3–18.

Department for Calculations and Statistics, Ihud HaKvutzot VehaKibbutzim and HaKibbutz HaDati. a: 1974. *Economic and Financial Summaries for 1972* (Hebrew).

———. b:1975. *Financial Summaries for 1972–73* (Hebrew).

Eisenstadt, S. N. a:1967. *Israeli Society*. London: Weidenfeld & Nicolson.

———. b:1968. (ed.), *The Protestant Ethic and Modernization*. New York: Free Press.

———. c:1973. "The Implications of Max Weber's Sociology of Religion for Understanding Processes of Change in Contemporary non-European Societies and Civilizations." In C. Y. Glock and P. E. Hammond (eds.), *Beyond the Classics?* New York: Harper & Row.

———. d:1981. "The Format of Jewish History—Some Reflections on Weber's *Ancient Judaism*." In W. Schluchter (ed.), *Max Weber's Studie über das antike Judentum*. Frankfurt: Suhrkamp. For an abridged English version, see *Modern Judaism* 1(1981):54–73, 217–34.

Elazar, D. J. 1978. "Covenant as the Basis of the Jewish Political Tradition." *Jewish Journal of Sociology* 20(June):5–37.

Featherman, D. L. 1971. "The Socioeconomic Achievement of White Religio-Ethnic Subgroups: Social and Psychological Explanations." *American Sociological Review* 36:207–22.

Fishman, A. a:1957. (ed.), *The Religious Kibbutz Movement*, Jerusalem: Youth and HeHalutz Department of the Zionist Organization.

———. b:1971. "Judaism in Its Relation to Empirical Reality: Max Weber's 'Active Asceticism' in the Framework of Jewish Religion in the Modern Era." *Molad 3(26):684*–90 (Hebrew).

———. c:1975. "The Religious Kibbutz: A Study in the Interrelationship of Religion and Ideology in the Context of Modernization." Unpublished Ph.D. dissertation, Hebrew University, Jerusalem (Hebrew).

———. d:1983. " 'Torah and Labor': The Radicalization of Religion in a National Framework." *Studies in Zionism* 6:255–71.

———. e:1983. "Moses Hess on Judaism and Its Aptness for a Socialist Civilization." *The Journal of Religion* 63:143–58.

———. f:1983. "The Religious Kibbutz: Religion, Nationalism and Socialism in a Communal Framework." In E. Krausz (ed.), *Studies of Israel Society*. Volume 2. New Brunswick: Transaction Books.

Glazer, N. 1958. "The American Jew and the Attainment of Middle-Class Rank: Some Trends and Explanations." In M. Sklare (ed.), *The Jews: Social Patterns of an American Group*. Glencoe: Free Press.

Glenn, N. D., and R. Hyland. 1967. "Religious Preference and Worldly Success: Some Evidence from National Surveys." *American Sociological Review* 32:73–85.

Glockel, G.L. 1969. "Income and Religious Affiliation: A Regression Analysis." *American Journal of Sociology* 74:632–47.

Golding, M. P. 1966. "The Juridical Basis of Communal Associations in Medieval Rabbinic Legal Thought." *Jewish Social Studies* 28:67–78.

Goldman, E. 1957. "On the Religious Personality in the Religious Kvutza." In A. Fishman (ed.), *The Religious Kibbutz Movement*. Jerusalem: Youth and HeHalutz Department of the Zionist Organization.

Goldschmidt, Y., and L. Shashua. 1976. "Economic Success, Equality, and Central Intervention in the Kibbutz Sector." *HaKibbutz* 3–4:214–20 (Hebrew).

Goldstein, S. 1969. "Socioeconomic Differentials Among Religious Groups in the United States." *American Journal of Sociology* 74:612–31.

HaKibbutz HaDati a:5702 [1942] *Alonim*, Shvat [February] (Hebrew).

———. b:5702 [1942] *Alonim*, Nisan [April] (Hebrew).

———. c:5720 [1960] *Amudim* 162 (Hebrew).

———. d:1961. "Society and Farm-Economy." Published in *Amudim* 181 (Hebrew).

———. e:1965. *Kibbutz Lifestyle Faces the Influence of the Abundant Society* (Hebrew).

———. f:1968. *Self-Imposed Austerity* (Hebrew).

———. g:1970. *The Individual and the Community in the Religious Life of the Kibbutz* (Hebrew).

Heilman, S. C. 1978. "Constructing Orthodoxy." *Society* 15(4): 32–40.

Hirsch, S. R. a:1836. *The Nineteen Letters of Ben Uziel*. New York: Funk & Wagnalls, 1899.

———. b:1854–6. *Judaism Eternal: Selected Essays from the Writings of Rabbi S. R. Hirsch*. 2 vols. London: Soncino, 1956.

———. c:1867–9. *Explanation to the Pentateuch*. Volume 2. New York: Judaica Press, 1971.

Hurvitz, N. 1958. "Sources of Middle-Class Values of American Jews." *Social Forces* 37 (December):117–23.

Kanovsky, E. 1966. *The Economy of the Israeli Kibbutz*. Cambridge: Harvard University Press.

Katz, J. a:1961. *Tradition and Crisis*. Glencoe: Free Press.

———. b:1971. "The Jewish National Movement: A Sociological Analysis." In H. S. Ben Sasson and S. Ettinger (eds.), *Jewish Society Through the Ages*. New York: Schocken Books.

Kibbutz Rodges. 5698 [1938]. *Dappim*, Tammuz (July) (Hebrew).

Lang, D. 1956. "This 'Earth of the Lord': Notes on the Religious Kibbutz." *Judaism* 5(Summer):212–16.

Laqueur, W. Z. 1964. *Young Germany*. London: Routledge & Kegan Paul.

Lazerwitz, B. a:1961. "A Comparison of Major United States Religious Groups." *Journal of the American Statistical Association* 56:586–79.

———. b:1964. "Religion and Social Structure in the United States." In L. Schneider (ed.), *Religion, Culture and Society*. New York: Wiley.

Leibowitz, J. a:1930. "Thoratreuer Zionismus." *Zion* (Berlin) 2:62–65.

———. b:1930. "Ein Versuch zur Klärung." *Zion* (Berlin) 2:142–49.

Lenski, G. 1961. *The Religious Factor*. New York: Doubleday.

Liebman, C. S. 1965. "Orthodoxy in American Jewish Life." *The American Jewish Yearbook* 66:21–97.

Mayer, A. J., and H. Sharp. 1962. "Religious Preference and Worldly Success." *American Sociological Review* 27:218–27.

Mayer, E. 1973. "Jewish Orthodoxy in America: Towards the Sociology of a Residual Category." *Jewish Journal of Sociology* 15:151–65.

Momigliano, A. 1980. "A Note on Max Weber's Definition of Judaism as a Pariah Religion." *History and Theory* 19:313–18.

Mueller, C. W., and W. T. Johnson. 1975. "Socioeconomic Status and Religious Participation." *American Sociological Review* 40:785–800.

Nordhoff, C. 1875. *The Communistic Societies of the United States*. New York: Schocken Books, 1965.

Parsons, T. a:1951. *The Social System*. Glencoe: Free Press.

———. b:1960. *Structure and Process in Modern Societies*. New York: Free Press.

Rosner, M., Y. Glick, and A. Avnat. 1979. "Consumption in the Kibbutz." Institute for Research of the Kibbutz and the Cooperative Idea, University of Haifa (unpublished data).

Sachar, H. M. 1957. *The Course of Modern Jewish History*. New York: Dell.

Scholem, G. 1971. *The Messianic Idea in Judaism*. New York: Schocken Books.

Schluchter, W. 1981. (ed.), *Max Weber's Studie über das antike Judentum*. Frankfurt am Main: Suhrkamp.

Shashua, L., and Y. Goldschmidt. 1974. "An Index for Evaluating Financial Performance." *The Journal of Finance* 29:794–814.

Sombart, W. 1911. *The Jews and Modern Capitalism*. Glencoe: Free Press, 1951.

Talmon, Y. 1972. *Family and Community in the Kibbutz*. Cambridge: Harvard University Press.

Unna, M. 1957. "The Elements of the Religious Kibbutz." In A. Fishman (ed.), *The Religious Kibbutz Movement*. Jerusalem: Youth and HeHalutz Department of the Zionist Organization.

Walk, J. 1961. "The Torah va'Avodah Movement in Germany." *Leo Baeck Institute Yearbook* 6:236–56.

Waxman, M. 1918. *The Mizrachi, its Aim and Purposes*. New York: Mizrachi Bureau.

Weber, M. a:1904–5. *The Protestant Ethic and the Spirit of Capitalism*. New York: Scribners, 1958.

———. b:1906–24. *From Max Weber: Essays in Sociology*. New York: Oxford University Press, 1946.

———. c:1915. *The Religion of China: Confucionism and Taoism*. Glencoe: Free Press, 1951.

_____. d:1916–17. *The Religion of India*. New York: Free Press, 1958.

_____. e:1917–19. *Ancient Judaism*. New York: Free Press, 1952.

_____. f:1922. *The Sociology of Religion*. Boston: Beacon, 1964.

Werblowsky, R. J. 1954. "Hanouca et Noël, ou Judaïsme et Christianisme." *Revue de l'Histoire des Religions* 145:30–68.

Wilhelm, K. 1957. "The Jewish Community in the Post-Emancipation Period." *Leo Baeck Institute Yearbook* 2:47–75.

11

A Mystic-Messianic Interpretation of Modern Israeli History: The Six-Day War in the Religious Culture of Gush Emunim

Gideon Aran

The Six Day War and its results had a startling impact on Israeli society. Its significance lay not only in the nature of the victory itself—a victory of fantastic, unexpected dimensions—but also in the shock of moving, in the space of a few days, from the brink of national destruction to unprecedented heights of strategic achievement. It was in this polarity that the force of the event lay, not least from a religious point of view.

Touching as it did, in one sense, the historical memory of the Holocaust or Jerusalem's destruction and, in another, the metahistorical eschatology of Redemption, the war forced Israelis to reconfront their relationship with Jewish peoplehood and with Judaism itself. This meant rediscovering a positive relationship with both the past of the Jewish people and the present-day Jews of the Diaspora. In both instances the confrontation was colored by overtones of revelation and was articulated in terms such as *eternal unity, common fate* and *destiny.*

Nationalism and statehood, permeated by the values of modernism and secularity, were placed in a new proximity and sympathy with the values of religion and tradition—a meeting that brought with it not only something of a renewed identification but also a heightened consciousness of the distinctions between them.

The confrontation with the Land of Israel was perhaps even more obvious and possibly no less significant than the rediscovery of Jewishness. The war reconnected the nation with its ancient "promised land." Here, too, there was a sense not of simple change and innovation but of rediscovery and reawakening of long-dormant impulses. The symbolism of returning to "the land" existed on the plane of the tangible, physical return to treasured landmarks and longed-for vistas as well as the conceptual—reestablishing the connection with the spiritual and cultural associations of the land. Here, too, as was true in the rediscovery of Jewish peoplehood, an attraction to religious motifs and traditional content played a natural and even essential role.

The Six Day War seemed, then, to be the pivotal moment in the path that led from Israeliness to Jewishness, and it is in that sense we shall be dealing with it.

Nowhere, perhaps, was the impact of the June war more highly pronounced than in the camp of the Kookists—adherents of the mystic-messianic theology of Rabbi Abraham Isaac Kook as interpreted and taught by his son Rabbi Zvi Yehuda Kook and cultivated in the Merkaz Harav Yeshiva in Jerusalem. Kookism would eventually find its political expression in the movement known as Gush Emunim. The ideology of the movement would propose an alternative to the prevalent forms of Zionism that were challenged by the new circumstances created by the Six Day War. The central image that connected the Kookists and the war was the well-known photograph of paratroopers who had just won in bloody battle weeping at the Western Wall. The Kookists became instantly intoxicated by this finally manifested "inner truth," and they were quick to herald the message that this and similar instances associated with the "liberation of the land" and of Jerusalem showed that the young generation was no longer aware of its Israeliness, but was now more attuned to the Jewishness of its people. Kookism found its home wherever there was a reaction against the sabra stereotype.

The Kookists were also keen on pointing out the crude antisemitic elements that were present in attacks on Israel in the media both before the war and afterward. The tendency to mix anti-Zionism with antisemitism underscored their argument that beneath the surface of the Zionist national renaissance—claims to the contrary notwithstanding—one could discern the ancient and irreducible force of Judaism. This exilic feature of Israel's existence ("the whole world is against us") was taken as a sign that the Kookist rejection of the national-political "normality" heralded in secular Zionism had been correct. In this connection the Kookists juxtaposed 1967 with 1948 and pronounced the former as the greater event in that it marked a basic change of spiritual direction. Independence was seen as the beginning of the illusory pursuit of "normality," whereas the Six Day War brought in its wake a welcome, more authentic, return to the idea of Jewish uniqueness and chosenness.

The Six Day War, in this view, reestablished the primacy of the land and the people of Israel over the Israeli state. Insofar as the biblical land was identified with traditional Judaism, it was set up in opposition to the state, which was identified as secular, modern and nationalist. Here is the root of the distinction between state and land in all subsequent rhetoric. Joel Bin-Nun, a devout Kookist, wrote explicitly about the dilemma of the "The State of Israel Versus the Land of Israel," claiming:

> [T]he Six Day War called a halt to the automatic identification of all Jewish values with the state of Israel. The divided, sundered Land of Israel rose up triumphantly to confront the state, drunk on the spirit of its victory.[1]

In the equation that posits a direct identity between the land and the lost tradition of Judaism—and implies that both negate mainstrain Zionism—we find another explanation of why territory became the "focal point of national spiritual ferment." At the apparent pinnacle of its achievement, the state, through its military conquest of the land, furnished the tools for its own ideological defeat.

The Kookists were alive to the irony involved here and even argued that those who sought a withdrawal to the borders of 1967, ostensibly for political reasons, "actually want to withdraw spiritually to the uncomplicated notion of the state qua state. . . . But the state of Israel can no longer hide the Land of Israel under its wing."

The Six Day War raised very basic questions, then, about Israeli identity. Some of these were actually old questions that had been shunted aside and ignored but that seemed now to gain sudden urgency and relevance. There was no longer any choice but to confront the problem of how to fill the framework of national sovereignty with national content. Innumerable articles and studies have made the point that the 1967 war created a crisis of legitimization and that the prewar value structure and modes of ideological rationalization ceased at that point to be effective.[2] Particularly in the face of international criticism and the demands of the other side, the secular, statist ideology found it hard to justify Israel's position in the territories without recourse to once-rejected principles deriving from the religious heritage. The early signs of a moral decline in Israel's public life seemed to reinforce the idea that the secular national idea was an empty vessel.

The Judaization of the Israeli identity was the result of a variety of other factors as well. Among the more important of these was the demographic shift in favor of the more traditional sector of the population, including those of a generally Oriental background.[3]

Kookism would thrive in this context, would seek to sharpen the dilemmas of Israeli identity and would offer as a solution its own version of legitimization. To the Kookists this was the hour for the self-assertion of Judaism, which had been forced for so long to leave the front seat to modern nationalism. The Judaism of Torah and observance, once vanquished by secular Zionism, now had the potent forces of Jewish peoplehood and the Land of Israel to support it and carry it beyond such Zionism. Even secular Israelis had some sense of the religious import of 1967; for the Kookists it meant nothing less than a rebirth.

They declared 1967 (not 1948 nor even the traditional rabbinic dating from Creation) to be the year zero, marking the start of a new era, the era of Redemption, which had begun with the Six Day War. Thus they spoke of the October War of 1973 as having taking place in "the sixth year of Redemption." The perception of the start of a new era, of a radical shift to a revolutionary religious consciousness, was articulated in thoroughly mythical language. Several months after the battle for Jerusalem, Joel Bin-Nun wrote in the journal of the National Religious party's "young guard":

> With the taking of the Temple Mount, we were suddenly thrust forward by a gigantic hand that propelled us out of the everyday and petty reality in which we had been submerged. At the same time it seemed that we could not possibly absorb all the divine and spiritual force that cascaded onto us from heaven.[4]

Here the man of faith is transported into a cosmic event. Divine powers intervene in earthly events. The "finger of God" directs the action and even touches the actors. The victory of Israel's army was the "victory of the Sons of Light over the Sons of Darkness." The battles at the various fronts became stages in the mystic restoration of the cosmos:

> This giant step forward cannot be fathomed simply by referring to the conquest of the land. That was only the catalyst for tremendous inner forces.[5]

The radical reinterpretation of Judaism along quasi-kabbalistic lines in the light of 1967 was based on an authentic religious experience. Specifically, it was a form of mystic-messianic exaltation. Key figures in the Kookist camp tended to describe it as "revelation" or "illumination." The motif of light (*Or, Orot*), as the emanation from the divine source of all that is good, true and creative—though sometimes dangerous—is a common religious-mystical metaphor. In Jewish mysticism it is certainly a central symbol. It is just as central in Kookist culture. The 1967 War caused a "flood of light" of "overwhelming intensity" in the words of Rabbi Moshe Levinger, a leader of Gush Emunim. The uninitiated, however, were blind to this light.[6]

In the immediate aftermath of the war, the Kookists plunged themselves into a frenzy of activity. According to their own testimony, they felt as if "possessed." Their compulsive energy found an outlet in ceaseless travels up and down the country to spread the good news and to arouse support. From the recollections of those who were involved and from other telling indicators, it would appear that behind this frenetic burst of activity lay a profound experience of spiritual trauma. This was manifested in their extreme restlessness and apparent confusion, on the one hand, and their exalted and self-assured manner on the other. It is true that a great proportion of the Israeli public at large might be said to have been transported into a strangely uneasy euphoria. However, the Kookists were different not only in the extremes to which they went in expressing their feelings but also in the way their emotions were supported, given depth and direction, by a rich vein of religious ideas. The Kookist worldview, which they had already imbibed, prepared them to experience the war as a great religious event and to avoid some of the emptiness and confusion that come in the aftermath of every war, even this one. At the same time the war did a great deal to reinforce and validate the earlier Kookist ideas.

The first phase of their activity took the form of ad hoc conventions of Merkaz Harav students and graduates, disciples of Zvi Yehuda Kook and of his father, Abraham Isaac. These were spontaneous events during which individuals testified how they personally had sensed overwhelming significance in the experience of the Six Day War. A collective myth of that experience was forged. It was at these gatherings, too, that leading figures emerged, political directions were determined and organizational structures took shape.

The most important function of these reunions, however, was to foster and strengthen a collective religious consciousness couched in a shared and considerably more focused ideological terminology. This became, in turn, the basis for a heightened self-assurance and an enhanced ability to appear in public in the name of Kookist values and ideas. This was, for example, the source of the Kookist missionary campaigns in which young members of the Merkaz Harav camp set up a network of small study groups, often with great impact. Personal contact, group meetings, lectures and public events all seemed to create the impression of a rising tide of interest in, and attraction toward, faith and tradition.

The sense of spiritual ferment found expression in print as well. After the Six Day War there was a sudden (albeit short-lived) spate of Kookist publishing activity. A variety of forums were created to give expression to the surge of active discussion of religious issues, and these were added to the already-existing "establishment" publications that also served as vehicles for the new ideas.[7] Reading the veteran publications at that time, we see a new interest in spiritual matters. We find an attempt to translate religious experience into an old–new theology, on the one hand, and into concrete geopolitical terms, on the other.

Among the newly created journals, *Morashah* took pride of place. It won financial backing from the youth of the Mizrachi-Hapoel-Hamizrachi party, despite its antiestablishment tone. It was at a conference on public relations, called at the urging of some of the earlier conventions, that it had been decided to create a sophisticated journal on the model of—and in conscious opposition to—that of the kibbutz movement, *Shdemot*. The opening statement of purpose in *Morashah* declared, ''Our path is that of religious Zionism—to be even more specific, Torah-true Zionism, in the spirit of Rabbi Abraham Isaac Kook.'' In this organ, whose every page bore out the editorial declaration, Kookism finally acquired a formal, institutionalized public platform. Yet, shortly after the October War of 1973 when Kookism turned to even more militant forms of activity, *Morashah* ceased publication. It is in its pages that we today can best study early Kookism.

The Land of Israel was a central topic in *Morashah,* as in other Kookist publications. Here were published the teachings of the ancient sages and of Abraham Isaac Kook about the land that have since become the hallmark of religious Zionist discourse. Here, too, we find the early stages in the debate over, and study of, the halakhic doctrine with regard to the geography of Israel's borders. The other central issue, capping the others and absorbed into them, was that of Redemption (*geulah*). The territorial dimension is a function of messianic progress. Expansion or withdrawal in terms of square miles is equated with forward or backward movements of the ''wheels of the Chariot of Redemption.'' One finds a plethora of citations from biblical and rabbinic texts—up to and including Zvi Yehuda Kook—and articles demonstrating the link between traditional texts and current political conditions. This marks the start of a growing trend toward a ''messianic philosophy of history''—caught somewhere between exegetical (or scholarly) and journalistic styles—seeking the messianic-mystical significance in worldly events.

Scattered among such material one occasionally also finds writings from secular sources: most frequently, the God-seeking confessions of early Zionist pioneers or else maximalist and activist expressions of nonreligious Zionism in its most radically nationalist form.

Finally, the material published in such post-1967 forums included essays affirming a deep religiosity and a kabbalistic conviction in the reality of hidden processes, of ''opposites finding common roots''—love and hate, beauty and ugliness, faith and despair, heaven and earth—a theme to which we shall return.

The Kookists, like their secular Zionist counterparts, fully appreciated the central significance of the war, but they created their own interpretation of the event, epitomized in their name for it: the ''war of Redemption.'' It was no coincidence that they turned the anniversary of the day on which Jerusalem was conquered into their particular holiday, tending to remove it from the general civic context and treat it as their own. Indeed, they set up Jerusalem Day as the rival of Independence Day, subordinating the sovereignty of the state to the liberation of the Temple Mount.

The first stage in the spiritualizing of the Six Day War was the well-known "prophecy" of Zvi Yehuda Kook uttered on Independence Day in 1967 at the Merkaz Harav Yeshiva—that is to say, before the start of the emergency situation that led to the outbreak of the war. In his holiday sermon, the rabbi told of his intense longings for the sundered portions of the land. The impact of his words was tremendous and in the light of subsequent events stood out in the memory of all his devoted pupils. Those who had been present in the crowd at the yeshiva spoke of a sense of spiritual exaltation. Later, this sermon became the Kookist manifesto. Especially affecting were the following lines:

> "They divided up my land." Yes—this is true. Where is our Hebron? Do we let it be forgotten? And where are our Shechem and our Jericho? Where are they? Can we ever forsake them? All of Transjordan—it is ours. Every single inch, every square foot . . . belongs to the Land of Israel. Do we have the right to give up even one millimeter?

The Kookists do not see the war in any context apart from these words, uttered before the war, but only fully comprehended afterward. They returned from the war declaring that their rabbi's words echoed in their minds as they went into battle and that they gave them strength and lent meaning to their role in combat. They found in his sermon the obvious explanation for the miracle that occurred and, by natural extension, the sermon itself came to be seen as a miraculous event. It became a prophecy. The Kookists tend to refer to it as the birth of Gush Emunim.

Among the sources claimed by the Kookists, then, is an act of divine revelation. As in any religion, there has been an attempt to fix the unique, charismatic moment in a ritualized context, making it reoccur mimetically. The sermon has come to be read (or its recording played) at the opening to Jerusalem Day observances and is a characteristic feature of Gush Emunim culture. From the Merkaz Harav Yeshiva, the young Jerusalem Day celebrants then pour through the midnight streets of the city, closely packed, carrying along or pushing aside anything in their path, singing and dancing their way to the Old City and the Western Wall. The mass ritual concludes with prayers at dawn at the Wall.

In point of fact Jerusalem Day is a public Israeli holiday with official status; but the Kookists have succeeded in appropriating it as their own, stamping it with their own special imprint. It is this Kookization of the annual celebrations that has, quite deliberately, infused the civic culture with the central tenets of Gush Emunim's redemptive theology. With it has come the renewed debate over the proper relationship between the Jewish state and the Land of Israel—a debate once stirred up by Territorialist proposals for a Jewish state outside Palestine and by the proposals for the partition of Palestine, but which had lain dormant since 1948. This time, however, the issue has been more complex, exposing the dialectical tension between traditional Judaism and modern Zionism.

The Kookists' injection of greater sacred connotation into the Jerusalem Day observances—as a way of assuming chief sponsorship while asserting the national significance of the event—was crowned with a measure of success when the official posters announcing the schedule of events for the day began to be published with imprints, side by side, of the state of Israel and the Merkaz Harav Yeshiva.

Layers of specific ideological meaning have been added over time. Ten years after the Six Day War it was announced that the Hebrew date of Jerusalem's reunification, the twenty-eighth of Iyar, was also the date of Abraham Isaac Kook's arrival in Palestine decades earlier.* The coincidence of dates is taken to signify an inner meaning linking the two events, enhancing the religious importance of each one. An internal circular distributed at his yeshiva by Zvi Yehuda Kook spoke of the dual significance of the day that saw not only the end of "the oppression of the gentiles" (Jewish rule over the Old City) but also the presence of "a new light in Zion" responding to the call of heaven (a reference to his father). Here was a prophetic manifestation, divine intervention, prefiguring in 1904 what was to occur sixty-three years later.

The religious basis of Jerusalem Day was called into question in 1977 when it fell very close to election day. For political and logistical reasons the government, therefore, decided to advance the Jerusalem anniversary that year by a week. This elicited a strong protest by the Kookist camp. They heatedly argued that tampering with the day marking "the union of earthly and heavenly Jerusalem" for mere mundane reasons was an act of blasphemy. Their proposal to shift the date of the national election instead was not accepted, and they proceeded with a "clandestine" plan to hold Jerusalem Day observances on the original date, to "simply summon the nation to prayers at the Western Wall" in anticipation of a massive popular response. In any case, the government's decision had no force in comparison with the "inherent" meaning of the "true" Jerusalem Day. In a telegram to the prime minister, the chief rabbis and the Knesset, the spokespersons for Gush Emunim added:

> It is a holy day for all Israel. Thanksgiving and prayer have been ordained for all generations on this occasion of Redemption. In our tradition, the dates of holy observances are invested with more than external, semantic meaning. . . . Rather, they give us the chance to relive the experience: "Remember ye this day."

Here it is worth noting that the attachment of transcendent importance to the specific date of Jerusalem's reunification did not occur immediately. It was only six years after the event, in 1973, that the date acquired its fully sacred meaning. The Kookist promotion of Jerusalem Day coincided with the political initiatives undertaken by Gush Emunim. Ironically, the implications of the Yom Kippur War—involving questions of territorial withdrawal, seen as spiritual retreat—tended to heighten the critical importance now associated with the messianic events of 1967.

In actual fact, it would appear that the "war of Redemption" had little to do with religion. It was carried out by secular state organs and, to a large extent, by secular people. Its motivations, objectives and timing were dictated purely by military and national factors. It would be difficult to deny that in the Six Day War it was the secular, sovereign Israeli state that was victorious; and it would be easy to argue that this was also a victory for mainstream Zionism as opposed to Orthodox non- or anti-Zionism. The results of the war could most plausibly be seen, at least tacitly, as a vindication of the "new Israel" over the alternatives more rooted in the Jewish

---

*The number twenty-eight in Hebrew letters is formed by kaf and ḥet, also spelling the word *koaḥ* (strength), as the believers are fond of pointing out.

past. The dissonance, then, between the revelation of Redemption, as the Kookists saw it, and its accomplishment by secular agencies was profoundly challenging to the religious consciousness. It was in this paradoxical atmosphere that Kookism thrived.

Another way of grasping the problem is by reference to the question of "Redemption without repentance." From the traditional religious point of view, the victories on the temporal-spatial plane contrasted sharply with the failures on the cultural-spiritual plane of religious dedication and ethical norms. These two sides of Redemption, were understood traditionally as working in tandem even when representing essentially different aspects of messianism. It was intensely disappointing that the crucial spiritual dimension of Redemption did not follow in the wake of the territorial one—but this was the very point at which Kookism stepped in and offered a rationalization.

Those who suffered from the seeming contradiction in the fact that the external manifestations of Redemption had not been accompanied by mass repentance, that the Jews of Israel remained subject to the hegemony of heresy and sin, could draw sustenance and confidence from the Kookists' vision of a better day to come. The messianic dialectic, they taught, was leading secular Zionism to play out its final act in history, after which it would fade from the scene and be supplanted by true faith. The ability of Zionism to fulfill its historical function was predicated on its secularism. By the same token Zionism's fulfillment would exhaust its *raison d'être* and would reveal secular Zionism to have been a passing episode. In this way Redemption without repentance—the epitome of heterodoxy according to contemporary rabbinic authorities—became a Kookist tenet. The embarrassing fact of the victory of secularism in its Zionist guise was rationalized in a way that turned it into the source of religious hope.

In the fall of 1967 Eliezer Schweid wrote about the period during and after the June war as the "Time of Return to Judaism" (*yemei shivah*). Subtitled "The Religious Dimension in the Experience of Victory and Liberation," Schweid's essay reflects very clearly the cultural mood of the time in Israel, and it is representative of what was a broad section of public opinion.[8] He wrote:

> Even people whose familiarity with religious concepts is limited or who feel too estranged from them to be able to live by them, have spoken of experiencing something akin to religious feelings. . . . Some actually went so far as to feel the need to perform some ritual act—prayer or thanksgiving—beyond their perfunctory marking of festivals or their normal habits of speech. These no longer seemed sufficient and they felt constrained to look further into areas [of religious expression] which they had previously encountered only as a subject taught in school. Thus the war has a significance beyond the military and political realms.

Schweid expands on the Jewish elements that the Six Day War brought back into the Israeli consciousness. He speaks not only of a return to Jewishness in the general sense of common fate and destiny but also of "return" or repentance in the traditional religious meaning of the term: a more rigorous observance and belief. He claims that the war, in a way that was quite different from other wars (which also posed basic existential questions), was uniquely characterized by an "experience of repentance . . . [and] of Redemption."

It is difficult to escape the impression that the aftermath of 1967 was indeed a time of looking for roots or a rediscovery of identity, including a more positive attitude to religion, a search for religiosity on both the personal and the collective level. In quite a number of cases this did lead to a new identification with Judaism in its more traditional aspects. The turn to faith and acceptance of greater observance were conspicuous phenomena at the time. This took various forms: study groups in Bible and Talmud sprang up; festivals were celebrated with special fervor; secular publications—especially those with a younger readership and even on kibbutzim—carried more articles on religion, tradition and Jewish customs; and there was more frequent citation of traditional sources in public discourse. A process of religious revival was traditionally considered to be a central aspect of messianic Redemption. The apparent resurgence of religious ideas and, among some, of religious observance (*ḥazarah biteshuvah*), gave believers the confidence to believe in an imminent consummation of Redemption.

But was there really a religious revival? Schweid himself posed the question: Was this, in fact, the sign of a dramatic cultural reorientation, the return of masses to the fold, or the reconciliation of secularists with traditionalists? His answer was that the potential had been there but was hardly realized. Deeply rooted worldviews and long-established modes of behavior rarely, if ever, change in one instant, even under the impact of traumatic events, and the exhilaration of a moment cannot be fully sustained over the long run. Shortly after the war, then, Schweid concluded that the great majority of Israelis were waking up from the ''trance'' and coming back to earth. Cultural values had not really changed; the secular-religious conflict remained; and the ambivalence toward national values, on the one hand, and religious values, on the other, had not been overcome.[9]

Only the Kookists viewed things differently. In their enthusiasm they failed to notice what had by then become apparent to almost everyone: that the movement back to tradition had been of limited depth and appeal. The proportions of the phenomenon had been overexaggerated. It was highly visible against the social horizon, but quantitatively weak. It did not really entail a systematic transformation of the Israeli collective identity; it certainly failed to translate itself into Orthodox norms of behavior. When the Kookists began to realize this, however, their energy only gained momentum. Without illusions about the likelihood of mass conversions by conventional means, they started to rely more heavily and explicitly on their own mystic-messianic ideology. They held to the belief that the brief ''time of return'' was not merely a passing phase, but a true indication of the hollowness at the core of secular Zionist identity, and, consequently, they assumed the existence of a deep hunger for faith.

Against this background of rising expectations, the failure of a mass return to materialize evidently contributed to the formulation of a fully fledged ideology of paradox. The Kookist faith originally grew out of the inherent dichotomy between religion and Zionism, creating a paradoxical tension in religious Zionism. Now, this faith was maintained through a theory that responded to the prolonged duration of this paradox.

The spiritual tension with which national-religious Zionists live—more than ever in the wake of 1967—is thus a source of both frustration and encouragement. It is this that explains the enthusiasm of the Kookists in their campaign to win the nation back to Judaism: not any more, however, in the old, conventional fashion, but through a "hidden," "kabbalistic" route—the route of ultra-Zionism as opposed to that of Orthodoxy.

Paradox lies at the very source of the mystic messianism of Gush Emunim, and it has become its central value. By identifying seemingly neutral or antireligious manifestations as the very sources of messianic Redemption, this dialectical point of view becomes a means not only of "explaining" the seeming contradiction between faith and reality but also of actually inspiring greater faith. The paradox then becomes the axis of religious revival. As in the cases of early Christianity and the Jewish millenarian Sabbateans,[10] a historic development that appeared to demonstrate the failure of faith becomes the cornerstone of a new religious conception and religious vitality. The Kookist system is built on the experience of believers who refuse to accept the verdict of history proclaiming their belief to be false. The more severe the test of reality, the greater is the weight attached to the "inner essence" of things. By the same token the exegetical tendency increases and the weight of empirical reality decreases. As the paradox deepens, its religious value increases.

The characteristic expression of this paradoxical system in its Kookist version is the idea of *segulah* in Judaism, that is, the indelible and undeniable property of unconditional holiness that adheres to the Jewish people, hiding a sacred spark in their hearts. With the help of this principle, it is possible to ascribe to phenomena, which seemingly negate religion, a special nature, qualifying them for the fulfillment of a sacred mission. Thus the emphasis shifts from conventional appearances to mysterious qualities. An eminent leader of Gush Emunim had this to say about the fact that the national enterprise in Israel considers itself a revolt against traditional belief and that it involves renouncing halakhic laws:

> Since I believe in *segulah,* I consider a man undergoing a test of fire on the Golan Heights or in the Sinai a Jew in the full sense of the word, even if he had never been exposed to formal Torah education.[11]

This concept of inherent virtue is a means toward overcoming tensions and contradictions. But from the moment the profane, which had threatened religion from without, is declared the realization of the sacred, this theology becomes vulnerable in a new way to an inner tension that it may not be able to contain.

There are some other contemporary equivalents to such a theology of the profane in different religions within varied historical settings. There, too, it serves as a way to defend traditional religion in the face of a rising secularism; they, too, appropriate the secular challenge and interpret it as the supreme realization of a unique religious essence. In Christianity, especially in Protestantism after World War II, certain church circles have interpreted progressive secularization as an essentially positive development manifesting pure Christian potential.[12] Trends within Russian Orthodoxy, in the desperate struggle against the Russian revolutionary state, have at times sought a secret holy nucleus hidden in Marxism-Leninism.

A peculiar paradox-oriented mentality has made its appearance among the Kookist believers, and it sometimes expresses itself in ways that border on the ostentatious or seem deliberately designed to shock the general public. Some especially revealing examples of this tendency can be found in the believers' language and peculiarities of style. Thus, their dress tends to include unconventional, even jarring combinations. Their blue jeans, flight jackets and commando-style boots stand out conspicuously while they study the Talmud in yeshivas, whereas black skullcaps, long beards, dark jackets and extravagantly long fringed garments are visually surprising for those who see them doing guard duty in their settlements. They have also found ways to turn language to the same purpose, using such phrases expressing incongruities as: "a K-47 assault rifle and Mishnah," and so on. Their even more startling linguistic innovations include juxtaposing expressions of holiness, normally enunciated with reverence, with secular words denoting routine, materialism and even coarseness: for example, "the accountancy of the Almighty," or "divine pumping," and so on. Such expressions are endlessly repeated with apparent nonchalance, but are, in fact, intentional and conscious. The believers enjoy the shocked reaction of their listeners, who recoil from such profanization of the sacred, whereas the believers themselves are seeking to sacralize the profane. The users of these paradoxical expressions are considered spiritually superior in their community.

These illustrations—a partial testimony to the birth of a novel religious terminology—reveal an original religious code. The rhetoric of paradox hints at the tensions experienced by the believers and the contradictions inherent in the actualization of Redemption itself. The believers' passion for paradox is linked to their compulsive attraction to those phenomena in the Israeli environment whose manifest, popular and formal appearance can be seen as contrary to their hidden nature, alleged to be their real and true nature. They systematically search for cases that lend themselves to interpretation in this way and may thus support their doctrine. Thus, the dominant reality of heresy and sin has only an apparitional existence. The reality hidden behind it is that of deep and compelling faith.

A theodicy based on paradoxical laws has given the adherents of this belief system self-confidence. The paradox and their ability to come to terms with it provide them with a feeling of uniqueness and superiority vis-à-vis their environment. This sense of advantage stems from their sense of absolute freedom. Their successful struggle with the paradox has been a liberating experience, and the liberty they have tasted is intoxicating. The opportunities open to them now to contain tensions, bridge gaps and solve contradictions are exhilarating. Breaking down logical and empirical laws and transcending the limits of conventional consciousness has produced an illusion of omnipotence. The believers, nourished by the mysterious and contemptuous of the manifest and the conventional, see themselves as above this-worldly laws. They are already in the domain of a new world, secret and redeemed.

Thus, they have attained total freedom to consummate their Jewishness fully. What they fail to attain in the sociopolitical realm, they can accomplish in the religious sphere. The very frustrations brought on by the actual circumstances fill their hearts with certainty of faith, the exclusive property of the enlightened. In Kookism there is an ideological rationalization of the defeat of religion in history. It is quite natural that the mystic-messianic rationalization endeavors to shift the center of gravity away from history as such. Yet, ironically, by the same token the believers confer increased value on history. After all, it was deep within history that the holy was found to reside. The law of paradox, intended to neutralize tension in the belief system, in fact, charges it with tensions of a higher order. Gush Emunim's unique belief system remains within the traditional boundaries that employ the old concepts of religious Judaism, yet implants with them an explosive dialectic.

The 1967 war brought historic reality and messianic vision into closer proximity with each other than ever before. Yet, not only messianism but also the halakhic law now appeared to gain new relevance and, to that extent, seemed to demand greater authority. Its primacy was bound up with the conceptual replacement of the state of Israel by the Land of Israel. The halakhah had never recognized the concept of a sovereign Jewish state; certainly, it could never conceive of a *secular* Jewish state. But the Land, as opposed to the state, was a category that had significance in Talmudic terminology. It was only natural that, as the land was reconstituted, there would be a growing urge to impose a code of law whose origins were in the Land. Rabbinical pronouncements on the Land's boundaries, on settling the land, were now deemed not simply relevant, but binding. Once this occurred, the rabbis were also sought out for their views on applying halakhic norms to such other spheres as the economy, the law and social relations.

What this meant was that in 1967 a potential conflict had been reopened between halakhic law and messianic fulfillment. The path to the actualization of both had been paved by the Six Day War. The sudden opportunity to consummate Judaism's history through messianism held within it the seeds of antinomianism, placing Redemption above the Law—originally constructed for exilic conditions. Likewise, the sudden opportunity to apply halakhah to additional spheres of life presented problems of its own. It would mean putting loyal adherence to a literal interpretation of the Torah to a severe, hypernomian test, for the ancient law was hardly applicable, without adaptation, to modern conditions.

Kookism is caught between messianism and fundamentalism. Both options are attractive, but both are also potentially embarrassing. Kookism oscillates between them, finding itself caught by the one whenever it attempts to avoid the other.

Notes

This essay is an excerpted version of part of a doctoral dissertation submitted to the Department of Sociology and Anthropology of the Hebrew University in 1987. A previous section was published in *Studies in Contemporary Jewry* 2 (1986), entitled "From Religious Zionism to Zionist Religion: The Roots of Gush Emunim." That essay dealt with the period prior to 1967.

1. *Nekudah,* no. 72 (April 1984).
2. An outstanding example, one written with particular force, is the collection of essays by A. B. Yehoshua, *Bizekhut hanormaliut* (Tel Aviv: 1980).
3. See, for example, Charles Liebman, "Religion and Political Integration in Israel," *Jewish Journal of Sociology* 17 (1975).

4. *'Alei mishmeret,* no. 32 (1968).

5. Interview with Rabbi E. Waldman, by Zvi Raanan in *Gush emunim* (Tel Aviv: 1980), 175–189.

6. Interviews with Moshe Levinger by the author.

7. Among the long-established publications in this category were *Zeraim,* the Bnei Akiva youth movement's journal; *'Amudim,* the newsletter of the Religious Kibbutz Federation; and the National Religious party's youth organ, *'Alei mishmeret.*

8. Eliezer Schweid, "Yemei shivah," *Petaḥim* 1 (Tishrei 5728/1967).

9. *Ibid.*

10. See the introduction to Gershom Scholem's *Sabbatai Ṣevi: The Mystical Messiah* (Princeton: 1975).

11. Hanan Porat, in *Petaḥim* (Nisan 5735/1975).

12. See, for example, Harvey Cox, *The Secular City* (New York: 1965).

Part V

The Sephardic Pattern

12

The Religiosity of Middle Eastern Jews

Moshe Shokeid

Introduction

National myths and public policies in Israel long assumed that the country's diverse Jewish immigrant groups would all eventually, and indeed within a short span of time, be absorbed and fused into a unified social, economic, political, and cultural entity, but this expectation is now giving way to widespread doubts as to its feasibility. Some of these doubts were expressed during the 1970s in a series of studies which demonstrated not only that there were still gaps between Israelis of Middle Eastern and North African extraction (often called Sephardim or Oriental Jews) and those of European extraction (Ashkenazim), as regards occupational and residential mobility, income and educational achievements, political representation,

Earlier versions of this paper were prepared for the International Seminar on Judaism and Secular Society and the International Seminar on East and West in Israel, held at Bar-Ilan University in the summers of 1980 and 1982 respectively. I am grateful to Shlomo Deshen, Jacob Katz, Robert Chazan, and Menachem Friedman for their helpful comments.

and social prestige, but that the gaps were widening.[1] The growing disillusionment on the part of Middle Eastern Jews (North Africans included) was dramatically revealed in the 1981 general elections by the emergence of a new ethnic party, Tami, which seemed to have better prospects of success and survival than any previous ethnic party. Moreover, the results at the polls obtained by most of the other parties seemed to reflect an intensifying ethnic polarity.[2]

A growing number of sociologists have been concerned with the social, economic and political factors that have led to the emerging ethnicity in Israel, but they have usually refrained from discussing more specifically the cultural elements that characterize Israeli ethnic divisions. The sociological perspective derived from the theories of modernization of the 1950s and early 1960s, which regarded Middle Eastern Jews as representing traditional societies and cultures, and expected them inevitably to move out toward the modern axis (which was apparently represented by the veteran European and mostly secularized Israelis),[3] had been seriously challenged,[4] but no alternative theoretical framework for understanding the dynamics of cultural continuity and change had been suggested. The absence of a clear treatment of these processes has possibly been influenced by the prevailing general sociological approach, which seems to perceive emergent ethnicity as an ephemeral phenomenon of little consequence. This has been inter-

---

1. See, for example, M. Hartman and M. Eilon, "Ethnicity and Stratification in Israel" (Hebrew), *Megamot* (1975): 124–129; S. Spilerman and J. Habib, "Development Towns in Israel: The Role of Community in Creating Ethnic Disparities in Labor Force Characteristics," *American Journal of Sociology* 81 (1976): 781–812; S. Smooha, *Israel: Pluralism and Conflict* (Berkeley: University of California Press, 1978); and S. Svirsky and D. Bernstein, "Who Worked Where, for Whom and for What: Economic Development in Israel and the Emergence of an Ethnic Division of Labor" (Hebrew), *Mahbarot le'Mekhar ule'Vikoret* 4 (1980): 5–66.

2. The major contest in the 1981 general elections involved the Labor party and the Likud. It has been confirmed, however, that a higher proportion of voters of European extraction voted Labor while a higher proportion of voters of Middle Eastern extraction voted Likud. See A. Arian, "Elections 1981: Competitiveness and Polarizations," *Jerusalem Quarterly* 21 (1981): 16–20; A. Diskin, "The 1981 Elections: Public Opinion Polls," *Jerusalem Quarterly* 22 (1982): 104; Y. Peres and S. Shemer, "The Ethnic Factor in the 1981 Elections" (unpublished research report, Tel-Aviv University, 1982).

3. See, for example, S. N. Eisenstadt, *The Absorption of Immigrants* (London: Routledge & Kegan Paul, 1954); D. Weintraub and M. Lissak, "Social Integration and Change," in *Agricultural Planning and Village Community in Israel,* ed. J. Ben-David (Paris: UNESCO, 1964); and R. Bar-Josef, "Desocialization and Resocialization: The Adjustment Process of Immigrants" *International Migration Review* 2 (1968): 27–45.

4. Smooha, *Israel: Pluralism and Conflict*; D. Bernstein, "A Critical Review of a Dominant School in Israeli Sociology" (Hebrew) *Mahbarot le'Mehkhar ule'Vikoret* 1 (1978): 5–19.

preted, inter alia, in terms of the exigencies of survival and the structure of opportunity (such as the result of residential and occupational enclaves) rather than as the manifestation of a common heritage.[5] Alternatively, Gans interpreted contemporary American ethnicity in terms of "symbolic ethnicity," which influences leisure-time activity, does not need a practiced culture, and is "largely a working-class style."[6]

Leaving aside intuitive assumptions and stereotypes, we know relatively little about the cultural components that characterize the ethnic structure of contemporary Israeli society.[7] Anthropological studies of Middle Eastern immigrants have provided detailed information about specific institutional characteristics, such as the patterns of family and kinship or the patterns of communal and religious leadership in particular communities of immigrants from Tripolitania, Djerba, or the Atlas Mountains.[8] However, because of the inhibitions and limitations inherent in the methodology of intensive participant observations in small communities, the authors of these studies have usually refrained from deducing relevant trends to wider ethnic populations.

Deshen, who gave more specific attention to the status of the ethnic cultures, observed during the late 1960s and early 1970s the revival of some ethnic customs and traditions among Tunisian Jews.[9] He interpreted this phenomenon as indicating a process by which cultural ethnicity has been

5. See, for example, *Urban Ethnicity*, ed. A. Cohen, A.S.A. Monograph 12 (London: Tavistock, 1974); and W. L. Yancey, E. P. Ericksen, and R. N. Juliani, "Emergent Ethnicity: A Review and Reformulation," *American Sociological Review* 41 (1976): 391–403.

6. H. J. Gans, "Symbolic Ethnicity: The Future of Ethnic Groups and Cultures in America," *Ethnic and Racial Studies,* 1979, pp. 1–20 (the quotation in the text is from p. 3).

7. See also the discussion of the state of research on Israeli ethnicity in H. E. Goldberg, "Introduction: Culture and Ethnicity in the Study of Israeli Society," *Ethnic Groups* 1 (1977): 163–186.

8. See, for example, S. Deshen, *Immigrant Voters in Israel: Parties and Congregations in a Local Election Campaign* (Manchester: Manchester University Press, 1970); M. Shokeid, *The Dual Heritage: Immigrants from the Atlas Mountains in an Israeli Village* (Manchester: Manchester University Press, 1971; new ed., New Brunswick, N.J.: Transaction, 1985); H. E. Goldberg, *Cave Dwellers and Citrus Growers: A Jewish Community in Libya and Israel* (Cambridge: Cambridge University Press, 1972); S. Deshen and M. Shokeid, *The Predicament of Homecoming: Cultural and Social Life of North African Immigrants in Israel* (Ithaca and London: Cornell University Press, 1974); M. Shokeid and S. Deshen, *Distant Relations: Ethnicity and Politics Among Arabs and North African Jews in Israel* (New York: Praeger and Bergin, 1982).

9. S. Deshen, "Political Ethnicity and Cultural Ethnicity in Israel during the 1960s," in *Urban Ethnicity,* ed. A. Cohen (London: Tavistock, 1974), pp. 281–309.

replacing political ethnicity among Middle Eastern immigrants. These observations and interpretations suited the euphoric, optimistic national mood following the 1967 war, which for some time camouflaged the persistence of social gaps. A few years later, Weingrod suggested the emergence of a working-class culture which involves Middle Eastern Jews in particular.[10] He related this culture mainly to certain typical leisure activities, such as the growing popularity of national ethnic festivals, the enthusiastic attendance at football games, the popularity of particular forms of music, etc. This observation requires, however, a closer investigation of various dimensions of behavior that may constitute a more complex definition of culture.

I do not intend to propose a specific definition of culture here. There is no doubt, however, that we cannot conceive of Jewish society at any stage of its history without considering the Jewish religion as a major component of its cultural presentation. The aim of this article is to indicate some trends in the cultural processes that characterize contemporary ethnic developments in Israel, as demonstrated by the role of religion in the life of Middle Eastern Jews. The religious component of Jewish culture has become increasingly problematic and a source of acute tension in recent generations as a result of the decline of social and cultural homogeneity in Jewish society at its various centers. This trend has been noticeable in Europe since the emergence of the Jewish Enlightenment (Haskalah) in the eighteenth century.[11] Among Middle Eastern or North African Jewry, however, the process started much later, in some places at the end of the nineteenth century, in other places not until the beginning of the twentieth century or even later.[12] In Israel, the question of the role to be played by religion in the nation's life has become a major source of conflict. A large segment of the population (and particularly those associated with the socialist elite which dominated the country for many decades) sees religious orthodoxy as an archaic survival of little relevance. Ashkenazi orthodoxy in its various shades, however, has demonstrated extraordinary viability. Apart from the ultra-Orthodox, who are concentrated in exclusive communities (such as Jerusalem, Benei-Berak, etc.), the more moderate "neo-Orthodox" group seems to have strength-

---

10. A. Weingrod, "Recent Trends in Israeli Ethnicity," *Ethnic and Racial Studies* 2 (1979): 55–65.

11. See J. Katz, *Tradition and Crisis: Jewish Society at the End of the Middle Ages* (New York: Free Press of Glencoe, 1961), pp. 245–274.

12. See, for example, the description of the process of change among the Jews in Morocco by A. Weingrod, "Moroccan Jewry in Transition" (Hebrew), *Megamot* 10 (1960): 193–208.

ened its hold on the younger generation,[13] as witnessed by the recent expansion of its modern rabbinical high schools (*yeshivot tichoniyot*) and the growing involvement of its youth with the Gush Emunim nationalistic movement.[14]

We are not concerned here with an analysis of religious change, as expressed, for example, in terms of secularization versus traditionalism. For the purposes of the present discussion we consider religious behavior to be an integral part of a broader cultural and social repertoire, although it is often arbitrarily separated from its more comprehensive context and analyzed independently in exclusively religious terms. Just as the changing position of religion in any particular group reflects on processes mainly related to the religious domain, it reflects no less on fluctuations in the status and the existential circumstances of the people involved. Thus, for example, A. Cohen demonstrated the Islamic religious revival which supported the ethnic-economic interests of the entrepreneurial Hausa traders in Yoruba towns.[15] In a study of a transplanted Atlas Mountains Jewish community, I found that the field of religious activity is a very sensitive vehicle for expressing the changing circumstances, aspirations, and achievements of individuals and groups.[16] This was demonstrated by changes in the style of worship. A different situation is described by Deshen, who revealed that the abandonment of religious symbols by Tunisian immigrants in an Israeli town was a result of their considering themselves religiously unworthy to perform the observances related to these symbols.[17] Their feeling of religious unworthiness reflected, however, a wider notion of failure and self-depreciation derived from the circumstances of their new environment. The role played by religion in expressing social developments and political conflicts has again been recently demonstrated in various parts of the Middle East, Israel included. Thus, on the one hand, certain revivalist religious trends have been identified among young Muslims in Israeli villages and

13. S. Deshen, "Israeli Judaism: Introduction to the Major Patterns," *International Journal of Middle East Studies* 9, (1978): 141–169.

14. A movement mainly dedicated to the establishment of Jewish settlements on the West Bank.

15. A. Cohen, *Customs and Politics in Urban Africa* (London: Routledge & Kegan Paul, 1969).

16. M. Shokeid, "An Anthropological Perspective on Ascetic Behavior and Religious Change" in *The Predicament of Homecoming: Cultural and Social Life of North African Immigrants in Israel,* by S. Deshen and M. Shokeid (Ithaca: Cornell University Press, 1974), pp. 64–94.

17. S. Deshen, "The Varieties of Abandonment of Religious Symbols," ibid., pp. 173–189.

towns,[18] and, on the other hand, religious activism among young, mostly Ashkenazi Jews has been the energizing force behind the establishment of new settlements on the West Bank. It is therefore interesting to find out whether and how Middle Eastern Jews express in religious terms their status in Israeli society.

Hypothesis and Method

The first encounter between Middle Eastern immigrants and the country's secularized dominant sector, as represented in particular by the major national bureaucracies, must have been a traumatic experience for the newcomers. Moreover, their concurrent meeting with the Ashkenazi religious establishment was by no means genial. Although the latter provided them with religious services and tried to recruit their youth to its educational institutions, the contacts between the Ashkenazi religious establishment and the Middle Easterners were disappointing, often painful, and ultimately of little consequence. On the whole, Ashkenazi orthodoxy in its various shades had little regard for the standards of religiosity and the ethnic traditions of the newly arrived co-religionists who had become its clients. Therefore, it could not reinforce their traditional religious patterns and did not succeed in recruiting many of the younger immigrants.

Social scientists assumed that Middle Eastern Jews would tend to assimilate with the dominant Ashkenazi segment of Israeli society. The observations providing the basis for the prediction that the Middle Eastern Jews would eventually be secularized were, however, greatly influenced by a perspective of religiosity which was anchored in the Ashkenazi tradition of orthodoxy as experienced or stereotyped by the researchers. This perspective inevitably leads to the conclusion that Middle Eastern Jews will eventually abandon their religious commitment completely, a conclusion supported by the absence of noticeable trends of religious revival and the lack of institutions of religious education among Middle Eastern Jews, in contrast to the remarkable vitality observed among the various sectors of Ashkenazi orthodoxy.[19] As a result of these assumptions, the newcomers

18. M. Shokeid and S. Deshen, *Distant Relations: Ethnicity and Politics Among Arabs and North African Jews in Israel* (new York: Praeger and Bergin, 1982), p.161.

19. See, for example, the discussion of religious education among Ashkenazi and Middle Eastern Jewry by S. Deshen, "Religion among Middle Eastern Immigrants in Israel," in *Israel: A Developing Society,* ed. A. Arian (Assen: Van Gorcum, 1980), pp. 235–246.

became to an extent "religiously invisible." Against this evaluation of the religious situation among Middle Eastern Jews, we argue that they have nevertheless developed a strategy of cultural accommodation with the surrounding dominant society, a strategy also employed by Middle Eastern Jews in earlier centuries. According to our observations, this has produced a religious path which appears to be midway between Ashkenazi orthodoxy, on the one hand, and Ashkenazi secularism, on the other. The symbolic presentation of this style is distinctive and appealing to the extent that it carries the potential of influencing political life in Israel, but it is not provocative and exclusivist to the extent of contradicting the national ideal of social integration. These observations, we hope, may also expand our understanding of the role and strategy of emergent ethnicity in contemporary civilization in general.

The data I draw upon are varied and it may not always satisfy a strict doctrinal approach. I report on participant observations which I carried out during the late 1960s and late 1970s in villages inhabited by Moroccan immigrants. During 1979 I carried out observations in several synagogues located in two neighborhoods of Tel-Aviv, and in 1981 I interviewed supporters of the new ethnic party, Tami. I also draw upon ethnographic data produced by other anthropologists, the available sociological surveys and interviews with leading Middle Eastern Jews recorded by the mass media. My discussion is supported by the reconstructions of Jewish life in the Middle East provided by historians and social scientists.

Precepts versus Tradition

During the 1950s Israeli sociologists, mainly involved with the then dominant theories of modernization, which often sought the variables most conducive to the accommodation of traditional societies with Western technology and culture, did not show much interest in the study of Middle Eastern Jews' religiosity. In the 1960s, however, a few sociologists began to include in their surveys questions about the religious attitudes of Middle Eastern Jews.[20] Thus the data produced from a national sample of eleventh-grade school students reported by Herman show that while Middle Eastern children were less religiously inclined than their parents, the proportion of

20. For example, J. Matras, *Social Change in Israel* (Chicago: Aldine, 1965) and S. N. Herman, *Israelis and Jews: The Continuity of an Identity* (New York: Random House, 1970).

Middle Eastern youth who considered themselves religious was higher than among Ashkenazi youth (34 percent vs. 22 percent). In addition, considerably more Middle Eastern youth defined themselves as *mesoratiim* (lit. "traditional")—a common term for believers who observe religious precepts selectively—44 percent verses 22 percent among Ashkenazi youth. The survey also revealed noticeable differences among the various groups of Middle Eastern Jews: Yemenite youth were highest in considering themselves religious (63 percent),[21] North African youth second on the scale (44 percent) and other Middle Eastern youth came lowest on this scale (21 percent). However, the majority of Middle Eastern youth who did not consider themselves religious defined themselves as *mesoratiim*.

The expansion of anthropological research in Israel since the mid-1960s had been accompanied by an increasing interest in the religious life of Middle Eastern Jews. In a study of an immigrant town, Deshen reported on the viability of ethnic synagogues: the regular participants, however, were mainly youngsters under fifteen years of age and adults above thirty-five.[22] Thus the generation of young adults was absent. Another observation, mentioned earlier, indicated that the immigrants' notion of religious depreciation reflected their deteriorating position in other spheres of life. We may assume that this low self-esteem also influenced parental authority over children's religious behavior, which may explain their absence from synagogue activities as well as the growing intergenerational disparity in religious conformity, as reported by Herman.[23] It is not surprising that ten years later Deshen reported that the ethnic synagogue had lost most of its thriving viability.[24] Its regulars appeared to be mostly aged, while the younger generations participated only occasionally and mainly at festivals and family celebrations.

Interpreting these observations, Deshen employed Sharot's comparison of the level of acculturation with the host culture among Jewish communities in Europe, the Middle East, and the Far East.[25] Middle Eastern Jewry occupies a midway position on a scale of acculturation whose extremes

21. Similar findings, based upon a study of Yemenites in an urban suburb, were reported by J. Katz and Z. Zloczower, "Ethnic Continuity in the Second Generation: A Report on Yemenites and Ashkenazim in a Small Israeli Town" (Hebrew), *Megamot* 9 (1958): 187–200.

22. S. Deshen, "The Ethnic Synagogue: Patterns of Religious Change in Israel" (Hebrew), in *The Integration of Immigrants from Different Countries of Origin in Israel,* ed. S. N. Eisenstadt and A. Zloczower (Jerusalem: Magnes Press, 1969), pp. 66–73.

23. Herman, *Israelis and Jews.*

24. Deshen, "Religion Among Middle Eastern Immigrants."

25. S. Sharot, *Judaism: A Sociology* (London: David & Charles, 1976).

represent, at one end, the high acculturation of Far Eastern Jewry (such as the now defunct Chinese Jewry) and at the other end, the Jewish communities of Europe, which until the nineteenth century remained remarkably segregated from their host societies. Sharot argues that the general disposition of the host religious doctrine toward minority religions determined the degree of the Jewish acculturation: the greater the tolerance demonstrated by the host society, the stronger the tendency on the part of the Jewish community toward accommodation with the host doctrine. This analysis is supported by the observation that the traditions, rituals, and beliefs of most Middle Eastern Jewish communities often displayed elements in common with those of their Muslim neighbors. To this assessment of the characteristics of the religiosity of Middle Eastern Jews, Deshen adds that oral tradition, as opposed to written tradition, played a greater role in the transmission of Middle Eastern Jewish culture. That is to say, as compared to East European Jews, Middle Eastern Jews were less likely to regard learned texts as depositories of culture. He therefore concluded that the religion of Middle Eastern Jewry was less differentiated externally, vis-à-vis Gentile culture, as well as internally, from other facets of Jewish culture.[26] The conclusions derived from these studies may provide an explanation for the patterns of religious behavior observed among Middle Eastern Jews in Israel. Since they are apparently predisposed to a relatively easy accommodation with the cultural pressures of their host society, whether Muslim or Israeli-Ashkenazi, they soon acculturated to the secular culture of the dominant veteran segment of Israeli society and accommodated with no protest to the attitude of superiority demonstrated by the orthodox establishment.

An anthropological study which I carried out during the late 1960s and again during the late 1970s among Moroccan immigrants in villages revealed a phenomenon different from what was observed in the town environment. The economic affluence afforded by farming, which eradicated the old communal stratification, enabled the families that had once been poor to utilize the religious sphere as a means of displaying their achievements in Israel, as, for example, through the acquisition of expensive Torah scrolls. Moreover, all generations participated regularly in synagogue activities. My observations revealed, however, persistent difficulties in the functioning of the traditional Moroccan religious leaders.[27]

26. Deshen, "Religion Among Middle Eastern Immigrants," pp. 241–242.
27. Shokeid, *The Dual Heritage*, and "The Decline of Personal Endowment of Atlas Mountains Religious Leaders in Israel," *Anthropological Quarterly* 52 (1979): 186–197.

In many parts of Morocco religious leadership was exercised by scholars whose authority was vested as much in their personal charismatic traits as in their family patrimony (i.e., *zekhut avot*—"merit of the fathers"). The attribute of *zekhut avot* was hereditary but at the same time was an inherent trait of moral superiority possessed by those who chose the religious calling. Such leaders were not formally appointed and did not receive a regular salary, but they were reputed for their extraordinary deeds and the power of their blessings. The characteristics of this leadership had a parallel in the religious leadership of the Muslim host society: *zekhut avot* might be compared to *baraka* ("blessing"), the virtue of sacredness attributed to the Moroccan *marabout* and his living descendants.[28] It was not easy for leaders of this type to accommodate to Israel's bureaucratic religious system. Moreover, while in Morocco the local communities had each supported several religious leaders who catered individually to their clients, in Israel the Ministry of Religious Affairs appoints only one salaried rabbi to each community. The unsuitability of the traditional leaders for this highly formalized system, as well as the tensions and conflicts resulting from the inevitable competition between the candidates who were available for such appointments, often led to the departure of the authentic communal leadership, whose members settled in the more heterogeneously composed new towns. Meanwhile, the ministry appointed its own candidates, who often did not gain the respect and affection of their congregants.[29]

During the late 1970s I carried out observations in two suburbs of Tel Aviv. One was a decaying public housing project dating from the 1950s. Its residents, of low socioeconomic status, were mainly of Middle Eastern extraction. The second suburb, situated nearby, was mainly composed of privately owned apartments, and its residents, a younger population of both European and Middle Eastern extraction, had moved in since the early 1970s. Eight ethnic synagogues were regularly operating in the old neighborhood: one Iranian, one Afghani, one Iraqi, two Egyptian, two East European, and a joint congregation of Tripolitanians and Moroccans.[30] Although spacious and richly decorated, the synagogues were usually poor-

---

28. See, for example, C. Geertz, *Islam Observed: Religious Developments in Morocco and Indonesia* (New Haven: Yale University Press, 1968), p. 50.

29. Shokeid, "Decline of Personal Endowment of Atlas Mountains Religious Leaders."

30. The suburb was mainly settled in the early 1950s, before the major immigration from Morocco in the mid-1950s. Therefore, the small number of residents of Moroccan extraction, who could not establish a separate Moroccan congregation, joined the Tripolitanian synagogue.

ly attended by the younger generations, who had moved out to better neighborhoods or did not feel obligated to attend services. The scene seemed to confirm Deshen's observations about the decline of ethnic synagogues. Nevertheless, these observations did not appear to represent an irreversible process.

In the nearby new neighborhood, I observed two ethnic congregations—one Moroccan and the other Yemenite. The congregants assembled in the local school, where they were allowed to use two classrooms for the daily early morning and evening prayers as well as for the Sabbath and festival services. The congregants were exerting pressures on the Ministry of Religious Affairs and the Tel Aviv Municipal Religious Council to provide the sites and financial means necessary in order to build proper separate synagogues. The Moroccan congregation, which I observed more closely, had been started by a forty-year-old congregant from Casablanca. He was the son of a religious leader in Tafilalt and had brought along a Torah scroll when he came to Israel in the early 1960s. On arrival he had settled in a development town, where he was employed in various teaching and clerical jobs. He moved to Tel Aviv in 1976 and soon after started to organize a *minyan* (ten adult males) for regular services. At first the *minyan* met at his home, but with the growth of the congregation it was allowed to operate in the school. In 1979 the congregation already owned four Torah scrolls, which had been provided by the ministry and by individual residents. When I attended Sabbath morning services during July (the peak of the summer season), twenty young and older men were present. The leader told me that usually thirty men attended services regularly, "but now there are some members who prefer to go to the beach." He added that he was careful not to burden the younger congregants with heavy religious demands. He knew that some of them did not wear a skullcap on weekdays and probably drove cars on the Sabbath, "but what is really important is that they come to the synagogue." He also told me that on the High Holidays many more residents of Moroccan extraction asked to participate in the services. On these occasions the services were held in the school's gymnasium. The holiday services provided the congregation with new recruits who sometimes became regulars. He did not hesitate to recruit new congregants whom he knew "were not particularly religious." Thus, for example, a regular congregant of about thirty years old told me that he did not wear a skullcap on weekdays but in the last few years had stopped driving his car on the Sabbath. "I keep the tradition which I got at Father's home," he ended as a sort of explanation.

At the end of Sabbath prayers the congregants went together to perform a short ceremony at the home of a non-member family which was mourning the loss of an elderly relative. On the way the leader mentioned that the congregants and other residents often invited him to perform family rituals and also consulted with him on various personal matters. He ended the conversation with the statement: "They treat me like a rabbi." Although the appearance and bearing of this congregational leader were "modern," his performance was very similar to that of traditional Moroccan religious leaders. His authority was personal, rather than based on formal criteria of learning and ordination, and also seemed to contain some features of *zekhut avot*.

During the High Holidays, the synagogues in the old neighborhood came to life. This phenomenon of religious revival was particularly noticeable among the Iraqi residents. The Iraqi synagogue, which was poorly attended most of the year, was fully packed, including many young adults and youth. Moreover, a new congregation was organized for the holiday season in the gymnasium of the local school. In addition, crowds of men, women, and children gathered around the synagogues during the services, so that each one appeared to be the center of a lively communal festival. Within the synagogues, large sums of money were contributed for the right to perform various honored parts during the service. The emergent congregations manifested noticeable features of communal bonds.[31] On Succoth (Tabernacles), when the attendance dropped considerably, I carried on a conversation with a group of regular congregants about religious life in Iraq and Israel. The beadle, an impressive man in his early sixties, argued somewhat impatiently: "There is no difference; it is all a matter of family comportment. If the father attends the synagogue, the children go along. But if the mother spends her time playing cards and the father whiles his time away in similar pursuits, the children will do just the same. And there are also the uncles whose behavior carries some influence as well. So you see, it all depends on the blood that runs in the family." He added that attendance at the synagogue in Iraq was also not regular, "but Rosh Hashanah and Yom Kippur are different days!" He was thus implying that in Iraq also, the attendance of congregants on the festivals was much more impressive.

---

31. This type of High Holidays communal congregation differs from that observed in many Ashkenazi synagogues, where the swollen congregations during the festivals are usually composed of unrelated participants.

Another congregant, in his early fifties, reacted as follows: "In Israel there are many parties [*miflagot*]: Iraqis, Iranians, Egyptians, etc. Everyone establishes his own synagogue; there is even another Iraqi synagogue here [on the High Holidays]. But on weekdays you can't assemble a *minyan!*" Although the latter expressed some bitterness about the organization of religious life in Israel, neither man complained about changes in the extent of religiosity among their compatriots, nor did they look back nostalgically.

The personal experiences of the historian Y. Nini are revealing in this context, reflecting similar characteristics among Yemenite Jews. He was born in a veteran village of Yemenite residents, which he left at a later stage for a nearby town. He was often questioned by observant older relatives about his absence from the synagogue services on the Sabbath. He answered in astonishment that he could not attend on the Sabbath because of the distance of the synagogue from his home. With no hesitation they suggested that he should come by car and park near the entrance to the village. He was also invited by relatives to participate in the Sabbath and festival services in another village whose residents had arrived from Yemen in 1948. They also suggested that he lead the prayers on the festivals. They knew he could not accept their invitation unless he came by car on these occasions. Eventually he came by car, parking at the center of the village. He was warmly received and was treated during the service as a guest of honor.[32]

Pertinent support for our observations is provided by Tessler, who carried out a study in Morocco during the early 1970s.[33] He reports that most of the Jews who remained in Morocco's towns (many of whom had migrated from villages), "are observant, but often by tradition rather than conviction" (p. 371). Ninety-two percent of his respondents kept *kashrut* at home, sixty percent attended synagogue every Sabbath, but only twenty-five percent observed the Sabbath strictly. When they were asked to report on aspects of daily life which most frequently reminded them that they were Jewish, the majority pointed out factors relating to family, friends, and the social milieu as often as those relating to worship and observance. This information recalls the many interviews with Jews of Moroccan extraction (the largest group of Middle Eastern immigrants) on Israeli radio and televi-

32. I am grateful to Prof. Yehuda Nini of Tel-Aviv University, who gave me permission to publish this information.

33. M. A. Tessler, "The Identity of Religious Minorities in Non-Secular States: Jews in Tunisia and Morocco and Arabs in Israel," *Comparative Studies in Society and History* 20 (1978): 359–374.

sion or appearing in the daily newspapers. The interviewees recurrently confess their attachment to *masoret* (lit. "tradition"). Such statements are often made by leading young figures who are not considered religious by most listeners and readers. For example, Mr. Shaul Ben-Simhon, president of the Association of Moroccan Jews, stated in a newspaper interview:[34] "Although I smoke on the Sabbath, I adhere to tradition [*ani mesorati*]. I am secularized, nevertheless I fast on Yom Kippur. I attend synagogue during the festivals, and I perform *kiddush* [the blessing over wine] every Sabbath. I consider the Sabbath feast as holy of holy [*kodesh hakodeshim*], and I dedicate the Sabbath completely to the family [*Shabbat kodesh lamish-pachah*]."[35] A similar attitude was reported by Mr. Raphael Edri, who at the time of the interview (1979) was the manager of a large national building concern and is presently a Labor member of the Knesset. He also defined himself as "traditional" (*mesorati*). He told his interviewer[36] that, although he drives a car on the Sabbath, he often dons phylacteries.[37] "It has been planted in our blood," he explained and continued: "My children attend a secular school, but during the Sabbath feast I make the blessing over the wine and the children wear skullcaps." Most revealing is Aharon Abu Hatzeira, son of the most venerated religious leader of Moroccan Jewry, who at the time of the following observation was serving as minister of religious affairs. At a political rally which he held on the campus of Bar-Ilan University[38] before the 1981 general elections, soon after he broke away from Mafdal (the National Religious party), he explained the meaning of the name of the new party he headed, Tami, whose initials stand for *Tenu'at Masoret Yisrael* (The Movement of Israel's Tradition): "Mafdal opened its ranks to those who observe *taryag mitzvot* [the 613 commandments prescribed in the Pentateuch; the word *taryag* is made up of the Hebrew letters *taf* = 400, *resh* = 200, *yod* = 10, *gimmel* = 3]. But there are

---

34. Levy Itzhak Hayerushalmi, *Ma'ariv* weekend supplement, Nov. 9, 1979, p. 30.

35. The Sabbath ritual and meals are made particularly noticeable by a family's symbolic presentation. Thus, for example, although women are exempt from performing positive precepts whose execution is bound to a specific time, they are obliged to observe the sanctification of the Sabbath. The primary *kiddush* is recited on the eve of the Sabbath before the start of the meal (see, for example, *Encyclopaedia Judaica*).

36. Hayerushalmi, *Ma'ariv* weekend supplement, Nov. 9, 1979, p. 30.

37. It seems that the interviewees attributed an equal value to most religious actions, as well as to their transgressions. Thus, for example, the *kiddush,* smoking on the Sabbath, fasting on Yom Kippur, the wearing of a skullcap, driving on the Sabbath, and donning phylacteries are presented as equal alternatives.

38. June 3, 1981.

many people who do not observe all the *mitzvot* [precepts], yet they do consider themselves Jews as the followers of Israel's tradition. Why should we close our ranks and exclude them? *Taf mitzvot* [400 precepts] or *resh yod mitzvot* [210 precepts] are also sufficient!!" A similar interpretation of Tami's ideology was offered to me by a young school principal whose family arrived in 1956 from the Atlas Mountains: "Tami is a party which cherishes tradition [*Tami miflagah mesoratit*]. Oriental Jews [*edot hamizrah*] are not extremists: they did not reside in the ghetto. If the Arab grew long hair, the Jew cut his hair and left a beard only. If the Arab wore a white gown, the Jew wore a black gown instead. But the Jew lived *with* [*hai 'im*] the Arab!" Referring to the complex reality of Jewish life in many Muslim countries, he was describing both a philosophy and a strategy of existence which had sustained Jewish cultural survival through an unabashed accommodation with social and cultural constraints (as forcefully phrased in his statement: "But the Jew lived with the Arab"). He was at the same time implying that the Ashkenazim tend toward extremism, as demonstrated both by their orthodoxy and by their secularism.[39]

Quite in line with this type of religiosity is the continuing popularity, particularly among North African Jews, of pilgrimages to the tombs of venerated scholars and saints, whether of ancient or more recent vintage. This phenomenon has been noticeable since the first years of immigration, the period which seemed to reflect most profoundly the weakening of religion in the life of Middle Eastern Jewry. Thus, for example, by the early 1960s the pilgrimage to the tomb of Rabbi Simon bar Yohai in Meron on Lag B'Omer was already the largest spontaneous gathering in the country. More than 100,000 pilgrims, the majority of Moroccan extraction, came to the annual celebration.[40] Tunisian Jews also hold lavish celebrations in honor of their late scholars.[41] The pilgrimages and celebrations attracted a

39. He went on to explain the pattern of voting in his village (composed of Moroccan settlers), which was divided between Tami and Likud (Premier Begin's party coalition). He thought that those who voted for Likud had acted against their own economic interests, since as farmers they were more likely to prosper under a Labor government, "but the propaganda presented the Labor party as the old Mapai [the Labor party, mainly under Ben-Gurion's leadership]. Mapai represents secularization! This is the party which, many years ago when the settlers arrived in the country, was suspected of prohibiting the learning of the Torah and which was enthusiastic in conscripting girls to the army." In accordance with this interpretation, the Labor party was now rejected because of its image as representing extreme secularism.

40. Shokeid, "Anthropological Perspective on Ascetic Behavior and Religious Change."

41. Deshen, "Memorial Celebrations of Tunisian Immigrants," pp. 95–121.

noticeably large number of younger people. Drawn, among other things, by the entertainment and social activities which the gatherings offered, the younger people were participating in these activities at the very time when they were neglecting synagogue life (as indicated by Deshen). The popularity of the pilgrimages continued in spite of the objections of the religious establishment, which also in North Africa had unsuccessfully objected to this phenomenon of folk religion. Manifestations of folk religion have not decreased since the 1960s. On the contrary, new pilgrimage sites have become popular. Particularly noteworthy are the North African scholars and saints whose spirits have apparently moved to Israel in recent years, as revealed in the dreams of their disciples. Ben-Ami, for example, observed that the worship of saints intensifies in times of crisis.[42] Immediately after the 1973 war he recorded instances of young soldiers and their parents expressing gratitude to family saints for the miracles they had performed on the battlefield.

Besides the spontaneous revival of traditional patterns of folk religion, a new type of ethnic-religious celebration has been evolving since the late 1960s: the Moroccan Memuna, the Kurdish Saharanei, and the Iranian Ruze-Baque. Although based on traditional elements, these celebrations have been greatly encouraged by the Israeli political establishment.[43] The largest celebration, the Memuna, on the day after Passover, has been held in Jerusalem.[44] The Saharanei celebration, which began during the 1970s, is held during Succoth at a more secluded country site.[45] The Ruze-Baque, the most recent of the celebrations, is also held on the day after Passover, in Ramat-Gan's National Park. These gatherings, which originally were family and communal events, have been transformed into nationwide ethnic-political festivals. They are regularly attended by national leaders and politicians, including the president, the prime minister, and the leader of the opposition. Although the activities at these celebrations bear little resemblance to the traditional family and communal festivities in Morocco,

42. I. Ben-Ami, "The Folklore of War: The Motif of Saints" (Hebrew), in *Dov Sadan*, ed. S. Verssess et al. (Tel Aviv: Hakibbutz Hameuhad, 1977), pp. 87–104.

43. A. Weingrod, "Recent Trends in Israeli Ethnicity."

44. For the origins and patterns of the Memuna, see, for example, H. E. Goldberg, "The Memuna and Minority Status of Moroccan Jews," *Ethnology* 17 (1978): 75–87, and Shokeid, *The Dual Heritage*, p. 32.

45. J. Halper and H. Abramovitch, "The Saharanei Celebration in Kurdistan and Israel" in *Jews of the Middle East: Anthropological Perspectives on Past and Present*, ed. S. Deshen and M. Shokeid (Tel Aviv: Schocken, 1984).

Kurdistan, and Iran, both the organizers and the participants perceive them as part of their diaspora heritage. This heritage is so intertwined with the religious aspects of the celebrations[46] that in 1980, accepting the inevitable, the Sephardi chief rabbi publicly gave his blessing to the Memuna.[47]

Familial and Communal Anchorage of Religious Action

The data suggest that religious vitality differs according to the extent of homogeneity or heterogeneity in the ethnic composition of settlements. Thus, a larger percentage of youth seem to participate in synagogue life among ethnic groups whose members are more concentrated in villages or urban suburbs.[48] But religion is not dying out with the passing of the older generation in the more heterogeneous settlements. Despite the shattering cultural crisis that Middle Eastern Jewry experienced in Israel, which involved, among other things, a depreciation in the status of their religious leaders and a diminution in the authority of religious observances in daily life, the religious domain still forms an important element in the cognitive, perceptive, and affective layers of social existence for a considerable portion of Middle Eastern Jewry.

In order to clarify these propositions we will first elaborate the sociological definition which indicates the features of religious activity among Middle Eastern Jews. The definition, largely developed by Deshen, relates to the minimal differentiation of religion from other cultural domains among Middle Eastern Jews.[49] This definition, which has greatly contributed to our understanding of Middle Eastern Jewish religiosity, fails, however, to consider the extent and the consequences of Middle Eastern Judaism's anchorage in the family and the community web of commitments. We argue that this type of lesser differentiation between religion and other social domains, which has deeply anchored Middle Eastern Judaism in familial and communal action, offers the religious domain indispensable support under

46. The Ruze-Baque, however, does not as yet carry any noticeable symbols of religious life.

47. There are two chief rabbis in the country, an Ashkenazi and a Sephardi. This system of rabbinical leadership was established during the British Mandate in Palestine.

48. This may explain, for example, the higher frequency of self-designations as religious among Yemenite youth as opposed to North Africans and members of other groups.

49. Deshen, "Religion Among Middle Eastern Immigrants in Israel," p. 241.

changing circumstances that deprive religion of many of its own resources. This perspective on the structure and content of religious action leads us toward a different interpretation of contemporary observations of Middle Eastern Jewish religiosity and toward a different evaluation of the prospects for religious life among Middle Eastern Jewry.

In Muslim countries, several factors related to the social environment and to material existence lent much binding force to the individual's familial and communal commitments. Genealogical bonds and territorial ascription were among the most important indicators of the social position of the individual in Muslim society.[50] Although the Jews did not adopt the ideological elements that sustained this system, the organizational components of the host society were, nevertheless, incorporated to some extent into Jewish society. The importance of genealogical and territorial bonds was particularly noticeable in small, remote, and isolated Jewish communities. Moreover, in many parts of the Muslim world, the weakness of the central political organization was reflected in the inability of the Jews to develop national or regional organizations. These constraints naturally buttressed the familial and communal dimensions in the composition of the individual's Jewish identity. The essential position of the family and the community is also indicated in the style of Middle Eastern synagogue services; for example, the seating arrangements, and the social activities that take place in the synagogue. Thus, all congregants, including children, participate as soloists in leading sections of the service, regardless of their musical skills or religious competence. The congregants are mainly seated along the walls of the synagogue hall facing each other, in contrast to the seating arrangements in Ashkenazi synagogues, where the congregants sit in rows facing the holy ark, and consequently can only observe the backs of most of the other congregants. Similarly, in the Middle Eastern synagogue service, those who have been called to take part in the reading of the scrolls of the Law make a round of the hall and greet each congregant before returning to their seats. The various modes of greeting (e.g., shaking hands, kissing cheeks, kissing on the brow) reflect the particular relationship with each congregant: kinship, friendship, and deference.[51] Traditionally, the old men in the

---

50. See, for example, the conception of Moroccan social organization as analyzed by L. Rosen, "Social Identity and Points of Attachment," in *Meaning and Order in Moroccan Society*, eds. C. Geertz, H. Geertz, and L. Rosen (Cambridge: Cambridge University Press, 1979), pp. 19–111.

51. See S. D. Goitein, *A Mediterranean Society*, 4 vols. (Berkeley: University of California

community, regardless of their religious competence and economic and social position, were treated with respect and were attributed with the power of blessing reminiscent of the reverence reserved for religious scholars and sacred objects. The deference expressed toward the old men buttressed their position as heads of their families and enforced family loyalties.

Economic life, however, more directly affected the patterns of religious life, social comportment, and identity. Itinerant peddlers and craftsmen who stayed for days, weeks, and even months with their Muslim clients could not regularly participate in synagogue life.[52] These difficulties were acknowledged by local religious leaders, as shown, for example, by the exception made by a Sefrou scholar for employees who could not attend public prayers.[53] Moreover, we do not find among Middle Eastern Jews pressures similar to those prevalent in European Jewish society regarding the severe avoidance of social relations with Gentiles, which aimed in Europe at maintaining religious and social barriers even when Jews were obligated to associate with Gentiles.[54] The data which I collected among Jews from southern Morocco demonstrate the frequent and relaxed contacts with Muslim patrons, neighbors, and clients. Since the religious leaders in the tribal and rural areas were not given full financial support by their communities, they too were usually obliged to interact regularly with Muslims with whom they had an economic relationship. Therefore, the religious leadership was not as remote as the European Jewish leadership from the reality of mutual relationships between Jews and Gentiles. Also, in their physical appearance and clothing the Jews in the Middle East were not ostentatiously different from their neighbors, unlike orthodox Jewry in Europe for many generations.[55] These observations indicate that Middle East Jewry did not

Press, 1967–83); 2:145; M. Shokeid, *The Dual Heritage,* pp. 149–152; A. Shtal, "The Order of Seating in the Synagogue as Reflection of the Type of Service" (Hebrew), in *Mikdash Me'at,* ed. Y. Ilan et al. (Jerusalem: Ministry of Education, 1975), pp. 46–56; S. Bar-Asher, "The Jews in North Africa and Egypt" (Hebrew), in *History of the Jews in the Islamic Countries,* ed. S. Ettinger (Jerusalem: Zalman Shazar Center, 1981), pp. 172–3.

52. M. Shokeid, "Jewish Existence in a Berber Environment," in *Jewish Societies in the Middle East: Community, Culture and Authority,* ed. S. Deshen and W. Zenner (Washington: University Press of America, 1982), pp. 105–122.

53. S. Deshen, *Individuals and the Community: Social Life in 18th–19th Century Moroccan Jewry* (Defense Ministry, 1983), p. 69; D. Ovadia, *The Community of Sefrou* (Hebrew) (Jerusalem: Center of Moroccan Studies, 1975), p. 90.

54. Katz, *Tradition and Crisis,* pp. 33–34.

55. S. D. Goitein, *Jews and Arabs: Their Contacts Through the Ages* (1955; reprint ed., New York: Schocken, 1974); Shokeid, "Jewish Existence in a Berber Environment."

develop a life-style of observances and prohibitions which consistently limited and stigmatized social interactions with Gentiles. The religious culture of Middle Eastern Jews, particularly in North Africa, was probably influenced by the Sephardi tradition developed by the Jews in the Iberian Peninsula until their expulsion in 1492. It was this tradition that also contributed to a more accommodating approach to the surrounding society and culture.[56]

Sharot and Deshen analyzed the close affinity of Middle Eastern Jewry to the culture of their host society in terms of its impact on the patterns and content of their religious activities.[57] My approach, however, emphasizes the relevance of this affinity in generating a mode of religiosity that is highly interwoven with the individual's bonds of family and community affiliation. Moreover, in spite of the economic, social, and political changes they underwent prior to their immigration to Israel (such as those following the process of urbanization in Morocco), Middle Eastern Jews still represented to a great extent a homogeneous society, in terms of a shared world view, maintained by all classes, in which a prominent position was occupied by the familial, communal, and religious realms. Although the same processes of social differentiation and communal disintegration that had occurred much earlier in European Jewry had already begun in some parts of Middle Eastern Jewish society, their impact and consequences were not, as yet, comparable. Similarly, while the close-knit kin and community networks of Middle Eastern Jewry disintegrated somewhat as a result of immigration, the extent of dispersion and actual decline of the family and community was by no means so pronounced as among European Jews in Israel. The immigration from Europe at the end of the nineteenth century was usually composed of individuals and small families, and this became irreversible as a consequence of the Holocaust. In stark contrast, Middle Eastern Jewry's immigration was usually composed of communities in their entirety. Although these communities often became dispersed in Israel, and in spite of the various constraints that affected the daily life of the immigrants and their offspring in their new environment, the individual Israeli of Middle

---

56. H. J. Zimmels, *Ashkenazim and Sephardim* (London: Oxford University Press, 1958). Zimmels claims, inter alia, that "as a general rule the Ashkenazim were stricter than the Sephardim" (p. 158) and, "while as far as general culture was concerned the Sephardim were certainly superior to their Ashkenazi brethren, the latter surpassed them in religious and moral conduct" (p. 261).

57. Sharot, *Judaism*; Deshen, "Religion Among Middle Eastern Immigrants in Israel."

Eastern extraction has not become dissociated from the actual bonds and obligations as well as from a general orientation toward a wider network of kin and community members.[58]

We relate the symbiosis of the religious, familial, and communal domains in Middle Eastern Jewish society in the diaspora, which survived until recent times, to the presence of a deep attachment to a diffused concept of *masoret beit abba* ("the tradition of the father's home") that is usually connected with synagogue life and, more specifically, to religious details connected with family ceremonial life on the Sabbath and the festivals. No doubt, the impact of religious obligations and the authority of religious leaders have greatly diminished, but the intensity and scope of family and communal ties, which have been traditionally interwoven with religious activities and meanings, have provided an important source for a diffused identification with religious symbols and an incentive for partial participation in religious activities at this stage of societal reorganization. The interpretations suggested by Sharot and Deshen for the apparently easy accommodation of Middle Eastern Jews with the secular culture of Ashkenazi Jews[59] ignore the impact exerted by the factors of familial and communal commitments in the process of religious change and adjustment among Middle Eastern Jews versus Ashkenazi Jews. The lack of powerful family and communal orientations may offer an explanation for the dominant patterns of religiosity among Ashkenazi Jews in Israel, which do not encourage the modes of "partial religiosity." It should be emphasized, however, that the Ashkenazi scene in Israel is considerably different from that in the United States and Western Europe, where partial religiosity is acceptable to the Reform and Conservative denominations and is not consistently denounced by the Orthodox sector.[60]

---

58. For my observations on the intensity of the feelings expressed during reunions of relatives who had settled in different localities, see Shokeid, "Evolution of Kinship Ties among Moroccan Immigrants," in *The Predicament of Homecoming*, pp. 210–236. For a more general conclusion on this subject, see M. Shokeid, "The Impact of Migration on the Moroccan Jewish Family in Israel," forthcoming in *Evolving Jewish Family*, ed. S. Cohen and P. Hyman (Holmes and Meier). In the latter paper I demonstrated, for example, the demographic stability, if not the expansion, of the North African nuclear family in Israel. See also D. Friedlander and C. Goldscheider, "Immigration, Social Change and Fertility in Israel," *Population Studies* 32 (1978): 316, and C. Goldscheider, "Family Change and Variation among Israeli Ethnic Groups," forthcoming in *Evolving Jewish Family*, ed. S. Cohen and P. Hyman (Holmes and Meier).

59. Sharot, *Judaism*; Deshen, "Religion Among Middle Eastern Immigrants in Israel."

60. During my stay in Britain in the 1960s I observed the phenomenon of selective preserva-

Particularly revealing have been our observations of the expressions of tolerance by Middle Eastern Jews toward partial participation in synagogue life. The attitudes of the leader of the Moroccan congregation that I observed in the new Tel-Aviv suburb are reminiscent of the attitudes expressed by Moroccan leaders in earlier generations, as, for example, the Sefrou scholar mentioned above who made allowances for congregants who could not easily attend prayer services. The mere identification of individuals with the synagogue congregation through partial participation, without acceptance of the full range of *mitzvot* in public and at home, was accorded by the leader a religious value in a scale of religiosity which ranks and rewards every believer according to his particular existential circumstances. The congregants perceive this scale as the natural order of religious life which endows contemporary leaders, as well as the scholars and saints of the past, with the spiritual power to supplement their religious deficiencies. These figures provide seasonal opportunities for religious elevation, as, for example, during the pilgrimages to the saint's tombs and other celebrations.

This mode of religiosity is characterized by spiritual and emotional involvement and the notion of belonging, rather than by the strict practice of religious observances. The general reaction of Middle Eastern Jewish religious leaders seem to provide some support for this approach. Even those of them who succeeded in preserving their leadership status in Israel did not encourage the kind of isolationist tendencies or more aggressive manifestations among their followers that are observed among certain segments of Ashkenazi orthodoxy. This accommodating reaction does not by any means imply that the Middle Eastern leadership is weak or has lost control under the new circumstances. Nonetheless, it is difficult for those whose expectations and evaluations of religious comportment are anchored in the Israeli Ashkenazi tradition to comprehend this seeming religious

---

tion of certain elements of religious life among the second generation of immigrants from Eastern Europe in Salford, where many Jews have concentrated. Successfully integrated in British economy and society, secular in their appearance in public and at home, they are also integrated in a close-knit network of family ties and community activities. They often participate in the Sabbath and festival services of Orthodox synagogues and preserve considerable elements of the customs related to the Sabbath and festival meals. Professor Jacob Katz has informed me that more recently, with the growing institutionalization of the *yeshivot,* their protagonists have started to protest and raise doubts about the value of partial observance. My experience in Salford, however, supports the hypothesis that wherever the individual remains embedded within a relatively close framework of familial and communal ties, he tends also to keep at least a partial commitment to religious traditon.

tolerance and the modest religious demands presented to the congregants in daily life. From the Ashkenazi perspective, there is not much religious substance in the selective preservation of religious observances that are mainly of folkloric value. The low evaluation in religious terms accorded to the modes of behavior reported here leads naturally to the conclusion that we are actually witnessing a process of secularization.

Masoret Religiosity and Ethnic Action

Beyond the possible debate about the religious value to be accorded them, Middle Eastern patterns of religiosity may indeed express distinct symbols of an ethnic culture. Congenial circumstances for the development of that symbolic estate are provided by certain structural factors, and particularly by the tendency of Middle Eastern Jews to concentrate geographically in villages, development towns, and urban suburbs. Moreover, this concentration in ethnic neighborhoods is associated with a shared socioeconomic status among residents.[61] *Masoret* religiosity as here described may both express and satisfy the growing dissatisfaction among Middle Eastern Jews and their increasingly more outspoken demand that their culture be recognized as a legitimate alternative to dominant Ashkenazi culture which is supposed to represent Israeli society. The melting pot ideology in Israel, as in other countries, has apparently aimed at social unification through a single, homogeneous culture. This ideology aimed no less at the quick acculturation of the recently arrived groups, whose members were often considered backward and traditional, into the social order and the cultural repertoire of the dominant veteran sectors. Secularization has been one of the most noticeable characteristics of the veteran Israelis of Ashkenazi extraction. It was they who staffed the governmental, municipal, Jewish Agency, and party bureaucracies that monopolized and allocated to the immigrants the major resources of livelihood and prestige. Among these bureaucracies the Labor party, which ruled the country for many years, was particularly influential. Actually, Middle Eastern Jews could usually choose between two alternatives offered, if not forced on them, by the Ashkenazi political establishment: firstly, the secular parties (preferably Labor), and

61. For an analysis of the phenomenon of ethnicity in American cities in terms of structural factors, see Yancey, Ericksen, and Juliani, "Emergent Ethnicity."

secondly, the religious parties (preferably Mafdal). Therefore, it is not surprising that Tami, an ethnic party that went to the polls for the first time in 1981 and showed better prospects than any other ethnic party that has emerged since 1948, has chosen to identify itself by the term *masoret*.[62]

The emergence and disappearance of ethnic parties in Israel has usually been analyzed in terms of situational factors.[63] Although we are not concerned here with the factors that triggered Tami's appearance on the political scene, nor with its future prospects, it is important to emphasize the cultural dimension, for we believe that it buttressed the personal and intra-party situation that led to the new party. Moreover, the same cultural dimension apparently also affected the results obtained at the polls by other parties. The new party's choice of its name appears to be consistent with our observations of the wide use of the term *masoret* by Middle Eastern Jews in explaining their religious situation. The concept of *masoret* conveys the symbols of a religio-familial-communal culture which is supposed to include also those who observe only *taf mitzvot* or *resh yod mitzvot,* as was openly declared by the party's leader. Thus, addressing itself to the vast constituency of Middle Eastern Jews, Tami made itself the representative of a distinct culture different from both the Ashkenazi secular culture, which has conspicuously and aggressively dissociated itself from traditional Judaism, and the Ashkenazi exclusivist orthodoxy, which compulsively observes *taryag mitzvot*.[64] The symbols and messages utilized by Tami offered indications about the characteristics of the cultural aspect of the developing ethnic-political framework of contemporary Israeli society.

Emergent ethnicity in Israel and elsewhere often seems to be a temporary phenomenon, as usually suggested by contemporary research. Thus, for example, it provides the first generation of immigrants with an instrumental means for claiming a larger share of public resources, and the third genera-

62. The election advertisements of Tami utilized the slogan "*masoret* is the thread which links all *edot* [ethnic groups]"; see, for example, *Ma'ariv,* June 11, 1981. The *edot* were identified in another advertisement as follows: ". . . those who came from North Africa, Egypt, Libya, Iraq, India, Cochin, Kurdistan, Yemen, and other Diaspora lands"; see, for example, *Yediot Ahronot,* June 12, 1981.

63. For a recent analysis of Israeli ethnic parties, see H. Herzog, "The Ethnic Lists to the Delegates' Assembly and the Knesset (1920–1977): Ethnic Political Identity?" (Hebrew) (Ph.D. diss., Tel-Aviv University, 1981).

64. It is beyond the scope of this article to discuss the more recent developments (since the 1984 general elections) that created a split in the Agudat Yisrael party which increasingly gained Middle Eastern voters. The new party, Shas, was headed by Sephardi Orthodox leaders.

tion with a nostalgic return to their ancestral culture.[65] I do not claim that the emergent ethnicity is a revival of an authentic ethnic heritage. It certainly is not, though it reflects traditional elements and influences. Nor is it the mere ephemeral outcome of structural opportunities,[66] or a primarily leisure-time activity of a working-class culture,[67] though it has certainly been influenced by structural opportunities and does sustain a type of leisure-time activity that often characterizes "working classes." The fact that "ethnic" and "working-class" cultural manifestations often filter upward (e.g., American black folk culture) indicates their role in creating new symbols which also attract the mainstream and may eventually be transformed into major national cultural symbols. The *masoret* religiosity adopted and proclaimed by Middle Eastern Jews, which has been influenced by their diaspora heritage as much as by their family, community, residential, and other structural opportunities in Israel, may under certain circumstances develop into a symbolic linkage with the more dominant cultural stream. With the growing disparity between the expanding Ashkenazi orthodoxy and the dominant secular sector, on the one hand, and the growing notion of cultural need concerning the symbolic realm of Jewish identity in the secular sector, on the other, *masoret* religiosity may be more than an ethnic peculiarity. Regardless of its possibly temporary nature, emergent ethnicity could have an important impact on mainstream culture,[68] much beyond what has usually been assumed.

65. M. L. Hansen, *The Problems of the Third Generation Immigrant* (Rock Island: Augustana Historical Society, 1938) and "The Third Generation in America," *Commentary* 14 (1952): 492–500.

66. As suggested, for example, by Yancey, Ericksen, and Juliani, "Emergent Ethnicity."

67. As suggested by Gans, "Symbolic Ethnicity."

68. A. Weingrod suggested that traditional immigrant groups influence the practices of institutions in the absorbing society through the process of reciprocal change. See "Reciprocal Change: A Case Study of a Moroccan Village in Israel," *American Anthropologist* 65 (1962): 115–131.

13

Secularization and the Diminishing Decline of Religion

Hannah Ayalon, Eliezer Ben-Raphael, and Stephen Sharot

The entrance of Jews into modernizing societies has been accompanied by a decline of religiosity, but when a low level of observance is reached the decline slows down or comes to a halt. A minimal level of religiosity does not inhibit the involvement of secular Jews in modern industrial society and it enables them to express their ethnic or national identity through symbols and rituals of their religious heritage. This diminishing decline perspective provides the framework for an analysis of the influences on the religiosity of four Jewish-Israeli groups, two Middle Eastern (Moroccan and Iraqi) and two European (Polish and Rumanian). A process of secularization, as measured by intergenerational declines in the performance of the mitzvot *(commandments), occurred in all four groups, but the intergenerational declines were greater in those groups whose older generation displayed high levels of religious observance. The relative importance of the independent variables influencing religiosity, such as father's religiosity, socio-economic status, and number of years lived in Israel, depend on the level of observance of the group. These generalizations are modified by attention to differences in the religio-cultural traditions and social locations of Israelis from Middle Eastern and European origins.*

Secularization, "the process by which religious institutions, actions, and consciousness lose their social significance,"[2] has commonly been viewed either as a dimension or as a consequence of modernization; industrialization, urbanization, the growth of science and technology, the spread of education, the development of the mass media, and the participation of the masses into political society have been seen as contributing factors in the decline of religion (Wilson, 1966, 1982; Berger, 1967). Secularization is not, however, an inevitable consequence of the many developments that have often been grouped together under the term "modernization," and the relationships of these two multidimensional processes vary considerably depending on the religious, cultural, and social contexts. In many Islamic societies developments such as urbanization and the expansion of higher education appear to have contributed to the contemporary resurgence of Islam (Arjomand, 1983). Even in the Western Christian context a decline in religiosity or religious practice did not always follow industrialization and urbanization, and there is considerable variation in the degrees and forms of secularization both among and within Western nations (Martin, 1978; Mol, 1972).

Whatever its limitations in other contexts, the modernization-secularization perspective appears to work well in the case of Western Jews. The precipitating factor in the decline of religiosity among Western Jews was their movement out of what had been semi-autonomous and highly boundaried communities. The transition into the wider society involved concentration in large urban centers, diffusion into the modern sectors of education, commerce, and industry, and participation in the political institutions of their respective nations. Increased social interaction with non-Jews and participation in modernizing societies were accompanied or followed by a considerable decline in Jewish religious practice (Sharot, 1976).

Since Jews in the traditional communities followed highly detailed religious prescriptions and proscriptions in their daily life, secularization was particularly obvious in the behavioral sphere. Changes in beliefs may have been no less drastic, but the emphasis of Judaism on the performance of numerous *mitzvot* (commandments) made the decline in religious practice far more apparent. Few secularized Jews went as far as to abandon Judaism, and attachment to the religious heritage continued to be expressed through a few selected rituals rather than beliefs.[3] The particular rituals that have been retained include family celebrations and observances that symbolize the historical continuity and integration of the Jewish nation, but they do not prevent involvement in modern society.

It would appear that there are limits to the decline of religion in even the most secular of societies. One reason for the continuation of at least minimal levels of practice and belief in many societies is the historical interpenetration of religion with ethnic or national identity. Although nationalism has in many instances involved a secularization of beliefs, societies whose historical identity has been anchored in religion have rarely adopted a modern national identity totally emptied of traditional religious content. There are few cases where the relationship between a "people" and a religion has been so close as among the Jews, and in the diaspora, where Jewish identity and the community's survival are perceived to be threatened by assimilation, Jewish religious practice has often been interpreted as a 'mask' for ethnicity. In Israel, Jews are more likely to take their Jewish identity for granted and intermarriage with non-Jews is rare, but for a variety of reasons, including the legitimation of their presence and an independent state in the area, most Israeli Jews are concerned to perpetuate their Jewishness. They do so by means of religious symbols and participation in at least a few religious rites (cf. Liebman and Don-Yehiya, 1983; Weissbrod, 1983).

From the last decades of the nineteenth century the process of secularization was accelerated for many Jews by their migration from the undeveloped societies of Eastern Europe, where participation in non-Jewish society was highly restricted, to the rapidly industrializing and relatively open societies of Western Europe and the United States. A few Eastern European Jews made aliya ('rose up' or migrated) to Palestine and established the new *Yishuv* (Settlement) whose secular features clashed with the old *Yishuv* of religious Jews. In Palestine it was the ideology of Zionist-Socialists and not entrance into a non-Jewish modern society that molded the secular character of the new *Yishuv* and Israeli state. Rapid industrialization began in Israel in the 1950s, but the new waves of immigrants that came in that period confronted a society whose veteran population and major institutional features were already highly secularized. This posed few problems for most immigrants from Europe, many of whom came from Communist societies in the 1950s, but it did entail cultural shock and considerable adaptation among immigrants from the Jewish communities of the Middle East.

In accord with the modernization-secularization perspective, it would be expected that the sharpest declines in religiosity are found in those communities who pass, possibly because of migration, from 'traditional' to 'modern' societies. Many immigrants attempt to retain their traditional lifestyles in the new milieux, but the second generation is likely to pull away considerably from their parents level of religious practice. Subsequent generations may continue the decline in religious practice, but where religion is tied to ethnicity or nationalism, the decline will diminish or come to a halt. Studies tracing religious observance over several generations of American Jews reveal an overall decline in religiosity with advancing generations, but this decline also lessens with each generation: the distance between the first and second generations is considerable, the difference between the second and third generations is much less, and in the more advanced generations there is a process of stabilization at a minimal level of ritual observance (Sklare and Greenblum, 1979; Goldstein and Goldscheider, 1968; S. Cohen, 1983).

The possibilities of conducting similar intergenerational comparisons in Israel are limited: nearly half of the population was born in the diaspora and the great majority of adults born in Israel are second generation. However, since Israelis migrated from communities of origin that varied in their degrees of traditionalism and secularization, it is possible to test the diminishing decline thesis by comparing the differences between the religiosity of adults socialized in Israel and their parents from a number of communities. This study focusses on the religious practice of adult male respondents and their fathers from four countries of origin, two Middle Eastern (Morocco and Iraq) and two European (Rumania and Poland).

Interviews were conducted in 1982/3 with a disproportionate stratified sample of 826 male residents of Beer Sheva, the largest town in southern Israel. The majority of respondents migrated to Israel in their childhood or youth (a minority were born in Israel), and are between the ages of 30 and 50. The sample was composed of about equal proportions of the four origin categories (about 200 in each), and it was further stratified to obtain a similar distribution of socio-economic status in each group of origin. This allowed a more sophisticated analysis that the crude division between Ashkenazim or European Jews and 'Oriental' or Middle Eastern Jews that has been the basis of most statistical analyses in Israel. The four origin categories were chosen because they are the largest in Israel and they cover the range of ethnic status in Israeli society; European groups are generally ranked higher than Middle Eastern groups, but within the broad categories Poles are ranked higher than Rumanians and Iraqis are ranked higher than Moroccans.

Ethnic status reflects, in part, the socio-economic distribution of the groups of origin: European Israelis are disproportionately concentrated in the upper middle and upper strata, and Middle Eastern Israelis are disproportionately concentrated in the lower strata. The overlap between geographical origins and soico-economic location is far from complete and our sample allows for the inclusion of categories that have been largely ignored in Israeli sociological studies: middle class Israelis from Asia and Africa and working class Israelis from European origins. Lists of appropriate respondents were made up from primary and secondary school records, supplemented in some schools by questionnaires administered to children, that gave the country of origin, years of education, and occupation of parents. Thus, a further perimeter of the sample was that all respondents were fathers of school-age children. If the parents were born in Israel, enquiries were made to discover the countries of origin of their parents. All the background details of respondents, including origins, education, and occupation, were checked when the questionnaires were administered by our interviewers.

An over-simplified distinction has often been made between Middle Eastern immigrants from "traditional" societies and European immigrants from "modern" societies. The majority of European immigrants to Israel did not come from the more advanced industrial societies, and this includes the two European groups in our sample from Poland and Rumania. Prior to World War II the majority of Jews in Poland and Rumania retained very high levels of traditional religious practice (on Polish Jewry see Heller, 1977). Nevertheless, the penetration of secular beliefs and ideologies, especially socialism and Zionism, into the traditional communities began much earlier and influenced far more Jews in Eastern Europe than in most Middle Eastern Jewish communities. The great majority of our respondents from Rumania and Poland immigrated to Israel after the war following the destruction of the traditional communities and the considerable secularizing effects of Communist regimes on those Jews who survived the Holocaust. Secularization was less advanced in Rumania where the majority of Jews survived the Holocaust and the post-war regime was more tolerant of Jewish cultural particularism and institutions than other Communist regimes (Vago, 1981).

The process of secularization began among some Middle Eastern communities, such as those from the Yemen and Kurdistan, only after they had immigrated to Israel. Of the two Middle Eastern groups in our sample, the Iraqis had been more influenced by Western trends prior to their immigration; a decline in religious practice was evident among a minority of Iraqi Jews even before World War I, but the British occupation and the entrance of some Jewish children into state schools from the 1920s were important secular influences on many Iraqi Jews (H. Cohen, 1973). There was considerable differentiation among Jews in Morocco in terms of their closeness to the Arabic or French cultures, but the majority who migrated to Israel tended to come from the least westernized, lower strata of Moroccan Jewry (Ben-Rafael, 1982). Thus, our four groups can be differentiated in terms of their level of secularization prior to their immigration; the least secularized were the Moroccan Jews, followed by the Iraqis, Rumanians, and lastly, the most secularized, the Poles.

The modernization perspective would expect that the process of secularization, as measured by intergenerational decline in religious observance, is occurring among the majority of Israeli Jews, but that the decline is sharper among the Middle Eastern communities whose origins are closer to the traditional religious society. However, in addition to level of religious observance prior to immigration, there are a number of other differences between Middle Eastern and European Jewish communities that are likely to affect their patterns of religious observance and secularization in Israel. One difference is that religion among Middle Eastern Jews is less differentiated from family and local community than among European Jews. The importance of genealogical lines and the related territorial belongingness deepened the importance of family and local community among Jews in Islamic countries, especially Morocco (Shokeid, 1984). The influence on Middle Eastern Jews of Israeli society, dominated by secular European Jews, was likely to be a secular one, but where the family and community of origin retain their strength many religious observances will remain widely practiced.

Another difference is that Jews in Middle Eastern societies were separated much less from non-Jews than had been the case in the traditional European societies (Sharot, 1976). There was less emphasis among Middle Eastern Jews on strict norms limiting relationships with non-Jews, and there was greater tolerance with respect to levels of religious observance. Shokeid argues that the absence of a militant defense of "orthodoxy" among Middle Eastern Jews and the continuing importance of family and community ties have contributed to the emergence of a *mesoriti* "traditional" or "partly religious" pattern in Israel.[4] Some observances have been widely abandoned but others are retained and Middle Eastern Israelis see themselves as continuing in the tradition of their fathers. In comparison, European Israelis are more polarized between a secular majority and a strictly orthodox minority who see little value in the "partly religious" pattern (Shokeid, 1984).

The meanings that Middle Eastern immigrants attributed to their *aliya* and their Jewish-Israeli identifications have differed from those of European immigrants. The distinction between Judaism and their Jewish ethnicity or nationality was undeveloped among Jews in the Middle East. The Zionist *halutzim* (pioneers) from Eastern Europe, and especially those of the second and third *aliya* (1904-1923), regarded their *aliya* as a revolutionary break from the religious way of life in their communities of birth. Later European immigrants were less anti-religious, but few imparted traditional religious meaning to their *aliya*. For most Middle Eastern Jews Zionism and the establishment of the Israeli state were affirmations of the tradition that they had upheld in their countries of origin. They responded to the Zionist appeal to make *aliya* and participate in the rebuilding of a unified nation because these notions were inherent in their attachment to Jewish law and ritual. The majority came to perceive the secular facets of their immigration and in the process of absorption they abandoned many of their former lifestyles, but traditional religious patterns have remained a major focus of a highly valued heritage and identity (cf. Ben-Rafael, 1982). Ethnic synagogues, based on community of origin, remain the rule among Middle Eastern Israelis, and *mizug hagaluyot* (fusion of the exiles) is not perceived to extend to the forms and style of prayer and liturgy (cf. Deshen and Shokeid, 1974; Shokeid and Deshen, 1982).

The socio-economic distribution and experiences of Jews of Middle Eastern origin in Israeli society might also limit a secular trend. The disproportionate concentration of Middle Eastern Israelis in the lower strata, their experiences of discrimination and feelings of relative deprivation have been emphasized in analyses of Israeli society as a plural society (Smooha, 1978) or in terms of an ethnic division of labor and dependency (Swirski, 1981), but the implications of these factors for religious practice have yet to be examined. In addition to limiting social interaction with European Israelis, the subordinate socio-economic and political position of Middle Eastern Israelis might also reinforce their religious practice indirectly by preserving their family and community patterns and their religiously informed identity.

Hypothesis and Variables

Respondents were asked if they practiced five specific mitzvot and they were asked also if their fathers practiced or, if deceased, had practiced, the same mitzvot. The five mitzvot were: donning *tephillin* (phylacteries) every day; not traveling on the Sabbath; separate utensils for milk and meat; *kiddush* (sanctification), the prayer recited over wine before the Sabbath meal; and fasting on *Yom*

Kippur (Day of Atonement). These were chosen to range from an observance (donning tephillin) that is kept by only a minority who practice all or most Jewish observances to an observance (fasting on *Yom Kippur*) that is practiced by most Jews including those who practice few other observances.[5] The five mitzvot were found to meet the requirements of a Guttman scale; for respondents, the coefficient of reproducibility was .93 and the coefficient of scalability .77; for respondents' fathers the coefficients were .93 and .79 respectively. Levels of observance were computed according to the number of mitzvot that were practiced, ranging from five to zero.

Three interrelated hypotheses, derived from the modified modernization or diminishing decline perspective, will be tested in this paper. The first is that the predominant intergenerational trend in religious practice will be one of decline in all four groups of origin. Although the four groups of origin in this study came from societies that varied in their levels of modernization, not one came from a predominantly secular community and it is expected that respondents' experiences of the largely secular Israeli society would result in a lower level of religious practice than their fathers.

The second hypothesis is that, the higher the level of religious observance of the fathers, the greater the distance in religiosity between respondents and fathers. This hypothesis is based on the argument that the pace of secularization between generations is greater where there is a wider distance between the comparatively traditional societies in which the older generation were socialized and the comparatively secularized societies in which the younger generation were socialized.

The third hypothesis is that, in addition to father's religiosity, the relative importance of the independent variables influencing respondents' religiosity will depend on the level of traditionalism or secularization in the communities of origin. In addition to father's religiosity and country of origin the other independent variables to be examined are: two components of the respondent's socio-economic status (education and occupational prestige), father's occupational prestige, year of immigration, respondent's age, and wife's continent of origin (Europe-America or Asia-Africa).

In analyzing the effects of status components on Jewish religiosity most previous studies have focused on education rather than on occupation. Cohen (1983), who found an inverse relationship between religious observance and education among Boston Jews, writes that higher education imparts values such as cosmopolitanism, cultural relativism, toleration, and individualism that undermine traditional religious commitment and practice. Education is most likely to affect the religiosity of those who are closer to the traditional base, and this was found to be the case by Goldstein and Goldscheider (1968) in their study of the Jewish community of Providence, Rhode Island; there was a significant inverse relationship between number of school years and religiosity only among the foreign born, and among the third generation post-college Jews had a slightly higher religious observance than those with a high school education. In their study of religiosity in Israel, Goldscheider and Friedlander (1983) found that the relationship between religion and education was not linear; the highest levels of religiosity were found among those with less than eight years of schooling, but there was an upturn of religiosity among those with twelve or more years of education.[6] The effects of education have generally been presented without controls for occupation,[7] but in Israel, in particular, it is important to measure the relative independent effects of education and occupation; the study of the Bible and the Talmud is a compulsory part of the curriculum in all schools, and a significant minority attend religious schools in the state system or under the auspices of a religious movement.

It is expected that occupation will have greater influence on levels of religiosity in the Middle Eastern groups because those in the more prestigious occupations are likely to be more closely associated with Israelis of European origin who make up the majority in these occupations and have an overall lower level of observance. The number of years lived in Israel will also affect a greater decline in religiosity in the Middle Eastern groups since the longer life experience in the more secular Israeli context will remove respondents further from the traditional base of their families' countries of origin.

The relationship between age and religiosity in Israel is likely to be a function of other factors such as generation and number of years lived in Israel. In the United States age had been found to have an independent effect; the concern of parents to transmit a Jewish identity to their children produces a rise in their observance as their children reach school age and continues until the children are of Bar Mitzva age (Sklare and Greenblum, 1979; Sharot, 1973; Cohen, 1983). The transmission of Jewish identity is less problematic in Israel and there are many alternative agencies other than religious observance and affiliation.

It is expected that the level of observance in the spouse's family of origin will influence the husband's pattern. Data was not collected on the religiosity of respondents' in-laws but it is evident that the average level of religiosity of in-laws from Africa and Asia will be higher than that of in-laws from Europe. Thus, a negative correlation can be expected between respondents' religiosity and European spouses and a positive correlation with Asian-African spouses. The spouses' origin will not, in most cases, reverse the respondents pull away from his parents, but it is likely to influence the level of decline that occurs. Spouse's origin has been found to be an important factor in the United States where comparisons are made between Central and Eastern European origins (Sklare and Greenblum, 1979; Himmelfarb, 1980), but in Israel, where the dominant form of Orthodoxy differentiates clearly between male and female religious roles, its effect is likely to be less.

FINDINGS

The data presented in tables 1 and 2 support the hypotheses that there is a general intergenerational decline in religiosity, that the sharpest declines are found in those groups from the most religious backgrounds, and that at the lowest levels of observance there is intergenerational stabilization.

The backgrounds of the two Middle Eastern groups are more religious than those of the two European groups, but there are important differences among Middle Eastern groups and it would be a mistake to counterpose two homogeneous religio-cultural blocs of "Western" non-religious Jews and "Eastern" religious Jews. The high level of observance of the great majority of Moroccan fathers is obvious; more than 80 percent practiced all the rituals and about a third more Moroccans than Iraqis practiced the first three rituals. In comparison there is little difference between Rumanians and Poles except at the level of the fifth ritual, fasting on Yom Kippur. Here the high level of secularity of the Polish fathers is obvious; more than a third did not observe any of the practices.

Turning to the respondents' patterns, the effect of Israeli society would appear to

Table 1

RELIGIOSITY OF RESPONDENTS AND FATHERS, AVERAGES ($\bar{x}$),
STANDARD DEVIATIONS (σ), AND COEFFICIENTS OF VARIABILITY (v)

	Respondents religiosity			Fathers religiosity			
	$\bar{x}$	σ	v	$\bar{x}$	σ	v	N
Moroccans	3.23	1.24	.38	4.44	.75	.16	202
Iraqis	2.18	1.21	.56	3.52	1.45	.41	204
Poles	1.11	1.30	1.17	1.83	1.84	1.01	179
Rumanians	1.69	1.32	.78	2.39	1.74	.73	203

blur any overall distinction in religiosity between Middle Eastern and European Jews. At the "strictly religious" end of the scale (donning tephillin) there is a clear difference between the Moroccans and the Iraqis, but there is no significant difference between the Iraqis and the two European groups. The difference between the Moroccans on the one hand and the three other groups on the other is clear also in avoiding traveling on the Sabbath. Moroccans continue to demonstrate a higher pattern of observance than Iraqis with respect to the third and fourth mitzvot, but here there are also significant differences between the Iraqis and the Europeans. At the end of the scale, fasting on Yom Kippur is observed by similar percentages of Moroccans, Iraqis and Rumanians, and it is the Poles who provide the more secular exception.

There are significant declines in intergenerational religiosity in all four groups. Among the Europeans the difference between the generations varies little regarding the different mitzvot, but among the Moroccans and Iraqis the intergenerational falls in observance are particularly sharp at the level of the first two "stricter" mitzvot. On the measure of kashrut, there are similar intergenerational differences in the Moroccan and Iraqi groups, but on the fourth observance (kiddush) the Iraqis continue the pattern of intergenerational discontinuity whereas between the two Moroccan generations there is little difference. The small intergenerational differences among all groups with respect to fasting on Yom Kippur suggests that once a low level of observance is reached a process of stabilization occurs.

In most cases, the higher the level of the father's religiosity and the "stricter" the mitzva, the greater the intergenerational discontinuity. However, there is considerable continuity in the observance of the last three mitzvot among Middle Eastern Israelis, especially the Moroccans. The high level of observance among Moroccan respondents of both the dietary law and kiddish suggests that they are unlikely to approach the low observance pattern of European Israelis for a considerable time.

The probability of a respondent observing the mitzvot is greatly increased if they were practiced by his father, but this probability decreased moving from the "popular" to the "stricter" mitzvot (column 4 in Table 2). A comparison of the coefficients of variability of the two generations (table 1) indicates that there has been some increase in polarization between "religious" and "secular" Jews, but this stems, in most part, from the fact that some respondents pulled more sharply away from their fathers and others. The last column in Table 2 shows that few respondents perform rituals that were neglected by their parents; this is true for all groups with only minor variations among the mitzvot.

Table 2

SPECIFIC RELIGIOUS OBSERVANCES AMONG RESPONDENTS AND FATHERS

	Respondents %	Fathers %	Difference Between Respondents and Fathers %	Respondents by Fathers' Practice %	N	Respondents Not Practiced By Fathers %	N
Don Tephillin							
Total	12.3	48.5	36.2	23.6	(90)	1.7	(7)
Moroccans	25.5	84.5	59.0	29.6	(50)	3.2	(1)
Iraqis	7.8	54.4	46.6	11.7	(13)	3.2	(3)
Poles	5.0	20.5	15.5	18.9	(7)	1.4	(2)
Rumanians	10.3	32.0	21.7	30.8	(20)	0.7	(1)
Not Travel Sabbath							
Total	20.4	49.8	29.4	33.5	(133)	7.5	(30)
Moroccans	39.1	87.0	47.9	40.0	(72)	33.3	(9)
Iraqis	18.1	52.9	34.8	23.0	(25)	12.0	(12)
Poles	9.9	27.5	17.6	30.0	(15)	2.2	(3)
Rumanians	13.2	28.9	15.7	35.6	(21)	4.1	(6)
Separate meat/ milk dishes							
Total	42.8	59.8	17.0	66.2	(315)	8.1	(26)
Moroccans	75.7	95.6	19.9	78.7	(155)	11.1	(1)
Iraqis	46.1	67.6	21.5	63.0	(87)	10.6	(7)
Poles	16.6	30.9	14.3	39.3	(22)	6.4	(8)
Rumanians	29.8	41.5	11.7	60.0	(51)	8.3	(10)
Kiddush							
Total	52.8	66.4	13.6	71.4	(375)	16.2	(43)
Moroccans	89.8	98.0	8.2	90.0	(181)	75.0	(3)
Iraqis	55.9	78.2	22.3	63.9	(101)	27.3	(12)
Poles	28.3	40.0	11.7	52.8	(38)	12.0	(13)
Rumanians	34.3	46.1	11.8	58.5	(55)	13.6	(15)
Fast Yom Kippur							
Total	80.4	87.8	7.4	87.6	(607)	29.2	(28)
Moroccans	93.8	99.0	5.2	94.7	(196)	0	(0)
Iraqis	90.1	97.5	7.4	90.9	(179)	60.0	(3)
Poles	52.8	63.5	10.7	71.7	(81)	20.0	(13)
Rumanians	85.2	88.2	3.0	84.4	(151)	50.0	(12)

The correlation matrix and the regression analyses demonstrate that the relative importance of influences on religiosity vary according to the level of religious observance of each group. The correlation matrix shows the important influence of fathers' religiosity on respondents' religiosity, especially among Poles and Rumanians. Most of the correlations with the other variables are lower, but they are all in the expected direction; there are negative correlations with respondents' occupational prestige, years of education, wives born in Europe-America, and fathers' occupational prestige. These negative correlations are especially prominent among the Moroccans and Iraqis. The only positive correlation for all groups is with age; older respondents tend to have higher levels of religiosity. Among Moroccans, the earlier the year of immigration, the lower the religiosity; among Poles and Ruma-

Table 3

CORRELATION MATRIX OF RELIGIOSITY AND INDEPENDENT VARIABLES

	Poles	Rumanians	Iraqis	Moroccans	Total Sample
Father's religiosity	.53	.59	.24	.34	.61
Occupational prestige	-.09	-.08	-.36	-.19	-.29
Years Schooling	-.09	.00	-.23	-.07	-.20
Wife's Continent of Birth (Europe-America)	-.04	-.18	-.28	-.17	-.41
Year Migration	-.12	-.13	.00	.22	.04
Age	.13	.01	.14	.11	.01
Father's Occupational prestige	-.15	-.02	-.15	-.11	-.15

nians, the later the year of immigration, the lower the religiosity.

The correlations between many of the independent variables and their differential impact in the four groups indicate the need for regression analysis. The regression analysis (Table 4) of the entire sample shows that the most important influence over respondents' religiosity is fathers' religiosity; this factor mediates almost completely the link between country of origin and religiosity.[8] The other variables that reach statistical significance for the entire sample are less important substantively. Both higher occupational prestige and wife of European-American origin reduce religiosity; the net contribution of these variables to the variance of religiosity beyond that of fathers' religiosity is -8 percent.

The separate regression analyses for the four groups of origin reveal different patterns. There is a greater distance in religiosity between respondents and fathers in the Moroccan group than in the European groups, but there is little difference between them in the extent that fathers' religiosity explains variance in religiosity among respondents; the metric coefficient between respondents' and fathers' religiosity in the Moroccan group is almost identical to that of the Poles and the Rumanians. The Iraqi respondents are the exception here; there is considerable divergence among them in the extent to which they moved away from their fathers' base.

The divergence in religiosity among both Moroccan and Iraqi respondents can be explained, in part, by the variables that relate to relative degrees of contact and involvement with the relatively secularized Israeli society. In the Moroccan group we find significant effects of year of migration and age on religiosity; younger Moroccans who have lived in Israel for a longer time tend to be less religious. (In table 4 due to control for year of immigration "age" refers to age of immigration.) Higher occupational prestige also reduces religiosity in the Moroccan group, but its effect among the Iraqis, most of whom migrated to Israel at the same time, is more prominent.

The stronger influence of father's religiosity and the weaker influence of SES in accounting for the variance in religiosity among Moroccans compared with the Iraqis may reflect the stronger intergenerational familial and community ties of that group. Evidence of the latter is provided by data that was collected from respondents on their three best friends. Whereas about half of the best friends of the Moroccans were also of Moroccan origin, only a quarter of the best friends of Iraqis were of Iraqi origin. The Iraqis were also likely to have more friends of European origin, and this was particularly the case among higher socio-economic status respondents. It is a reasonable assumption that the assimilation of a larger proportion of Iraqi Jews in Ashkenazi circles both reduces their religiosity and increases the variance in religiosity within the group.

Starting at lower levels of religiosity reduces the effects on Polish and Rumanian respondents of their differential involvement in secular society. Among Poles only higher occupational prestige of fathers reduces respondents' religiosity. Significant influences on the religiosity of Rumanians are wife's continent of origin and years of schooling. Rumanians married to wives of Asian-African origin tend to be more religious. There is a positive correlation between years of schooling and religiosity in the Rumanian group; the correlation is marginal in magnitude, but it should be noted that when occupational prestige and other variables are held constant there is no negative correlation between education and religiosity in any group.[9] It may be suggested that more years in school in Israel effect a decline in religiosity since more educated youth move into higher status occupations where the influences of modernity are greater, but since education in Israel is not unequivocally secular it has little if any independent effect on religiosity after occupation is controlled.

CONCLUSION

The hypotheses derived from the diminishing decline framework have, for the most part, been supported: an intergenerational erosion of religious observance occurred in all four groups of origin, but the distance between the generations was greater in the Middle Eastern groups who were closer to the traditional base and whose members' religiosity was affected more by factors that strengthened the effects of the comparatively modern milieu (socio-economic status and number of years in Israel). It is clear, however, that the process of secularization does not follow a fixed pattern in line with modernization regardless of cultural and social structural differences among groups. Israelis of Moroccan origin may have drawn further away from their fathers than European Israelis but they have retained a comparatively high level of observance. The difference between the Moroccans and the European groups remains considerable and in unlikely to disappear in the near future. At the present rate of intergenerational erosion among Moroccans it would take another three generations before they drop to the current Polish level of observance of the dietary law and another six generations before they reach the current Polish level of observance of kiddish. If the Moroccans conform to the pattern of diminishing decline, their movement toward the minimal Polish practice would take even longer.

The comparative high level of Moroccan religious observance has been attrib-

Table 4

INFLUENCES ON RELIGIOSITY: REGRESSION COEFFICIENTS

Independent Variables	Moroccans b	β	Iraqis b	β	Poles b	β	Rumanians b	β	Total Sample β
Father's religiosity	.42*	.25*	.22*	.26*	.43*	.61*	.44*	.59*	.46*
Year migration	.05*	.23*	-.01	-.01	.02	.13	-.01	-.06	.04
Father's occupational prestige (1)	-.01	-.12	-.01	-.11	-.01*	-.17*	.00	.06	-.06
Age	.03*	.15*	.02	.09	.00	.02	.00	-.02	.04
Occupational prestige (1)	-.01	-.16*	-.02*	-.28*	-.01	-.14	-.01	.06	-.16*
Wife's Continent birth (2)	-.54	-.12	-.38	-.12	-.10	-.03	-.64*	-.18*	-.16*
Years of Schooling	.03	.07	.02	.05	.05	.15	.06*	.18*	.09*
Iraqi (3)									-.07
Polish (4)									-.11*
Moroccan (5)									.07
	a = 2.04 R^2=.20		a=2.16 R^2=.24		a=-.53 R^2=.33		a=2.40 R^2=.41		R^2 =.45

*Coefficient is more than twice its standard error

(1) According to Hartman's prestige scale for Israel
(2) Dummy Variable: '1' Wife of European-American origin
               '0' Wife of Asian-African origin

(3) Dummy Variable: '1' Iraqi '0' Non-Iraqi
(4) Dummy Variable: '1' Pole '0' Non-Pole
(5) Dummy Variable: '1' Moroccan '0' Non-Moroccan

uted to its anchorage in strong familial and community ties (Shokeid, 1984) and to the importance of religion in the identity of Moroccan Jews (Ben-Raphael, 1982). These factors may have been reinforced by the concentration of Moroccans in the lower strata and their experiences of relative deprivation and social rejection in Israel. If this is the case, only a considerable weakening of ethnic stratification is likely to accelerate the intergenerational erosion in religious practice among Moroccan Israelis and produce a temporary exception to the diminishing decline of religiosity.

NOTES

1. We wish to thank the Ford Foundation for the principal funding, received through the Israel Foundations Trustees, and the Research Fund (Anonymous) of Ben-Gurion University of the Negev for a supplementary grant. Authors are in alphabetical order to denote equal contributions.

2. We follow here Bryan Wilson's definition of secularization (Wilson, 1966, 1982). For useful discussions on the meanings of secularization, see Shiner, 1967; Hill, 1973.

3. A recent survey of Israeli Jews found that only 64 percent expressed a belief in God and 35 percent said that they believed in the coming of the messiah, but 74 percent fasted on Yom Kippur, 88 percent lit Hanukah candles, and 99 percent participated in the Passover Seder night meal (Ben-Meir and Kedem, 1979).

4. In Israel there are few non-orthodox synagogues (on Reform and Conservative Judaism in Israel see Tabory, 1983), and Israeli Jews differentiate themselves mainly in terms of *dati* (religious, roughly equivalent to orthodox in America), *mesoriti* ("traditional"), meaning a less orthodox or less strict level of ritual observance, and *lo-dati* (non-religious) or *hiloni* (secular). (For overviews of religion in Israel see Deshen, 1978; Yaron, 1976).

5. In deciding which mitzvot to include in our questionnaire we had the benefit of the findings of a recent study in which Israelis were questioned regarding their performance of twenty mitzvot (Ben-Meir and Kedem, 1979). No clear-cut divisions in levels of religiosity were found; there was a continuum of religiosity ranging from the "strictly religious," 14 percent of the population who performed fourteen or more of the twenty mitzvot, to the "non-religious," 39 percent who performed six or fewer of the mitzvot. Observance of the individual mitzvot ranged from 1 percent who did not use electricity on the Sabbath to 99 percent who participated in the yearly Seder meal at Passover.

6. A problem with the Goldscheider and Friedlander study is that they had few questions on specific mitzvot and they did not cover the range from those practiced by the orthodox to those practiced by the majority. In constructing a typology of religiosity they combined both objective (specific mitzvot) and subjective measures (respondents' evaluations of the importance of religion in their homes and their parents' homes). Since definitions of particular levels of observance as "religious," "traditional," or "non-religious" vary among groups of origin, especially between European and Middle Eastern Israelis, the inclusion of such subjective measures poses problems in comparing "religiosity" across groups and across generations. Studies in Israel that have depended solely on respondents' evaluations of their levels of religiosity, include Herman (1970) and Antonovsky (1963).

7. Cohen's analysis of the Boston surveys is unusual in measuring the relationship of occupation (controlling for education and other factors) and religiosity, but his discussion is limited to a comparison between salaried and self-employed and between professionals and all other occupations. As for income, Cohen found that this had little influence on ritual practice. Himmelfarb (1980) reported a small negative relationship between education and "total religiosity," but a larger positive relationship between income and "total religiosity."

8. The product-moment correlation coefficient between "Moroccan" as a dummy variable and religiosity is .46 indicating the relatively high religiosity of this group. The parallel beta coefficient has neither substantive nor statistical significance.

9. The product-moment coefficient between religiosity and years of schooling is nil, and the positive beta effect indicates the suppressive effect of the other independent variables.

REFERENCES

Antonovsky, Aaron
   1963   "Israeli Political-Social Attitudes." Amot (Hebrew)6:11-22.
Arjomand, Said Amir
   1983   "Social Change and Movements of Revitalization in Contemporary Islam."
           Working Paper Series, Department of Sociology, SUNY.
Ben-Meir, Yehuda and Peri Kedem
   1979   "Index of Religiosity of the Jewish Population of Israel." Megamot (He-
           brew)14:353-362.
Ben-Rafael, Eliezer
   1982   The Emergence of Ethnicity: Cultural Groups and Social Conflict in Israel.
           Westport, Conn.: Greenwood Press.
Berger, Peter L.
   1967   The Sacred Canopy. Garden City, New York: Doubleday.
Cohen, Hayyim, J.
   1973   The Jews of the Middle East 1860-1972. New York: John Wiley and Sons.
Cohen, Steven M.
   1983   American Modernity and Jewish Identity. New York: Tavistock.
Deshen, Shlomo
   1978   "Israeli Judaism: Introduction to the Major Patterns." International Journal of
           Middle East Studies. 9:141-169.
_____ and Moshe Shokeid
   1974   The Predicament of Homecoming: Cultural and Social Life of North African
           Immigrants in Israel. Ithaca, New York: Cornell University Press.
Goldscheider, Calvin and Dov Friedlander
   1983   "Religiosity Patterns in Israel." American Jewish Year Book. 83:3-39.
Goldscheider, Sidney and Calvin Goldscheider
   1968   Jewish Americans: Three Generations in a Jewish Community. Englewood Cliffs,
           N.J.: Prentice Hall, Inc.
Hartman, Moshe
   1975   Occupation as a Measure of Social Class in Israeli Society (Hebrew). Tel Aviv:
           Tel Aviv University.
Heller, Celia A.
   1977   On the Edge of Destruction. New York: Columbia University Press.
Herman, Simon J.
   1970   Israelis and Jews: The Continuity of an Identity. New York: Random House.
Hill, Michael
   1973   A Sociology of Religion. London: Heinemann.
Himmelfarb, Harold S.
   1980   "The Study of American Jewish Identification: How It Is Defined, Measured,
           Obtained, Sustained, Lost." Journal for the Scientific Study of Religion. 19:48-
           60.
Liebman, Charles S. and Eliezer Don-Yehiya
   1983   Civil Religion in Israel: Traditional Judaism and Political Culture in the Jewish
           State. Berkeley: University of California Press.
Martin, David
   1978   A General Theory of Secularization. Oxford: Basil Blackwell.
Mol, Hans (ed.)
   1972   Western Religion. The Hague: Mouton.
Sharot, Stephen
   1976   Judaism: A Sociology. New York: Holmes and Meier.

   1973   "The three-generation thesis and the American Jews." British Journal of Sociol-
           ogy. 24:151-164.
Shiner, Larry
   1967   "The concept of secularization in empirical research." Journal for the Scientific
           Study of Religion. 6:207-220.

Sklare, Marshall and Joseph Greenblum
1979   Jewish Identity on the Suburban Frontier. Chicago: University of Chicago Press.
Shokeid, Moshe
1984   "New Religious Trends of Middle Eastern Jews." Pp. 78-91 in Shlomo Deshen and Moshe Shokeid (eds.), Jews in the Middle East. Anthropological Perspectives on Past and Present. Tel Aviv: Schocken Publishing House (Hebrew).

_____ and Shlomo Deshen
1982   Distant Relations: Ethnicity and Politics among Arabs and North African Jews in Israel. New York: Praeger.
Smooha, Sammy
1978   Israel: Pluralism and Conflict. London: Routledge and Kegan Paul.
Swirski, Shlomo
1981   ". . . Lo Nehkshalim Ela Menahkshalim" (Orientals and Ashkenazim in Israel: The Ethnic Division of Labour). Haifa: Mahbarot Le'Mehkar U'Lebikoret (Hebrew).
Tabory, Ephraim
1983   "Reform and Conservative Judaism in Israel: A Social and Religious Profile." American Jewish Year Book. 83:41-61.
Vago, Bela
1981   "Jewish Assimilation in Rumania and in Hungary." Pp. 105-126 in Bela Vago (ed.) Jewish Assimilation in Modern Times. Boulder, Colorado: Westview Press.
Weissbrod, L.
1983   "Religion as National Identity in a Secular Society." Review of Religious Research. 24:188-205.
Wilson, Bryan R.
1966   Religion in Secular Society. London: Watts.

_____
1982   Religion in Sociological Perspective. Oxford: Oxford University Press.
Yaron, Zvi
1976   "Religion in Israel." American Jewish Year Book. 76:41-90.

14

Saints' Sanctuaries in Development Towns

Eyal Ben-Ari and Yoram Bilu

ABSTRACT: Since the 1970s new sacred sites for Jewish saints have been established in a number of Israeli development towns. In this paper this phenomenon is interpreted as a mechanism by which some of the social and cultural qualities of those urban settlements are being transformed. Development towns, which were "planted" in the periphery of the country by the central organs of the young Israeli state during the 1950s, turned into "residual communities," i.e., into localities populated by people heavily dependent on government aid and subject to external manipulation. From the 1960s, however, these towns have been the site of growing local political activism and an emerging sense of local identity. It is proposed that the interplay of these opposing sets of factors has formed the preconditions for the establishment of holy sites in development towns. The establishment of one sacred site in Northern Israel is depicted in detail in order to illustrate the mechanisms underlying the machinery of sanctifications.

Introduction

Since the early 1970s a number of Israeli development towns have been the site of a largely unnoticed but nevertheless constant urban transformation. This transformation (which has occurred in such places as Beit She'an, Safed, Hatzor-Haglilit, Kiriyat Gat and Ofakim) has been the outcome of the establishment of new sacred sites of Jewish saints.[1] Typically the sanctification of such sites, which serve as pilgrimage centers and healing shrines, has been effected either through a translocation of a saint from Morocco, or through a discovery or renewal of a sacred place in the locality on the basis of folk beliefs and local traditions. While these patterns of sanctification of space are usually the outcome of the spontaneous initiative of individuals, they nevertheless have a number of notable consequences for the transformation of the physical and social environment of the development towns where they occur.

These consequences are especially notable against a background of what are taken to be the main social and cultural characteristics of these towns. These "planted" communities (Cohen 1970) were founded during the 1950s and early 1960s in Israel's urban periphery (Matras 1973) and now encompass between one-fifth and one-sixth of the country's population.[2] These towns have been characterized (especially in regard to the initial phases of their development) in some of the following terms: lacking in social consolidation (Spiegel 1966:180-181); lacking a sense of community-wide identification and responsibility (Berler, 1970:144; Aronoff 1973:39); marked by unamicable relations among people (Altman and Rosenbaum 1973:323); having relatively little civic identification and citizen participation (Kramer 1973:49); and as dependent on outside government and public bodies (Marx 1975; 1976).

Yet despite such negative portrayals, the establishment of saints' shrines has brought about a measure of change in many of what are taken to be the major parameters of urban transformation. Spatially, the changes have been circumscribed to such matters as the erection of new facilities around the sites, e.g. synagogues, abattoirs, covered compartments for lighting candles, public bathrooms, improvised parking lots, signboards, and areas for visitors. Socially, the effects of the new holy sites have been in the mobilization of locally based kith and kin in and around such activities as escorting visitors, ritual slaughtering, preparing refreshments, and cleaning the surroundings. While some of this aid is proffered throughout the whole year in order to help maintain the site, most of it is given before and during the *hillula*, the annual celebration commemorating the death anniversary of the patron-saint. In more successful cases, these *hillulot* (pl.) may become the foci of mass pilgrimages, the number of pilgrims far exceeding the population of the local community. A less tangible, but no less important effect of the erection of the sites has been the development of a greater sense of localism in terms of attachment to place and an assertion of civic pride. Finally, the image of the communities within which the sites are located has grown in importance as these settlements have sometimes gained recognition by national leaders, and more often by municipal officials, religious figures, and pilgrims from all over the country.

The social science literature on Israel's development towns normally does not include suitable conceptual tools for dealing with the changes wrought by the construction of saintly sites. The earlier studies found within this literature contain thorough analyses of the planning devices which determined the placement and initial development of these towns and of the mechanics of migration which affected their subsequent growth and stagnation. The more recent literature is marked by detailed probes of local politics and its influence on the dynamics of these urban settlements. While these types of analyses furnish an excellent background for an examination of the case at hand, they do not seem to fit its peculiarities. An examination of the establishment of these new sites thus necessitates an analysis of a relatively unexplored mechanism of urban transformation which is of central import for the understanding of these settlements: the sanctification of space.

Three related analytical issues, or sets of issues, suggest themselves in this regard. The first has to do with the dynamics of the sanctification of urban space. It involves elucidating the ways in which sites are consecrated in the context of a wider map of religious significance, and legitimated and accepted among a group of believers. The second question is related to the social preconditions for the emergence of this process of sanctification. Here we must deal with the "urban peripherality" of the phenomenon, i.e. with its emergence in communities marked by a high percentage of Middle Eastern Jews, relatively low status, and a working class population "locked into" their communities for a number of decades. The third set of questions, clearly a derivative of the former two sets, is about the effects of the sanctification of space. It entails drawing out the specific effects of erecting such sites for the local allocation of resources, the dynamics of communal social networks, and the development of a sense of "home" among the populace of these settlements.

Beginnings: Central Planning and Household Migration

The initial shaping of the spatial and social character of Israel's development towns was effected primarily through the use of one mechanism: the formal policy making and planning processes undertaken by the country's central government.[3] The use of this mechanism grew out of the special circumstances which Israel faced during the first years of its existence. Up until 1948, Israel's Jewish population was concentrated either in one of the three main cities (Jerusalem, Tel Aviv, and Haifa) or in small agricultural settlements. The intermediate sized towns, like Ramle, Lod, or Tiberias, were either comprised totally of Arabs or had an Arab majority. With the flights of Arabs from the country during the 1948 war, most of these medium sized towns were left nearly vacant and the need for similar sized Jewish settlements became apparent. It was against this background that the establishment of the development towns throughout the country was begun.

While other countries such as Australia, Brazil, or the Soviet Union have had programs which were designed to promote the development of frontier areas, Israel stands as an exception in this regard. For in Israel there "has been practically no significant settlement of peripheral areas independent of deliberate, policy-originated and policy-supported settlement" (Matras 1973:3). Israel has not been the scene of a "gold rush," nor of the discovery of any important oil fields or mineral deposits which propelled governments to formulate planning policies for frontier areas. The initial mechanism for the construction of development towns, then, was that of formal decision making: that is, a process which involved the formal proceedings and decrees of a highly centralized government machinery. Through the use of this essentially political mechanism (Cohen 1976:54), the features of these towns (their location, detailed planning and implementation, social make up, industrial infrastructure, and physical layout) were all controlled and carried out by large and centralized government and public agencies. In this process the country's "urban frontier" was politically organized in terms of super and sub-ordination: each town was granted some rights over its territory but was at all times subject to the overall regulation of the central government.

At the same time this political organization of space had an explicit collective orientation. For these thirty or so new, or as they came to be known, development towns were seen to be instrumental in achieving four national objectives (Shachar 1971; Comay and Kirschenbaum 1973; Cohen 1977): providing housing and employment for large numbers of immigrants; establishing regional centers which would service their rural hinterlands; dispersing the population from the over concentrated cores of the main cities; and securing Jewish presence in areas of sparse population for defense purposes.

These, then, were the lines along which the development towns were begun and which determined their initial social character. As Cohen (1970:489) notes, these were essentially "planted" communities:

> The planned character of the new towns as well as the framework of their development --an apparatus of governmental and other public, central institutions --attest to the fact that they are "planted" communities, established by decree for overall social purposes, and have not evolved in accordance with the pressures and demands of local conditions. This means that these communities and their inhabitants are, or are at least considered to be, passive objects of manipulation by central agencies.

These "planted," or what Suttles (1972:ch.4) perhaps more aptly terms "contrived" communities then, were artificially created settlements. They were artificial both in that they were set up by large external agencies on the basis of national priorities and in that their establishment was effected despite the lack of existing social institutions and "natural" networks.

An understanding of the beginnings of these towns involves an examination of another transformative mechanism which began to operate almost as soon as people were placed in these towns. This second mechanism (the patterning of migration) is related to the constant movement of people in and out, as well as within, the development towns. If the previous mechanism of planning and policy making was essentially a collective one, this device involved the individual household. Here the determining considerations did not have to do with national priorities. Rather, they involved considerations about the location of the development town in respect to "other resources, productive facilities, or populations linked with the realization of different goals" (Cohen 1976:52). In the case of development towns, this implied accessibility to better accommodations, job opportunities, relatives, higher status areas, or cultural and educational opportunities.

As we shall see, given the nature of the land and property markets, governed as they are by the forces of exchange and pricing, and given the peculiar characteristics of the populations settled in the development towns, the effects of this mechanism had serious implications.[4] This is because for many of the new immigrants who arrived in the country the peripheral settlements served as temporary places of abode until they acquired the resources to move to other, more desirable communities. In short, the trend that evolved in most of the development towns was that of a selective in- and out-migration:

> Major difficulties were encountered by these new towns in attracting immigrants from Europe or America, or even veteran and native born Israelis of higher socio-economic status. The turnover rate was high, with immigrants who had improved their socio-economic status after a few years in the development towns generally tending to move towards the older cities on the coastal plain (Ben Zadok and Goldberg 1984:18).

On a national scale what emerged were serious disparities: the peripheral new town steadily came to be characterized by a high ratio of Middle Eastern Jews and by a low socio-economic status. In other words, they came to be spatial loci within which a relatively distinct socio- economic and ethnic stratum crystallized (Weintraub and Krauss 1982:377).

The people who remained within the towns tended to have modest occupational aspirations or to require the housing and welfare assistance which were available to them as residents of such settlements. The towns thus grew to become "residual communities" (Kramer 1973:49), to become "sinks" for the less resourceful immigrants (Spilerman and Habib 1975:805). As Marx (1976) notes, the single word most aptly describing these communities in their initial stages is that of dependence. Thus, for example in many towns external agencies tended to exploit internal divisions and to impede the growth of a sense of community identification and responsibility (Aronoff 1973:39). Moreover, the transient nature of many settlements entailed by the high population turnover (Altman and Rosenbaum 1973:324) led to the development of indifference in regard to the future of the town and to the obstruction of spontaneous action on the basis of common interests (Berler 1970:144).

It was thus the conjoint operation of these two mechanisms , governmental direction and selective migration, that determined to a large degree the rather bleak circumstances of the development towns during the first decade or so of their existence. Yet, at the same time, many of these circumstances appear to have been associated with the relative youth, with the earliest stages of development, of the settlements (Matras 1973:13). For alongside these processes new mechanisms which were slowly transforming the urban experiences of these towns began to operate.

Continuation: Local Activism and Attachment to the Locality

From the late 1960s a new mechanism began to bring about changes in the urban environment of many development towns. Centered essentially around the workings of local activism and local government, this mechanism has been described variously as interest articulation, making demands, or political participation. Against the background of the social circumstances of these "planted" communities, however, the effecting of this mechanism should not be taken for granted. Indeed, it is not surprising to learn that many of the inhabitants of these towns were either indifferent to politics or did not believe in the efficacy of their actions (Bernstein 1984:25ff.).

But this was a different period, one in which the new political and civic sentiments that began to emerge after the 1967 war started to pervade many public issues. In very abbreviated terms, these new sentiments "the ethnic issue" grew out of the rising aspirations of the younger elite, and the resentment of many second generation youths of Middle Eastern origins over their predicament (Cohen 1983:120 -121).

From the point of view of the "Middle Eastern" majority who resided in the development towns, the implication of these wider trends was the appearance of a combination of a sense of legitimacy in expressing their demands, and of a perception of the political efficacy of these expressions.

These, however, were not vague or ill defined perceptions, but ones which were firmly rooted in the changing content of local politics. As Deshen (1982:24) puts it, the local political level developed from the grass roots in these settlements as "a new power arena which was wide open to the new immigrants."

A number of studies have documented the effects of the changing qualities of local politics in development towns. Thus we are told of the emergence of local electoral lists which are independent of the national political parties (Ben-Zadok and Goldberg 1984:23); the strengthening of localism, i.e. an affirmation of local interests and a distinction between local and national policy (Ben-Zadok and Goldberg 1984:20); the rise of ethnic representation in local municipal and workers' councils and the increase of influence on decision-making (Avineri 1973; Yishai 1984:286); the growth of a greater sense of attachment to the local community (Deshen 1982:28); or, outside the formal arena, the establishment of local newspapers (Caspi 1980:13), and the appearance of protest movements (Hasson 1983:178; Bama'aracha 1985). As Ben Zadok and Goldberg (1984:27) phrase it, "the stereotype of a 'manipulated subject' does not fit the present new town resident."

It is important to note that while local activism is also an essentially political mechanism, its focus and effects differ from the political devices which figured in the initial shaping of the development towns. While both processes involve formal policy making and the promulgation of ordinances and decrees, the loci of their operations differ. From the point of view of the development towns, while the devices used during their beginnings involved directions coming from above, local activism implies the use of negotiations as the means for accomplishing things. While the national collective priorities figured as the central considerations earlier on, now it is local (albeit still collective) criteria which are taken into account in the decision -making processes.

Alongside this new mechanism, other less tangible processes began to operate within the development towns. These processes (which have to do with the creation of a sense of attachment to the locality) have only been alluded to in the literature on Israel's urban periphery. The general lack of attention to the development of sentiments of belonging to and ties with the local community is related, no doubt, to the way these towns were portrayed in the earlier literature. Indeed, within the earlier studies, the creation of local sentiments was seen to be especially difficult within the context of artificially created locales like the development towns. This is because such settlements, as mentioned earlier, were viewed as having a transient nature, as populated by people with previous attachments elsewhere, and as marked by a general lack of "natural," informal social ties.

Despite this view, for a large part of the permanent population of the development towns, the simple facts of living for a long time in the settlement and of coming into contact with others there were significant for the creation of ties within and with the locality. Thus, a close reading of the literature on the towns reveals a constant, if somewhat subdued, emphasis on some of the following qualities: Soen (1973; 1976 -1977) underlined the strong relationship between length of residence and presence of kith and kin in the development towns and identification with them; Berler (1970:144) categorized the phenomenon, in somewhat derogatory tones, as ethnic particularism and cited a number of studies which illuminated the link between the continued residence of relatives in the settlements and the strengthening of attachment to them. Deshen (1974) highlighted the development of active neighboring ties centering around religious activities, while Effrat (1977:66) hinted at the creation of what one might call "urban villages" in one town. And finally, Goldberg (1984a:15) gives examples of the growth of "home territories" of different groups in a northern settlement.

In brief, what all of this seems to point to is the operation of a process through which attachment or a sense of belonging to the locality is created. As Guest (1984:1) rightly notes, the growth of such sentiments (in older as well as in newer "contrived communities") is related to the interplay of two elements: territorial contiguity and ecological stability. Taken together, these two requirements make possible the "natural" maturation of local ties and the emergence of a sense of sharing a common experience and identity. To quote Guest (1984:16),

> Such simple acts as living for a long time in an area and interacting with nearby others make social claims upon us... We become caught up in webs of social relationships which have no rational basis but are meaningful and important for us.

It is the interplay of the four mechanisms discussed above which formed the background   or more aptly the pre-conditions   for the emergence of the processes by which holy sites were established in a number of development towns.

The Establishment of Holy Sites:
The Case of Rabbi David u-Moshe

In order to facilitate an exploration of the way holy sites are established it may be helpful to trace the specifics of one case: that of the "House of Rabbi David u-Moshe" in Safed. In later sections, which will deal with the analysis of this case, we shall have occasion to refer to relevant comparative material from other development towns.

In 1973 a forestry worker named Avraham Ben-Haim dedicated a room in his small Safed apartment to a Jewish Moroccan saint, Rabbi David u-Moshe. This saint was one of the most popular saints in Morocco and his *hillulah* would draw thousands of people from all over the Maghreb country to this sanctuary located in the High Atlas mountains. The dedication itself came after a dream-series in which the Rabbi had appeared and claimed that he had left his tomb and that he wanted a new abode in Avraham's residence. Avraham published these dreams as "announcements to the public" which were circulated among Moroccan synagogues throughout the country. The impact of those announcements was remarkable, and within a few years the new tomb was transformed into a major pilgrimage center which serves as a full-fledged substitute for the original sanctuary. As a consequence the saint's residence draws to it a constant flow of supplicants all year long. It is by far the most successful of the sacred loci which have been created through individual initiative, and has been designated as an obligatory station in the "saint map" of Northern Israel by many North African immigrants.

Having traced the general contours of this case, let us begin to explore it in greater detail. Avraham was a native of a fairly large southern Moroccan village near Marrakech. Despite its remoteness from rabbinical centers, the village was a place where Jewish life could be lived fully and piously. His father was an unsophisticated man who earned his living as a shoemaker, but who did not fail to inculcate in his children from an early age a deep-seated faith in the *tsaddiqim* (holy, pious men). Indeed, Avraham's childhood recollections are replete with memories of visits to the tombs of the local village saints. In addition, Avraham views his Moroccan past with affection and sentiments. He describes life in his native village as characterized by peaceful and harmonious relations both among the Jews and between them and the Muslims, plentiful and uncontaminated natural resources, and a Jewish lifestyle which was marked by strict observance of laws and spirituality. If this is an idyllic view, it is in no small measure the outcome of the strong contrast with the hardships encountered in an Israeli development town.

In his mid-twenties and already married, with an infant daughter, Avraham came to Israel in 1954 and was immediately sent to the town of Safed. Life was not easy in the new neighborhood which had been created according to the model of development towns on the site of a small Jewish settlement. The apartment was tiny and during the first years was devoid of running water and electricity. Avraham found that he had to give up his former occupation of shoemaker and soon began to earn a living as a forest worker, which is one of the lowest-ranked jobs in terms of status and salary.

Since his immigration and settlement in Safed Avraham has lived in Shikun Canaan, as the immigrant housing project is known. Since his parents and most of his siblings were settled in the same neighborhood, the extended family has managed to preserve a sense of "togetherness" which was typical of their life in Morocco. Indeed, as the family's married children also tend to find residence nearby, and with the fourth generation (now) being born in the 1980s, an impressive cross -generational   stability   (not unlike what is found in other development towns) has been established.

In 1972, a year before Rabbi David u-Moshe's first visitation, Avraham's closest brother was killed in a car accident. Avraham's religious faith had never before been so seriously shaken, but it was the *tsaddiq* who put an end to Avraham's prolonged distress. In one of his first oneiric apparitions, he took Avraham to a magnificent garden and picked one of the most beautiful roses that grew there, explaining that in the same way God selects the best people to reside with him. Under the saint's explicit demand, Avraham stopped his mourning and complaints.

The death of his brother undoubtedly created in Avraham a state of emotional turmoil which constituted a "suitable" background for the appearance of the *tsaddiq*. The event which immediately precipitated this appearance, however, was related to his intention to move from his apartment to a bigger place in another neighborhood. This change was prevented at the last moment by Rabbi David u-Moshe's announcement in 1973 that he desires the old apartment as his permanent residence. It is through his appearance that Avraham and his family have become bound to their place.

Interestingly, a firm decision to change the place of living by moving to a less peripheral town or neighborhood, eventually annulled by a *tsaddiq*, underlies the creation of other sacred sites as well. The town of Beit She'an, for example, has recently been the locus of intense hagiolatric revivals and two sites have been established there in adjacent neighborhoods. In both cases, the precipitating factors underlying the establishment of the new sites were the firm intentions of the future initiators to move to another place. The same pattern was discerned in other sites in the southern development towns of Ofakim and Yeru'ham.

The recurrent precipitating factor well reflects an ambivalence that initiators to be (along with many residents of development towns) have felt towards their communities. On the one hand, these are areas which are marked by lack of employment, and educational opportunities and by a rather poor public image. On the other hand, many of those people find themselves linked to their locality through various networks of friends and family. In many of these instances, however, the conflict is solved by the *tsaddiq* who sanctifies the old place of living and impels its inhabitants to stay there.

The revelations of Rabbi David u-Moshe in 1973 marked a dramatic change in Avraham's life. From then on the saint's oneiric messages became his sole guidelines for action. One of these first messages was to write down his dreams and to distribute them in all the Moroccan communities in Israel. In complying with the *tsaddiq*'s command, Avraham transformed his private vision into a public affair, shared and supported by many.

Following the phase in which Avraham's house emerged as the saint's chosen abode, there was a long period of effort aimed at developing the site and securing the economic basis of the *hillula*. Gradually, the apartment and its environs were turned into a shrine complex. While the complex itself is located in the standard, rather unattractive house which seems indistinguishable from other apartment blocks in the neighborhood, at its center is situated the saint's room. Placed within it are a marble tablet, which acts as a substitute for the absent gravestone, a donation box and various ritual objects, a bookcase designed as an Holy Ark, an ornamental chair for use in circumcisions, and a narrow bench for praying. These are placed against a colorful (almost eye-dazzling) array of carpets, tapestries and amulets which lend the room an aura of ceremoniality.

On the day of the *hillulah* the tiny room becomes the focus of a mass celebration in which some 15,000-20,000 people take part. Although the inhabitants of Safed and its hinterland are over-represented among the celebrants, many pilgrims come on a one-day journey from all over the country. While most of the participants in the *hillulah* are of

Moroccan extraction, in recent years, groups of Libyan and Tunisian Jews have also participated in the celebration.

Having reached the neighborhood the visitors are channeled into a narrow alley where a small but variegated market spontaneously emerges at the time of the *hillulah*. The commodities which are sold comprise the peculiar mix of sacred and secular which is so typical of pilgrimage sites (Meeker 1979:209). Holy books, oil and candles, and popular portraits of renowned *tsaddiqim* are offered alongside a variety of edibles, garments and ornaments. Beggars and sellers of blessings (also an indispensable part of the pilgrimage setting) are grouped at the end of the trail near the entrance to the apartment which has been enlarged and reshaped into an area for servicing the pilgrims. However, since this area too is small, most of the celebrants locate themselves wherever they find an empty space, be it a yard of a neighboring house or a nearby sidewalk.

In the absence of a formally imposed ritual structure, the only act deemed compulsory during the *hillulah* is a visit to the saints' room. From the early house of the evening until late at night a long line is formed opposite the entrance to the apartment. Some sturdy men, recruited from a group of relatives, neighbors, and friends who voluntarily participate in the organization of the *hillulah*, regulate the massive flow of human traffic.

Inside the *tsaddiq*'s room an atmosphere of fervor and ecstasy prevails. The devotees, particularly women, enter the room displaying gestures of submission. They kiss the marble tablet and the carpeted walls and utter their prayers and wishes with great excitement. Before leaving they place generous sums of money in the donation-box. On their way out, the visitors have ample opportunity to survey the rest of the apartment, the modesty of which stands in sharp contrast to the grandeur of the richly decorated room of the *tsaddiq*.

Most of the celebrants conclude their visit to the saint's room by lighting candles in his honor. In other pilgrimages, where the tombs are located in the open, candles are lit very close to the grave. In "Rabbi David u-Moshe's House" a special, covered compartment on the far side of the front yard is used for this purpose. Pilgrims throw candles inside the compartment, which soon becomes a fiery furnace, and is the focus of much excited praying and crying. Another place of note are three small booths adjacent to the house where teams of local volunteers deliver food for free to the celebrants. The food is prepared during the week preceding the *hillulah* by a group of female relatives and neighbors supervised by Avraham's wife.

Toward the late evening the *hillulah* becomes a formidable spectacle of mass celebration. The streets near the house are jammed with parked vehicles. Visitors continue to flow towards the house, pushing their way to the *tsaddiq*'s room. Policemen from the nearby station are called to control the heavy traffic. The crowded front yard becomes the scene of varied social activities as groups from places throughout the country intermingle, old acquaintances meet again, and new associations are formed. Women whose vows have been granted offer trays of sweets to the people around; popular singers attract the celebrants with traditional songs in praise of Rabbi David u-Moshe; and local political figures appear to congratulate the pilgrims.

The shift from this climax of mass-celebrations to the ending of the *hillulah* is quite abrupt, for by midnight most of the visitors have already left for their homes. Many of the people to be found around the site on the morning following the *hillulah* belong to the core of relatives and friends who help Avraham's family in putting the place back to its ordinary state. Soon the neighborhood reassumes its shabby provincial character.

Inspired by the positive response to his project, Avraham has sought to maximize its potential by absorbing other saints into it. Rabbi David u-Moshe, Avraham's patron-saint, has remained the dominant figure in the site, but the house bearing his name has become in recent years a pantheon on saints as six other *tsaddiqim* successively appeared in Avraham's dreams and expressed their wish to have their *hillulot* celebrated in his place. Well dispersed throughout the whole year, the seven *hillulot* have strengthened Avraham's web of associations with the *tsaddiqim*. For, by incorporation of these other saints, Avraham has expanded the one-day temporal marker of holiness to a sacred annual calendar which regulates the rhythm of life course of his family and neighbors.

Clearly Avraham has succeeded in creating a "sacred space" (Eliade 1954) in erecting the house which serves Rabbi David u-Moshe and the other six saints and a "sacred time" in and around the *hillulot* days of these *tsaddiqim*. Yet an understanding of the process of consecration or sanctification (Cohen 1976:57) of space in development towns involves explicating a complex mix of elements: the specific cultural tools through which sanctification is effected, the preconditions for its emergence and the spatial and social implications for the local community.

Sanctification: Preconditions and Machinery

The sanctification of space is always carried out through the symbolic idiom, the traditional "tools" that a specific culture provides. The cultural tools by which the holy sites were consecrated in Israel's development towns are part of the indigenous Moroccan traditions (Jewish as well as Muslim) of maraboutism and hagiolatry (Westermark 1926; Eickelman 1967; Geertz 1968; Gellner 1969).

The presence of saints was a basic given in the culturally constituted reality of Moroccan Jews and Muslims. Indeed on the basis of recent studies (Ben-Ami 1984; Goldberg 1983) it has become clear that almost all of the Jewish communities had their own patron-saints. The high points of veneration of these saints were the collective pilgrimages to their sanctuaries. But what is of importance in regard to these holy men is that they provided one of the central idioms through which people articulated and came to terms with their experiences (Crapanzano 1977:1). Thus, in addition to collective pilgrimages, visits to saints' tombs were often conducted on an individual basis in times of trouble. Devotees lit candles in honor of these holy men, held festive meals for them, and in many cases the relationship with a saint spanned an entire life course. The adherent displayed due respect for "his" saint, visited his tomb on the *hillula*, and expected that the latter would intercede on his behalf whenever he faced any difficulties or problems.

This hagiolatric tradition formed the background for the actions of people like Avraham Ben-Haim in Safed. The specific psychological mechanism through which the holy sites were established is related to the role of visitational dreams. The role of dreams in sustaining and facilitating the innovation of cultural traditions has been documented in a number of societies (Bourguignon 1972; Lanternari, 1975; O'Nell 1976; Stepen 1979). In Morocco the role of visitational dreams in discovering and in maintaining linkages to saints has long been a feature of both Jewish and Muslim practices. In Avraham's case dreams appear as devices which aided him on numerous occasions: in deciding to stay in Safed, in gaining confidence to negotiate with contractors and municipal officials, or in providing justification for his actions.

Yet the following question still remains[5]: in what way is this kind of sanctification of space related to the peculiarities of development towns? One answer may have to do with the high percentage of Middle Eastern, and especially North African, immigrants in these settlements. This argument would posit that such towns are populated by people who would be predisposed to use these kinds of cultural devices. Yet, surely, such an explanation is at best only partial. While Maghrebi immigrants reside in many different kinds of Israeli settlements, urban as well as rural, the phenomenon of establishing holy sites appears only in development towns. A fuller explanation may thus lie in the way this sanctification fits with the basic conditions (or more specifically, with a basic predicament) shared by certain residents of development towns

A brief digression by way of Cyrenaica may help to illuminate this point. Meeker (1979:210-211) in a revealing insight shows how the veneration of saints' tombs among the Bedouin of Cyrenaica is related to the basic social circumstances of certain men: i.e. to what he called their "vulnerable domestic interests." These men were caught in a situation in which they had an interest in the land on the

one hand, but did not possess the suitable political resources for controlling access to it on the other. By positing
a fixed link between a man and the land through the form of
a saints' tomb these men attempted to usurp a measure of
ownership of the land. Through the vehicle of saints' tombs,
they thus sought to come to terms with their situation by
transposing an essentially precarious political and economic situation into an immutable religious one.

It is a similar process, we contend, that goes on in regard to many of the holy sites recently established in Israel's development towns. It is a process which is most obviously observed in relation to the problematic nature of deciding whether to leave or stay in these peripheral settlements. On the one hand, residents of development towns
live in places which are characterized by few employment
and cultural opportunities, and by a constant flow of in- and
out-migration. They reside in towns which are often viewed
by Israelis with a mixture of condescension, mild disdain
and paternalistic concern (Goldberg 1984a:7). Moreover,
many of these people (and especially those who are not
politically oriented) are vulnerable. They lack the political
and economic ability to restructure their living environment.

Yet for these people a move out of the development
town (even given that they possess the requisite resources)
is not an act that is easily realized. For on the other hand,
there are residents who have never left their hometowns
since their immigration to Israel. In their case the sentiments
of being an integral part of the locality (whether through local activism or through networks of friends and neighbors)
are often reinforced by the transgenerational continuity of
families in the town: witness the four generations of Avraham's family in Safed.

The establishment of holy sites in Israel's development
towns can now be more fully understood. These holy sites
were established in towns which were shaped into two opposing directions by the mechanisms which operated during the decades of their existence. The juxtaposition of the
"negative" consequences of the earlier devices of planning
and selective migration, and the "positive" outcomes of local
activism and creation of a sense of belonging created a

dilemma for residents of many development towns. This dilemma (whether to leave or to stay and somehow change the town) was resolved for some people through the establishment of holy sites. It was resolved by the transposition of the "real" contradictory situation onto an otherworldly plane, that is, onto a plane in which persons became decisively "fixed" to their local communities.

While the above explanation illuminates the relation between the holy sites and their erection in Israel's urban periphery, it leaves unexplored the specific operations on these sites' space. These operations are related to the movement and establishment of (to create a metaphor) the other-worldly immigrants, the saintly settlers. Three points merit underlining in this regard. The first involves the special potential inherent in the visitational dreams for overcoming the restrictions imposed by a lack of political and economic resources. This kind of dreaming (in ways akin to what Sack [1980:149] calls mythical thinking) makes possible the negation or suspension of spatial distance. This implies that the visitational dreams facilitated the migration of saints between Morocco and Israel without the limitations faced by the thousands of "real" immigrants who made such journeys. It allowed (to put this somewhat crudely) the movement of the holy men without the need to incur the costs of transportation or the difficulties of crossing international borders.

Second, this mechanism of sanctification makes possible a linking between the symbolic space of society and "real" space. This is similar to the way an act of settlement or construction serves such a function in societies all over the world (Tuan 1977:104; Sack 1980;155). Thus, the installment of a saint in a development town serves to do two things: to recreate the special cultural forms of Jewish life in Morocco and to inscribe the holy site on the map of Jewish holy places in Israel

The third, and perhaps most concrete, point is related to the effects of housing the saintly immigrants on the development towns as built-up systems. Given the limited resources of the innovators at the beginning it was natural that the constructional effects of establishing the sanctuaries were limited to only a partial restructuring of the sites themselves. As Choay (1968:31), in a distinctly continental parlance, puts it,

> The acceleration of history reveals the vice inherent in all built-up systems: a permanence and a rigidity which makes it impossible for them to continually transform themselves according to the rhythm set by less rooted systems such as language, technology, clothing or painting. Against this permanent threat, the modern city's own means allow it but one meagre defense: partial restructuring.

Put less abstractly, this means that the expression of the special logic or rhythm of sanctification (for example sumptuousness or ceremoniality) was limited more or less to the existing structures and houses. Thus the rich display of the centrality of the saints' abode in Safed was limited to a tiny room in a "regular" residence with only a modest reconstruction of the housefront. This holds true for other places such as Yeruham, Ofakim, or Beit She'an. In all of these places the recently erected saints' shrines are contained in small rooms or huts within their initiators' apartments or yards. This is not to deny that sanctification often takes place on a grand architectural scale. It is rather to underscore the fact that it can find a measure of expression even within the limits of "ordinary" residences and neighborhoods.

Conclusion: Implications and Suggestions

The establishment of holy sites in Israel's development towns is not limited to the installation of saints in "new" locations. A number of other devices for the sanctification of holy sites have been in operation in Israel's urban periphery. One such vehicle has been the consecration of tombs of local *tsaddiqim* (mainly from the Talmudic period) which have been pilgrimage centers from as early as the Middle Ages. Two examples of this process are the Jewish Moroccan appropriation of Talmudic sages' tombs in Hatzor

Haglilit and Yavneh. In both cases long-existing traditions of holy sites have been "colored" by North African practices.

Aside from "annexing" old-time native pilgrimage sites, new centers have been established around the tombs of contemporary rabbis who were allotted saintly attributes in their lifetimes or, more often, posthumously. The most impressive examples of this trend are the mass pilgrimages to the tomb of Rabbi Haim Houri (a Tunisian rabbi who died in 1957) which is located in the municipal cemetery of Beersheba (Weingrod n.d.), and to the tomb of Baba Sali of the venerated Abu Hatsera family in Netivot. Other minor, local-bound *hillulot* following this pattern take place in such places as Ashdod, Ofakim and Migdal Ha'Emek.

Against this background it appears that sacred sites may well continue to emerge in large communities of traditionally-oriented North African Jews. Indeed, these processes (though short of encompassing all such Jews in Israel) are too recurrent to be considered sporadic or episodic. In such places as Beit She'an, Hatzor, and Safed, the traditional pattern of a community with "its" own *tsaddiq* has been reestablished. The messages carried by such actions are as follows: "One should not turn one's face to Morocco when looking for Rabbi David u-Moshe's help; one should go to Safed instead." "Beit She'an is not a place to be disregarded and deserted for it contains a site of utmost sanctity."

These kinds of messages are related in turn to the significance of the *tsaddiq* to the town in which the site has been erected. The appearance of a saint in a development town may contribute to (as well as reflect) a change in the image of the place. As noted before, the *tsaddiq* accords the town an aura of sanctity, through which it is "cathected" with the holy man's divine grace. In this way, the residents' sense of belonging to the locality acquires a wider meaning. The sense of attachment, if you like, is placed within a larger meaning-giving system, within a holy map of pilgrimage sites in Israel.

Yet the growth and implications of these contentions cannot be understood apart from the changing context of ethnic consciousness in Israel. For it is in this context that the legitimacy of a whole range of cultural tools for contending with the difficulties faced by the Middle Eastern immigrants to Israel are anchored. Thus, the installation of saints in new locations should be seen in the context of the tenacious preservation or revival of such sponsored, as well as spontaneous, practices as folk healing, Middle Eastern music and dance (Cohen and Shiloah 1985), ethnic festivals, lecture series, museum exhibits, radio programs dedicated to aspects of Jewish culture in the Muslim world, ethnic journals, or the memoralization of rabbis (Goldberg 1977:170-176).

Contrary to a naive "melting-pot" conception, the relative improvement in the socio-economic conditions of the North African Jews in Israel has facilitated an awareness of their distinctive ethnic identity. The folk veneration of saints and the establishment of their sanctuaries have (along with a whole array of practices outlined above) provided many Middle Eastern Jews in Israel with a set of cultural means to deal with their situation. To underscore this by way of example, by furnishing his community with a viable idiom, Avraham's project has become a cultural resource of considerable importance. The appearance of saints in Israel's urban periphery has thus facilitated a process through which the inhabitants of these areas (once the reluctant or passive victims of arbitrary policies promulgated by the central government) have actively contended with their situation, become more rooted in their localities, and strengthened local patriotic sentiments. As such, the *hillulot* in various sites partake of the nature of "ethnic renewal ceremonies" (Gluckman 1963; Weingrod n.d.): i.e., rites which reflect the growing confidence of an emigre group in being part of the contemporary Israeli scene while, at the same time, indicating a strong sense of ethnic distinctiveness.

A recognition of these trends raises, in turn, a question about the "Middle Eastern" quality of Israel's development towns. In a wide-ranging paper in which he compared the urban experience of Israel with that of the Arab world, Cohen (1979:18) suggested the following: that despite government efforts to the contrary, Israel's development towns have undergone a process of Levantinization, a reversion to the "habitual lethargy" of the Levant. According to Cohen (1979:87) in these towns, the

> customs and life ways to which the inhabitants were accustomed prior to immigration took over, neutralizing in many respects the forces of incorporation emanating from the center of Israeli society. This Levantinization process was probably reinforced by the formation of eth-noclasses of Afro-Asian origin in these towns, itself an unintended consequence of the new town policy.

At first glance, the establishment and activation of new centers for the veneration of saints in some of the country's development towns seems to fit this characterization. Yet, as we have rather relentlessly been stressing, this phenomenon puts into question Cohen's description of a reversion to an "habitual lethargy" which is devoid of potential for innovation and an active contention with the changing circumstances of the towns. By way of conclusion it may perhaps be apt to highlight a number of these innovative and active aspects of the phenomenon under study.

The establishment of saints' tombs should be seen, first of all, as one out of a number of alternative mechanisms which people and organizations use to change their physical and social environments. Thus we propose that, in dealing with the patterns of transformation of Israel's development towns, different kinds of mechanisms (and mixes of mechanisms) should be taken into account. More specifically, this implies going beyond the stress of the instrumental and political devices--planning, migration and activism--which have figured as the prime foci of research on Israel's urban periphery, towards an examination of the "cultural" resources which are at people's disposal in order to transform their urban settlements. These kinds of resources, in other words, may be the only viable means through which people such as Avraham in Safed (who belongs to the rank-and-file in terms of background and political acumen) may have.

In this regard, if the cultural resources which individuals use are remarkably similar to those used in the Levant (or more specifically in the Maghreb) this is because people naturally utilize the social techniques which their tradition bequeaths them. Thus neither the mere existence of these techniques nor their similarity to Moroccan traditions are necessarily reasons for believing that they contribute to a lethargic passivity. As Goldberg (1984b) rightly notes, culture or tradition should not be seen as a monolithic force from the past but as a system of meanings, parts of which are actively utilized by persons in changing social circumstances.

In this regard, however, we would suggest two additional problems for further research.[6] The first has to do with a refinement of our general assertion that there is a relation between saints, shrines and development towns. Since these towns differ historically in the way they have been subject to the macro-forces of planning, migration and local activism, one may well ask the following question: how are these differences related to variations in the kinds of shrines which are being built, and to the diversity of processes through which they are being sanctified? The second problem involves comparing the establishment of saints' shrines with other mechanisms by which the residents of the development towns have produced symbolic manifestations of themselves and rationalized their continued residence in the settlements. Here the question is how does the saintly sanctification of space differ functionally and symbolically from such activities as building synagogues or community centers, congregating in cafes or on neighborhood corners, or the operation of youth clubs or sports organizations?

These contentions and questions should not be misconstrued as an argument for the establishment of saints' tombs as a panacea for all of the problems of development towns in Israel. One cannot make the easy assumption that all such difficulties will be solved to the extent that the inhabitants of such settlements become (politically or "culturally") active. For governments and private corporations vary greatly in their ability to take effective action. As Spiegel (1966:184; see also Handelman and Shamgar-Handelman 1978) noted two decades ago, many, if not most, of the problems of these towns are related to the twin factors of population stabilization and the creation of more and better jobs. What we do argue for, however, is a richer appreciation of the means which people utilize in order to come to terms with and change their social and physical circumstances.

ACKNOWLEDGEMENTS

Thanks are due to V. Azarya, E. Cohen, H. Goldberg, R. Kahane, A. Seligman and to two anonymous reviewers for comments on earlier drafts of this paper, and to the Harry S. Truman Research Institute for generous help in assisting us to complete it.

NOTES

[1] During 1981-982, Yoram Bilu conducted extensive observations and interviews in several sites in Israel where local or Moroccan traditions of saint veneration had been renewed. Most of the material was gathered in two locales in Northern Israel: Safed and Beit She'an. In order to render the picture more complete, however, he also conducted research in Hatsor Haglilit, Ofakim, and Kiriyat Gat.

[2] No one definition of development towns exists. Following Goldberg (1984a:2), however, we refer to those towns on the country's geographical periphery in the Galilee (North) and Negev (South).

[3] A good, if abbreviated, historical overview of the growth of development towns in Israel can be found in Goldberg (1984a: chap.1).

[4] For reasons of brevity the main argument in the text will emphasize migration into and out of the development towns. An important parallel mechanism which we leave unanalyzed involves intra -town mobility (Don and Hovav 1971-1972; Efrat 1977).

[5] Greater detail regarding the psychological aspects of this case can be found in Bilu (1986) and Bilu and Abramovich (1985).

[6] We are greatly indebted to an anonymous reviewer for aiding us in formulating these questions.

REFERENCES CITED

Avineri, S. (1973). Israel: Two Nations? IN Israel: Social Structure and Change, M. Curtis and M.S. Chertoff (eds.). New Brunswick, NJ: Transaction, pp. 281-305.

Altman, E.A. and B.R. Rosenbaum (1973). Principles of Planning and Zionist Ideology: The Israeli Development Town. Journal of the American Institute of Planners 39:316-325.

Aronoff, M.J. (1973). Development Towns in Israel. IN Israel: Social Structure and Change, M. Curtis and M.S. Chertoff (eds.). New Brunswick, NJ: Transaction, pp. 27-46.

Bama'aracha, (1985). The "Struggle-85" Movement: Activists in Urban Neighborhoods and in Development Towns. Bama'aracha 292:26 (Hebrew).

Ben-Ami, I. (1984). Folk-Veneration of Saints Among Jews in Morocco. Jerusalèm: The Magnes Press (Hebrew).

Ben -Ami, I. (1981). The Folk-Veneration of Saints Among Moroccan Jews; Traditions, Continuity and Change. The Case of the Holy Man, Rabbi David u-Moshe. IN Studies in Judaism and Islam, S. Morag et al. (eds.). Jerusalem: Magnes (Hebrew), pp. 283-345.

Ben-Zadok E. (1985). National planning - The Critical Neglected Link: One Hundred Years of Jewish Settlement in Israel. International Journal of Middle Eastern Studies17: 329-345.

Ben-Zadok E. and G. Goldberg (1984). Voting patterns of Oriental Jews in Development towns. Jerusalem Quarterly 32: 16-27.

Berler, A. (1970). New Towns in Israel. Jerusalem: Israel Universities Press.

Bernstein, D. (1984). Political Participation: New immigrants and Veteran Parties in Israeli Society. Plural Societies 5:13-32.

Bilu, Y. (1986). Dreams and the Wishes of Saint. IN Judaism Viewed From Within and From Without, Harvey Goldberg (ed.). New York: New York University Press, pp. 285-313.

Bilu, Y. and H. Abramovich (1985). In Search of the Sadiq: Visitational Dreams Among Moroccan Jews in Israel. Psychiatry 48:83-92.

Bourguignon, E. (1972). Dreams and Altered States of Consciousness in Anthropological Research. IN Psychological Anthropology, F.L.K. Hsu (ed.). Cambridge, MA.: Schenkman, pp. 403-434.

Brown, K.D. (1976). People of Sale. Manchester: Manchester University Press.

Caspi, D. (1980). The Growth of Local Newspapers in Israel: Trends and Appraisals. Bar Ilan University: Institute of Local Government (Hebrew).

Choay, F. (1968). Urbanism and Semiology. IN Meaning in Architecture, G. Baird and C. Jenks (eds.). London: Barrie, pp. 27-37.

Cohen, E. (1983). Ethnicity and Legitimation in Contemporary Israel. The Jerusalem Quarterly 28: 111-124.

Cohen, E. (1979). Urban Hierarchy, Urban Policy and Urban Social Change in Israel and the Arab World: A Comparative Analysis, IN Contemporary Urbanization and Social Justice, J. Beuujeu-Garnier and S. Reichman (eds.). Jerusalem: Ministry of Energy and Infrastructure, pp. 70-94.

Cohen, E. (1977). The City in the Zionist Ideology. The Jerusalem Quarterly 4:126-144.

Cohen, E. (1976). Environmental Orientations: A Multidimensional Approach to Social Ecology. Current Anthropology 17(1): 49-70.

Cohen, E. (1970). Development Towns: The Social Dynamics of "Planted" Urban Communities in Israel. IN Integration and Development in Israel, S.N. Eisenstadt et al. (eds.). Jerusalem: Israel Universities Press, pp. 587-617.

Cohen, E. and A. Shiloah (1985). Major Trends in the Dynamics of Change of Jewish Oriental Ethnic Music in Israel. Popular Music 5: 199-223.

Comay, Y. and A. Kirschenbaum (1973). The Israeli New Town: An Experiment at Population Redistribution. Economic Development and Cultural Change 22: 124-134.

Crapanzano, V. (1975). Saints, Jnun and Dreams: An Essay in Moroccan Ethnopsychology. Psychiatry 38:145-159.

Deshen, S. (1982). Social Organization and Politics in Israeli Urban Quarters. The Jerusalem Quarterly 22: 21-37.

Deshen, S. (1974). Political Ethnicity and Cultural Ethnicity in Israel During the 1960s. IN Urban Ethnicity, A. Cohen (ed.). London: Tavistock, pp. 281-309.

Don, Y. and H. Hovav (1971-1972) The Measurement of Population Mobility: A Case Study of an Israeli Development Town. Economic Development and Cultural Change 26: 703-721.

Efrat, E. (1977). Residence and Internal Migration in the Immigrant City of Ashdod. Ir-Ve'eizor 4: 61-71 (Hebrew).

Eickelman, D.F. (1976). Moroccan Islam. Austin: University of Texas Press.

Elazar, D.J. (1973). Local Government as an Integrating Factor in Israeli Society. IN Israel's Social Structure and Change, M. Curtis and M.S. Chertoff (eds.). New Brunswick, NJ: Transaction, pp. 15-26.

Eliade, M. (1954). The Myth of the Eternal Return. New York: Pantheon.

Firey, W. (1947). Land Use in Central Boston. Cambridge, MA: Harvard University Press.

Geertz, C. (1968). Islam Observed. New Haven: Yale University Press.

Gellner, E. (1969). Saints of the Atlas. Chicago: Chicago University Press.

Gluckman, M. (1963). Order and Rebellion in Tribal Africa. London: Cohen and West.

Goldberg, H. (1984a). Greentwon's Youth: Disadvantaged Youth in a Development Town in Israel. Assen: Van Gorcum.

Goldberg, H. (1984b). Historical and Cultural Aspects of the Phenomenon of Ethnicity (Hebrew). Megamot 29(2-3): 233-249 (Hebrew).

Goldberg, H. (1983). The Mellahs of Southern Morocco: Report of a Survey. The Maghreb Review 8(3-4): 61-69.

Goldberg, H. (1977). Introduction: Culture and Ethnicity in the Study of Israeli Society. Ethnic Groups 1:163-186.

Guest, A.M. (1984). Robert Park and the Natural Area: A Sentimental Review. Sociology and Social Research 69(1): 1-21.

Handelman, D. and L. Shamgar-Handelman (1978). Social Planning Prerequisites for New and Expanded Communities. Contact 10(3): 86-122.

Hasson, S. (1983). The Emergence of an Urban Social Movement in Israeli Society: An Integrated Approach. International Journal of Urban and Regional Research 7(2): 157-174.

Hasson, S. (1981). Social and Spatial Conflicts: The Settlement Process in Israel During the 1950s and the 1960s. L'Espace Geographique 3: 169-179.

Kramer, R.M. (1973). Urban Community Development in Israel. IN Israel: Social Structure and Change, M. Curtis and M.S. Chertoff (eds.). New Brunswick, NJ: Transaction, pp. 47-66.

Lanternari, V. (1975). Dreams as Charismatic Significants: Their Bearing on the Rise of New Religious Movements, IN Psychological Anthropology, T.R. Williams (ed.). The Hague: Mouton, pp. 221-235.

Marx, E. (1976). The Social Context of Violent Behavior. London: Routledge.

Marx, E. (1975). Anthropological Studies in a Centralized State: Max Gluckman and the Bernstein Israel Research Project. Jewish Journal of Sociology 17: 131-150.

Matras, J. (1973). Israel's New Frontier: The Urban Periphery. IN Israel: Social Structure and Change, M. Curtis and M.S. Chertoff (eds.). New Brunswick, NJ: Transaction, 3-14.

Meeker, M.E. (1979). Literature and Violence in North Africa, Cambridge: Cambridge University Press.

O'Nell, C.W. (1976). Dreams, Cultures and the Individual. New York: Chandler.

Sack R.D. (1980). Conceptions of Space in Social Thought: A Geographic Perspective. London: Macmillan.

Shachar, A.S. (1971). Israel's Development Towns: Evaluation of National Urbanization Policy. Journal of the American Institute of Planners 37(6): 362-372.

Soen, D. (1976-1977). Primary Relations in Poor Urban Neighborhoods and in Development Towns in Israel. Ir-Ve'eizor 3: 65-73 (Hebrew).

Soen, D. (1973). Migdal-Ashquelon: A Social Analysis. IN Cities in Israel, A. Schachar et al. (eds.). Jerusalem: Akademon, pp. 600-618 (Hebrew).

Spiegel, E. (1966). Neue Stadte/New Towns in Israel. Stuttgart: Karl Kramer.

Spilerman, S. and J. Habib (1976). Development Towns in Israel: The Role of Community in Creating Ethnic Disparities in Labor Force Characteristics. American Journal of Sociology 81(4): 781-812.

Stephen, M. (1979). Dreams of Change: The Innovative Role of Altered States of Consciousness in Traditional Melanesian Religion. Oceania 50: 3-22.

Suttles, G. (1972). The Social Construction of Communities. Chicago: Chicago University Press.

Tuan, Y.F. (1977). Space and Place: The Perspective of Experience. London: Arnold.

Weingrod, A. (n.d.). Rabbi Haim Houri: The Saint of Beersheva. Typescript.

Weintraub, D. and V. Kraus (1982). Spatial Differentiation and Place of Residence: Spatial Dispersion and Composition of Population and Stratification in Israel. Megamot 27(4): 367-381 (Hebrew).

Westermark, E. (1926). Ritual and Belief in Morocco. London: Macmillan.

Yishai, Y. (1984). Responsiveness to Ethnic Demands: The Case of Israel. Ethnic and Racial Studies 7(2): 283-300.

Ychtman-Ya'ar, E., S.E. Spiro and J. Ram (1978). Reactions to Rehousing: Loss of Community or Frustrated Aspirations? Urban Studies 16: 113-119.

15

The Religion of Elderly Oriental Jewish Women

Fieldwork conducted among elderly, Oriental Jewish women living in Jerusalem reveals a religious world centred around guarding over ancestors and descendants. The article identifies and labels the 'domestication of religion' as a process in which people who profess their allegiance to a wider religious tradition personalise the rituals, institutions, symbols and theology of that wider system in order to safeguard the well-being of particular individuals with whom they are linked in relationships of care. It is argued that individuals (such as the Oriental women) who have a great deal invested in interpersonal relationships, and who are excluded from formal power within an institutionalised religious framework, tend to be associated with a personally-oriented religious mode.

An intense concern with the well-being of their extended families characterises the religious lives of many elderly, Oriental Jewish women. In numerous rituals—spontaneous, formal, private and communal—they guard the living, dead and unborn people with whom they have close relationships. The religious world of these women highlights the need for a conception of religion which takes into account the interpersonal nature of much of human religiosity. Inspired by Fustel de Coulanges's notion of domestic religion,[1] in this article I shall describe a process that I call *domestication*—a process in which people who profess their allegiance to a wider religious tradition personalise the rituals, institutions and perhaps even the theology of that wider system in order to safeguard the health, happiness and security of particular people with whom they are linked in relationships of caring and interdependence. Domestic religion, concerned with the lives and deaths of specific and usually well-loved individuals, is continually re-created whenever human beings personalise or 'domesticate' aspects of an impersonal, universally-oriented religious culture.

During 1984 and 1985 I conducted fieldwork among Oriental Jewish women in Jerusalem. These women, who came to Israel from Kurdistan, Iraq, Iran, Yemen and North Africa, attend a Senior Citizens' Day Centre located in one of Jerusalem's old, Oriental neighbourhoods.[2] These women are specialists in the domestication of religion. They are also poor, illiterate, powerless in terms of the rabbinical establishment, and extremely committed to and dependent upon networks of kin and neighbours with whom they maintain intimate and daily contact. I suggest that individuals (such as these women) who have a great deal

Man (N.S.) **23**, 506–521

invested in interpersonal relationships, and who are excluded from formal power within an institutionalised religious framework, tend to be associated with a highly personally-oriented religious mode. Similar religious emphases have been noted for Muslim women (Beck 1980; Jamzadeh & Mills 1986), urban Hindu Women (Beech 1982), Spanish Christian women (Christian 1972), Black Carib women (Kerns 1983), Christian women in rural Greece (Danforth 1982), and rural Hindu women (Thompson 1983; Wadley 1980). While I am not suggesting that it is only women who meet these criteria, within many and probably most cultures it is indeed women who are most visibly involved with and/or expert in the domestication of religion. To reiterate, the religious process that I describe here is characterised not by gender but by theme; its association with women is an empirical observation (cf. Gilligan 1982: 2).

Previous studies of women and religion have focused upon several major motifs. First, there have been many analyses and critiques of women's official status within institutionalised religious frameworks (Davis 1975; Lawless 1983; al-Hibr 1982; Mukherjee 1983; Pomeroy 1975; Reuther 1979).[3] In addition, several studies have explored ritualised or symbolic female rebellion against male-dominated religious frameworks (Bilu 1980; Kraemer 1980). A number of studies have concentrated upon exceptional women, founders of new sects, and women who have broken away from traditional female paths (Binford 1980; White 1980; Burfield 1983; Durrant 1979; Harvey 1979). A fourth area of interest has been women's involvement in pilgrimage, church attendance and possession cults—religious activities that are carried out by clearly defined populations in clearly defined and separated sacred spaces and times (Moberg 1962; Bourguignon et al. 1983; Mernissi 1977). Another fairly large group of studies emphasises female physiology as a symbol, source or determinant of participation in various rituals (Hoch-Smith & Spring 1978: 1–2; Lowie 1952; Gutmann 1977; Gross 1980).

A somewhat different approach has emerged in those very few recent studies which have looked at the ways in which women's religious activity supports and legitimates women's everyday, profane activities (Falk & Gross 1980: xvi; Rushton 1983). My analysis in this article may be seen as growing out of this type of approach; the interpersonally-oriented religiosity of the Oriental women certainly validates, supports and legitimates their familial concerns. However, the *essence* of the religiosity depicted here is not the relatively small number of rituals that directly relate to specific aspects or activities of women's prosaic and diurnal lives. Far more significant is the overarching world-view or paradigm that in fact determines the ways in which these women interpret and participate in diverse and seemingly unrelated religious phenomena and rituals. This existential mode has been described by the educational psychologist Carol Gilligan as a moral 'voice' that speaks of 'the realization that self and other are interdependent, and that life, however valuable in itself, can only be sustained by care in relationships' (Gilligan 1982: 127).

Background

The elderly, Oriental women of this study are exceedingly pious. They participate in numerous religious rituals each day—they recite blessings, donate small sums of money to charity, kiss sacred objects, attend Judaica lessons, prepare for the Sabbath and holidays, frequent holy tombs and pray in the local synagogues. A substantial portion of their meagre financial resources is directed towards supporting religious institutions and funding religious rituals. The sacred permeates all aspects of their lives—nearly every conversation ends with someone looking upwards and saying: 'Everything is in God's hands', or, 'God is great, and everything will turn out for the best'. Time, for these women, is marked off by the Sabbath and holidays. Birth, marriage and death are surrounded by hundreds of rituals whose meaning is that life is not a random, natural process, but a significant part of a divinely created and ordered universe. In short, for these women time, space, life, death, love and tradition are potentially sacred—'You just need *emunah* [faith, belief]'.

'Official' rabbinic Judaism is noteworthy for its preoccupation with male religious sentiments and religious duties. The *halacha*[4] or legal literature describes male-dominated rituals in great detail, but says almost nothing about female spiritual life. Most women's rituals are extra-*halachic*, although the women of this study, probably because of their illiteracy, are oblivious to that distinction. Very little about Jewish women's religious experience appears in written sources of any period, and the sparse ethnographic literature on pious Jewish women has concentrated primarily on the social role of Ashkenazi women (see Berger-Sofer 1979; Finkelstein 1980; Frank 1975; Jayanti 1982; Myerhoff 1979).

The women described here define their religio-cultural affiliation and identity in terms of the male-oriented great tradition of orthodox Judaism. Official Judaism stresses learning—being conversant with sacred texts is the path to power in the Jewish world—and the distinction between those who are literate and those who are illiterate has traditionally been made along gender lines. Although not all men who know the Hebrew alphabet can be considered religious specialists or representatives of the great tradition, it is significant that women as a group did not (until very recently) have access to sacred writings.[5]

The women's experience of religion is highly gender-specific: they conduct their religious lives mainly among other women and talk about their religious concerns and behaviour from a gynocentric perspective. For example, the women describe a 'religious person' in the same way that they describe a 'religious woman', while their description of a 'religious man' is very different. They believe that their female religious world is just as holy, traditional, spiritually powerful and important to the continued existence and well-being of the Jewish people as that of the male rabbis, cantors, circumcisers, scholars, judges, exegetes, poets, writers, priests and teachers. The women do not consider that their female rituals are superstitious, optional, local, magical, syncretistic or in any way tangential to Jewish life. Indeed, the vast majority of their religious practices are culled from the official Jewish great tradition.

Ancestors and descendants

The Oriental women of Jerusalem, like all human beings, live out their lives among people with whom they are connected in webs of relationship—of love, concern, and care.[6] The religion of these women sacralises those relationships: the women described here participate in the holy by caring for their kin and, by extension, the entire Jewish people. In this and the following sections I shall trace the thread that organises the women's religious world—the paradigm through which they interpret and approach the sacred. Personal relationship serves as the core component of that world and the personally-oriented religious world of the women interacts with the great tradition of rabbinic Judaism.

These women see themselves as the spiritual guardians of their families. The religious role of guarding one's family is a function of both age and gender; men and younger women have much more limited contact with ancestors and have almost no responsibility—in the spiritual sphere—for the welfare of their descendants. (Younger women are of course in charge of the *physical* well-being of their families.) The organising principle in the religious lives of these women is that they enlist the aid of ancestors in helping descendants, and they educate descendants to remember ancestors. As Kerns writes (1983: 103) of Black Carib women in Belize, 'Ritual and kinship share a central meaning: the interdependence of the generations and the lifelong responsibility of women for . . . kin'. What is described in this article is a self-defined, self-selected religious role. It must be emphasised that the religious establishment does not tell the women to function as guardians of their extended families; the rabbis give but minimal instruction on how to care for ancestors and descendants properly.

In referring to the women as the spiritual guardians of their families I am using the word 'family' in the broadest possible sense of ancestors and descendants, biological and mythical. For the women of this study, what differentiates 'family' from the rest of the world is that with family members one has a personal, reciprocal relationship.

Saints. The women of this study attribute to all dead members of their kin groups, with the possible exception of a particularly hated husband or in-law, something of the status of a saint. The minimal definition of a saint is someone who has a special relationship with God, someone whose request to God is especially likely to be answered. The women expand the Jewish notion of saint to include almost all dead relatives. Thus the category of saint includes Biblical figures such as Abraham, Rachel or Elijah, historical figures such as the Talmudic Rabbi Meir baal HaNess, modern miracle-workers such as the popular Moroccan Baba Sali who died three years ago, and parents and grandparents who are buried in local cemeteries.

The living can remain in communication with dead saints via prayer, ritual and pilgrimage. The dead communicate with the living primarily through dreams in which they provide guidance, advice and information (close relatives such as late husbands and such Biblical figures as Elijah the Prophet have figured in the dreams of several of my informants). The women go to the graves of saints to discuss their problems with the saints, to enlist help for their resolution, and to urge the saints to extend their protection to safeguard the health and happiness of children and grandchildren. In exchange, the women promise to perform specific acts, such as giving money to charity or lighting candles to honour the saints' memories. They also tend the graves of family members by cleaning and putting flowers on them. The dead saint is seen as being in direct relationship with those of his/her kin living on earth (see Benaim 1980; Ben-Ami 1981 for a fuller discussion of this notion). The women speak as if the saint is physically present in the grave; they say, for example, that they 'visited Elijah the Prophet' or 'are going to visit Rabbi Meir'. They believe that by touching or kissing the tomb they can come into closer contact with the person who was buried in it. The dead saint is thought to come out of the grave at night to bless objects such as oil left near the tomb.

The graves of family members are visited on the eve of the New Moon and on the anniversaries of their deaths. The graves of more famous saints are visited on anniversaries of their deaths (*hilulot*) and whenever the Senior Citizens' Day Centre organises a bus to the saints' tombs.[7] The women describe these visits as opportunities 'to ask for mercy and to cry on the graves'. When asked why they visit the tombs, one woman explained 'because we are homesick for our ancestors'. Most of the popular saints are male, which reflects the predominance of men in Biblical stories, later Jewish literature, and the Orthodox rabbinate (which is exclusively male).

The relationship between the women and their dead is a reciprocal one. The dead help the women by giving advice (usually in dreams) and by interceding with God on the women's behalf. Gifts such as new curtains to cover a tomb, flowers, candles and money for its upkeep encourage the saint to intercede. The women also help their ancestors by collecting (purchasing) blessings on the anniversaries of their deaths, when the women request rabbis to say special blessings in memory of the deceased. The women both seek the assistance of the dead saints and keep guard over them, in much the same way that, as we shall see, old women guard living Jews.

The assistance that the women ask of the dead is almost always for a child, grandchild or great-grandchild who is ill, unemployed, unmarried or infertile. In other words, what is being described here is a chain with two intermediary links. The child has a problem, the elderly woman asks the saint to intercede, and God actually grants the petition.

Daughters. In Oriental Jewish culture, as in many other cultures, it is daughters (and to a lesser extent daughters-in-law) who have responsibility for aging parents (cf. Hess & Waring 1983). Sons who own cars may help their parents with transportation, and religiously observant sons may visit their widowed mothers on the Sabbath to recite the appropriate prayers and blessings (since the women are illiterate, most find it difficult to learn the Hebrew prayers that their husbands had always said but that as widows they must now say for themselves). But the daughters bear the burden of day-to-day and emotional support of aged and sick parents. Daughters of widowed mothers are expected to telephone or visit their mothers daily, to help their mothers negotiate the intricacies of the Health Service, to help to clean their mothers' houses, and above all to be available for endless discussions of the health problems of all members of the extended family. Daughters of widowed fathers are expected to keep house for their fathers, to bring them food and cook for them, to do their laundry and to make any other domestic arrangements. Thus, the spiritual role of caring for dead ancestors may be seen as an extension of the female day-to-day task of caring for aging parents. The Oriental daughter who cleans the house for her living parents, will some day tend their graves. In the same way that she is responsible for the emotional support of her elderly mother, she is responsible for the spiritual support of her deceased ancestors.

Children and soldiers. The elderly women generally have close and loving relationships with their children and grandchildren. While most describe their relationships with their husbands as at best problematic, there is no such ambiguity regarding their children—they love and admire their children and grandchildren, and are vitally concerned with their health and happiness. The women enjoy describing the difficult conditions under which they brought up their children—the shortage of food, financial problems, lack of adequate housing and the never-ending housework. They are proud of their success in raising good and financially independent children, and say that their success was achieved with the help of God (not the help of their husbands). Since children are so greatly loved and valued, it is not surprising that the greatest misfortune to befall a woman is barrenness, and the greatest sorrow is the death of one's children. Infant mortality was common in Asia and North Africa in the early decades of this century, and one Kurdish women cites the not a-typical case of a neighbour 'who had ten children, nine of whom died in youth'.

These women, who have worked hard for so many years providing for their children, do not relinquish responsibility for their descendants when they themselves are no longer healthy and strong enough to do laundry and clean the house. Instead, they transfer their role of caretaker to the spiritual realm, devoting time, thought and money to safeguarding children and grandchildren by way of prayers, blessings and the soliciting of saints' intervention. The women frequently give small contributions to rabbis (usually for rabbinical seminaries) in return for their blessing. The blessing that the women request is sometimes for themselves, particularly if they have recently been ill, but more typically for one of their children. The problem that requires a blessing can be financial, health, marital, or almost anything else (cf. Kerns 1983: 177–9).

The women expand the category 'children' to include all the members of Israel's Defence Forces, frequently saying that 'All of the soldiers are like my own children'. When visiting the holy graves and on other ritual occasions the women bless each other with words such as, 'May there be health for all of Israel, may there be peace, may all of the soldiers return in peace'.[8] In the words of one informant, 'Every soldier is like my eye, even the Druze soldiers'. She meant that all soldiers in Israel's Defence Forces, even the non-Jewish Druze who serve in the Army, were as precious to her as her own eyesight. While it is common to express the value one places on an individual (almost always a child or grandchild) by saying that he or she is as dear and irreplaceable as one's own eyes, it is significant that the woman used this intimate metaphor to describe her feelings about non-Jewish soldiers.

Just as the women believe that they have a reciprocal relationship with the blessed dead—whose graves they tend and whose spirits in turn intercede with God on their behalf—so they see their relationship with the soldiers as being reciprocal. The rabbi who conducts Judaica lessons at the Senior Citizen's Day Centre expressed this idea: 'By carefully observing the holidays [according to Jewish law] we can convince God to protect the soldiers on the borders, and the soldiers who ensure the security of the Jewish State make it possible for civilians like us to be good [practising] Jews'.

The women believe that it is their duty to care for the soldiers, and that their own actions can affect the soldiers' safety; e.g., the women make a point of not wearing dark coloured clothing while grandsons are serving in the Army in case this causes misfortune to the boys. They use the word *mitzvah* (divine ordinance) to describe all their work of helping the soldiers, both spiritual and more prosaic assistance such as donating money to the Soldiers' Welfare Fund or volunteering to pack uniforms and ammunition at a local Army base.

Unborn children. The elderly women of this study also devote a great deal of time to ensuring that the next generation of Jews will be born. A particularly frequent reason for visiting the tombs of saints is to pray for a daughter, daughter-in-law, or granddaughter who has difficulty conceiving. The dead Jew in the tomb is expected to be interested in his or her as yet unborn descendants, and this interest is often mediated by old women. According to Jewish law and Oriental Jewish custom a man can divorce his wife if she is barren. Thus, the women's concern with fertility reflects their dependence upon good relationships with both God and husbands.

Pregnancy and childbirth are believed to have both practical and supernatural aspects, and elderly Oriental women have special knowledge of both fields. Profound belief in the singular ability of God to grant fertility and an auspicious hour for giving birth, are combined with centuries of women's folk knowledge about pregnancy and childbirth. Typical of the comments is the adage that in order to be safely and speedily delivered a woman should cover her head (a sign of female piety), kiss the *mezuzah* (a small box attached to all doorways in traditional Jewish homes in which certain Biblical verses are written), ask God to help, do good deeds and continue to have sexual relations with her husband up to the last minute. What the pregnant woman sees and hears is believed to affect the foetus. Listening to a conversation about distressing matters can have injurious consequences, while going on a pilgrimage to a saint's grave would cause the baby to be born with a 'good soul'. The women's concern with fertility is twofold: not only do they want their daughters to have the joy of raising children; they are also very concerned with the continuity and continued existence of the Jewish people.

Process

The religion of the women is thus supremely personal. Their religious world revolves around an axis of relationship—with ancestors, with descendants, with unborn children. In this section we shall see how their personal religious concerns interact with, and indeed define their participation in, the great tradition of literate, male-oriented, orthodox Judaism. Shokeid has convincingly shown that the 'flexibility of meaning and interpretation of symbols and norms seem to be an important feature of the ritual domain' (Shokeid 1974: 89). The three examples that follow show how the women of this study elaborate, de-emphasise, modify, circumvent and personalise elements and aspects of the male (official) model of religion (White 1981).

Example 1: synagogue attendance. The great tradition frequently provides the external form or language to a more personal religious content. Women are not required by Jewish law to attend synagogue; observant Jewish men are expected to attend synagogue twice each day. In Yemen and Kurdistan women did not attend synagogue at all (there were no women's sections) and in most Israeli synagogues today the women's section consists of a balcony which is closed off by a curtain. The elderly Oriental women with whom I worked have begun, in old age, to attend synagogue regularly. They generally cannot hear the men's service (they are sitting too far away) or understand most of the Hebrew, and their presence is considered superfluous in terms of a prayer quorum (for which ten men are needed). The women play no part in the male synagogue service, nor do they conduct an autonomous female service.

The male synagogue service comprises written prayers and readings from the Bible. On Mondays, Thursdays and the Sabbath, portions of the Torah (Pentateuch scroll) are read out loud at synagogue. The Torah is removed from behind a covered cabinet in the men's section to the accompaniment of song and held up for the congregation to see at the beginning or end of the public reading. In many synagogues it is passed among all male congregants for them to touch or kiss the holy scroll. The men follow the Torah reading in their individual copies of the Pentateuch, and the content of the weekly reading is the most common topic for sermons.

Many elderly Oriental women attend synagogue faithfully, making a special effort to come on Mondays, Thursdays and the Sabbath, because they believe that the time when the Torah is held up is particularly efficacious for requests to God on behalf of their families. Women are not required by *halacha* to attend synagogue, take no part in the official synagogue service, can barely hear or understand the formal service from their seats in the ladies' gallery, but still come to synagogue at times determined by Jewish law in order to make personal petitions. This is a case in which an official ritual—synagogue attendance—has given the external form to the personal religious content of guarding family members. The women use the male great tradition ritual as the forum for expressing their own religious concerns.

Example 2: Festival of the New Moon. The women themselves distinguish between personal and non-personal religious rituals. The next ritual that I shall describe is particularly important because it is a developmental one: the same women, when younger, performed it as a non-personal ritual, but in old age reinterpreted it as personally-oriented.

The Festival of the New Moon is a women's holiday. While it is probably rooted in ancient beliefs connecting women's and lunar cycles, Jewish written sources give the credit for turning the Festival of the New Moon into a holiday celebrated by women more than men to the generation of righteous women who refused to give their jewellery to make the golden calf (*Pirkei de Rabbi Eliezer*, 45). Many if not most modern Jews are unaware when there is a new moon in the sky. Observant male Jews celebrate the Festival of the New Moon only by reciting a few additional Psalms and prayers during the morning prayer service and by adding an extra paragraph to the Grace after meals. The women of this study, who cannot even read a calendar, are extremely aware of the Festival of the New Moon, and on the day before make an effort to visit cemeteries, both those of their families and historical shrines such as Rachel's Tomb in Bethlehem.

Unlike the case for the Sabbath and most holidays, there are few laws governing behaviour on the Festival of the New Moon. The only special prohibitions observed by the women concern laundry and sewing (work that can be postponed). The only ritual enacted by all the elderly women is lighting candles for the dead on the evening of the New Moon. Most of them light numerous candles, aiming to light one for each dead relative. One informant explained that on the evening of the Festival they (women of her ethnic group, Iraqi) light candles for family members, wise men and scholars, and saints who have died. When they light the candles they do not recite a formal Hebrew blessing—they 'pray that the soul of the deceased should be in *Gan Eden* [Heaven]'. The type of candle is not important. She herself lights a combination of remembrance candles, big candles, small candles, Sabbath candles, Chanuka candles or whatever else she happens to have in the house.

What is relevant here is that according to my informants they did not light the Festival of the New Moon candles when young. One woman explained that when she herself was newly married there were no dead relatives for whom to light. As a young wife she would light only one candle 'for the Festival of the New Moon' (as opposed to 'for dead relatives'). Upon questioning, however, it became clear that she now lights candles for relatives who were already dead when she was newly married, for distant relatives that she must have had when she was younger, and for Jewish saints who died two thousand years ago: even as a young woman she would have had ancestors for whom to light. But it is only as an old woman that she has begun to light a multitude of candles each month. The women, then, differentiate between lighting New Moon candles as a calendrical ritual and lighting New Moon candles as a personal–relationship ritual, and they shift from one to the other in the course of their lifetimes.

Example 3: Planting trees. When Jews from Europe began returning to Palestine at the end of the nineteenth and beginning of the twentieth century, the land was mostly barren swamp or desert. Thus, reforestation became an important goal for the early Zionists. On *Tu b'Shvat* (the traditional Jewish holiday on which all trees are reckoned to become one year older) in 1985 the women of this study were taken by the Senior Citizens' Day Centre to plant trees in a new forest. As they planted the saplings they said, 'In the merit of my planting this tree, my family should have good health/happiness/everything we need'. Planting trees on *Tu b'Shvat* is a modern, secular ritual, normally performed by Scouts, other youth organisations or tourist groups for the express ecological and political purpose of reforestation. When the elderly, Oriental women were taken to plant trees they created their own ritual, utilising a traditional verbal formula and conception of the relationship between God and humans. Contributing to the State and Land of Israel by planting trees in a new forest is assumed by the women to merit divine reward.[9] The expected divine reward is expressed in personal terms—health for a child, fertility for a granddaughter.

Worthy of comment is the fact that these illiterate, uneducated women feel competent to create a new ritual within a broader religious system that has been more or less frozen for a great many years. While rabbis continue to argue over the *halachic* legality of reciting additional Psalms of praise (*Hallel*) on Israeli Independence Day, these elderly women are firmly convinced that any contribution to the modern Jewish State is deserving of divine reward. They did not ask a [male] rabbi before performing this new ritual. Designed to enlist God's protection for their families, it lies within the women's sphere and in the women's judgement does not need rabbinical approval.

Domestic religion

Following Geertz, most anthropologists today see religion as dealing with ultimate concerns such as life, death and suffering (Geertz 1969). Yet life, death and suffering are also the paradigmatic *domestic* concerns—it is in a domestic context that life is conceived, nurtured, declines and often ends. Ironically, the term 'domestic religion' has been used by anthropologists and historians to indicate a relatively minor subset of religious observances. In the new fifteen volume *Encyclopedia of Religion*, for instance, in a total of but seventeen pages various writers record examples of the domestic observances of Jews, Christians, Muslims, Hindus, Chinese and Japanese (1987: vol. 4, 400–17).

The notion of domestic religion is an important one, particularly but not exclusively for women, yet few writers have attempted to define either the parameters or the characteristics of domestic religiosity. Within the academic literature the term 'domestic' is used ambiguously, sometimes referring to the architectural category 'house', at other times to familial concerns regardless of where the action takes place. The first of these usages is problematic in that it arbitrarily and generally inaccurately excludes sites such as cemeteries from the realm of the domestic, while it includes rituals that physically take place in the house but that are otherwise unconnected to the life of the home. (For example, an Orthodox Jewish man who wakes up too late to join the prayer quorum at the synagogue and instead closes himself into his study to recite the formal morning prayer service is indeed conducting a religious ritual at home, but neither content nor structure of the ritual seems domestic.) The second use of 'domestic' has some meaning in those (very few) modern, differentiated societies in which there is a clear distinction between kinship and non-kinship related activity (Eisenstadt 1973: 23–4). But in the many simpler societies that anthropologists usually label as 'kin-based' (see Schneider 1984 for a critique of this term), this conception of domestic religion cannot differentiate a particular sub-category within the religious world.

Domestic religion clearly shares symbols, beliefs, a ritual framework and a sacred history with the non-domestic religion of the same wider tradition: a Christian theologian writes a theology of the crucifixion and a Christian woman whose child is ill kisses the cross hanging on her living-room wall. Simultaneously, if there is meaning to the cross-cultural category of domestic religion, we should expect that the domestic religions of Jews, Christians, Muslims, Hindus, etc. share certain other beliefs, moods, motivations, themes and behaviour patterns.

It seems that the muddle surrounding the concept of domestic religion is a result of treating it as a cluster of discrete rituals rather than as a religious mode. The difference between the theologian's theology of the crucifixion and the woman's kissing of the crucifix when her child is ill is above all a matter of intent: the crucifix-kisser is concerned with the lives and deaths of particular people, not merely with life and death as abstract problems. I propose characterising the domestic religious realm very broadly as the arena in which the ultimate concerns of life, suffering and death are *personalised*. Thus domestic religion has to do with the lives, sufferings and deaths of *particular*, usually well-loved, individuals. This conception of domestic religion is useful in that it allows for the possibility that the same symbol or ritual may, on different occasions, or on one occasion but for different people, be both domestic and non-domestic. A New Moon candle may be lit 'for the holiday' or 'for the dead'. Domesticity, then, is not an inherent characteristic of any particular ritual, place or event—it is a human interpretation of that ritual, place or event.

The women of this study (like the Hindu, Muslim and Christian women observed by Beech 1982; Beck 1980; Danforth 1982, etc.) use their relationship-focused concerns as a point of entry into the great tradition, while they simultaneously reinterpret aspects of the great tradition to meet their own relationship-focused religious needs. Domestic religion is not a particular subset of rituals, but a spiritual theme that pervades and organises the religious lives of many human beings. Throughout this article I have pointed out ways in which domestic religion interacts with the great tradition; I have described a *process* that I identify as '*domestication*'. As an analytically meaningful term, domestication of religion refers to the personalisation of religion, to the process in which people who profess their allegiance to a wider tradition use the rituals, symbols, institutions, mythology and even the theology of that wider system to address their personal, domestic religious concerns. In addition, human beings live in communities in which larger groups of people share common histories and interests. Thus, I see continuity rather than fracture between domestic and non- or less-domestic religion. The example of the soldiers cited earlier highlights this point: the women move easily from concern with 'my own children' to 'the soldiers, all of whom are like my children'.

In describing the religious lives of the Oriental Jewish women, I emphasised how rituals or symbols become transformed when they enter or leave the domestic realm. When a literate Jewish man listens to the Torah reading in synagogue he is obeying a divine law, learning about the history of the Jewish people, and participating in the life of the community. When an illiterate Oriental Jewish woman listens to the Torah reading in synagogue, she is seeking the most efficacious moment, the moment when the channel of communication between human and God is most open, to ask God a personal favour for a particular, loved person (cf. Tapper & Tapper 1987; also see Turner's (1964) notion of the multi-vocality of symbols). A pervasive problem in much of the academic study of religion is the tendency to treat the first set of motivations as more noble, beautiful, important, eternal, primary or true than the second set. This sort of treatment is ethnocentrism at its worst: there is no reason to assume that the experience of the holy is any more immediate to a monk in a cell or a Talmudic scholar in a seminary than to a woman lighting candles to protect her family.

It is against this background that Gilligan's work on moral development becomes critical for anthropólogists of religion. Gilligan points out that re-searchers using the classic six-stage Kohlberg scale of moral development have found that women's moral judgments seem to remain in the third stage of the scale—the stage at which morality is equated with helping and pleasing others—while men more often reach the sixth stage—where morality is understood as the subordination of relationship to universal principles of justice.[10] (In terms of the nomenclature that I have suggested in this article, women's moral decisions exemplify the domestic mode, men's the non-domestic.) Gilligan contends that 'the failure of women [noted throughout the psychological literature] to fit existing models of human growth may point to a problem in the representation, a limitation in the conception of human condition, an omission of certain truths about life' (Gilligan 1982: 1–2). Gilligan's critique is two-pronged: she questions the legitimacy of a developmental scheme in which male moral modes are deemed to be more highly developed than female ones, and in which relationship and care are subordinated to universal rights.

The androcentric model of moral development of Gilligan's critique bears an uncanny resemblance to the evolutionist models propounded by Frazer (1911–1915) and other late nineteenth- and early twentieth-century scholars who posited a progressive scale in which 'magic' precedes 'religion', and the model for 'religion' was literate, philosophically- and universally-oriented, Western religion. Modern anthropologists are sagacious enough to avoid Frazer's evol-utionist and terminological errors. However, language denoting religion in such terms as 'folk' (Christian 1987; Harrell 1986; Noy 1980; Foster 1953; and others), 'common' (Hornsby-Smith et al. 1985), 'popular' (Brooke & Brooke 1984; Overmyer 1980), 'customary' (Hornsby-Smith et al. Reilly 1985), 'prac-tical' (Leach 1968), 'peasant' (Wolf 1966), 'local' (Christian 1981), and 'the little tradition' (Redfield 1956; Obeyesekere 1968) does tend to brand certain popu-lations[11] and sets of rituals as unsophisticated (Leach 1968), 'magical or superstitious' (Hornsby-Smith et al. 1985: 247), or in some way derivative, subordinate or marginal.

What seems to me far more significant in all of these 'religions' is an overarching emphasis upon the personal: in all of these religious frameworks ultimate concerns tend to be expressed in the language of personal relationship, and personal relationship becomes a major determinant of participation in religious activity.[12] In fact, I suggest that the domestication process identified in this article has already been hinted at, albeit in a diffuse and often ambiguous manner, in most of the studies cited above.

The Oriental Jewish women of Jerusalem participate in the sacred through caring for their kin, and they care for their kin through participating in the sacred. These particular women are ritual specialists, 'devotional . . . virtuosi' (Christian 1972: 160) of the personal/sacred mode. As illiterate females they are excluded from significant aspects of 'great tradition' Judaism, and as daughters, mothers and grandmothers they depend financially and emotionally upon their ancestors and descendants. However, their concern with loved ones and their exclusion from ecclesiastic hierarchies are far from unique. Just as Gilligan's re-assessment of theories of moral development revealed a relationship-oriented moral voice, I believe that a serious and clear-sighted re-assessment of human religiosity will demonstrate the centrality of relationship in the religious lives of most lay people and even of many religious specialists. The old women of Jerusalem allow us to glimpse an existential theme that underlies many religious rituals, moral decisions and human interpretations of the holy.

NOTES

[1] Fustel de Coulanges in *The ancient city* (first published 1864), described the earliest religion of Greece and Rome as 'domestic religion', and 'A family was a group of persons whom religion permitted to invoke the same sacred fire, and to offer the funeral repast to the same ancestor' (1956: 42).

[2] Most of these women came to Israel before the establishment of the State in 1948. I met with them at the Senior Citizens' Day Centre, at their homes, and at synagogue, and accompanied them on trips to holy tombs and other shrines. Although the municipal senior citizens' day centres are formally open to all senior citizens, only women attend this one, and most activities held there are religious in nature. My field method consisted of a combination of participant-observation, small-group interviews, and in-depth interviews with the more articulate informants.

[3] This overview of the literature on women's religious lives is intended as illustrative, not exhaustive.

[4] *Halacha* is the total system of Jewish law, and governs almost every aspect of life. Its main attributes are that it is written, developed and studied by men as a religious pursuit, and changes very slowly.

[5] In the *Talmud* 'Sotah' 20a, it is written that it is forbidden to teach one's daughter Torah. It is well documented that among the Jewish community in Yemen it was widely believed that if women learned to read, natural disasters would occur (Gilad 1982: 62). In the modern Jewish world the *halacha* concerning women has not significantly changed, though young women now attend school and learn to read.

[6] Obviously, in different societies people love and care for different categories of people: major affective bonds may be with parents, siblings, children, friends, aunts or uncles, spouses, etc. However, I have not as yet seen an ethnographic or historical study of a culture in which there is no interpersonal relationship that is considered loving or caring.

[7] Other popular organisations also organise bus trips to tombs. Pilgrimage is a central feature of modern Israeli religion.

[8] In the context of the Senior Citizens' Day Centre, 'the soldiers' must also be seen as a neutral and unifying symbol for the women to discuss. All of the women are Zionists and all have descendants who are soldiers, thus they can all participate in conversations and rituals about soldiers without risk of boredom, argument, or envy.

[9] Concerning innovative ritual dealing with Zionist themes, also see Shai (1980).

[10] When Gilligan refers to male or female moral development she is indicating two different themes or modes of thought, not an absolute correspondence.

[11] The literature suggests no consensus about who the 'folk' of folk religion are. Christian (1987), for example, stresses the agricultural component of folk religion; Foster (1953) defines folk religion as an urban phenomenon; and for Redfield (1956) the folk of the little tradition are the unreflective masses. There is a similar lack of consensus concerning the content of folk, common, etc. religion.

[12] I am not suggesting that all this terminology should be abandoned—most of the nomenclature is useful in certain contexts, and some is in fact specific to certain populations. Nor am I suggesting that all folk, popular, etc. rituals must have an overriding personal focus; e.g. popular passion plays may not be primarily relationship-oriented.

REFERENCES

al-Hibr, A. (ed.) 1982. *Women's Studies International Forum, Special Issue on Women and Islam* **5**: 2.

Beck, L. 1980. The religious lives of Muslim women. In *Women in contemporary Muslim societies* (ed.) J. I. Smith. London: Associated Univ. Presses.

Beech, M. H. 1982. The domestic realm in the lives of Hindu women in Calcutta. In *Separate worlds: studies of purdah in south Asia* (eds) H. Papanek & G. Minault. Columbia, Missouri: South Asia Books.

Benaim, S. Y. 1980. *Le pélerinage juif des lieux saints au Maroc*. Casablanca: Published by the author.

Ben-Ami, I. 1981. Folk veneration of saints among the Moroccan Jews. In *Studies in Judaism and Islam* (eds) S. Morag *et al*. Jerusalem: Magnes Press.

Berger-Sofer, R. 1979. Pious women: a study of women's roles in a Hassidic and pious community: Mea She'arim. Thesis, Rutgers University.

Bilu, Y. 1980. The Moroccan demon in Israel: the case of 'evil spirit disease'. *Ethos* **8**, 24–39.

Binford, M. 1980. Julia: an east African diviner. In Falk & Gross 1980.

Bourguignon, E., A. Bellisari & S. McCabe 1983. Women, possession trance cults, and the extended nutrient-deficiency hypothesis. *Am. Anthrop.* **85**, 413–16.

Brooke, R. & C. Brooke 1984. *Popular religion in the Middle Ages*. London: Thames & Hudson.

Burfield, D. 1983. Theosophy and feminism: some explorations in nineteenth century biography. In Holden 1983.

Christian, W. 1972. *Person and God in a Spanish valley*. New York: Seminar Press.

—— 1981. *Local religion in sixteenth century Spain*. Princeton: Univ. Press.

—— 1987. Folk religion: an overview. In Eliade 1987.

Coulanges, F. de 1956. *The ancient city*. Garden City: Doubleday.

Danforth, L. M. 1982. *Death rituals of rural Greece*. Princeton: Univ. Press.

Davis, N. 1975. *Society and culture in early modern France*. Stanford: Univ. Press.

Durrant, S. W. 1979. The Nisan shaman caught in cultural contradiction. *Signs* **5**, 338–47.

Eisenstadt, S. D. 1973. *Tradition, change, and modernity*. New York: John Wiley.

Eliade, M. (ed.) 1987. *Encyclopedia of religion*, New York: Macmillan.

Falk, N. & R. Gross (eds) 1980. *Unspoken worlds: women's religious lives in non-western cultures*. San Francisco: Harper & Row.

Foster, G. 1953. What is folk culture? *Am. Anthrop.* **55**, 159–73.

Finkelstein, E. 1980. A study of female role definitions in a Yeshiva high school. Thesis, New York Univ.

Frank, B. 1975. The American Orthodox Jewish housewife: a generation study in ethnic survival. Thesis, City Univ., New York.

Frazer, J. G. 1911–1915. *The golden bough: a study in magic and religion*. London: Macmillan.

Geertz, Clifford 1969. Religion as a cultural system. In *Anthropological approaches to the study of religion* (ed.) M. Banton. London: Tavistock.

Gilad, L. 1982. Yemini Jewish Women. Thesis, Cambridge Univ.

Gilligan, C. 1982. *In a different voice*. Cambridge: Harvard Univ.

Gross, R. 1980. Menstruation and childbirth and ritual as religious experience among native Australians. In Falk & Gross 1980.

Gutmann, D. 1977. The cross-cultural perspective: notes toward a comparative psychology of aging. In *Handbook of the psychology of aging* (eds) J. Birren & K. Schaie. New York: Nostrand Reinhold.

Harrell, S. 1986. Men, women, and ghosts in Taiwanese folk religion. In *Gender and religion: on the complexity of symbols* (eds) C. W. Bynum *et al.* Boston: Beacon Press.

Harvey, Y. K. 1979. *Six Korean women: the socialization of shamans* (Am. ethnol. Soc. Monogr. **65**). St Paul: West.

Hess, B. & J. Waring 1983. Family relationships of older women: a women's issue. In *Older women* (ed.) E. Markson. Lexington: Lexington Books.

Hoch-Smith, J. & A. Spring (eds) 1978. *Women in ritual and symbolic roles.* New York: Plenum Press.

Holden, P. (ed.) 1983. *Women's religious experience: cross-cultural perspectives.* London: Croom Helm.

Hornsby-Smith, M., R. Lee & P. Reilly 1985. Common religion and customary religion: a critique and a proposal. *Rev. relig. Res.* **26**, 244–52.

Jamzadeh, L. & M. Mills 1986. Iranian Sofreh: from collective to female ritual. In *Gender and religion: on the complexity of symbols* (eds) C. W. Bynum *et al.* Boston: Beacon Press.

Jayanti, V. 1982. Women in Mea Shearim. Thesis, Hebrew Univ., Jerusalem.

Kerns, V. 1983. *Women and the ancestors: Black Carib kinship and ritual.* Urbana: Univ. of Illinois Press.

Kraemer, R. 1980. Ecstasy and possession: women of ancient Greece and the cult of Dionysus. In Falk & Gross 1980.

Lawless, E. 1983. Shouting for the Lord—the power of women's speech in the Pentecostal religious service. *J. Am. Folkl.* **96**, 434–59.

Leach, E. 1968. *Dialectic in practical religion.* Cambridge: Univ. Press.

Lowie, R. H. 1952. *Primitive religion.* New York: Grosset & Dunlap.

Mernissi, F. 1977. Women, saints, and sanctuaries. *Signs* **3**, 101–12.

Moberg, D. 1962. *The church as a social institution: the sociology of American religion.* Englewood Cliffs, New Jersey: Prentice-Hall.

Mukherjee, P. 1983. The image of women in Hinduism. *Wom. Stud. int. Forum* **6**: 4, 375–81.

Myerhoff, B. 1979. *Number our days.* New York: E. P. Dutton.

Noy, D. 1980. Is there a Jewish folk religion? In *Studies in Jewish folklore* (ed.) F. Talmage. Cambridge, Mass.: Association for Jewish Studies.

Obeyesekere, G. 1968. Theodicy, sin and salvation in a sociology of Buddhism. In *Dialectic in practical religion* (ed.) E. Leach. Cambridge: Univ. Press.

Overmyer, D. 1980. Dualism and conflict in Chinese popular religion. In *Transitions and transformation in the history of religions* (eds) F. E. Reynolds & T. M. Ludwig. Leiden: E. J. Brill.

Pomeroy, S. 1975. *Goddesses, whores, wives and slaves: women in classical antiquity.* New York: Schocken Books.

Redfield, R. 1956. *Peasant society and culture.* Chicago: Univ. Press.

Reuther, R. R. 1979. *Religion and sexism: images of women in the Jewish and Christian tradition.* New York: Simon & Schuster.

Rushton, L. 1983. Doves and magpies: village women in the Greek Orthodox Church. In *Women's religious experience* (ed.) P. Holden. London: Croom Helm.

Schneider, D. 1984. *Critique of the study of kinship.* Ann Arbor: Univ. of Michigan Press.

Shai, D. 1980. Changes in the oral tradition among the Jews of Kurdistan. *Contemporary Jewry* **5**, 2–10.

Shokeid, M. 1974. An anthropological perspective on ascetic behavior and religious change. In *Predicament of homecoming* (eds) S. Deshen & M. Shokeid. Ithaca: Cornell Univ. Press.

Tapper, N. & R. Tapper 1987. The birth of the prophet: ritual and gender in Turkish Islam. *Man* (N.S.) **22**, 69–92.

Thompson, C. 1983. Women, fertility and the worship of gods in a Hindu village. In Holden 1983.

Turner, V. 1964. Symbols in Ndembu ritual. In *Closed systems and open minds: the limits of naivety in social anthropology* (ed.) M. Gluckman. Chicago: Aldine.

Wadley, S. 1980. Hindu women's family and household rites in a north Indian village. In Falk & Gross 1980.

White, S. J. 1980. Mother Guru: Jnanananda of Madras, India. In Falk & Gross 1980.
White, S. R. 1981. Men, women and misfortune in Bunyole. *Man* (N.S.) **16**, 350–66.
Wolf, E. 1966. *Peasants*. Englewood Cliffs, New Jersey: Prentice-Hall.

Part VI

Secularism and Reform

16

Hanukkah and the Myth of the Maccabees in Ideology and in Society

Eliezer Don-Yehiya

MODERN national movements tend to make use of traditional festivals in order to nourish their political myths.[1] A myth may be defined as a tale possessing symbolic significance so that relevant lessons can be drawn from it. The present article examines the manner in which the Zionist movement made use of the Festival of Hanukkah to create and disseminate a national myth, the myth of the Maccabees (who fought against Greek rule of Judea, in 167–158 B.C.E. and who were also known as the Hasmoneans). The focus is mainly on the decades 1880–1948, before the establishment of the State of Israel, but the changes in the pattern of Hanukkah celebrations since independence will also be considered and set in the broader context of recent developments in Israel's political culture.

Hanukkah was one of various Jewish traditional festivals which the Zionist movement employed to assert the continuity of Jewish identity and the national right of the Jews to the Land of Israel. However, although the secular Zionist groups continued to celebrate the traditional religious festivals, they changed the manner of the celebration and also reinterpreted some of those festivals, with the aim of replacing their original religious content with new national or social myths.[2] The leaders of the Zionist Labour movement in particular grasped the importance of the political potential of Jewish festivals. One of them, Berl Katznelson, commented: 'The Jewish year is filled with days which for sheer depth have no parallel in other peoples. Is it in the interest of the Jewish workers' movement to squander these latent forces?'.[3]

The approach to the traditional festivals was selective, and the principle of selection applied both to the festival itself and to its attendant ceremonies and customs. A guiding principle was the degree to which the traditional festival could be imbued with a national or social aura, and serve to reinforce a political myth. As a result, some holy days underwent a change of status: those which occupied a central place in traditional Judaism, such as Rosh Hashanah (the Jewish New Year) and Yom Kippur (the Day of Atonement) were set aside because of their purely religious character while those with a less pronounced religious context, such as Hanukkah, were brought into prominence.

The renewed importance given to Hanukkah was apparent from the early beginning of the organized Zionist movement in 1882. Zionist clubs and associations were named after the Hasmoneans or the Maccabees, while Hanukkah was chosen as the preferred time to hold conferences and parties; it was also a popular theme of nationalist sermons and speeches.[4] It must be remembered that Theodor Herzl concluded his book, *The Jewish State*, with the words: 'The Maccabees shall rise again'.

Before the establishment of the State of Israel, Hanukkah was celebrated by the Jewish community of Palestine (Eretz–Israel) as an important national holy day and Zionists of all persuasions participated in the regenerated ceremonies associated with the festival. In the Labour movement, attempts were also made to imbue Hanukkah with a 'social' element by proclaiming it as a celebration of class, as well as of national, liberation. Thus, in 1910, Yitzhak Ben-Zvi (who later became the second president of Israel) depicted the Hasmoneans as 'simple peasants' who liberated their people from foreign rule, as well as from exploitation by Jewish priests and 'capitalists', who enriched themselves 'at the expense of the people'.[5] A peculiar attempt to use Hanukkah for class-struggle propaganda was made by the Palestinian Jewish Communists, who supported the anti-Zionism of the Arabs and who went so far as to portray the anti-Jewish riots of 1929 as a popular uprising of Arab peasants against Zionist efforts to dispossess them. In 1929, the Communist Youth League of Palestine published a pamphlet in which the leader of the Palestinian Arabs and self-confessed foe of Zionism — the Jerusalem Mufti, Hadj Amin al-Husseini — was portrayed as the equivalent of Mattathias the Hasmonean, since both were spiritual leaders who encouraged the emergence of a national class-liberation movement:[6]

> It may well be that the symbol in whose name the Hasmonean muftis fought was of a fanatic–religious character, but the real cause for which the peasant masses rose up was that of a movement of liberation from foreign domination and cruel exploitation.

However, the vast majority of the Jewish community of Palestine continued to regard Hanukkah as chiefly expressing the values associated with the struggle for national liberation. This perception was shared by the two rival movements which competed for hegemony in the Zionist movement and in the Jewish community of Palestine (the *Yishuv*): the Labour movement which was established in 1905 and the Revisionist movement which was founded in 1925. However, the two movements differed in their approach and in their interpretations of Jewish historical myths.

Both Labour and the Revisionists used myths which revolved around heroic deeds and struggles for national independence; but the Revisionists emphasized the theme of combating foreign rule without hesitation and without compromise, however dangerous the fight, and even if their own nation was not willing to encourage such a rebellion. The Revisionists glorified the Zealots who revolted against the Romans in 66–70 C.E. as well as Bar-Kokhba's fighters who also rebelled against the Romans in 132–35 C.E. Bar-Kokhba's last stronghold was Betar and this was also the name of the youth movement of the Revisionists, while their most radical group was called Brit Habiryonim, after the most militant of the Zealots.

Although other Zionist groups also admired the fighters against the Romans, they gave pride of place to the Hasmoneans who had waged war only after grave acts of provocation and of suppression by the Greek rulers. Such a reaction was more in tune with the 'defensive ethos' (to use Anita Shapira's term)[7] of the Labour movement and of other moderate groups in the *Yishuv*, while the revolts against Roman rule were more in line with the militant ethos of the Revisionists.

We can even detect a certain ambivalence in the attitude of some Revisionists towards the Hasmoneans. This is related to the fact that many Zionist leaders, writers, and poets, who inspired the Revisionist movement, were admirers of the Hellenistic culture which was anathema to the Hasmoneans. The Revisionists saw themselves as disciples of the renowned Zionist leader, Max Nordau. In an article published in 1900, Nordau urged the cultivation of a 'muscular Jewry', which he associated especially with Bar-Kokhba, whom he described as 'a hero who never knew defeat' and who embodied 'the Jewry that is steeled in war and is enamoured of weapons'.[8] Nordau also lauded, as representatives of 'muscular Jewry', the young Hellenizing Jews who took part in wrestling competitions and who were among the bitter enemies of the Hasmoneans.

One of the poets who was held in high esteem by the Revisionists and who exercised a powerful influence on them was Shaul Tchernichovsky (1875–1943), a great admirer of Hellenistic culture, who bluntly blamed the Maccabees because they had sought to eradicate Hellenism. In his 1926 poem 'My Melody' the poet rhetorically asks: 'Who are you, my blood that seethes within me? The blood of the Maccabees?' and replies: 'No! ... the blood of the conquerors of Canaan is my blood'.[9] One of the Zionist leaders who admired Hellenistic culture was the founder of the Revisionist movement, Ze'ev Jabotinsky, who in 1905 declared:[10]

Mankind will be eternally grateful to Hellenism, which was first to point to sports as the best educational means for creating, by prolonged training and will-power, a type imbued with spiritual beauty and courage. The Hellenes were the first to establish special gymnasia for this purpose.

Abba Achimeir, the prominent radical Revisionist, was even more forthright in his 1932 article in which he expressed more admiration for the Hellenistic culture which the Hasmoneans fought against than for the traditional Jewish culture which they were defending. He argued that in contrast to traditional Judaism, which was mainly a spiritual phenomenon, Hellenism gave expression to the 'earthly-political' approach which he favoured.[11] Achimeir's attitude towards Judaism later changed, as did the approach of some other Revisionist leaders, including Jabotinsky.[12] In an article published in 1941, Achimeir described Hellenism as an expression of 'civilization', which was an internationalistic, materialistic, and technological cultural phenomenon, but devoid of national distinctiveness.[13] Judaism, in contrast, could be perceived as a typical example of an authentic national culture , expressing 'an intensive inner independent spiritual life'. From this point of view, the Hasmoneans' revolt against the Greeks symbolized the clash between cosmopolitan 'civilization' and national 'culture' — and Achimeir clearly preferred the latter.

The ideological differences between the Revisionists and Labour also became apparent in their differing concepts of the Hanukkah festival and of the Hasmonean revolt. The Revisionists saw the revolt as exhibiting heroism in battle and self-sacrifice for the cause of national independence, while their political rivals interpreted that revolt as a popular uprising of peace-loving peasants who had to defend themselves against their cruel oppressors.

However, despite their differences, the various secular movements in the *Yishuv* certainly were united in looking upon Hanukkah as a celebration of political activism and of a national awakening. The only exception were the 'Canaanites'. Their leader, the poet Yonathan Ratosh, rejected the myth of the Maccabees since this myth was an affirmation of the continuing connection between Zionism and Judaism which the Canaanites vehemently opposed.[14] Ratosh's attitude towards the Hasmoneans is linked with his reservations about the Second Temple period as a whole. He explained that in that era, the original Hebraic culture of Eretz–Israel was driven out by non-territorial Judaism which had been imposed on the people by the returning Babylonian exiles.[15]

The Canaanites depicted the Hasmoneans not as Hebrew fighters in a campaign for national liberation against foreign rule, but as Jewish religious fanatics who were primarily fighting their internal adversaries, the Hellenizers. Although that struggle occurred in Eretz–Israel, the Hasmoneans did not fight for the cause of a political–territorial nation, but for that of a dispersed and self-enclosed religious sect. Adaya Horon, the Canaanite historian, has claimed that the only original purpose of the war of the Hasmoneans was to secure 'independence of worship in Jerusalem and its environs with freedom to take revenge on "the wicked" — the Hellenizers among them ... No national liberation was involved'.[16] Horon added that although Judaism and Hellenism were mutually incompatible, there was no conflict whatever between the Greek and the Hebrew cultures. Indeed, the Greeks were heavily influenced by the early Hebrews.[17]

Some principles held by the Canaanites, notably their radical 'negation of the Diaspora', corresponded to ideas which were widespread among young native-born Palestinian Jews.[18] However, their rejection of the myth of the Maccabees, as well as the sharp distinction they drew between the 'Hebrew history' of the Biblical period and the 'Jewish history' which followed, never gained acceptance beyond marginal circles in Jewish society in Eretz–Israel.

Ironically, the Canaanite conception of Hanukkah resembles that of the Haredim (ultra-Orthodox Jews). For both groups, who rejected Zionism out of diametrically-opposed reasons, Hanukkah is a religious holy day, and the struggle of the Hasmoneans cannot serve as the source of a national–political myth. However, the difference between the Haredim and the Canaanites is that the former exalt the religious character of Hanukkah, whereas the latter excoriate it. As for the Zionists, secular and religious alike, they were of the opinion that the fact that Hanukkah was rooted in the Jewish religious tradition should not hinder its use for the promotion of national goals.

It is worth noting here that the festival of Hanukkah has potentialities which cannot easily be found in other traditional celebrations, which are loaded with religious meaning and require strict observance. That was why the secularized version of the Passover *seder* was confined mainly to the kibbutz movement. Many Jews who were not Orthodox, but who still respected the religious tradition, balked at the introduction of changes in the consecrated order of the *seder*, just as they objected to the transformation of *Shavuot* (the Feast of Weeks or Pentecost) in the kibbutz into a harvest festival in which the traditional meanings, notably the giving of the Torah, were discarded.[19] On the other hand, since Hanukkah was less ritualized than Passover or *Shavuot*, it could more easily be re-interpreted as a modern–national festival.

Nevertheless, even Hanukkah can illustrate the problems entailed in the use of a traditional religious festival for the dissemination of a political myth. The first difficulty is that, historically, the revolt of the Maccabees against the Greeks began as an uprising of traditional Jews against religious decrees enacted by the Greek ruler with the encouragement and active support of the Hellenizers, who wished to impose on the Jewish people an alien secular culture. This was an obstacle for those Zionists who aimed to make the events and heroes of Hanukkah the source of a national political myth, devoid of a religious content.

Virtually every national or social movement must at some point decide how to resolve the problem of the gap between myth and fact. One solution is simply to disregard the inconvenient facts, or to present them in a new light by reinterpreting them. Secular Zionism resorted to the former option in its reinvention of the Hanukkah festival: 'problematic' aspects of the Hasmonean revolt were ignored or played down, and the accent was placed on elements which seemed to lend themselves especially to the aims of the Zionists. Thus, the causes of the revolt were not stressed and the spotlight was directed at the heroism and courage of the fighters and at the continued struggle for political independence even after the religious decrees were abolished. Israel Eldad aptly summed up the stratagem when he noted that Zionism 'appropriated the form but not the content of the war of the Hasmoneans'.[20]

Hasmonean goals were also reinterpreted in a manner which placed the emphasis on 'loyalty to the people' and on 'preserving national distinctiveness', without specifying the actual components of that distinctiveness. Thus, even the Zionists who admired Hellenistic culture denounced the Hellenizers for deserting their people in favour of foreign rulers. Nordau observed that the new 'muscular Jews' of the Bar-Kokhba Zionists' sports club 'had still not attained the degree of heroism of our forefathers who would burst into the arena in their masses ... in order to take part in the competitions'. However, he added: 'Morally speaking, we are already at ... a level higher than theirs'. This was because the Jewish athletes in Hasmonean times were ashamed of their Jewishness and strove to conceal their origin, whereas the modern Jewish sportsmen openly displayed their national pride.[21]

The second problem about the Zionist conception of Hanukkah is that that conception cannot be reconciled with the traditional interpretation of the festival. The Talmud has very little to say about the wars of the Hasmoneans, and almost nothing about their connection to Hanukkah. Instead, the central theme is the 'miracle of the cruse of oil' which was found in the Temple and which continued to provide fuel to burn in the candelabrum for eight days, although the amount of oil was sufficient for only one single day. This miracle is represented as the source of the major celebration of the festival — lighting the candelabrum for eight days. The war against the Greeks is certainly given an important place in the prayer 'For the Miracles' which is recited on Hanukkah, but the prayer does not praise the courage or strength of the Jews as the factors which ensured their victory, but refers to God's deliverance of his people because of their piety:

> And You in Your great mercy stood by them in their hour of distress ... You delivered the strong into the hands of the weak, the many to the few, the

defiled to the pure, and the evil-doers into the hands of those who devote themselves to the study of Your Torah.

Thus, God was the only true redeemer and the principal task of the Jews was to consecrate the Temple for His worship and to offer Him prayers of thanksgiving:

> Afterward Your sons came to the sanctuary of Your house, and cleaned Your Palace and purified Your Temple and lit lights in the chambers of Your holy place. And they set aside these eight days of Hanukkah to praise and exalt Your great and holy name for Your miracles and Your wonders and Your deliverance.

Clearly, then, the traditional conception of Hanukkah does not accord with the modern Zionist view of the festival as the victorious struggle of the people for self-redemption, which was achieved through their own efforts alone, without divine help. But the Zionists claimed that their own version of Hanukkah was the more accurate one and that it was the political passivity of traditional religious Jews which caused them deliberately to ignore the heroic exploits of the Hasmoneans and their struggle for national liberation.[22] The words of the prayer 'For the Miracles' were condemned for the same reason. A Jerusalem writer, Shlomo Jonas, stated in an article published in 1893 that this prayer praised the Lord for the deliverance of His people but omitted to refer to the brave fighters who had achieved that victory:[23]

> We recite [in that prayer] ... You fought ... You judged ... You avenged ... You delivered ... [but] Who wrought all these things? Who did all this? Who was the emissary of the Lord? Who was the man of battle? Where is Judah the Maccabee who defended his brothers with his sword and his bow ...? Judah the Maccabee might as well never have existed for all his mention in this prayer!

In another article published in 1911 the Socialist Zionist writer, Zerubavel (Yaakov Vitkin) commented on the striking contrast between martyred Jews in the Diaspora, the helpless victims of pogroms, and the new Jews, who bore arms and fell in the defence of their homeland.[24] These Jews, members of *Hashomer*, the first Jewish defence organization, were renewing the heroic tradition of the Hasmoneans and of the insurgents against the Romans. In Zerubavel's view, that tradition had been abandoned in the Diaspora, which had sanctified 'passive martyrs' and had consigned to oblivion activist heroes. Those responsible were 'the passive Torah bearers ... who carried the name of God on their lips but whose hearts were far from every feeling of freedom and liberty'. The author observed: 'Martyrs are evoked at a time of weakness, heroes are emulated at a time of courage and action'. That was why the pioneers of the national renaissance tended to identify with the Hasmoneans and with the other heroes of the Second

Temple: 'The Hasmoneans did not make do with prayers ... The Biryonim did not expect miracles ... They shed their blood for the people's freedom'.

The village of the Hasmoneans, Modi'in, became a shrine for the Zionist youth movements and a place of pilgrimage. Zerubavel pointed to the contrast between Modi'in and Miron, the pilgrimage site in the Galilee, which has been a centre of prayer and ritual for traditional Jews. While Modi'in is a symbol of activism and courage, Miron symbolizes the passive waiting of traditional Jews for a miraculous salvation from the heavens. The author asked: 'Miron and Modi'in ... which is stronger? Which will triumph? Which will determine the course of our current history?'

Zerubavel's approach was not favoured by all the spokesmen of secular Zionism. Even in his own Labour movement, there were those who maintained that the central theme of the Hanukkah celebration should not be military activism but spiritual heroism. That was the stand taken by Berl Katznelson, who stressed the virtue of selfless devotion to the Jewish faith associated with Hanukkah, as exemplified in the story of Hannah and her seven sons who were willing to sacrifice their lives rather than surrender to apostasy. In an article published on Hanukkah in 1944, Katznelson entered the debate about the fiercely condemnatory proclamation issued by the rabbinical establishment against Jewish pig farmers in the Holy Land. He quoted the legend dating back to Hasmonean times about a pig which dug its hoofs into the wall around Jerusalem 'and the whole land did shake from one end to the other'. Katznelson declared his support for the rabbis, reasoning: 'How shall we tell our children about the selfless devotion of ... Hannah and her seven sons — if the very cause for which they were killed has no meaning in our own way of life?'.[25]

However, Katznelson also did not concur with the traditional concept of Hanukkah, since it stressed the miraculous salvation from above, in contrast to the Zionist emphasis on the theme of self-liberation. This clash between the two approaches to the festival was apparent from the very beginning of modern Zionism. In 1903, a rabbi deplored the actions of the Zionists who, he claimed[26]

> magnified the festival of the Maccabees and augmented their strength and power, and this is truly a great mistake ... For under natural conditions they were incapable of winning the war, and [they were victorious] only because they were completely just men and sought with selfless devotion to save our sacred religion.

The fiercest opponents of the Zionist version of Hanukkah were the Haredim, who also dismissed Zionism as a movement which ran counter to the spirit of religious tradition. They claimed that the manner of the Zionist celebrations of Hanukkah was closer to the outlook of the Hellenizers than it was to that of the Hasmoneans, although the Zionists were pretending to be praising the latter. They added that the Zionists expressed admiration for the values fostered by the Hellenizers under the influence of a foreign culture, such as the worship of physical strength. Yitzhak Breuer, a major Haredi leader, commented:[27]

> The Hellenizers loved their people and their land in their own fashion . . . They loved the land but loathed the Land of Torah, loved the people but despised the People of the Torah, loved Greek licentiousness but hated the burden of Torah . . . It is not for the Jewish State that the Hasmoneans fought but for the People of the Torah. They did battle against the kingdom of evil when it threatened the People of the Torah with destruction . . . They also fought against the wicked among their own people . . . This was a kulturkampf . . . Greek culture triumphed over the whole world, and only the Torah culture was able to withstand it.

As for the religious Zionists, they sought to reconcile the national myth of the Maccabees with the traditional elements of Hanukkah. They held that the struggle of the Hasmoneans was fuelled by both religio–spiritual and national–political goals. Rabbi Yeshayahu Shapira, the Hapoel–Hamizrachi leader, considered the exploits of the Hasmoneans to be a shining example of the special obligation on the Orthodox community to rally to the cause of national redemption:[28]

> In the days of the Hasmoneans, the banner of the revolt was raised expressly by Torah followers, and they risked their lives for the liberation of the land and of the Jewish spirit. Today, we face a similar war, a war for the redemption of our land and a war for the liberation of the Jewish spirit from the alien cultures that we have absorbed.

A unique approach to Hanukkah was presented by a group which called itself 'Covenant of the Hasmoneans' and advocated a fusion of religiosity with radical Messianic nationalism. The Hasmoneans were their models because they exemplified the ideal fusion of the religious believer and the hero–warrior. In *Hahashmonai* (The Hasmonean), they published an article at the time of the 1944 Hanukkah festival which asserted that the lesson of the revolt against the Greeks was that the national struggle should be conducted in a revolutionary and uncompromising style: 'It is not by building and ploughing and sowing well, or even by defending ourselves with arms that we will attain . . . liberty, but by establishing the irrevocable fact by irrevocable means: "Who shall be sole ruler here?" '[29]

As Orthodox Jews, the members of the 'Covenant' had to confront the problem of the apparent contrast between their militant nationalistic attitude and the political passivity of traditional religious Jewry. They resolved that problem by blaming the conditions of Jewish exile for the abandonment of the heritage of heroism associated with the

Hasmoneans. Another article in their publication stated that 'heroism and pride were deeply-rooted qualities in the Jewish people from its very beginnings ... The Torah does not teach submission and weakness. It is a source of strength and pride'. However, the 'distortion and disruption' caused by the exile had brought about a 'warped attitude towards heroism'.[30] Moreover, it was argued that as a result of the 'shortcomings of the Diaspora', the Torah sages 'cannot be considered as exemplars in other matters such as heroism in battle'.[31]

Other religious Zionists also claimed that it was not religious tradition but rather conditions of exile which were the source of Jewish historical passivity. However, in contrast to the members of the 'Covenant', they sought to link Hanukkah to the values of labour and land settlement rather than to militant–nationalistic values — an approach more in keeping with the ethos of the Labour movement than with that of the Revisionists. Thus, Rabbi Shapira concluded his article on Hanukkah with the statement that the battle for the nation's political and spiritual deliverance 'is no longer waged by the sword, but through the redemption and settling of the land'.

In spite of the objections of the ultra-Orthodox, Hanukkah became a festival which provided the *Yishuv* with symbols of solidarity, national cohesiveness, and political mobilization, and was intended to imbue the Jewish population (and the younger generation in particular) with the virtues of heroism and a readiness for self-sacrifice in the pursuit of national goals. So it was that the pioneers and the defenders of the *Yishuv* were depicted as 'new Maccabees' — a title which was especially claimed for the underground organizations (the Haganah, Irgun, and LEHI) which repeatedly adopted symbols associated with Hanukkah and the Maccabees.

Hilda Schatzberger has shown that each of these organizations used the exploits of the Maccabees to legitimize its goals and its methods of operation.[32] For example, the Haganah (which was controlled by the official *Yishuv* leadership) stressed that the army of the Hasmoneans was an army of defenders and of popular liberators which had the unwavering support of the people. On the other hand, the Irgun depicted the Maccabees as freedom fighters who of their own initiative rose in revolt against foreign rule, without reference to the official leaders of their Jewish community and indeed against the will of these leaders. LEHI claimed that the Hasmonean revolt provided a precedent for the use of terrorism as a legitimate method of combat. Its spokesmen reminded their critics of Mattathias (the priest and father of the Hasmonean brothers) who killed the Hellenizing Jew who offered a sacrifice to a statue erected in Modi'in, and sparked off the revolt. All three underground organizations, in common with most Zionist groups in the *Yishuv*, drew a parallel between the Maccabees (whose war was that of 'the few against the many') and the struggles waged by the underground fighters and the defenders of the *Yishuv* against forces vastly superior in both numbers and material.

The myth of the Maccabees was also associated with the whole gamut of activities connected with self-defence and with the land-settlement operations carried out in the *Yishuv*. The festival of Hanukkah was celebrated in public ceremonies and at mass events to foster in the people the Hasmonean spirit of heroism and devotion to the national cause. According to the historian Ben-Zion Dinur,[33] the ceremonies included:

> lighting the candles with great ostentation, lectures and speeches in syna-gogues and community halls, in schools and kindergartens, on the Has-moneans' war of freedom ... so that the whole people might know ... what the heroes did, what a people is capable of accomplishing if moved by faith, by trust, by the ability to lay down its life ...

The period of Hanukkah was also perceived as a time of 'national reflection' in which individuals as well as the whole Jewish community must engage in self-examination, asking themselves: 'What brick did I bring to the great edifice we are building — a home for the Jewish people in its land?'[34] Hanukkah was also used for various Zionist activities. The days of the festival were described as 'days of convoca-tion for the whole movement, days of assemblies and conferences'.[35] The Jewish National Fund, which was engaged in buying land for Jewish settlement, chose the days of Hanukkah for its mass fund-raising operations. These included a special campaign which appealed particularly to the religious sector of the *Yishuv*. In 1939, for example, the Sabbath preceding Hanukkah was set aside as 'a Sabbath dedi-cated to the land and its redemption'. The official announcement stated that 'on this Sabbath speeches will be delivered in all houses of worship, ... in which the need to expedite the redemption of our Holy Land ... will be explained'. The religious–Zionist daily *Hatzofe* published proc-lamations of the chief rabbis urging the religious public to contribute to the land-redemption project.[36]

On the other hand, the Hanukkah celebrations aimed at the general public almost entirely ignored the festival's religious–traditional sig-nificance. The decrees of the Greek ruler against Jewish religious observance were depicted as merely an incidental effect of the subju-gation to foreign rule, not as the root cause of the Hasmonean revolt. The 'miracle of the cruse of oil' was openly belittled since it was believed that it was a salient example of the passive approach which characterized traditional Diaspora Jewry. Indeed, a popular song, widely heard during Hanukkah, stated: 'No miracle befell us, no cruse of oil did we find'. The divine intervention of the Lord was replaced by reference to the heroic people who delivered the Jewish community by their own courage and strength. A children's song chanted at

Hanukkah altered the Biblical verse: 'Who can utter the mighty acts of the Lord?' (Psalms, 106: 2) to 'Who can recount the exploits of Israel?'. The very name 'Maccabees', traditionally considered to be an acronym for the verse, 'Who is like unto thee, O Lord, among the gods?' (Exodus, 15: 11) was given a new rendition by a Zionist functionary: 'Who is like unto thee among the nations, Israel?'[37] Although religious circles condemned the festival's growing secularization, religious Zionist schools were actually following this trend, and songs such as 'Who can recount the exploits of Israel?' were also sung in their Hanukkah celebrations. (But after the establishment of the State of Israel, the original Biblical words were restored in those schools.)

Traditional practices in the celebration of the festival, such as the lighting of the candles in the *Menorah* (candelabrum), were observed but they were reinterpreted: the candles were said not to be in memory of the miracle of the cruse of oil, but to betoken the light of national deliverance. Furthermore, the ceremony of lighting the candles which traditionally took place in the home was now observed in the town square or other place of public assembly; and instead of the traditional blessings, there were speeches, declarations, and songs of a national–political character, and torches were lit and were carried through the streets in festive parades.

The lighting of the candles or torches was sometimes accompanied by special ceremonies designed to reflect the festival's regenerated meaning. One elaborate event was a pilgrimage to Modi'in where members of the youth movement, Maccabi, lit a torch and relayed it in a marathon to light Hanukkah candles along the way. On the first occasion of such a ceremony in Modi'in, the audience was told that the torch which was being kindled there would be carried by runners who were the descendants of the Maccabees 'not only to light the Hanukkah candles but to light up the hearts of Hebrew youth and to herald unity and national action'.[38] The Modi'in marathon became part of a series of sports events which were held during the Hanukkah period.

In many other cultures it is customary to celebrate national holidays with parades, torch marathons, and other ceremonies involving fire and light as symbols of awakening, heroism, and fortitude.[39] But in the Hanukkah celebrations there was also the interplay between the lighting of the candles and of the torches. While the first custom symbolized continuity with the Jewish tradition, the lighting of the torches symbolized the motif of renewal and of a change from that tradition. In contrast to the small, modest candles used in the private homes, the torches were carried with great flourish while their light shone over great distances. Thus, they could also be said to represent the renewal of the flame which had been largely extinguished or hidden in the Jewish people during the Diaspora, but which was now rekindled, to illuminate the movement of national revival.

The various new ways of interpreting and celebrating Hanukkah prompted some observers to claim that the traditional holy day had been in fact replaced by a new festival which differed from the older one in content and even in name. Thus, while the Hebrew word Hanukkah (which means 'dedication') refers to the religious dedication of the Temple in the wake of its liberation from the control of the Hellenizers, the preferred name now was the 'Festival of the Hasmoneans'. The historian, Joseph Klausner, who was one of the mentors of the Revisionist movement, stated:[40]

> Hanukkah is an ancient festival, but a modest one. The Festival of the Hasmoneans is a new holy day, but full of high spirits and popular gaiety. What was Hanukkah? ... 'For the Miracles' ... the lighting of the little candles ... at home, potato pancakes and playing cards for the adults, spinning tops for the toddlers. And what is Hanukkah now? — The Festival of the Hasmoneans, a holiday filled with cheering, a big national holiday which is celebrated by the Jewish people in all its dispersions with parties and speeches, songs and ballads, hikes and parades ... This is our Festival of the Hasmoneans as it is today, and does any nation have a national holiday as great and as consecrated as this?

The establishment of the State of Israel apparently led to a decline in the importance of Hanukkah in Israeli political culture. It is no longer a major national event, with public assemblies, declarations, and speeches, or with mass parades. One reason for this decline was that there was now a new annual national celebration — Independence Day. Another reason is related to the attitude of David Ben-Gurion, Israel's first Prime Minister, who wished to glorify the Biblical period and its heroes, not the Hasmoneans or other heroes of the post-Biblical period. For, although Judah the Maccabee or Bar-Kokhba were undoubtedly brave heroes, they were eventually defeated and were unable to preserve and consolidate the political independence for which they had fought; hence they could not serve as role models for Ben-Gurion's *Mamlachti* (Statist) approach, which put the emphasis on enduring military and political achievements. Moreover, Ben-Gurion did not wish to engage in a confrontation with the religious sector of Israel, which opposed the secularization of traditional festivals. He explained that since the Bible was accepted or revered by all sections of Jewish society, secular as well as religious, it was the most fitting source for national myths and symbols.[41]

In a Knesset debate in 1955 about military decorations, Ben-Gurion rejected the proposal to name medals after leading figures of the Second Temple period such as Judah the Maccabee or Bar-Kokhba. He insisted that only Biblical heroes were worthy of having medals named after them, because they surpassed in stature all those who came after them, including the Hasmoneans and the leaders of the revolts against the Romans. He argued that 'the Israeli child, the Israeli youngster ...

needs to feel that our history did not begin in 1948, nor in 1897, and not even in the days of the Maccabees', but that it had its origins in the Biblical era, 'the period of Jewish glory and independence ... the period of independent spiritual creativity which forged the Jewish people and brought us to this day'.[42]

Ben-Gurion was of course aware that his approach differed from that of 'classical' Zionism in whose mythology 'the theme of the Maccabees and Bar-Kochba ... was placed on a pedestal, not historical events which had occurred earlier and were more crucial'. According to him, the cult of the Hasmoneans had its roots in 'the protest of the Zionist generation against the Talmud which tried to obscure and conceal the Maccabees' enterprise'. But unlike their forebears, the Jews of modern Israel did not need 'heroes of protest' against the Talmudic approach. What they needed were 'educational heroes' such as the Biblical figures 'who were set apart both by their primacy and by being anchored in an authentic historical–literary source which was accepted and revered by the whole Jewish people'.[43]

Ben-Gurion's attitude also marked the crucial difference between conditions in the Holy Land before and after the establishment of the State of Israel. Before independence, Zionism needed to make use of the myths glorifying the overthrow of foreign domination of the Jewish nation, and this was also true of the underground organizations during the *Yishuv*. But the myths and symbols employed before 1948 were no longer relevant after Independence. New myths and symbols were now necessary, such as would help to consolidate and intensify the loyalty of Israelis to their State, stress the necessity of civil obedience to the State's laws and institutions, and ensure that Israeli citizens would be ready to act in defence of their country and for the realization of its goals. That was why Ben-Gurion favoured the Biblical heroes who had established themselves as legitimate leaders in the kingdoms of the First Temple.

Ben-Gurion was not solely responsible for the decline in the public importance of the Hanukkah festival as a national celebration. That decline was part of a process of cultural change which has been manifested in the growing tendency in Israeli society to discard the secularized and politicized new versions of the Jewish festivals and to return to the more traditional private and domestic forms of celebration. Thus, Hanukkah celebrations in Israel either regained traditional religious features or became a sort of popular entertainment. In neither case do they carry ideological or political messages.

Many Israeli Jews do not perceive Hanukkah as a saliently national festival. In a public opinion survey which Charles Liebman and I conducted with the help of the Pori Institute in 1975, only a little over a third (35.1 per cent) of the respondents said that they regarded Hanukkah primarily as a national festival; 21.9 per cent considered it to be a primarily religious festival and 14.6 per cent regarded it primarily as a family celebration. The other respondents defined Hanukkah as a 'religious–family' occasion (5.4 per cent), 'religious–national' (9.2 per cent), 'national–family' (6.3 per cent), and a 'religious–national–family' celebration (4.9 per cent).[44] As this was the first such survey, no statistical data were available for comparison. However, we can conclude on the basis of everything that we know about the way that the festival used to be celebrated in the *Yishuv* period and in the early years of the State, that the percentage of those who regarded Hanukkah as a distinctly national holiday had probably been far higher in those years.

The changes in the public perceptions of the festival are also reflected in the patterns of its celebration. Today, Hanukkah is celebrated mainly in the circle of family and friends, in the home or in parties. The 'little candles' and the spinning tops, the potato pancakes and the doughnuts have once again become the festival's primary symbols. Such changes should be seen within the context of a far more comprehensive transformation in Israeli political culture, as discernible in the way that Israelis celebrate their other festivals.

The present discussion of this development is confined to the most general terms. Two distinctive but interconnected processes are at work: on the one hand, there is a departure from the earlier tendency towards the deliberate and explicit secularization of religious festivals and ceremonies, and a return to their original traditional formulas; on the other hand, there is also a retreat from the 'nationalization' or 'politicization' attempts which marked the ceremonies of Jewish festivals during the *Yishuv* period and the early years of the State. Both trends reflect a weakening of commitment and fidelity to collective values, as well as the abandonment of myths and symbols which were used to express those values.

This whole process is linked in turn to the great decline in the status of secular ideologies, such as Socialist Zionism, or Ben-Gurion's version of *Mamlachtiyut* (Statism). These ideologies were intended to replace traditional Jewish religion as a symbol-system which would underpin the cohesiveness of Jewish society and be a source of inspiration for the achievement of national goals.[45] With the decline of these ideologies, institutionalized and politicized structures of festivals and ceremonies were abandoned in favour of more traditional or more individual and spontaneous styles which do not reflect clear and well-defined ideological commitments. A related development is the attenuation of political authority in Israeli society, as evidenced in the refusal of large sections of the Israeli public to accept the dictates of the establishment concerning the management of social and cultural affairs, including symbolic and ceremonial behaviour. A salient example is the change in the patterns of Independence Day celebrations, which is manifested in the trend away from symbols and ceremonies of clearly collective significance towards practices of a more 'private' and pluralistic nature, and the declining role of political leaders in the regulation of the celebrations.[46]

The only exception to the current trends of divesting Hanukkah of its political and heroic overtones is to be found in the symbol-system of Gush Emunim. In that movement, which advocates a mixture of devoutly religious and national values,[47] Hanukkah symbolizes the uncompromising struggle for both religious and national goals. Danny Rubinstein describes the occasion of a lecture given in 1980 by one of the spiritual leaders of Gush Emunim, Rabbi Shlomo Aviner, on the subject of 'The Miracle of Hanukkah'. The rabbi declared that the chief feature of the festival was a commemoration of the victory of the heroic Hasmoneans over their people's oppressors. But that victory, the rabbi added, was achieved because the Jewish fighters were divinely inspired with spiritual power, which proved miraculous just like the miracle of the cruse of oil.[48] Here we have a conception which stresses the centrality of the heroism of the Hasmoneans in the struggle to liberate their people, but which asserts that the source of that heroism was divine inspiration.

The members of Gush Emunim consider themselves to be the successors of the Maccabees. Gush Emunim played a dominant role in 'The Movement to Stop the Withdrawal from Sinai', which was engaged in 1982 in a struggle against the implementation of the Camp David agreements with Egypt. Members of that group described themselves as 'the Hasmoneans of their generation, the few against the many, fired with the spirit of truth and faith'.[49] The case of the Hasmoneans was used by the political radicals of Gush Emunim in their polemic against their rivals of the Israeli left. In an article published on Hanukkah 1987, Dan Be'eri commented caustically that Hanukkah celebrations hailing the heroism of the Maccabees were increasingly becoming 'something both creaking and grating', and the reason for this was that:[50]

> Just between ourselves, the Maccabees were at bottom pretty fascistic. They were also terrorists and religious fanatics who thrust the nation into mortal danger. They operated out of irrational, Messianic motives, and fomented a civil war. They also spurned the nation's legitimate legal institutions, which enjoyed the solid support of a broad consensus, whereas they were a radical, violent minority. They ... despised progress and universal cultural values. So, is it the deeds of these people that we are instilling in Jewish youth, not to mention the miracle of the cruse of oil? This must be stopped at once! It's all very well and fitting for Orthodox Jews. But it cannot be a Zionist holiday, glorious and positive, a source of inspiration for a progressive and humanistic society.

Dan Be'eri was a member of the 'Jewish Underground' which was active in the occupied territories in the years 1980–84, and he had received a prison sentence in 1985 for his part in the plot to blow up the Dome of the Rock — the Muslim shrine on the Temple Mount. At the trial of Be'eri and his comrades, one of the defence's arguments was that 'this court would also have convicted Judah the Maccabee for removing the idols from the Temple'. The same reaction was implicit in a comment by the father of one of the accused: 'This court is situated on Salah al-Din Street and not on Judah the Maccabee Street: that's the whole problem in a nutshell'.[51]

Gush Emunim made efforts to link Hanukkah to its settlement activities. On Hanukkah 1976 it established its first settlement in the occupied territories at Sebastia, and on Hanukkah 1981 it launched a countrywide campaign to stop the Sinai withdrawal, using the slogan, 'Do not uproot what is planted'. However, despite the importance which Gush Emunim has attached to Hanukkah, it has not been able to restore its standing as a central national event. One reason for this is that Hanukkah could not compete with new national festivals, such as Independence Day — and since the Six-Day War of 1967, also Jerusalem Day, which has acquired special importance and is indeed particularly celebrated by Gush Emunim. But the important factor is that while Gush Emunim can boast of its achievements in establishing Jewish settlements in the occupied territories, it can hardly boast of having made a deep impression on Israeli culture.

There has clearly been a great weakening in the link between Hanukkah celebrations in Israeli Jewish society and the national myth of the Maccabees. The prevailing tendency now is to observe the festival in a manner which reflects a mild fusion of national and traditional elements and which to a large extent is characteristic of Israeli political culture in general.

NOTES

[1] See Henry Tudor, *Political Myth*, London, 1972.

[2] Charles Liebman and Eliezer Don-Yehiya, *Civil Religion in Israel*, Los Angeles, 1983.

[3] Berl Katznelson, 'Well-springs' (Hebrew) in B. Katznelson, *Ketavim* (Writings), Tel Aviv, 1947, vol. 6, p. 391.

[4] Azriel Shohat, 'Names, Symbols and Ambience in Hibat Zion' in *Shivat Ziyon* (Hebrew Annual), vols 2–3, 1951, p. 248.

[5] A. R. (Yitzhak Ben-Zvi), 'The Miracle of Hanukkah' in *Ha-achdut* (Hebrew weekly), no. 10, December 1910.

[6] Quoted by G. S. Yisraeli (Walter Laqueur), *MPS–PKP–Maki* (Hebrew), Tel Aviv, 1953, p. 69.

[7] Anita Shapira, *Visions in Conflict* (Hebrew), Tel Aviv, 1988, pp. 23–71.

[8] Max Nordau, 'Muscular Jewry' (Hebrew) in M. Nordau, *Ketavim* (Writings), vol. 1, Jerusalem, 1955, pp. 187–88.

⁹ Shaul Tchernichovsky, 'My Melody' in *Poems* (Hebrew), Jerusalem, 1959, p. 278.

¹⁰ Quoted on the basis of hearsay evidence in Moshe Bela, *The World of Jabotinsky* (Hebrew), Tel Aviv, 1975, p. 133.

¹¹ Abba Achimeir, 'Hellenism in Judea and Judaism in Hellas', in A. Achimeir, *Revolutionary Zionism* (Hebrew), Tel Aviv, 1966, p. 237.

¹² See Eliezer Don-Yehiya and Charles Liebman, 'Zionist Ultranationalism and its Attitude towards Religion', *Journal of Church and State*, vol. 23, no. 2, 1981, pp. 259–74.

¹³ Abba Achimeir, 'The Hanukkah Miracle in the Past and the Present' in *Revolutionary Zionism*, op. cit. in Note 11 above, pp. 255–56.

¹⁴ Yehoshua Porat, *The Life of Uriel Shelah* (Hebrew), Tel Aviv, 1989, p. 139.

¹⁵ See Yonathan Ratosh's foreword in Y. Ratosh, ed., *From Victory to Defeat* (Hebrew), Tel Aviv, 1976, pp. 21–26.

¹⁶ Adaya Horon, 'The Primeval Hebrew', in Ratosh, op. cit. in Note 15 above, p. 254.

¹⁷ Ibid., pp. 209–15.

¹⁸ Baruch Kurzweil, 'The Essence and Sources of the "Young Hebrews" Movement ("Canaanites")', in B. Kurzweil, *Our New Literature: Continuation or Revolution?* (Hebrew), Jerusalem, 1965, pp. 270–300.

¹⁹ See M. Glickson, 'Beautiful Is the Harvest Festival with the Festival of the Giving of Our Torah' (Hebrew) in Yom Tov Levinsky, ed., *Sefer Hamoadim* (The Book of Festivals), Tel Aviv, 1950, vol. 3, p. 284.

²⁰ Israel Eldad, 'The Logic of Hanukkah 1981', *Nekuda* (Hebrew weekly), no. 22, December 1981, p. 5.

²¹ Nordau, op. cit. in Note 8 above, p. 188.

²² Many historians reject this view. See Yehoshua Efron, 'The Revolt of the Hasmoneans in Modern Historiography' in *Historians and Historical Schools* (a collection of essays in Hebrew; the name of the editor is not given), Jerusalem, 1963, pp. 117–43.

²³ The article, 'Commandments Require Devotion', was first published in the Hebrew weekly, *Hatzvi* in December 1893. It was reprinted in Yehoshua Kaniel, ed., *Ben-Yehuda in Prison* (Hebrew), Jerusalem, 1983, pp. 3–4.

²⁴ Zerubavel, 'Yizkor (Fragments of Ideas)' in *Ha-achdut* (Hebrew weekly), nos 11–12, 1 February 1911. See also Jonathan Frankel, 'The Yizkor Book of 1911: A Note on National Myths in the Second Aliyah', in H. Ben-Israel *et al.*, eds., *Religion, Ideology and Nationalism*, Jerusalem, 1986, pp. 335–84.

²⁵ Berl Katznelson, 'How Far the Love of Israel (In the Wake of the Debate over Hanukkah)' in B. Katznelson, *Ketavim*, vol. 12, Tel Aviv, 1950, p. 57.

²⁶ Quoted in Ehud Luz, *Parallels Meet*, New York, 1988, pp. 123–24.

²⁷ Yitzhak Breuer, *Moriah* (Hebrew), Jerusalem, 1982, p. 89.

²⁸ Rabbi Yeshayahu Shapira, 'The Lesson of the Partition Vote', *Hatzofe* (Hebrew daily), 16 December 1939.

²⁹ B. Duvdevani, 'Is This the Beginning of the Revolt?', *Hahashmonai*, December 1944 (Hebrew).

³⁰ 'Chapters of the Covenant of the Hasmoneans', ibid., Spring 1944 (Hebrew).

³¹ Ibid., Spring 1946.

[32] Hilda Schatzberger, *Resistance and Tradition in Mandatory Palestine* (Hebrew), Ramat-Gan, 1985, p. 58.

[33] Ben-Zion Dinur, 'Festival of the Hasmoneans', *Sefer Hamoadim*, op. cit. in Note 19 above, p. 197.

[34] Ibid.

[35] Ibid.

[36] *Hatzofe*, 16 December 1939.

[37] Ernest Simon, 'Are We Still Jews?', *Luah Ha'aretz* (Hebrew Annual), 1952, p. 99.

[38] 'The Torch Race from Modi'in', *Sefer Hamoadim*, op. cit. in Note 19 above, p. 212.

[39] George L. Mosse, *The Nationalization of the Masses*, New York, 1975, pp. 40–44.

[40] Yosef Klausner, 'Hanukkah — Symbol and Warning', *Sefer Hamoadim*, op. cit. in Note 19 above, pp. 189–90.

[41] Eliezer Don-Yehiya, 'Judaism and Statism in Ben-Gurion's Thought and Policy', *Haziyonut* (Hebrew Annual), vol. 14, 1989, pp. 51–88.

[42] *Knesset Proceedings*, 1955, p. 1792 (Hebrew).

[43] Ibid., pp. 1791–92.

[44] These are unpublished results of the survey, which was conducted for our study on civil religion in Israel.

[45] This subject is discussed extensively in Liebman and Don-Yehiya, op. cit. in Note 2 above.

[46] Eliezer Don-Yehiya, 'Festivals and Political Culture: Independence Day Celebrations', *The Jerusalem Quarterly*, no. 45, Winter 1988, pp. 61–84 (see especially pp. 82–83).

[47] Eliezer Don-Yehiya, 'Jewish Messianism, Religious Zionism and Israeli Politics: The Origins and Impact of Gush Emunim', *Middle Eastern Studies*, vol. 23, no. 2, April 1987, pp. 215–34.

[48] Danny Rubinstein, *On the Lord's Side: Gush Emunim* (Hebrew), Tel Aviv, 1982, pp. 141–43.

[49] Quoted by Gideon Aran in *Eretz Israel Between Politics and Religion: The Movement to Stop the Withdrawal from Sinai* (Hebrew), Jerusalem, 1985, p. 12.

[50] Dan Be'eri, 'Hanukkah of the Zionists', *Nekuda* (Hebrew), no. 116, December 1987, p. 8.

[51] See Haggai Segal, *Dear Brothers* (Hebrew), Jerusalem 1986, p. 258.

17

Death Customs in a
Non-Religious Kibbutz

Nissan Rubin

This paper examines the development of mourning customs from the early stages of the kibbutz, where the sacred in terms of Jewish tradition was rejected as a matter of ideology, and where secular tradition had not yet developed. Coinciding with the eradication of traditional symbols, there was a search for alternate symbols to replace those rejected by the revolutionary kibbutz pioneers. Hence, a process of creation and innovation of new rituals was introduced, either by the adoption of ritual elements from outside sources or by the transformation of existing Jewish symbols through the infusion of new content. These replaced the sacred transcendental symbols of traditional Jewish life with symbols which were to be no less sacred, but found their origins and definition in secular ideology and collective identity. As long as ideological fervor was strong, secular formulations of ritual could be preserved. With the waning if ideological fervor, some of the secular elements of mourning customs disappeared and more traditional content was reinstated.

Secularization in modern society sometimes carries with it processes of secular ritual. These may be observed on many levels, from national rituals to local, individual and rites of passage rituals. Research on secular ritual has grown around new concepts such as non-religious sanctity (Moore and Myerhoff, 1977). Writers such as Turner (1982a) and Moore and Myerhoff (1979) have developed theoretical frameworks for secular ritual. Earlier, Gluckman (1958) dealt with dedication rituals in socially loosely integrated communities. Similarly, there has been interest in secular funeral ritual in the United States (Huntington and Metcalf, 1979) and in European socialist countries (Fried and Fried, 1980; Binns, 1979; 1980).

Little has been written about the way in which secular ritual emerges, develops and changes. The present study is devoted to the question of change in secular ritual and uses the kibbutz as a test case. In this study the major focus is the development of mourning rituals in the kibbutz as a particular example of developing secular ritual. We connect changes in its secular ritual with changes in kibbutz social structure. These changes

This is a revised version of a paper that was presented in 1982 at the 10th World Congress of Sociology in Mexico City and in 1983 at a seminar of the Department of Anthropology at Harvard University while I was a Visiting Scholar at the Poject for Kibbutz Studies. I am grateful to Glenn M. Vernon and to Charles Waddell for their comments during the Congress as well as to the seminar participants, especially S. J. Tombiah and the members of the Project, for their helpful comments.

I also thank Shlomo Deshen, Bernard Lazerwitz, Ernest Krausz, Michael Harrison and Shimon Cooper and two anonymous reviewers for reading the manuscript and offering their important comments, and Helene Hogri for her editorial assistance.

allow for shifts in meaning and emphasis which permit further social development. We begin with an examination of the background upon which the Israeli kibbutz was founded in order to provide a basis for our theoretical discussion.

BACKGROUND

The early kibbutzim were established in Israel in the second decade of the twentieth century by young Zionist pioneers who had emigrated from Cental and Eastern Europe. Most of these pioneers were socialists who had been influenced by the revolutionary movements in Russia; some had even been actively involved. Their immigration to Israel was motivated by national and social aims, i.e., by the desire to establish a homeland based on egalitarian socialist principles. These revolutionaries actively rebelled against the Jewish tradition and lifestyle in the Diaspora (Talmon-Garber, 1962).

The life of Orthodoxy Jewry in 19th and early 20th century Eastern Europe revolved around the active execution of the day-to-day obligations imposed by the Law (Torah). Intense ritual vitality in daily life gave the individual group members a sense of closeness with the sacred. Routine participation in regular ritual performances was the fullest expression of identification with Jewish society. Those who rejected tradition and looked ahead to Gentile society went through a process of secularization, but those young people who identified with socialist Zionism or Zionism in general did not escape from their Jewish identity. The Socialist Zionists considered themselves representatives of Jewish historical continuity, because Zionism was, after all, a movement of *return* to Zion. This return rejected any connection with the era of the exile and Rabbinic Judaism and focussed instead on the biblical period and that of the Second Commonwealth. Kna'ani (1976: 32-33) defines these Zionists as continuing Jewish tradition while rejecting all religious obligations and belief in the Almighty.

The Zionist pioneers who immigrated to Israel in the early 1900s found themselves in one of the most run-down areas of the Ottoman Empire. The central government and local rulers made various decrees and regulations which were without rhyme or reason. The 1908 rebellion of the Young Turks did not improve the situation. Life in Palestine remained one of insecurity, isolation and poverty under a corrupt regime of unpredictable behavior (Giladi, 1983: 97).

Against this background, communes of wandering youth were organized in which there were no plans for fixed residence. The groups wandered in search of work among the veteran farms and among the farms set up by the Zionist movement. These youths did not want a permanent residence or place of work; they preferred to apply their energies to pioneering, moving onward whenever a new task was presented. The commune's membership changed rapidly and some communes disintegrated while others were newly formed. These were not favorable conditions for the establishment of family or for developing a stable lifestyle (Giladi, 1983: 104-108). In the political twilight zone of the Turkish regime, these vibrant wanderers, who sought self-perfection and the correction of all national and worldly ills, found the communal existence a mode of survival in face of alienation and isolation.

The twilight zone was however temporary; first, because the young grow older and cannot wander forever — hence the establishment of the early kibbutzim during Ottoman rule. Second, the conquest of Palestine by Great Britain after World War I led to more reasonable administrative arrangements which made it possible to develop a sense of stability and security. Meanwhile, the Zionist establishment began intensive settlement activities and the conditions for wandering disappeared.

Most of the early pioneers were young (17-25) and had migrated alone without their families (Kna'ani, 1976: 93-94). The first kibbutzim were very small, numbering no more than 20 persons. Settlements were set up in a desolate and hostile environment without benefit of basic services and infrastructure, and the struggle for survival demanded sacrifice. Suffering and death were a part of everyday life; sickness, accidents and attacks by hostile elements took their toll. There were also quite a number of suicides.[1] It became important to give meaning to the tribulations of life. As Jewish religious values had already been rejected, alternative symbols were likely to be generated to reflect the new existential experience (see Douglas, 1973). Among these were symbols related to death and mourning.

Death from old age was unknown in the early kibbutz, and despite the death of some young members, mourning did not become a pressing issue for many years. Only when the kibbutz became multigenerational, after second and third generations grew up and parents of members were absorbed, was the kibbutz society forced to deal with death of the elderly. The issue of death became particularly salient in the 1960s, when the founders' generation began to pass on. In July 1970 the Inter-Kibbutzim Social Committee published a one-page mimeographed code of mourning that was distributed to all the kibbutzim and in March 1978 a revised two-page edition was circulated. The code in both editions differed from Jewish tradition (Rubin, 1982; Ben Gurion, 1979).

Our observations and research have shown that the development of mourning customs and rituals in the kibbutz took an interesting course. It began with a total rejection of religious ritual and symbols based on the desire to eliminate religious meaning and a sense of "holiness" from their revolutionary settlement of the land of Israel (Kna'ani, 1976: 101; Azili, 1984: 10-17; Liebman and Don Yehiya, 1983a), and creation of an alternative set of rituals. Though some of these rituals retained the structure of tradition while making changes in content, others were completely new, invented for newly introduced holidays, such as May Day, Settlement Day, the Hebrew Book Festival, and the Festival of Shearing (Sheep).[2] All the rituals were meant to be non-religious.

As the kibbutz evolved, a sense of sacredness began to develop around this set of rituals, a sacredness similar to what Moore and Myerhoff (1977: 20) label non-religious sanctity. For this reason, the kibbutz supplies us with an interesting example of a modern, integrated, strongly ideological secular community in which the system of secular ritual expresses the ideology and cohesiveness of the community.

Of the four kibbutz movements in Israel, we deal here with three which are generally

---

1. There are estimates that in the early 1920s, close to 10% of the deaths reported in the workers' newspaper were the result of suicide (Tsur, 1976:33).

2. For details on Settlement Day, see Lilker (1982); on the Hebrew Book Festival and the Festival of the Shearing, see Nagid (1953: 313). Members of kibbutzim from Hashomer Hatzair movement proposed celebrating class holidays: May 1 was to be the workers' holiday; November 7 was to be celebrated as the outbreak of the Bolshevik Revolution and February 12 was to be celebrated as the anniversary of the Social Democratic Uprising in Vienna in 1934 (see Azili, 1984: 31, 43).

described as "secular."[3] We do not distinguish between them since, by and large, the individual kibbutzim of all three accepted the revised code of mourning with minimal variation (the Religious Kibbutz Movement follows the Orthodox Jewish code of mourning). Since the three movements are self-declared revolutionary secular movements and reject much of Jewish tradition, they provide an important field for the study of the development and crystallization of newer rituals and symbols.

In the present paper, we show first that when a society sees in the collective the source of the sacred, a secular religion[4] develops which requires the commitment of the individual to society. This suggests that collective patterns of mourning develop which replace traditional mourning rites. We also show that rituals of mourning in the kibbutz reflect the quality of existential experience in the different periods of kibbutz history. In the earlier periods, when the community fought for survival and was forced to deal with particularly difficult living conditions, ritual was of a more spontaneous and effervescent nature. Later, as the kibbutz became established and conditions improved, ritual became more formalized and lost its spontaneity. According to Lilker (1982: 60), the ideological fervor of the collective was weakened, i.e., when the group begins to make fewer demands on the individual because it has more or less achieved its goals, the rigid adherence to new symbols and rituals is lessened. Consequently, a paradoxical process begins, which, for lack of a better term, we call the "secularization" of secular religion. This is expressed by a willingness to accept some of the previously rejected rituals and symbols, an attitude which had been considered "sacrilegious" several decades earlier.

SECULARISM AND SECULAR RELIGION IN SOCIALIST ZIONISM AND IN THE KIBBUTZ MOVEMENT

Socialist Zionism, in the first half of this century, had characteristics of secular religion; it was a system of symbols and action which gave ultimate meaning to human existence (Bellah, 1964). The ideology of Socialist Zionism reflected a quest for a new social order and a rejection of the traditional Diasporan order. If the Zionist movement was primarily secular, Socialist Zionism was even more so. Socialist Zionism actively rejected the major part of the values and practices of traditional Eastern European Judaism, sometimes vehemently (Kna'ani, 1976: 98-92).

As Don-Yehiya and Liebman (1981) observe, the socialist movement in Israel, of which the kibbutz was a part, resisted a religion of revelation and accepted the Bible only as a source of social values. God was expunged from ritual and replaced by the land, nation and social class as sources of ultimate values. The well-known traditional prayer, "Hear O Israel, the Lord our God, the Lord is One," was transformed in one kibbutz text to, "Hear O Israel, Israel is our Destiny, Israel is One" (cited in Don-Yehiya and Liebman, 1981: 128), reflecting an absolute change in value orientation even though the change

3. On the kibbutz movements, see, for example Darin-Drabkin (1962). Recently, the three secular kibbutz movements have merged into The United Kibbutz Movement.

4. We prefer to use the term "secular religion" rather than "civil religion," since, as Liebman and Don-Yehiya (1983b) state, the latter need not be totally secular. God can be a basis for civil religion, as, for example, in the American version (Bellah, 1967; Gehrig, 1980). Moreover, civil religion is generally conceived as providing legitimacy for the social order, while secular religion and traditional relgion can direct the individual against social order.

was only in content while the traditional pattern of wording was retained. The texts of new ritual were paraphrases of the old religious texts. Almost every new ritual used the formulations of the older traditional texts to generate sentiment. The sources of transcendental holiness were replaced with a more immanent source.

A comparison between the traditional *kiddush* ("sanctification of the day") made at the beginning of the *seder* (the main Passover meal) and the new kibbutz version illustrates this point:

> Blessed art thou Lord our God, King of the universe, who hast chosen and exalt us above all nations, and hast sanctified us with thy commandments. Thou Lord our God, has graciously given us Sabbath for rest, holidays for gladness and festive seasons for joy . . . Thou didst choose and sanctify us above all people. . . . Blessed art thou, O Lord, who hallowest the Sabbath, Israel, and the festivals (*Daily Prayer Book,* 1977: 598-600).

> Blessed art thou Lord our God, King of will, who hast chosen us to sanctify us with work, and hast given us days for work . . . because Thou hast chosen the workers and made them holy . . . Blessed art thou O Lord, who hallowest labor and its festivals (Tsur et al., 1981: 319).

While the later version retains the traditional pattern of the *kiddush* and even contains God's name, the change in content distorts the religious motif and places the ritual in a nearly secular frame. In place of the profane weekday and the sacred Sabbath, we find the sacred work day and the profane Sabbath — a day of no work. Many kibbutzim cancelled the traditional day of rest on the seventh day and allowed each kibbutz member to choose his own day of rest during the week. Nevertheless, the rest day, whenever it took place, continued to be called *shabbat* (Sabbath).

Another example is the *kaddish* prayer, which is one of the high points in burial ritual. The kaddish, which begins "May the name of the Lord be glorified and sanctified," was sometimes reformulated as "May the lust of life of the Hebrew man be glorified and santified" (Ben-Gurion, 1963). Also, Berl Katznelson (1887-1944), an outstanding moral leader of the labor movement, wrote a memorial prayer in March 1920 in memory of eight pioneers who had been killed in defense of Tel-Hai in Upper Galilee. The prayer begins, "Let Israel remember the souls of its sons and daughters" instead of the traditional, "Let God remember . . ."

It is apparent that if the people, the land and the social class become the source of the sacred, and labor becomes the sacred itself, then the nature of sacrifice would change as well. The legitimate right to a land of Israel is acquired not by Godly decree, but by self-sacrifice on the altar of national and social goals for renewal of the homeland and of Jewish society (Don-Yehiya and Liebman, 1981:128). In Douglas' (1973) terms, the cosmology became adjusted to the community's existential state.

MOURNING PATTERNS IN THE EARLY KIBBUTZ

Early kibbutz members were not generally kinsmen, and upon the death of one member there was no familial obligation to mourn; even so, we may assume that people living in primary groups grieved for one another. Written sources describing this period (1910-1920) provide some information as to mourning practices. Traditional patterns of mourning seem to have been maintained, with significant change taking place in the verbal content of mourning.

In one of the early tales of kibbutz life, "The First Grave" by Shlomo Zemach (1886-1974, an author who immigrated to Palestine in 1904), the only girl in a group of twelve young people died of an illness. The doctor, who was called from a nearby town, offered to send people from the town to attend to her burial there. The members of the kibbutz, however, declined the offer, and three of them went to a nearby hill to dig a grave. The story goes:

> After we finished the work, we returned to the cabin, someone brought water, another went to dismantle a fence and make a bier . . . We washed her body very well and dressed Shlomit in holiday dress and wrapped her in a white sheet, put her on the bier and took her outside . . . We walked upright . . . no one said a word, the bier passed from shoulder to shoulder . . . we took hold of the sheet and lowered her body . . . into the grave. We then covered the grave with earth . . . we stood in our places . . . we didn't know what to do . . . then Amiram's shoulders began to shake . . . he approached the grave and with a voice choked with tears said . . . 'May the name of the Lord be sanctified and glorified . . . ' When we returned home, we could not sit . . . we went outside and sat in sadness like lost children (Zemach, 1912).

Several things can be inferred from this story. First, the cemetery is a part of the community's collective identity and an expression of its ideological independence. Therefore, the kibbutz would not send its dead away but rather tended to them on its own terms (Lilker, 1982:221). Second, though the burial did not conform to traditional Jewish East European practice (e.g. men never wash the bodies of dead women, the dead are carried in the arms, and Psalms are recited), traditional patterns were evident. Thus, the body is washed - similar to the purification of the dead (tahara); it is wrapped in a white sheet similar to the traditional linen shrouds; the pall bearers take turns; and the *kaddish* is recited at the conclusion, the high point, of the funeral.

The modified symbols gave the kibbutz members a new sense of existence: the pallbearers walk upright to express their determination; they carry the bier on their shoulders in defiance of the hardship involved (on their silence, see below). The mourning ritual expressed growth and renewal rather than deterioration and degeneration because it was practiced in a society consciously in the midst of growth processes (see Huntington and Metcalf, 1979: 12). Sacrifice was legitimated by the resulting contribution to renewal, and this is what is being expressed in the above-mentioned ritual. This feeling was also reflected in the prose, poetry and art of this period (Nagid, 1983: 318-21).

Similar observations are supported by testimony on two other funerals. The deaths occurred one after the other in 1913 and in the same area. Yosef Zaltzman, an outstanding member of kibbutz Kinneret, was murdered at the age of 23, in an ambush on his way home from the fields. The ambush took place from behind a zyzphum (a thorny bush with deep roots) and the grave was dug at the spot where the man fell, at the side of the road. The bush was uprooted and a tree planted in its place. After the burial, someone began to eulogize the dead man. A.D. Gordon, a noted ideologist of the labor and kibbutz movement at that time, who was present, interrupted saying, " 'Stop, stop, the words are profane!' " and in tears burst forth with the *kaddish* " (Habas, 1967: 56). The second death took place nearby, in the Segera farm in lower Galilee, when Ya'akov Feldman, a member of *HaShomer* (a watchman organization, founded in 1909 to protect Jewish settlements), was killed. Before the funeral, the body was moved and where he fell, a tree was planted. When the people returned from the funeral, the young men broke out in a popular song: "Here we will live, and here we will create a life of freedom" (Habas, 1947: 376).

Burial of the deceased on the spot in which he fell is reminiscent of early Talmudic Law, based on Deuteronomy 21: 1, which states that the slain are buried where they were found (BT, *Baba Kamma* 81a). Renewal of the old practice, however, is at odds with the law of rabbinic authorities who discontinued this custom (Avidan, 1978: 28). Recitation of the *kaddish* is another traditional element present but its context is new as it occurred only after the traditional eulogy was canceled. The uprooting of the bush was a major innovation. The uprooting of such bushes took much of the time and energy invested in preparing land for agriculture, and reflected the victory of the settlers over nature. It was a sign of being rooted to the soil and a steadfast belief in continuity even in the face of death. The planting of the tree and the spontaneous song of the youth also express the determination of the kibbutz members to grow and to establish new roots.

We have one other testimony of song and dance in mourning. When it became known that Yitzchak Turner, a member of the watchmen, died of pneumonia, his friends sat in silence for a long time. Then,

Fleisher . . . started to hum quietly to himself and this tune grew into a loud shocking song. . . . The others slowly came around and began to hum silently. He clasped his hands and stomped his feet and cried. "Hey, Hey friends, with passion, Turner didn't want tears, he wanted life and growth . . . " A *hora* dance began, with painful hearts and dancing feet . . . until early morning and from the dance circle to the sheep (Habas, 1947: 540).

While death is the absolute expression of nonactivity, quiet and order, song, dance and movement are expressions of vitality and action (Huntington and Metcalf, 1979: 109-118). The more a society feels threatened by death, the more it tends to emphasize symbols of vitality.

The complex of symbols revealed in the above-mentioned examples reflect the chaos in which both the individual and society find themselves in mourning. They also reflect the state of kibbutz society within this period is departing from an old world and attempting to create a new one. It is in a state of transition, a twilight zone of neither here nor there or perhaps both here and there. Therefore, social symbols reflect a mixture of old and new, of tradition and of change. The contrast between silence and singing is heightened, reflecting, according to Turner (1976: 90-102), an intermediate or liminal state. Both the silence and the dance are not ordinary things, and mixing them reflects a state of transition.[5]

CHANGES IN SECULAR RELIGION AND IN MOURNING

In its revolutionary stage kibbutz ideology was collectivist and anti-familist; this went hand-in-hand with egalitarian principles which see the family as a divisive force in the collective (Talmon-Garber, 1962). With the growth of the second and third generation in the kibbutz, it became evident that the family, far from being a threat, was supportive of the collective. Family metaphors became the genre for the kibbutz as a whole (Talmon-Garber, 1970: 18). Death of an individual was a loss for the whole community: "When

5. Huntington and Metcalf (1979: 46-49; 109-18) deal with the universality and the meaning of drumming, noise and silence in mourning. Drumming or noise indicates boundaries in time just as a wall makes boundaries in space. The opposition of noise and silence is similar to that of black against white or hairy against smooth which dramatize and emphasize the transition taking place.

a child dies in our children's house, we are all bereaved . . . when a member dies, we are all orphaned . . . this turns the mourning of the individual into a loss for the whole society" (Ben-Gurion, 1963: 4). This collective feeling generated the kind of collective ritual observed above.

In contrast to the more spontaneous responses — song and dance — in the 1910s, a period of silence characterized kibbutz funerals of the 1920s to 1950s. Behavior was restrained and decorous in comparison to the traditional Eastern European Jewish funeral. Yehuda Ya'ari (1900-1982, a novelist of kibbutz life, immigrated to Palestine in 1922). He tells of the embarrassment and the dead silence at the funeral of one of the early members of kibbutz Bet Alfa (established in 1922). "We didn't know what to do or how to behave. The *kaddish* was forbidden and it was almost forbidden to cover one's head (as is the custom at traditional Jewish funerals). We felt terrible, just stood still and kept quiet and no one had the nerve to leave." Yoseph Baratz (one of the founders of kibbutz Dagania established in 1910), told of the death of one of his comrades who was killed in 1920 near Tiberias. "Here, too, the burial took place in silence. No one opened his mouth . . . " As late as 1936, reports of the silent funeral still abound. A kibbutz member, wrote, "Blistering days hardened the hearts / Heat waves dried the tears / The people stood orphaned and alone . . . (in silence)" (cited in Azili, 1984: 12). In accordance with the collective world view, the whole kibbutz took part in a funeral of a member and postponed all entertainment for a 3-to-7 day period according to the size of the kibbutz (Rubin, 1982: 15-17). As long as no active form of funeral behavior was innovated, the period of silence was the major identifying characteristic of the kibbutz funeral (Rubin, 1982; Ben-Gurion, 1979).

Gradually, antagonism against traditional Jewish religion relaxed: "Happily, we have passed through the period of antagonism toward tradition . . . the period of our pioneering adolescence has passed . . . we feel a desire for something better formulated than the feverish release of days passed" (Shelem, 1956: 176). One of the early founders of the kibbutz reflected, "We could maintain a Bohemian atmosphere in the early years as long as life was not complex . . . and there was no stability . . . but when the kibbutz entered a more fixed path, when children are born, the thread of generations is spun . . . then the need for a stable way of life becomes clear and, thus, we need formal patterns of behavior" (Maletz, 1960: 21).

The past acquires a nostalgic flavor and the "secular" ritual seem somewhat rootless: "In the kibbutz, we invested much energy in the creation of our own festivals. First, they were dry and tasteless. Only when we began to include traditional elements did we begin to feel the content and the beauty of the ritual" (Bittman, 1965: 475). This made it possible to begin to return to the spirit of tradition in ritual: "If there were a man who would try to deface a stone artifact of generations past . . . we would surely declare him wild . . . yet, when we deface Sabbath and festivals by removing all content from them, no one takes notice" (Mano'ah, 1967: 16).

As the kibbutz grew and could no longer remain a small intimate community, the sense of ideological purity began to dissipate. The kibbutz became segmented into networks of varying degrees of closeness and some of the more revolutionary symbols lost their ability to generate sentiment. The door was open to the regeneration of old symbols, especially those which are shared by all Jews. This was not a process of return to orthodox

Judaism, but a tolerant combination of modernity and tradition (Gelb, 1979: 178).

Among those who questioned the new rituals were those who challenged the silence of the kibbutz mourning ritual. Quiet is meaningful when the community, as a whole, feels the pain or loss. Extended silence creates solidarity in an intimate group, but ceases to be cohesive when participants do not feel the same degree of closeness to the departed. Words become necessary to awaken feelings and participation. It is not surprising that in kibbutz Yagur, (near Haifa), whose members insisted that no eulogy be made in order to maintain equality among the dead, the cry arises, "We cannot accept the silent funeral — the assembled need a way to express themselves" (Ben-Gurion, 1963: 19).

More and more, we find cautious attempts to reexamine traditional patterns. There were those who were as yet unwilling to introduce religious texts into traditional ritual. A member of kibbutz Meoz Hayim, in the Beit Shean Valley, writes, "They say that traditional customs are the result of religious beliefs of which we can have no part of; that they are the result of superstition, but did we not accept the salutation, *mazal tov* (good luck) . . . or the toast, *lehayim* (to life) on wine?" (Ben-Gurion, 1963: 11). These examples are neutral from a religious perspective; the greetings are traditional yet not religious. Referring to those who claim that their ancestors had fixed patterns for their whole life-style "even [one] for the last hours of life: *el maleh rahamim* [God full of mercy], *kaddish* and *zidduk hadin* [prayers for the dead]," the author proposes not a return to these prayers but acceptance of their validity. He also suggests the selection of appropriate texts, "ancient as well as modern," for integration into the ritual (Ben-Gurion, 1963: 9). This is quite contrary to the words of Yitzchak Tabenkin, one of the founders of the kibbutz movement, who said in the 1920s, "neither *kaddish*, nor *zidduk haddin*" (Ben-Gurion, 1963: 7).

There are kibbutzim which reintroduced some elements of the religious funeral. In Sedot Yam, in the coastal plain, a generally accepted veteran of the kibbutz with some traditional orientation conducts the traditional prayers. In kibbutz Kinneret the prayers are said by the regional rabbi or a close relative of the deceased. A member of kibbutz Degania said that in Jewish tradition, it is accepted that the son say *kaddish* for his parents, but "in our kibbutz, the *kaddish* is said by our comrade, Yehiel, and in neighboring kibbutzim, it is said by a ritual practitioner or other outsiders . . . The *kaddish* is called the orphan's *kaddish*, our dear sons . . . must give us the last honor at the death of a father or mother" (Ben-Gurion, 1963: 15).

DISCUSSION AND CONCLUSION

Deshen (see Deshen and Shokeid, 1974: 151-62) claims that secularization as a concept is not delicate enough to describe the transition from the pole of religious to the pole of secular. Deshen suggests a four-part typology: eradication, creation, innovation and profanation. This typology seems applicable to changes in secular religion as well; specifically it suits the varieties of change found in mourning rituals in the kibbutz. It can be shown that these changes in ritual are connected to structural changes resulting from historical processes.

The stormy existence of the first pioneers explains the spontaneous nature of their mourning ritual in the second and third decade of the twentieth century. Rejection of the past led to rejection of ritual, of festivals and of the sabbath. Yet, death could not be ignored; the departed had to be buried and the mourning was expressed in an effervescent and spontaneous way. In this period, we see an eradication of traditional symbols coupled with 1) the generation of new symbols and rituals often adopted from outside sources; and 2) transformation of existing Jewish symbols through the infusion of new content (respectively, creation and innovation in Deshen's typology).

These existing symbols were taken from the supply available in the Bible, while rabbinic interpretation was rejected. Such developments did not entail a process of vitalization (Wallace, 1956 and 1968; Spindler and Spindler, 1971; and Turner, 1982b), since vitalization movements mark a return to fundamentalist forms and a reinforced connection with the supernatural. Nor is this an instance of the secular hedonistic revitalization which Manning (1977) had described. Rather it is a regeneration of symbols.[6] In other words, there was no return to Orthodoxy; items which kibbutz members did not consider limited to the supernatural were selected from tradition. Thus, for example, when the kibbutz employs traditional liturgy, it does so without the implications of religious prayer. Lilker (1982: 146) remarks that Israeli librarians do not catalogue the kibbutz Passover *Haggadot* with traditional liturgy. The use of old symbols with new content substantiates Avraham Shlonsky's (1900-1973, one of the foremost Hebrew poets who immigrated to Palestine in 1923), seemingly contradictory statement, "We came here to begin from the beginning because we came to continue the way" (cited in Nagid, 1983: 313).

From the 1920s on, there were repeated attempts to modify and renew certain ritual symbols, such as the Passover *seder* and the beginning of the first fruit on Pentecost (Lilker, 1982). We no longer hear of spontaneous mourning, and yet for many decades no attempt is made to create new funeral rituals; only silence is accepted (Azili, 1984: 45). It is not until the end of the 1960s, with the aging of the kibbutz founders and especially their parents (who had been absorbed in the kibbutz), that a search began for new rituals to express the spirit of the kibbutz. At this point the kibbutz was already socially and economically established and earlier ideological fervor had died down.

Evidence points to a tendency toward traditionalism among the elder generation. Yet, even younger members came to demand recognition for traditional Jewish symbols which had been rejected in the past, and this was answered by objections from among those who feared a gradual return to traditional customs (Lilker, 1982:60). Even as the debate was going on, religious elements began to be introduced in kibbutz ritual. This too was not a matter of vitalization since it does not imply a return to orthodoxy. It may well signify the weakening of the secular religion. The ideology which was supported by secular religion lost validity when it achieved many of its goals and, as a result, a new process of eradication, creation and innovation was possible, this time involving the absorption of traditional religious elements. In this way, secular religion of the kibbutz moved closer to the civil religion of the nation (see Liebman and Don-Yehiya, 1983b).

6.   The regeneration of ritual in kibbutz differs from that noted by Myerhoff (1982: 130-31) in a modern urban setting. In contrast to the *ad hoc* non-repeated rituals invented by individuals for personal use, kibbutz rituals are collective and reflect greater planning, i.e., they are decided upon by the individual kibbutz or even the entire kibbutz movement. And once agreed upon, they are not easily changed.

REFERENCES

Avidan (Zemel), A.M.
1978   *Darkei Hessed.* Jerusalem: Igud Lochamey Yerushalayim (in Hebrew).
Azili, A.
1984   *The Attitude of HaShomer Hatzair to Religion and Tradition (1920-1948).* Givat Haviva: Documentation and Research Center (in Hebrew).
Bellah, R.N.
1964   "Religious evolution." *American Sociological Review* 29: 358-74.
1967   "Civil religion in America." *Daedalus* 96: 1-21.
Ben-Gurion, A. (Ed.)
1963   *Mourning.* Tel-Aviv: HaHistradrut HaKalit Shel HaOvdim (mimeo) (in Hebrew).
1979   "Memorial procedures in the kibbutz." Pp. 487-91 in A. De Vries and A. Carmi (Eds.), *The Dying Human.* Ramat-Gan: Turtledove.
Binns, C.A.P.
1979   "The changing face of power: Revolution and accommodation in the development of Soviet ceremonial system: Part I." *Man* 14: 585-608.
1980   "The changing face of power: Revolution and accommodation in the development of Soviet ceremonial system: Part II." *Man* 15: 180-87.
Bittman, I.
1965   "Jewish way of life." *Niv HaKevutza* 14: 473-76 (in Hebrew).
BT
1935   *(The Babylonian Talmud), Baba Kamma.* Trans. by E.W. Kirzner. London: Soncino Press.
Daily Prayer Book
1977   Trans. and annot. by P. Birenbaum. New York: Hebrew Publishing Company.
Darin-Drabkin, H.
1962   *The Other Society.* New York: Harcourt, Brace and World.
Deshen, S. and M. Shokeid
1974   *The Predicament of Homecoming.* Ithaca and London: Cornell University Press.
Don-Yehiya, E. and C. S. Liebman
1981   "The symbol system of Zionist socialism: An aspect of Israeli civil religion." *Modern Judaism* 1: 121-48.
Douglas, M.
1973   *Natural Symbols: Explorations in Cosmology.* New York: Vintage Books.
Fried, N. F. and M. H. Fried
1980   *Transitions: Four Rituals in Eight Cultures.* New York and London: Norton.
Gehrig, G.
1980   *American Civil Religion.* Ann Arbor, Michigan: University Microfilm International.

Gelb, S.
1979   "The dying human in the kibbutz." Pp. 477-79 in A. de Vries and A. Carmi (Eds.), *The Dying Human.* Ramat-Gan: Turtledove.
Giladi, D.
1983   "The period of the second aliya." Pp. 96-113 in S. Stempler (Ed.), *The Yishuv in Modern Time: Landmarks in the Pre-State Period.* Tel-Aviv: Ministry of Defense (in Hebrew).
Gluckman, M.
1958   *Politics, Law and Ritual in Tribal Society: An Analysis of a Social Situation in Modern Zululand.* Manchester: Manchester University Press.
Habas, B. (Ed.)
1947   *Second Aliya Book.* Tel-Aviv: Am Oved (in Hebrew).
1967   *The Yard and the Hill.* Tel-Aviv: Am Oved (in Hebrew).
Huntington, R. and P. Metcalf
1979   *Celebrations of Death: The Anthropology of Mortuary Ritual.* Cambridge: Cambridge University Press.
Kna'ani, D.
1976   *The Second Worker Aliya and Its Attitude Toward Religion and Tradition.* Tel-Aviv: Sifriat Po'alim (in Hebrew).
Liebman, C.S. and E. Don-Yehiya
1983a   "The dilemma of reconciling traditional culture and political needs: Civil religion in Israel." *Comparative Politics* 16: 53-66.
1983b   *Civil Religion in Israel: Traditional Judaism and Political Culture in the Jewish State.* Berkeley: University of California Press.
Lilker, S.
1982   *Kibbutz Judaism: A New Tradition in the Making.* New York: Cornwell Books.
Maletz, D.
1960   "The culture of the kibbutz." Pp. 13-24 in S. Warm (Ed.), *Bussel Book.* Tel-Aviv: Mifaley Tarbut VeChinuch (in Hebrew).
Manning, F. E.
1977   "Cup match and carnival: Secular rites of revitalization in decolonizing tourist oriented societies." Pp. 265-81 in S. F. Moore and B. G. Myerhoff (Eds.) *Secular Ritual.* Assen/Amsterdam: Van Gorcum.
Mano'ah, Y.
1967   "Shabbath and Jewish festivals." *Shdemot* 24: 11-17 (in Hebrew).
Moore, S. F. and B. G. Myerhoff
1977   "Secular ritual: Forms and meanings." Pp. 3-23 in S. F. Moore and B. G. Myerhoff (Eds.), *Secular Ritual.* Assen/Amsterdam: Van Gorcum.

Myerhoff, B. G.
1982   "Rites of passage: Process and Paradox."
        Pp. 109-35 in V. Turner (Ed.), *Celebrations:*
        Studies in Festivity and Ritual. Washington,
        D.C.: Smithsonian Institution Press.
Nagid, H.
1983   "The Hebrew revolution." Pp. 306-60 in S.
        Stempler (Ed.), *The Yishuv in Modern Time:*
        Landmark in the Pre-State Period. Tel-Aviv:
        Ministry of Defense (in Hebrew).
Rubin, N.
1982   "Personal bereavement in a collective en-
        vironment: Mourning in the kibbutz." *Ad-*
        vances in Thanatology 5: 9-22.
Shelem, M.
1956   "Jewish festivals in the kibbutz." *Niv*
        HaKevutza 5: 59-75 (in Hebrew).
Spindler, L. S. and G. Spindler
1971   *Dreams Without Power: The Menomeni In-*
        dians. New York: Holt, Rinehart and
        Winston.
Talmon-Garber, Y.
1962   "Social change and family structure." *In-*
        ternational Social Science Review 14:
        468-87.
1970   *The Kibbutz: Sociological Studies.*
        Jerusalem: Magnes Press (in Hebrew).
Tsur, M.
1976   *Doing It The Hard Way.* Tel-Aviv: Am
        Oved (in Hebrew).

Tsur, M. T. Zevulun, and H. Porat (Eds.)
1981   *The Beginning of the Kibbutz.* Tel-Aviv:
        HaKibbutz HaMeuchad and Sifriyat Po'alim
        (in Hebrew).
Turner, V. W.
1976   *The Forest of Symbols.* Ithaca, New York:
        Cornell University Press.
Turner, V. W. (Ed.)
1982   *Celebrations: Studies in Festivity and Ritual.*
        Washington, D.C.: Smithsonian Institution
        Press.
Turner, V. W. and E. Turner
1982   "Religious celebrations." Pp. 201-19 in V. W.
        Turner (Ed.), *Celebrations: Studies in*
        Festivity and Ritual. Washington, D.C.:
        Smithsonian Institution Press.
Wallace, A. F. C.
1956   "Revitalization movements." *American*
        Anthropologist 58: 264-81.
1968   "Nativism and revivalism." Pp. 75-80 in
        International Encyclopedia of Social
        Sciences, vol. 11. New York: Macmillan and
        The Free Press.
Zemach, S.
1912   "The first grave." *HaPoel Hatzayir:* 11-12 (in
        Hebrew).

18

Americans in the Israeli Reform and Conservative Denominations

Ephraim Tabory and Bernard Lazerwitz

Historically, American religious movements have provided a major vehicle for the formation and maintenance of ethnic groupings (Herberg, 1960; Wells, 1970). In the United States, American identity traditionally is seen as overshadowing all ethnic backgrounds. It is fully legitimate, however, to belong to any religious movement. Some of the denominations affiliated with, in effect, provide a shield for ethnicity, in addition to their religious plausibility structures (Niebuhr, 1957).

Clearly, this sociological conclusion applies to American Jews. One very important function of the American Jewish denominations is to provide an institutional framework for social contacts with fellow Jews and for the expression of Jewish ethnic values (Sklare and Greenblum, 1967; Dashefsky and Shapiro, 1974).

What happens, though, in a democratic, industrialized society where a wide range of ethnic differences is perceived to be a normal state of affairs and where the religious norms strongly favor one mode of religious expression and organization? Will, then, a reverse picture to that of the United States develop? In other words, will ethnicity shield religiosity and provide legitimacy for religious "deviance"?

It is possible to study this question within the context of Israeli society. There, as a result of continuing streams of migration from most Western countries, Eastern Europe and the Balkans, Southwest Asia, North and South Africa, together with "old-line" population components of Jews, Moslems, and Christian Arabs, the country has a wide variety of ethnic groups. However, these groups are linked together by their separate religious heritages into Jews, Moslems, and Christians. Of course, within these major religious blocks, there are additional ethnic subdivisions such as the classification into Ashkenazic Jews, who are descendants from the originally Yiddish speaking communities of Germany and Eastern Europe, and Sephardic Jews, descendants of the Spanish and Portuguese Jewish communities destroyed by the Inquisition together with Jews from Moslem countries.

For the majority Jewish population of Israel, regardless of ethnic background, the religious form recognized as "legitimate" by the masses is Orthodox Judaism. Orthodoxy is founded upon the rabbinic tradition that has developed over the last 2,000 years. It is somewhat differentiated by ritual variations and rabbinical decisions into two major Jewish subdivisions—Ashkenazic and Sephardic (or Oriental).

About 30 percent of the Jewish population regard themselves as Orthodox and adhere to traditional religious positions. They avoid riding on the Sabbath, eat only kosher food, and send their children to state-run religious schools. Many of the other 70 percent of the Jewish population regard themselves as traditional, which means that they follow many religious rituals, but do ride on the Sabbath, will deviate from strictly kosher food practices at times, and send their children to the secular branch of the public school system. A relatively small group of Jews regard themselves as fully secular and lead lives remote from Orthodox customs, apart from those that find expression within national holidays or general educational practices. (See Abramov, 1976, for a detailed picture of religion in Israel.)

Into this system have come nearly 30,000 American Jews, most of them since 1970. This American migration has provided an impetus for the establishment of non-Orthodox, more liberal, denominations. Furthermore, these "imported" denominations are the American Reform and Conservative denominations that historically have been shaped to a very great degree within an American environment strongly permeated with the Protestant tradition (Tabory, 1980).

This recent and rapid growth of the American Jewish group in Israel permits an excellent controlled focus upon the issue raised above. Namely, what happens to the ethnic-religious balance when one shifts from a society, the United States, in which religious diversity is considered good, but ethnic manifestations are not encouraged, to one in which the situation is reversed, namely, to a society in which Jewish ethnic differences are regarded as normal, but non-Orthodox religious diversity is discouraged.

The added advantage of focusing upon Americans in Israel and the Jewish denominations that they have developed is that they are a relatively homogeneous group. Almost half of the American immigrants were born in the United States (40 percent); they are English speakers, and they reflect in their lives much that is clearly American down to playing softball. Research by Antonovsky and Katz (1979), Engel (1969, 1970), Goldscheider (1974), Herman (1970), Jubas (1974), Katz (1974), Avruch (1981), Lazerwitz and Dashefsky (1979), and Sherrow and Ritterband (1970) shows the strong degree of Americanism brought to Israel by these American migrants and their definite display of ethnic group characteristics.

In addition, one can study two fairly successful American denominations, the Reform and Conservative, within an Israeli context. This paper utilizes a cross-cultural situation to examine what happens to American

Jews, and their two major denominations, within a multi-ethnic sociological context that discourages their religious expression. Under these conditions, it is expected that ethnicity will shield religious expression—the formation of Conservative and Reform synagogues in Israel.

METHODOLOGY

The data for this paper are derived from three sources. Data on the members of the Reform and Conservative denominations in Israel are based on a mail survey of a sample of their members conducted in 1978. The response rate was 86 percent, with 977 questionnaires being returned. Twelve percent of the Reform members and 33 percent of the Conservative members had emigrated from the United States. An examination of the ethnic composition of the denominations from a broader English-speaking perspective reveals that 19 percent of the Reform members and 48 percent of the Conservative members emigrated from English-speaking countries. In addition, general denomination activities were observed during the 1976-1981 period, and extensive interviews were conducted with all national and congregational leaders.

Data on all Americans in Israel are based on a secondary analysis of data from the immigrant absorption surveys conducted by the Israel Central Bureau of Statistics from 1969 through 1975. This data set yielded 560 American respondents (Lazerwitz and Dashefsky, 1979).

Finally, data on Jews in the United States are from the national Jewish population survey (NJPS) conducted in 1970-71. Almost 6,000 views were obtained in that study (Lazerwitz and Harrison, 1979).

AMERICANS IN ISRAEL

Given their self-selection process, it is to be expected that Americans in Israel should differ in important ways from Jews, as a whole, in the United States. For instance, Lazerwitz and Dashefsky (1979) report that American migrants to Israel are more Jewishly identified than American Jews in general. As a group, American Jews living in Israel are more than three times as likely as the U.S. Jewish adult population to have attended synagogue service regularly when last in the United States. They were more likely to have fasted on their last Yom Kippur in the U.S., and they were more than seven times as likely to have had a U.S. Jewish day school education than U.S. Jewish adults as a whole. Also, Americans in Israel, in contrast to the U.S. Jewish adult population, are more likely to be children of American born parents, highly educated, and to have held a professional position in the United States. Their stronger Jewish identification apparently combined with these latter traits to make them especially sensitive to the incompatibilities arising out of their situation as highly identified Jews living in a Christian based democratic society.

According to Lazerwitz and Dashefsky (1979), over a third of the Americans who came to Israel identify themselves as Orthodox Jews. (Only 11 percent of American Jews identify themselves as Orthodox according to Lazerwitz and Harrison, 1979.) Twenty-two percent of the American immigrants prefer the Conservative denomination and 15 percent prefer the Reform.

These data are significant for the religious behavior of Americans in Israel. While the Reform and Conservative denominations in the United States are the most popular forms of institutionalized Judaism, Orthodoxy is predominant in Israel. Israeli Orthodox Judaism is passively tolerated, and even subscribed to, by many nonobservant Israelis (Tabory, 1981a; 1981b). Thus, Orthodox American immigrants can readily fit into Israel and one of its 7,000 Orthodox synagogues.

Reform and Conservative immigrants have a more difficult time in that there are only a handful of non-Orthodox synagogues in Israel. Reform and Conservative Judaism are not indigenous to Israel. Indeed, the Israeli Reform and Conservative denominations may be considered "American" movements to the extent that most of their congregations were founded by American expatriates; many current leaders are of American origin; and there are extensive relationships with the American Reform and Conservative denominations.

AMERICAN MEMBERS OF THE REFORM
AND CONSERVATIVE DENOMINATIONS

There were 369 American immigrant families officially members of the Reform and Conservative denominations in Israel. These families included 990 people. The number of U.S. born persons in Israel in 1978 was estimated to be 27,600 (Lazerwitz and Dashefsky, 1979). Forty percent of all American migrants were under 30 and, thus, not prone to joining any synagogue (Lazerwitz and Harrison, 1979). Even discounting the Orthodox from the remaining persons, however, it is clear that no more than 10 percent of the potential American members actually join the Reform and Conservative denominations in Israel.

In looking at the sociodemographic data of Table 1, it may be seen that the American synagogue members are older than other Americans in Israel. The difference in educational levels between the Americans in the denominations and the other groupings is impressive. The Americans have both a greater amount of secular *and* Jewish education. Twenty-six percent of the American Reform members and forty-four percent of the American Conservative members have had more than nine years of Jewish education. Likewise, 39 percent of the Conservatives and 27 percent of the Reform American members in Israel have at least an M.A. degree. Their professional job percentages reflect their education. While professional occupations in Israel are not necessarily the highest paying jobs, they are, as indicated by Hartman (1975), the most prestigious.

The high levels of secular education and professional occupations among Americans in the Conservative denomination are so predominant as to make the Conservative denomination have a higher social status than the Israeli Reform denomination. This is a clear reversal of the pattern found in the United States (Lazerwitz and Harrison, 1979).

Religious Characteristics of Members

The strong religious commitment of the American members in Israel is seen in Table 2. For analytical purposes, the members in Israel are compared with synagogue members in the United States as well as with the

Table 1

SOCIAL CHARACTERISTICS OF AMERICAN REFORM AND CONSERVATIVE SYNAGOGUE MEMBERS

	American Members in Israel		All Israelis[a]	All Americans in Israel	U. S. Jews (NJPS)
	Conservative (N=152)	Reform (N=60)			
	... in percent ...				
Parents were foreign born	36	38	9	40	20
Prefer Orthodox	10[b]	3[b]	17[c]	28	11
Jewish Day School Education	53	45	26	29	4
Married	79	78	75	60	80
Ages 18-29	8	1	18	42	15
College Degree	67	64	8	42	33
Professional Job in U.S.	--	--	--	40	29
Professional Job in Israel	80	57	23	--	--

[a]Sources for data on all Israelis: Israel Central Bureau of Statistics, Statistical Abstract of Israel 1979, Number 30: Table II/23 (Parental Background); Table XXII/16 (Jewish Day School - i.e., in Israel, "religious" schools); Table II/20 (Marital Status); Table II/18 (Age); Table XXII/2 (Education--refers to 16+ years of education); Table XII/17 (Occupation).

[b]Attended such congregations in the U.S. on a regular basis.

[c]Percentage identified as "religious" in Ben-Meir and Kedem (1979).

general Israeli population (which includes Orthodox persons). Across all categories, American synagogue members in Israel are more "religious" than their counterpart members in the United States. In fact, a greater percentage of these Reform members in Israel observes the religious practices than do Conservative synagogue members in the United States. (The data for non-American Reform members in Israel are closer to the data for American Conservative members than to American Reform members.) To the extent that the membership data are reflective of the general trends in these Israeli synagogues, they indicate a more traditional orientation toward religion in the liberal synagogues in Israel than in those of the United States.

Among those Americans in Israel who join these two liberal religious movements, 80 percent affiliate with the Conservative denomination. Most of those Americans who joined the Reform denomination did so when there were no, or only a few, Conservative congregations to be found. Even now, a quarter of the American Reform members in Israel identify themselves as "Conservative" when given an "Orthodox-Conservative-Reform" choice. Over three-quarters of the American Conservative mem-

Table 2

RELIGIOUS PRACTICES OF AMERICAN REFORM AND CONSERVATIVE SYNAGOGUE MEMBERS

	Members in Israel		All Israelis[a]	Members of U. S. (NJPS)	
	Conservative (N=152)	Reform (N=60)		Conservative	Reform
	... in percent ...				
Attend Synagogue at Least Weekly	48	53	30 Men 9 Women	20	16
Fasted Last Yom Kippur	89	83	56	--	--
Light Sabbath Candles	86	83	60	56	31
Sabbath Blessing Over Wine	73	67	34	33	20
No Bread on Passover	93	93	78	69	41
Kosher in Home	74	53	--	42	6
Separate Meat and Milk Dishes	68	40	33	31	2
No Travel on the Sabbath	30	8	15	--	--

[a]Source: These data were generously provided by Dr. Peri Kedem and are based on special computer runs of the Ben-Meir and Kedem (1979) report. Except for synagogue attendance, the figures refer to Israelis of European or other Western backgrounds. Data on synagogue attendance, which refer to all Israelis, are based on Katz and Gurevitch (1976:89).

bers in Israel classify themselves as Conservative Jews in comparison with 57 percent of the American Reform members who classify themselves as Reform. Assuming a continuous stream of American immigrants in the future, it is likely that the gap between the percentage of American members in these two denominations will widen still more.

Ethnicity in the Synagogues

The Americans (and other English speaking members) tend to be concentrated in particular congregations. In 1978 there were only twenty-two Reform and Conservative congregations in Israel. In only two of the ten Reform congregations did the English-speaking presence rise above 50 percent. Only in three of the twelve Conservative congregations did the English-speaking presence *fall* below 50 percent. The importance of the local congregations as ethnic enclaves is expressed by comments made by their leaders. For example, when asked what their religious movements are trying to achieve in Israel, one American leader stated:

We are rather egocentric. We are concerned about our own synagogue. Many of us came with our families, but left behind family, and the congregation is like one extended family.

Supporting the argument that affiliation with the congregations may be attributable to a desire to be with persons of similar ethnic background is the fact that many persons joined the denominations for the first time in Israel. Only about half of the American Conservative members in Israel attended a Conservative synagogue abroad, and only about a third of the Reform members attended a Reform synagogue in the United States. In addition, 60 percent of the American Conservative members and 30 percent of the American Reform members say that a fair number of their friends are to be found in their synagogue. No matter if the members affiliated with the congregations are in search of friends, or whether friendship is a by-product of belonging, the synagogue is an important social context for a considerable number of them.

The ethnic foundation of the denominations is understandable when viewed in the framework of religion and migration. Religious affiliation has often been found to serve a positive function for immigrants in the process of absorption in a new society (Mol, 1961). Yet, what is striking in the present case is that only a minority of Americans in Israel joined one of the denominations.

Perhaps an "ethnic" religious movement is utilized by a sizable percentage of a social group only when the group's members are socially and economically deprived, as in the cases discussed by Niebuhr (1957). The data show that these Americans belong to the highest educational and occupational strata in Israeli society. Socially, American culture is much respected in Israel, and Americans are among the most popular immigrants (cf. El-hanani, 1979). In general, then, these persons do not need an ethnic movement that functions primarily as an aid in their absorption process.

American Ethnic Identity in Israel

A strong point of the Conservative movement in the United States is its educational network. The system of schools affiliated with this United States denomination provides many Jews with an institutionalized means of transmitting the minimal amount of Jewish knowledge necessary to maintain a sense of kinship with the Jewish people. In Israel, this purpose is largely served by the state "secular" school trend. In these schools, the Hebrew language is spoken as the vernacular; the Bible is studied as history and literature. Thus, many American Jews can fit into Israeli society by adopting an Israeli identity apart from a specifically religious identity. These persons do not need an additional religious framework to complete their social absorption.

Then, there are some Americans who affiliate with the dominant Israeli Orthodox denomination. There are no data on the actual number of persons involved, but some of the Conservative leaders interviewed mentioned that they themselves occasionally attend Orthodox synagogues, and that they know of other fellow denomination members who do so. The reasons they give for this are related to the traditional nature of religious life in Israel and to their own identities in that context. As one leader explained, in Israel "one rises in holiness, and one does not descend." The implication is that the more traditional Orthodox denomination is a "holier" or more authentic embodiment of Judaism.

Sensitivity to their larger social environment also characterizes the Israeli Conservative and Reform denominations and influences their goals and aims (Tabory, 1982a). There is a strong desire on the part of the leadership (as seen in their interviews) to reduce the degree to which their denominations can be considered "imported" organizations.

Charges that the denominations are "only American" organizations have been raised by Orthodox circles. To some extent, such charges are used to try to prevent the more liberal denominations from gaining a stronger foothold from which to challenge Orthodoxy as the "true, legitimate" manifestation of Israeli Judaism. An example of the attempt to derogate them is the way the Hebrew Orthodox press writes the English term "rabbi" in Hebrew characters when referring to Reform and Conservative clergy, rather than referring to them by the Hebrew term, *rav*. The use of the Hebrew term might imply recognition of the denominations, while "rabbi" is foreign and demeaning.

An example of the way the liberal Israeli denominations attempt to downplay their "foreign" nature is in their use of language. While English must be employed for newsletters and in announcements for the many members who do not know Hebrew well, it is employed reluctantly. The fear that the use of English will lead the movements to be seen as "American" has even led to the adoption of an Orthodox prayer book by several Conservative congregations. The United States Conservative denomination prayer books contain a substantial amount of English. In Israel, Conservative denomination leaders are fearful that the use of such an "English" prayer book would reinforce the charge that the movement is "imported." It is noteworthy that the use of an Orthodox prayer book does not bother many of the leaders or their followers.

There are other ways in which the congregations have "traditionalized" their religious practices to accord more with those generally accepted in Israel. The use of musical instruments in Sabbath services, common in U.S. congregations but forbidden in Orthodox rituals, has been omitted in some Reform congregations and is not to be found in any Conservative service. This practice is notable because musical instruments could be a major feature emphasizing the ways in which the "liberal" movements enhance their prayer services. Many leaders in Israel, however, fear that the use of musical instruments is "too foreign" a practice. (Most Conservative leaders oppose it, also, on religious grounds.)

Overall, the desire of the leaders of the denominations and their members to be accepted in Israel has moderated both their religious practices and their attitudes regarding the degree of aggressiveness to be utilized in achieving greater state recognition (Tabory, 1982b).

DISCUSSION

In Israel, there is a great degree of tolerance toward affiliation with specifically ethnic organizations, such as the Association of Americans and Canadians in Israel, and other "immigrant" organizations or even ethnically identified Orthodox synagogues, such as Yemenite, Moroccan, or Hungarian Hassidic ones. Israelis perceive their society to be quite pluralistic, ethnically (Smooha, 1978).

On the other hand, Israelis appear to look askance at religious variance that departs from the framework of Orthodoxy. At the very least, Reform and Conservative Judaism do not attract any significant number of native Israelis. Religious differentiation, in accord with the basic patterns of Orthodoxy, which is based on ethnic-cultural-customs, is, however, acceptable. Indeed, traditional Judaism demands adherence to the particular customs of one's membership group, provided they are in accord with historic religious laws. Such group variations are not perceived to be a denominational split of Judaism. Reform and Conservative Judaism, however, do challenge Orthodoxy and deviate from what the Orthodox Rabbinate regards as proper religious laws and customs. In Israeli society, hence, these two denominations have questionable legitimacy.

The majority of American immigrants to Israel also do not join Reform or Conservative congregations. The ethnic identification with fellow Jews provided by these denominations in the United States is not needed in Israel by American Jews. Many Americans in Israel, according to Avruch (1981), "traditionalize" their identities. That is to say, their ties to their kin, language, religion, and other particularistic, often ascriptive, groups and identities overtake or preclude ties to universalistic, achieved identities. This has an impact on their orientation to society, and they seek less to introduce reform and change, than to be accepted.

With regard to religion, most Americans in Israel do what the Israelis do and join Orthodox synagogues or melt into the secular population. Yet there is a nucleus of Americans who do join the Reform and Conservative denominations because they are committed to religion, but not to Israeli Orthodoxy. These persons wish to apply their "modern" approach to religion, acquired in the United States, to Israel. They seek to blend their new with the Israeli old.

It is in this context that the ethnic factor adds a particular twist to the case at hand. The hypothesis of this study was that in Israel, Reform and Conservative members would use an ethnic identity to shield their religious "deviance." This has not occurred in a clear-cut manner because these persons do not want their denominations to be seen as foreign "sects." On the contrary, the members wish to be accepted as an integral part of Israeli society. To this extent, these Israeli denominations have modified some of their American religious patterns that might cast them as imported religious movements. Rather, they wish to be perceived as the agents of religious change in response to gradually growing needs of Israeli society. Their "modern" approach to religion is clearly American inspired. Indeed, the members are quite proud of their American *cultural* ethnicity. It is their organized ethnic *group* identity that they seek to downplay.

As religious Americans, the members of these denominations have become disillusioned with traditional religion in Israel. This is confirmed by the fact that so many of them did not actually attend services in American Reform or Conservative synagogues. It is submitted that it is the desire to maximize their Jewish identity in Israel in a manner still in keeping

with middle class American values that leads them to be religiously innovative in Israel.

It is to be noted that religious innovation among Americans in Israel
is not limited to Reform and Conservative Judaism. A network of Orthodox synagogues patterned after, and affiliated with, the American Young
Israel Orthodox movement has also been established by Americans in
Israel. While these synagogues are in line with mainstream Orthodoxy,
the intentions of the leaders are to "improve" synagogue life in Israel in
line with modern Orthodox patterns established in the United States.

Among the members of all three Jewish religious trends, Orthodox,
Conservative, and Reform, there are attitudes of superiority about an
"American" way of religion that is independent of the fact that many of
these persons are of higher social class than the general Israeli population.
Instead of being "greenhorns," Americans in Israel are almost a self-
proclaimed elite.

In conclusion, we turn to a formal consideration of the hypothesis,
that ethnicity might shield religion, just as religion at times shields ethnicity. In the Israeli case, the higher status position of the Reform and
Conservative denominations does not require a "shield" to legitimate
affiliation with the religious movements *per se*. The claim that these denominations are "merely" ethnic enclaves does not justify affiliation with
religious movements that are considerably different from the dominant
religious pattern. The American origin, however, does serve as a shield,
to the extent that it provides the members with cultural legitimacy for
joining synagogues that they want to support. It is probable, although
beyond the scope of the present discussion, that the prominent American
cultural identity of the denominations provides a similar shield even for
those persons whose backgrounds are not that of English-speaking countries.

NOTE

1. The authors gratefully acknowledge the financial assistance of the National
Institute of Mental Health, United States Public Health Service (Grant Number
IR03 MH 24972-01A1) for the study of Americans in Israel; Bar-Ilan University; and the Memorial Foundation for Jewish Culture. In addition, the authors
thank the Council of Jewish Federations and Welfare Funds for permission to
use the NJPS data from the survey it commissioned and the Israel Central
Bureau of Statistics for access to the North American data from its Immigrant
Absorption Survey. The comments of the anonymous reviewers of this journal
were very helpful, and their contribution is also acknowledged.

REFERENCES

Abramov, S. Zalman
    1976   Perpetual Dilemma: Jewish Religion in the Jewish State. New York:
           World Union for Progressive Judaism.
Antonovsky, Aaron, and David Katz
    1979   From the Golden to the Promised Land. Jerusalem and Darby, Pa.:
           Jerusalem Academic Press and Norwood Editions.
Avruch, Kevin
    1981   American Immigrants in Israel: Social Identities and Change. Chicago:
           University of Chicago Press.
Ben-Meir, Yehuda, and Peri Kedem
    1979   "Index of religiosity of the Jewish population of Israel." Megamot
           24: 353-62 (Hebrew).
Dashefsky, Arnold, and Howard Shapiro
    1974   Ethnic Identification among American Jews. Lexington, Mass.: Lex-
           ington Books.

El-hanani, Edith
1979 "Feelings of deprivation and patterns of response among two ethnic communities in Israel." M.A. Thesis, Department of Sociology, Bar-Ilan University, Israel.
Engel, Gerald
1969 "Comparison between American permanent residents of Israel: part I, American background." Journal of Psychology 72:135-39.
1970 "North American settlers in Israel." American Jewish Year Book 71: 161-87.
Goldscheider, Calvin
1974 "American aliya: Sociological and demographic perspectives." In M. Sklare (ed.), The Jew in American Society. New York: Behrman House.
Hartman, Moshe
1975 Occupation as a Measure of Social Status in Israel. Tel-Aviv: The General Federation of Labor and Tel-Aviv University (Hebrew).
Herberg, Will
1960 Protestant, Catholic, Jew. Garden City, N.Y.: Doubleday.
Herman, Simon
1970 American Students in Israel. Ithaca: Cornell University Press.
Jubas, Harry
1974 "The adjustment process of Americans and Canadians in Israel and their integration into Israeli society." Unpublished Ph.D. Dissertation, Michigan State University.
Katz, Elihu, and Michael Gurevitch
1976 The Secularization of Leisure: Culture and Communication in Israel. Cambridge: Harvard University Press.
Katz, Pearl
1974 "Acculturation and social networks of American immigrants in Israel." Unpublished Ph.D. Dissertation, State University of New York at Buffalo.
Lazerwitz, Bernard, and Arnold Dashefsky
1979 "Success and failure in ideological migration: American Jews in Israel." Paper presented at the 1979 conference of the American Sociological Association.
Lazerwitz, Bernard, and Michael Harrison
1979 "American Jewish denominationalism: a social and religious profile." American Sociological Review 44:656-66.
Mol, J. J.
1961 "Churches and immigrants: a sociological study of the mutual effects of religion and immigrant adjustment." R.E.M.P. Bulletin 9 (Supplement):1-86.
Niebuhr, Richard H.
1957 The Social Sources of Denominationalism. New York: Meridan Books.
Sherrow, Fred, and Paul Ritterband
1970 "An analysis of migration to Israel." Jewish Social Studies 32 (July): 214-23.
Sklare, Marshall, and Joseph Greenblum
1967 Jewish Identity on the Suburban Frontier. New York: Basic Books.
Smooha, Sammy
1978 Israel: Pluralism and Conflict. London: Routledge & Kegan Paul.
Tabory, Ephraim
1980 "A sociological study of the reform and conservative movements in Israel." Unpublished Ph.D. Dissertation, Department of Sociology, Bar-Ilan University, Ramat-Gan, Israel.
1981a "State and religion: religious conflict among Jews in Israel." Journal of Church and State 23:275-83.
1981b "Religious rights as a social problem in Israel." Israel Yearbook on Human Rights 11:256-71.
1982a "Reform and Conservative Judaism in Israel: aims and platforms." Judaism 31:390-400.
1982b "Religious freedom and nonorthodox Judaism in Israel." Journal of Reform Judaism (Spring):10-15.
Wells, Alan
1970 Social Institutions. London: Heinemann.

19

Religion and Democracy in Israel

Charles S. Liebman

Judaism and Democracy

This chapter is concerned with exploring the influence of the Jewish religion (hereafter religion or Judaism) on democracy in Israeli society. The aphorism that is so often heard in U.S. constitutional law courses—"the Constitution is what the Supreme Court says it is"—is not quite true. By the same token, the aphorism that "Judaism is what 'the rabbis' say it is" is also not quite true. But there is enough truth in both these statements to caution us against seeking to understand the imperatives of either system without recognizing that each is subject to new interpretation by its authoritative interpreters.

Statements by religious spokesmen about democracy generally refer to the formal properties of the system: majority rule and some guarantee of individual rights. Although some religious leaders have interpreted Judaism as incompatible with democracy, others view the two systems as completely harmonious.[1] Obviously, if the Knesset were to pass a law contrary to *halakah* (Jewish law), a religious Jew, by definition, would feel obliged to follow the dictates of halakah rather than the law of the Knesset. But, as Haim David Levy, the present chief rabbi of Tel Aviv, has suggested, such a circumstance is a purely hypothetical one, and he finds difficulty in conceiving that such a situation could arise.[2] I agree, although not for the same reasons Levy suggests. In order for such a situation to arise, two conditions would have to be met. First, the Knesset would have to pass such a law, with all the consequences involved in deliberately defying the religious tradition and the religious elite. In other words, not only would the present political constellation have to change, but the whole climate of attitudes toward Judaism (to be discussed below) would have to change. Second, all rabbis of scholarly stature would have to declare the law to be contrary to halakah, with all the consequences that such a defiance of the authority of the state would entail.

For the sake of argument, let us assume that these two conditions were met. All such an event would do is establish a situation that is no different, in theory, from a situation that arises when an individual is faced with a contradiction between positive law and his own moral convictions. The democratic system is in no danger as long as this sort of thing doesn't happen too often or too many people do not find the law incompatible with their moral conscience. There is no major or peculiar incompatibility between halakah and democracy in practice because Jewish law is subject to interpretation.

Conflict does occur, however, when we come to assess the role of religion in forming public attitudes and values that serve as preconditions to the functioning of a democratic system. The following is a list of such attitudes or values, which, one might anticipate, are also influenced by one's religious commitment.

- Basic respect for law and authority. Democracy places more limited means of coercive control in the hands of its political elite than does an authoritative system of government. Respect for law or the willingness of the citizenry to voluntarily acquiesce to laws they do not personally favor is probably more important to the survival of a democracy than it is to other systems of government.
- A large measure of tolerance for the opinions of others, regardless of how sharply one disagrees with these opinions and without regard to the type of person expressing the opinion.
- Relatively great concern about the process of the political system and relatively less concern about the outcome or output of the system.
- As an extension of the previous point, high commitment to what Robert Bellah calls a liberal constitutional regime rather than to a republic,[3] in which there is low commitment to the notion that the state has a role to play in shaping the moral character of its citizens or in achieving some other preordained goal. A belief, instead, that the function of government is to serve the needs of its citizens as the citizens define their needs.
- Given the presence in Israel of national and religious minorities who are self-conscious concerning their collective identity, a special tolerance toward non-Jews and some recognition of their group as well as their individual rights.

Other things being equal, high religious commitment is probably correlated with a respect for law and authority. That, at least, is my impression. Whether this is empirically so; under what circumstances it is more or less so; and if this relationship exists to what is it attributable are all considerations awaiting further study. If this correlation holds true, it may be accounted for by a generalized respect for law and authority that is a byproduct of religious socialization, but it may also stem from the relatively greater success of religious institutions in socializing their youth to the value of respect for law and authority (in other words, secular institutions seek the same goal, but religious institutions socialize their youth more effectively). It may also stem from one or more other factors. Whatever the reasons, respect for authority and the rule of law, in my opinion, are strengthened by religious commitment.[4]

Such a relationship does not hold for the remaining values important to stable democracy. Commitment to Judaism does not encourage a respect for the opinions of others or the rights of others to express themselves freely when such expression is contrary to basic beliefs of Judaism, especially when those who express this opinion are nonreligious Jews. This is not only because expressions of such beliefs (for example, denial of the existence of God) are contrary to Jewish law, though senti-ments not in sync with such law have led to demands for the censoring of plays.[5] The religious believer, other things being equal, is accustomed to the notion that there is an absolute truth; that right and wrong, morality and immorality, good and evil, are absolutes that are readily distinguish-able. Such a believer therefore considers it folly to permit the expression of ideas and values that one knows to be wrong, immoral, or harmful, especially when such notions are expressed by secularists, whose indiffer-ence, if not antagonism, to basic religious values suggests that they or their intent may be evil. According to a leader of the National Religious Party, art has a purpose, but, instead of fulfilling that purpose, the theater, television, and press disseminate material offensive to religion and harm-ful to Israel's security. Everything published or presented to the public "must be in accordance with moral and educational standards," he argued on the floor of the Knesset.[6]

This argument is related to a conviction that is central to the thinking of religious Jews: the notion that a proper state is one that shapes the moral outlook of its citizens. It is therefore incumbent upon the state to adopt measures that will further this goal. A religious world view socializes the Jew to the notion that the ideal state, the proper Jewish state, is not simply an instrument to serve a variety of interests or needs of the population, but a framework that assists the Jew in his moral and spiritual elevation. This attitude is shared by all religious Jews, non-Zionists as well as Zionists.

The state therefore has a purpose. To return to Bellah's distinction noted above, the religious Jew favors a republic, not a constitutional democracy. It is insufficient, as far as religious Jews are concerned, to be told that the government has adopted some law in accordance with "due process" (i.e., proper procedures) or that the majority of the population in addition to a majority of the Knesset favor a particular law. From a religious point of view, Israel has a special purpose, and no government and no majority has the authority to override that purpose. Thus, according to a resolution adopted by the Council of Jewish Settlements in Judea, Samaria, and Gaza, if Israel should surrender sovereignty over Judea or Samaria, it would "represent a *prima facie* annulment of the State of Israel as a Zionist Jewish state whose purpose is to bring Jews to the sovereign Land of Israel and not, perish the thought, to remove them from the land of Israel and replace them with a foreign sovereignty."[7]

The idea of a republican rather than a constitutional democracy, the vision of a moral state rather than one that simply services the needs of its citizens, is a Zionist, no less than a Jewish, ideal. Both Israel as a Zionist state and Israel as a Jewish state imply limitations on democracy. The notion that Israel has a moral purpose that Knesset law cannot overrule is not confined to the religious population.[8] Thus, for example, the decision of the Knesset to prohibit parties that advocate abolishing the Jewish nature of the state was passed with virtually no public protest.

However, it remains true that religious Jews interpret the consequences of Israel's condition as an ideological state more broadly than do nonreligious Jews. To put it another way, the policy consequences of Israel being a Jewish state are much broader from the point of view of the religious Jew, than are the consequences of Israel's being a Zionist state to the secular Jew.

The most serious conflict between attitudes necessary for the maintenance of a stable democratic society in Israel and attitudes fostered by high religious commitment has to do with the rights of Arabs. Judaism in Israel has become increasingly particularistic and ethnocentric. It promotes little tolerance for the individual rights of non-Jewish citizens, and even less for group rights of minorities. In the minds of most religiously committed Jews, the Arabs represent a danger and a security threat, and strong measures, including denial of their civil rights, is justified.[9] I would summarize the dominant tendency as one that grudgingly acknowledges the right of non-Jews to live in Israel, to live their private lives in accordance with their religious or cultural norms, but only insofar as doing so has no influence on other Jews or on the public life of the state. Even this tendency stretches the limits of halakic tolerance as the halakah is understood by many rabbinic sages.

Tkhumin (the most distinguished annual dealing with matters of Jewish law and public issues from an Orthodox perspective) published a learned essay on the status of Moslems in Israel according to Jewish law.[10] The author seems to phrase his words carefully, and there is no trace of polemic in the tone of the article, a fact that makes the conclusions all the more striking. According to the writer, under the ideal conditions envisioned by Jewish law, non-Jews in the land of Israel ought to live in servitude to Jews. In fact, their very right to live in the land of Israel is problematic. A Jew is permitted, though not required, to save non-Jews if their lives are in danger, and non-Jews should not benefit from free public services. These, the author stresses, are basic principles according to which Jews want to build their society. The halakic imperative to subjugate non-Jews living under Jewish rule may be relaxed because of political constraints, but Jews ought never lose sight of the ideal society to which Israel should aspire. However, the editor of the volume challenged the author's understanding of halakah in a note to the article.[11]

The deemphasis on universal standards of morality on the part of many rabbinical leaders extends beyond the Jewish-Arab dispute. For example, the then chief rabbi of Ramat-Gan, in a letter to the National Religious Party daily *Hatzofeh,* decried the practice of childless Israeli couples adopting Brazilian children who then undergo conversion. Such children, he wrote, will be raised as Israelis, but not all of them will identify with the Jews. "After all, it is clear that children inherit characteristics from their parents." He then cited texts to prove that non-Jews are not blessed with the quality of mercy with which Jews are blessed, but, on the contrary, are cruel by their very nature.[12]

The attitudes and values described above are derived from a religious perspective. Behind them lies a worldview that is formed, in part, by basic halakic notions that divide the world into right and wrong, good and evil, pure and impure. It is true that these attitudes and values do not carry the force of halakic norms. They do not obligate anyone to observe or follow them; indeed, they are rarely articulated. They are conveyed by indirection and in a matter-of-fact manner, as basic assumptions, not only of Judaism, but of human nature and the cosmos. For that very reason, they are more difficult to challenge and are more readily dispersed among population groups, especially poorly educated Jews of Sephardic background who are not punctilious in observing halakic norms but who do internalize many presuppositions of the religious tradition as they are conveyed by the present religious elite.

On the other hand, attitudes and values are amenable to development and change without having to overcome legalistic hurdles. Indeed, attitudes and values concerning the Jewish tradition have undergone dramatic change, as I have tried to show elsewhere.[13] The question is why has Israeli Judaism undergone a transformation in the direction of particularism and ethnocentrism rather than moralism, universalism, and political liberalism? In other words, why has Israeli Judaism undergone a transformation that makes it appear less, rather than more, compatible with the preconditions for a stable democratic society?

Religious Changes in Israeli Life

The transformation of Judaism in Israel can only be understood as the result of two processes that are probably interrelated. The first is the growing deference of the nonreligious population to the religious elite's definition of Judaism, the Jewish tradition, and the Jewish religion. The second is the changes that have taken place in the religious elite's own definition of Judaism. Both processes are easy enough to demonstrate, but it is rather difficult to account for them.

The Rise of the Religious Elite

In the past, secular Zionists asserted their own definitions of Judaism in contrast to the definitions of both religious Zionists and religious anti-Zionists.[14] Indeed, it was clear to Ahad Ha'Am and his leading disciples that the appropriate custodians of the Jewish tradition were Jewish scholars and Hebrew writers rather than rabbis.[15] This point of view was inevitable since, in their eyes, the Jewish tradition was a national and not a religious one. But the efforts to transfer custody of the tradition from the rabbis failed. That failure has been especially noticeable since 1967.

The influence of the rabbis has come at the expense of custom (community practice) and the role of Judaic scholars.[16] This is true among both the religious and the nonreligious population, being especially prevalent among those aligned with the political right. They perceive religious Jews as political allies and religion as a powerful instrument to legitimate their national-political demands. Disproportionate numbers of Sephardic Jews, the bulk of those who define themselves as *masorati'im* (traditional in their religious orientation), share this mood. Others who share this mood include some who define themselves as *hiloni* (secular) as well. Ariel Sharon, the favorite political leader of the radical right, is quoted as saying, "I am proud to be a Jew but sorry that I am not religious."[17]

In the last few years, as divisions between doves and hawks have sharpened, one hears both nonreligious and religious leaders affirm that fidelity to religion and loyalty to the state are associated. Prime Minister Yitzhak Shamir, for example, was quoted as saying:

> The left today is not what it once was. In the past, social and economic issues were its major concern. Today, its concern is zealousness for political surrender and, on the other hand, war against religion. It is only natural that someone whose stance is opposed to the Land of Israel will also oppose the Torah of Israel.[18]

The deference accorded to religion by secular elements of the population has strengthened the religious elite (i.e., rabbinical leaders) at the expense of other religious spokesmen, intellectuals, and even politicians who were more sensitive to currents within the nonreligious world in general as well as in Israeli society. Religious spokesmen need no longer concern themselves with secular alternatives to the religious tradition or respond to alternate conceptions of Judaism that stress universalist or ethical components within that tradition. Secular Judaism no longer poses an ideology that competes with religious Judaism. Therefore, those most capable of leading the battle against the competition, politicians but especially religious intellectuals, find their influence has declined and the balance of authority within the religious world has shifted in favor of the rabbinical elite, who, by virtue of their narrow training, career opportunities, and significant referents, tend to be more particularistic and xenophobic.

The Transformation of Israeli Judaism

The Jewish tradition over which the rabbis reign is not, as we noted, the same tradition over which they held sway in the past. The tradition has been nationalized, among both nonreligious and religious Zionists, through a selective interpretation of sacred texts and of Jewish history, and has taken place independently of the rabbinical elite's influence. Emphasis is given to the sanctity and centrality of *Eretz Yisrael,* the Land of Israel. In the past, Zionists celebrated their radical departure from the the Jewish tradition in their efforts to reclaim and settle the land. Today, Israelis celebrate their continuity with the tradition in this regard. What is all the more remarkable is that Eretz Yisrael has come to symbolize both loyalty to the state of Israel and to Judaism. Baruch Kimmerling points out that the term Eretz Yisrael has increasingly replaced the term state of Israel in the pronouncements of national leaders, especially those on the political right.[19] To be a good Jew means to live in the land of Israel under conditions of Jewish autonomy.

The nationalization of the Jewish tradition means its particularization as well. I do not wish to argue that this is a distortion of the Jewish past. I suspect that the effort to interpret Judaism as moralistic and universalistic, an effort that is basic to the U.S. Jews' understanding of Judaism, is less faithful than is the Israeli version to what Jews throughout the ages understood as their tradition.[20] The present interpretation also contrasts with the Zionist effort to "normalize" Jewish existence. Classical Zionists suggested that anti-Semitism was a consequence of the peculiar condition of the Jews as perennial "guests" or "strangers" in countries not their own. It was not, they claimed, the result of any special animus toward Jews as such. Zionists believed that once the Jews had a country of their own, their condition would be normalized and anti-Semitism would disappear. The

Zionists were aware of the fact that this cornerstone of their credo contradicted traditional Jewish conceptions of anti-Semitism.

For the most part, Israeli Jews no longer believe this to be true. Anti-Semitism, they are likely to believe, is endemic. "The world is all against us," as the refrain of a popular song went, suggests that there is nothing that Jews in general or Israelis in particular can do to resolve the problem. The Jew is special because he is hated, and he is hated because he is special. This is the lesson of Jewish history, and it serves to anchor the state of Israel within the currents of Jewish life. In summary, Zionism, the ideology of Jewish nationalism, has been transformed and integrated into the Jewish tradition. The tradition, in turn, has been nationalized. Erik Cohen describes this trend as

> a reorientation of the basic principles of legitimation of Israel: a trend away from secular Zionism, especially its pioneering-socialist variety, towards a neo-traditionalist Jewish nationalism which, while it reinforces the primordial links among Jews both within Israel and the diaspora, de-emphasizes the modern, civil character of the state.[21]

The rise of particularism has implications for the interpretation of ethics and morality as well. Emphasis on law (and ritual) means a deemphasis on the centrality of ethics. But, in addition, religious Jews in Israel have redefined "morality" in particularistic rather than universalistic terms. According to the rabbi who pioneered the establishment of extremist education within the religious Zionist school system, Jews are enjoined to maintain themselves in isolation from other peoples. Foreign culture is a particular anathema when its standards are used to criticize Jews.[22] According to another rabbi, "between the Torah of Israel and atheist humanism there is no connection"; there is no place in Judaism for "a humanistic attitude in determining responses to hostile behavior of the Arab population." According to a leader of Jewish settlers on the West Bank, "Jewish national morality is distinct from universal morality. Notions of universal or absolute justice may be good for Finland or Australia but not here, not with us."[23]

Ideological Convergence Among Religious Parties

It is customary to distinguish between two segments of the religious population in Israel. One is the haredi, often referred to as the ultra-Orthodox, who look to the past as a source of legitimacy and are hostile to Zionism, the ideology of Jewish nationalism (i.e., an ideology that conceives of the Jews as a people defined by a national rather than a religious essence and that aspires to the normalization of Jewish life). The other strand is associated in the public mind with Gush Emunim, ultra-nationalistic and preoccupied with the political and religious consequences of their belief that Jews are living in a messianic age (i.e., a period of imminent redemption).

If we identify the two strands as distinct movements and then look at the more extreme elements in each strand, we will find that the two share little in common. The most extreme haredim are hostile to the state of Israel. Even among less extreme haredim, those who define themselves as loyal citizens of Israel, there is a tradition of political passivity with respect to non-Jews, an anxiety about antagonizing the nations of the world, and a desire to find a peaceful accommodation with the Arabs, even if it requires surrendering territory that Israel has held since 1967.

Within the other strand, among many of the most extreme ultranationalist messianists, opposition to any surrender of territory, retaining the Greater Land of Israel under Jewish sovereignty, and settling the length and breadth of the land with Jewish settlers supersedes every other religious obligation. Belief in the imminent coming of the messiah encourages activity of the most extreme form. "I am not afraid of any death penalty, because the messiah will arrive shortly," proclaims Rafi Solomon, charged with an attempt at the indiscriminate murder of two Arabs.[24] Nationalism within this ideological camp "is the highest form of religion."[25] This allows compromise on virtually every other religiopolitical demand. In order to further their cause, religious ultranationalists have not only formed alliances with secular Jewish nationalists, but they have justified this alliance as the fulfillment of a positive religious commandment. Religious Jews who are active in ultranationalist nonreligious parties, and they include a number of prominent rabbis, tend to be most moderate in the "religious" (as opposed to the "nationalist") demands they make of the Israeli polity. Indeed, these demands never exceed that which the secular members of these parties have been willing to concede.

One could, therefore, make a good case for distinguishing between two religious groupings and argue that they have virtually nothing in common at the political level.

The alternate argument, and one offered here, is that the two religious strands are converging. This convergence is not evident in the assertions of the extremists and ideological purists in each camp, but rather in its effect on the larger population of religious Jews who were heretofore readily identifiable as either haredi or religious Zionist. Today, one can point to the emergence of new groups and/or changes in the ideology of established religious parties that integrate both strands.

Support for this approach is found in the growing usage of a label that was coined as a derogatory term about ten years ago: *haredi-leumi* (a nationalist haredi). To the best of my knowledge, the term was first used by a moderate, anti-haredi leader of the religious Zionist youth movement, Bnei Akiva. He was very concerned with the growth of haredi tendencies within his movement and unhappy, though perhaps less distressed, by the emergence of ultranationalist tendencies as well. The term "haredi-leumi" was certainly intended as a term of opprobrium. The term is now borne with pride by a growing number of religious schools; by a rapidly growing religious youth movement, Ezra, which recently adopted this label; and by an increasing number of religious Jews who, according to a poll conducted by the religious weekly *Erev Shabbat,* decline to identify themselves as either haredi or religious Zionist but prefer to be called haredi-leumi.

No less persuasive are developments among religious parties in Israel. Of the four religious parties that won seats in the Twelfth Knesset elections (November 1988), three were identified in the media as haredi. Nominally, all of them might be properly called anti-Zionist. Together, these parties won thirteen seats. Eleven of the thirteen seats, however, went to two parties whose platform and/or constituents and/or leadership was especially close to the leading secular nationalist party of the right (the Likud). The largest of these parties is Shas. It increased its number of seats from four to six in the elections. While its platform did not call for the annexation of the occupied territories, its television campaign was critical of the Israeli government for not adopting harsher measures in the suppression of the intifada. Despite the predictions of the pundits, generous promises by Labor with regard to religious legislation, but especially its promises of public funds and political appointments, led Shas leaders to seriously consider joining a Labor-led coalition following the election. However, demonstrations by Shas's own supporters and a reminder that the party leadership had explicitly promised during the campaign that it would not join with Labor rather than the Likud, restrained the party leaders from taking this step.

The next largest haredi party, Agudat Israel, increased the number of its seats from two to five. While Agudat Israel is reputed to be virulently anti-Zionist, it happily accepted the support of two important groups whose religiously based opposition to any Israeli withdrawal from the occupied territories equals that of Gush Emunim. These two groups do not view the state of Israel or the present era in the same messianic and apocalyptic terms as Gush Emunim's spiritual leaders, nor do they attribute the same metaphysical significance to events that began a century ago when nonreligious settlers initiated the present Zionist settlement of the land. They are no less adamant, however, about the religious imperative of maintaining Jewish sovereignty over the territories. When the

Likud-Labor alliance broke up and Agudat Israel agreed to form a coalition with Labor, two of its parliamentary representatives bolted, thereby sabotaging Labor's hope to form a government under its leadership.

The growth of haredi parties and their ability to attract voters from nonharedi segments of the population has been accompanied, at the ideological no less than the pragmatic level, by their de facto adoption of a nationalistic orientation and the muting of their ideological objections to Zionism,[26] although this tendency does not encompass all haredim.

At the religious-Zionist end of the continuum, the National Religious Party and its constituents, heretofore characterized by religious moderation and an accommodationist, rather than a rejectionist, orientation toward modernity and secular culture, show increasing signs of rejecting modernity and asserting a rather reactionary interpretation of the religious tradition. This is evident in the increased allocation of school time to the study of sacred text in religious-Zionist schools, in increasing insistence upon separating the sexes in institutions identified with religious Zionism, and in the increased emphasis on religious observance by many religious-Zionists. Whereas the National Religious Party's platform on the future of the territories has been increasingly radicalized and now virtually mirrors that of Gush Emunim, it, and other institutions of the religious-Zionist camp, adopt "religious" stances in other matters that increasingly resemble those of the haredim. Thus the counterpart to the nationalization of the haredim is the "haredization" of the religious Zionists.

In summary, the argument presented here is that there is less and less point in distinguishing among the segments of religious Jewry, at least for purposes of assessing its impact on democratic ideas and structures within Israeli society. This does not mean that all religious Jewry or all the religious parties are cut of one cloth. There are different orientations that one can distinguish among parties, groups within the different parties, and among individual political and religious leaders. The argument, here, however, is that these differences are not reflected in the traditional distinction between religious Zionist and haredi, and that one can identify a mainstream within religious Jewry in Israel, whose core assumptions, attitudes, and values are in many cases in conflict with the system of assumptions, attitudes, and values that undergird a stable democratic polity.

However, it is also worth noting that the religious parties have been affected by the democratic structure of Israeli political life. Slightly less than 20 percent of Israeli Jews define themselves as *dati,* (religious), roughly one-third of whom are haredi. The majority of Israeli Jews, unlike, for example, the masses of Moslems, are not "religious" in belief or behavior, although many, probably most, harbor a feeling of sympathy for the religious tradition. When asked about their religious identification, 35 to 40 percent prefer to define themselves as "traditional" rather than "secular." Many are distressed, though not to the point of doing much about it, by the ignorance of religious rite and custom they find among their own children. But even this general mood is often accompanied by anticlerical feeling. Under the circumstances, religious leaders are reluctant to demand the total imposition of Jewish law, even if they might harbor the hope for such an eventuality. What they have called for, in more outspoken terms, is the maintenance of what is called a "Jewish street," i.e., the conduct of *public* life in accordance with Jewish law. In fact, they have been more anxious to maintain victories they have already secured rather than expand the scope of religious law.

The key demands of the religious parties in the 1988 Knesset elections, were, in fact, defensive demands. In many instances, the religious parties simply sought to retain the fruits of legislative and administrative victories they had secured in the past. The most important of these included Sabbath closing laws passed by municipal councils, which a 1988 court decision held invalid because the Knesset had never explicitly empowered local councils to pass such laws. Closely related was the demand for the expansion of the authority of rabbinical courts in matters of personal status (especially marriage and divorce), an authority that has undergone some erosion by virtue of decisions by secular courts. (The legal status of the latter is superior to the former.) However, for the haredi parties, two of the three in particular, the most important defensive demand was the continuing assurance that *yeshiva* (plural: *yeshivot*) students (students at schools for advanced religious study, which means virtually all haredi youth) would continue to benefit from draft exemptions as long as they are enrolled in yeshivot.

A second type of demand included increased benefits, or what the religious parties called "equalizing" public funding for their educational and philanthropic institutions. The haredi parties also called for greater housing benefits for young couples; Shas was especially interested in government recognition of its schools as an independent system eligible for public funding while maintaining administrative autonomy. These demands, while marginally burdensome to the Israeli taxpayer, hardly presaged an onslaught on the democratic structure of the Israeli polity or, for that matter, on individual religious freedoms.

An effort to expand religious influence in Israeli society was reflected in two types of demands. One was of a generally symbolic nature: amending the "Who Is a Jew?" law. Amending the "Law of Return" to preclude recognition by Israel of non-Orthodox conversions performed abroad (popularly known as the "Who Is a Jew?" law) would have affected no more than a handful of Israelis, but it was of great symbolic importance because it would have established the authority of Orthodox rabbis in determining whom the state of Israel recognizes as a Jew. The second type of demand was in the area of culture and education. Proposals in this regard were rather vague. They included the demand that the government ought to do something about introducing more Jewish (read religious) education. The National Religious Party also talked about the need for more national (read ultranationalist) education. There were also hints at the need to preserve Israeli culture against negative influences (an allusion to pornography and probably to antireligious and/or antinationalist expressions as well). Opposition to the construction of the "Mormon University" (in fact, a branch of Brigham Young University) on Mount Scopus in Jerusalem also falls into this category.

These demands, it should be noted, were phrased very carefully, generally in a positive, rather than a negative vein, under category headings that talked about the need for the unity of the Jewish people. Except for the proposal to amend the "Who Is a Jew?" law, these demands were quickly surrendered in the negotiations over the establishment of a coalition government following the election. Furthermore, although Agudat Israel, and to some extent the National Religious Party, did feel strongly about the need to amend the Who Is a Jew? law, neither conditioned their joining the government on a change in that law. It might be argued that such surrender was necessary because once the two major parties (Likud and Labor) had agreed to form a unity government, the bargaining position of the religious parties was severely reduced. However, following the dissolution of the unity government, the religious parties again held the balance of power. Most of them refused an alliance with the left despite evidence that the Labor Party would concede to virtually any demand they made. Their demands from the Likud were fairly modest in the realm of legislation. No amendment to the "Who Is a Jew?" law, no banning of the Mormon University, no censorship of pornography, no changes in the secular school system occurred. What did materialize was a law banning the sale of pork, a law placing some minor limitations on how a woman can request a legal abortion (it is not clear that the law will have any effect on the number of legal abortions performed in Israel), a law permitting local municipal councils to determine whether places of entertainment may or may not open on the Sabbath (a law whose impact may be to extend the number of such places now open), and a law banning lascivious advertisements.

How are we to account for the generally moderate nature of the demands raised by the religious parties? Part of the explanation rests on the importance that some religious parties now place on their "nationalist" agenda, an agenda that, by their definition is, of course, "religious."

Nevertheless, the religious parties are sufficiently sensitive to the distinction between "national" and "religious" in the eyes of the secular public in order to avoid jeopardizing their "nationalist" agenda by emphasizing their "religious" agenda. Even if one accepts that settling, and/or annexing, or at least refusing to surrender parts of the Greater Land of Israel is a "religious" issue, the emphasis on this issue rather than others suggests an order of priorities.

Second, at least two of the religious parties, Shas and Agudat Israel, increasingly attract nonreligious voters. Shas's attraction to ethnic nonreligious voters is well known, but the fact that Agudat Israel has become an increasingly attractive option to voters of low socioeconomic status has received less attention.[27] The success both these parties had in attracting such voters and the fact that they became outlets for social protest among some nonreligious Jews may have led the parties themselves to temper the narrowly religious focus of their demands.

Third, more active participation in the democratic process may have sensitized party leaders to the fact that excessive demands in the area of religious legislation threaten them with public backlash whose shadow, even now, looms on the horizon. The religious parties are aware of their minority position in Israeli society and are anxious to avoid confrontations with the nonreligious majority at both the political and the social level—a confrontation they can only lose.

Finally, benefits from public funds that the leaders of the secular parties have showered on the haredi parties may be the most important factor in moderating demands for religious legislation. Large segments of haredi society benefit from these funds and are unwilling to jeopardize them by raising demands that the majority will refuse to meet. It is especially dangerous for a religious party to raise demands of a religious nature that go unmet. They then stand charged with a willingness to compromise religious principle for the material benefits to be derived from participation in a governing coalition. They may prefer, therefore, to moderate their demands to begin with.

Can Democracy Survive in a Jewish State?

Assuming we are flexible about what we mean by democracy and a Jewish state, democracy can, of course, survive in a Jewish state. If democracy means a state without moral purpose, one that functions simply to attend to the interests of its citizens as they define them, to provide services its citizens demand without an effort to further some ultimate vision of the good society and the good citizen—then democracy is incompatible with a Jewish state, a Zionist state, or any other kind of ideological state. I don't think such a state can survive, but that is another question entirely. If by a Jewish state we mean a theocratic state, one ruled by a religious elite or in which the laws are subject to the approval of a religious elite, or a state in which the Torah is the ultimate constitutional authority, then democracy and a Jewish state are also incompatible.

But if by democracy we mean majority rule, individual liberties, and minority rights guaranteed by law, within a set of parameters that are derived from a reasonable understanding of Judaism and the Jewish tradition, then democracy and a Jewish state are not incompatible, although accommodating these two values may require painful compromises for those committed in good faith to only one or the other value. Separation of religion and state is no solution because a Jewish state is, by definition, one in which religion plays a public role and is accorded public status.

The resolution lies in an accommodation that by definition is less than perfect. The route to that accommodation rests in part on the good faith of all the parties to find such an accommodation, and no less important in the definition that is accorded to democracy, but especially to Judaism. It should be clear from this that everyone has a stake in how everyone else defines these conceptions.

Policy Recommendations

This chapter has argued that Judaism, as it is presently perceived, in Israel does not reinforce attitudes and values that undergird a democratic system. This stems in part from tendencies inherent within Judaism and democracy and from particular perceptions of Judaism and democracy. There are, therefore, three areas in which recommendations are appropriate.

First, recommendations that would encourage the political elite to make accommodations necessary to maintain a society that is both as Jewish as is possible within the parameters of a democratic society and that is as democratic as possible within the parameters of a Jewish state are needed. I emphasize the political elite because their role is critical in the process.

Religious leaders must understand that whatever "ultimate" hopes or "messianic" visions they may harbor about the ultimate constitution of Israeli society, reference to a Torah state or a state ruled by halakah suggests a very limited commitment to a democratic society. Even if they do not mean what they say, and I strongly suggest that they do not, they are socializing their youth to antidemocratic values, raising false expectations about the nature of the political system, and casting doubts upon the Jewish commitments of those who eschew this value. Religious leaders should be encouraged to consider how meaningless the slogan "a state in accordance with halakah" has been to them in the past, and whether they would not do better to either abandon the notion or rephrase it so that their public understands that it is not a program for implementation in the here and now. Studies of what "a state in accordance with halakah" has meant in the past to religious leaders in Israel, and how distinguished rabbis and politicians have reinterpreted this "principle," may be of some help in this regard. But it is equally important for nonreligious leaders to indicate that while no one would deny the right of religious Jews to express their hope for a halakic state, the expression of such a hope is offensive to the nonreligious and casts grave doubts about the willingness of religious Jews to arrive at a basic accommodation with the nonreligious.

Political elites who define themselves as secular must appreciate that privatization of religion is a peculiarly Protestant notion that is simply not applicable in the case of Judaism—unless, of course, they are prepared to surrender the notion of a Jewish state.

The framework of accommodation, therefore, includes the surrender by the religious of the ambition to realize a state in accordance with halakah and the recognition by the nonreligious that a Jewish state means that the Jewish religion will be reflected in the public life of the society, the recognition that Jewish law will in one form or another find expression in public law. Within this framework, political negotiations based upon everyone's sense of what is fair and just and on the relative balance of political power each side possesses can take place. It would be inappropriate to try and to elaborate what such a settlement would ultimately look like.

The second set of recommendations deals with perceptions of democracy and of Judaism. The effort to define democracy in the most libertarian of terms presents the democratic system in sharp conflict with Judaism or any religious system of life. The definition that Ze'ev Sternhall, for example, offers of democracy as a system of government that places the individual and not collective goals at the center of its concern or the essence of democracy as "the rights of humans to be masters of themselves ... the expression of man's recognition that all sources of political, social and moral authority inhere in man himself" and that "society and state exist in order to serve the individual ... and are never ends in themselves"[28] is an example of such a conflict. Therefore, it is important to reinforce perceptions of democracy that emphasize group, as well as individual, interests, that comprehend minorities in cultural, ethnic, religious, and perhaps even national terms, rather than as a set of individuals organized on an ad hoc basis in order to secure a particular right. And, as we have pointed out, it is important to stress that the stability of a democracy depends, among other factors, on a sense of moral order and moral vision that the members of that society share.

The third set of recommendations deals with perceptions of Judaism. In this chapter, I have argued that Israelis define Judaism in narrow, particularistic, and nationalistic terms, but that this is only one alternative conception of Judaism. How can perceptions of Judaism, on the part of Israelis in general and the religious public in particular, be transformed so that they are more compatible with a democratic society?

The presence of Conservative and Reform Judaism in Israel would probably contribute to that end. Forced to articulate their perception of Judaism in ideological terms and compete with alternative conceptions of Judaism, we may find that Orthodoxy in Israel comes to resemble more closely Orthodox Judaism in the United States and Western Europe. (This is not the place to describe the salutary effect that such a development would have on Conservative and Reform Judaism in the United States if they were forced to formulate their Jewish conceptions, as they would in Israel, with greater fidelity to sacred text.) There is also little doubt that the particularization of Judaism in the hands of the religious elite, and the acquiescence of the religious public in this narrowing of Jewish vision, finds support in the failure of other alternatives, the bankruptcy of secular Zionism as a system of ideas and behavior being the most important. The emergence of any alternative definition of Judaism that demonstrates both intellectual vigor and the capacity to inspire a way of life would generate a new breed of religious thinkers who would be forced to confront these new developments.

Notes

Parts of this chapter have appeared in revised form in an essay, "Religious Fundamentalism and the Israeli Polity," in Martin Marty and R. Scott Appleby, eds., *Fundamentalism and the State* (Chicago: University of Chicago Press, 1992), pp. 68–87. I have also drawn upon material from my book, co-authored with Steven M. Cohen, *Two Worlds of Judaism: The Israeli and American Jewish Experience* (New Haven, Conn.: Yale University Press, 1990).

1. The late Rabbi Meir Kahane was not a great rabbinical scholar, but he anchored himself in rabbinic text and certainly represented one stream within the Jewish tradition. According to Kahane:

> The liberal west speaks about the rule of democracy, of the authority of the majority, while Judaism speaks of the Divine truth that is immutable and not subject to the ballot box or to majority error. The liberal west speaks about the absolute equality of all people while Judaism speaks of spiritual status, of the chosenness of the Jew from above all other people, of the special and exclusive relationship between God and Israel. (Meir Kahane, *Uncomfortable Questions For*

Comfortable Jews [Secaucus, N.J.: Lyle Stuart, 1987], p. 159.)

Other rabbis, less politically extreme than Kahane, express opinions that cover a wide spectrum. I am indebted to my colleague, Asher Cohen, who located many such sources, only a few of which are cited here. Zvi Weinman writes that even if all the Knesset members were religiously observant Jews, the democratic system is tainted because it can, in theory, decide matters contrary to the Torah. See Zvi Weinman, "Religious Legislation—A Negative View," *T'khumin* 7 (1986), in Hebrew. *T'khumin* is the most highly regarded periodical dealing with problems of society and state from the perspective of Jewish law.

According to another distinguished rabbi, "The democratic approach, whose substance is consideration for the will of the people, their demands and their needs, is among the foundation stones of Israeli *halakha*" (Nathan Zvi Friedman, "Notes on Democracy and *Halakha*," *T'khumin* 4 (1984), p. 255, in Hebrew). Eliezer Schweid concludes his discussion of Rabbi Chaim Hirshenson's ideas about a democratic state according to halakah with the observation that "the political system that the Torah intended is democratic in its basis" (Eliezer Schweid, *Democracy and Halakha: Reflections on the Teachings of Rabbi Chaim Hirshenson* [Jerusalem: Magnes Press, 1978], p. 75, in Hebrew). Finally, to Rabbi Sol Roth, "it is clear that the fundamental principles of democracy, namely, representative government and rule by majority, inhere in a Jewish tradition" (*Halakhah and Politics: The Jewish Idea of a State* [New York: Ktav, 1988], p. 141).

2. Haim David Halevy, *Dat V'Medina [Religion and State]* (Tel Aviv: Arzi Printers, 1969), pp. 49–60, in Hebrew.

3. Bellah distinguishes between liberal constitutionalism built on the notion that "a good society can result from the actions of citizens motivated by self interest alone when those actions are organized through proper mechanisms" and a republic that "has an ethical, educational, even spiritual role" (Robert Bellah, "Religion and the Legitimation of the American Republic," in Robert Bellah and Phillip Hammond, *Varieties of Civil Religion* [New York: Harper and Row, 1980], p. 9). The point and its application to Israeli society is discussed more fully in Charles S. Liebman and Eliezer Don-Yehiya, "The Dilemma of Reconciling Traditional Culture and Political Needs: Civil Religion in Israel," *Comparative Politics* (October 1983), pp. 53–66.

4. On the lack of respect for the authority of law in Israel, see Ehud Sprinzak, *Every Man Whatsoever Is Right In His Own Eyes: Illegalism in Israeli Society* (Tel Aviv: Sifriat Poalim, 1986), in Hebrew.

5. The effort, for example, to remove or at least censor the play, *The Messiah,* because of exclamations of heresy is described in Uri Huppert, *Back to the Ghetto: Zionism in Retreat* (Buffalo, N.Y.: Prometheus Books, 1988). Although the book is a polemic, extremely one sided, and misleading in many respects, the treatment of this incident is, to the best of my knowledge, an accurate one. On the other hand, Minister of Interior Aryei Deri, a leader of Shas, a Sephardic, haredi party, the most ostensibly "primitive" of all religious parties, abolished the censorship of plays in an order issued in August 1989.

6. The speech by Rabbi Haim Druckman was reprinted in *Nekudah,* March 2, 1983, and is described in Charles S. Liebman, "Jewish Ultra-Nationalism in Israel: Converging Strands," in William Frankel, ed., *Survey of Jewish Affairs, 1985* (London: Associated University Presses, 1985), pp. 28–50.

7. The statement was issued November 4, 1985, reprinted in *Davar,* November 22, 1985, and translated into English in International Center for Peace in the

Middle East, *Israel Press Briefs,* 40 (December 1985), p. 17. There are many similar statements.

8. In addition to Sprinzak, *Every Man,* see Boaz Evron, *A National Reckoning* (Tel Aviv: Dvir, 1988), pp. 392–395, in Hebrew.

9. Religion acts independently of education and ethnicity in the formation of Jewish attitudes toward Arabs. The religious Jew is more likely to harbor prejudice and less likely to respect the political rights of Arabs. Ephraim Yuchtman-Yaar's chapter, "The Israeli Public and the Intifada: Attitude Change or Entrenchment?" in this volume (Chapter 12) provides additional documentation of this phenomenon, which is supported by every survey of Israeli public opinion with which I am familiar.

10. Elisha Aviner, "The Status of Ishmaelites in the State of Israel According to *Halakha,*" *T'khumin* 8 (1987), pp. 337–359, in Hebrew.

11. Overtones of this attitude in the political realm are evident in an incident that occurred during the tense days preceding the January 15, 1991, deadline for an Iraqi withdrawal from Kuwait. The general secretary of the National Religious Party demanded that in the event that Israel calls up reserves as a consequence of a U.S.-Iraqi conflict, activists from the Peace Now movement not be drafted. He indicated that the Palestinian population in the West Bank and Gaza might respond to the war by heightening the intifada. In such a case, the Israeli army would have to resort to harsh measures and Peace Now activists, according to the general secretary, would be unwilling to participate in such measures and might create a false impression in the world media (*Ha'aretz,* January 11, 1991, p. 3). Underlying this demand, in my opinion, was the belief (hope, fear) among some Israelis and Palestinians that a U.S.-Iraqi war would serve as the pretext for the Israeli army to undertake a massive expulsion of Palestinians.

12. *Hatzofeh,* June 20, 1988, p. 4. I have deliberately eschewed citing individuals known for their political extremism or forums that encourage the expression of extremist positions. Among the most horrendous in this regard are the anthologies *Tzfiya,* three of which have appeared to date. In the last issue, a rabbi from Merkaz Harav writes on the differences between Jews and non-Jews (David Bar Haim, "Israel is Called—'Man,'" *Tzfiya* 3, (n.d.), pp. 45–73, in Hebrew). After bringing proof texts, he concludes that "non-Jews are considered as animals . . . the status of non-Jews in Jewish law resembles the status of animals and there is generally no distinction between them" (p. 61). A number of articles in the anthology are overtly racist, some written by rabbis of some distinction. The most depressing aspect is not that there are learned rabbis who hold such views but that the religious establishment finds no cause to condemn them.

13. See Charles S. Liebman, *Attitudes Toward Jewish-Gentile Relations in the Jewish Tradition* (Cape Town: Kaplan Centre, University of Cape Town, 1984), and Charles S. Liebman and Steven M. Cohen, *Two Worlds of Judaism: The Jewish Experience in Israel and the United States* (New Haven, Conn.: Yale University Press, 1990).

14. Ehud Luz, *Parallels Meet: Religion and Nationalism in the Early Zionist Movement, 1882–1904* (Philadelphia: Jewish Publication Society, 1988).

15. See, for example, Haim Nahman Bialik, "HaSefer HaIvri," in *The Collected Work of H.N. Bialik* (Tel Aviv: Dvir, 9th ed., 1947), pp. 194–201, in Hebrew. The Jews were not unique in this regard. Anthony Smith describes "the new priesthood" as the "secular intellectuals committed to critical discourse" and the blueprint of a new society formed by "the romantic vision of the scholar-intellectual, redefining the community as a 'nation' whose keys are unlocked by the 'scientific' disciplines of

archeology, history, philology, anthropology and sociology" (Anthony Smith, *The Ethnic Origins of Nations* [Oxford: Basil Blackwell, 1986], p. 161).

16. See, for example, Yosef Dan, "The Hegemony of the Black Hats," *Politika* 29 (November 1989), pp. 12–15, in Hebrew.

17. *Maariv,* "Weekend Supplement," March 10, 1986, p. 12.

18. *Maariv,* December 20, 1987, p. 6.

19. Baruch Kimmerling, "Between the Primordial and the Civil Definition of the Collective Identity: *Eretz Israel* or the State of Israel?" in Erik Cohen, Moshe Lissak, and Uri Almagor, eds., *Comparative Social Dynamics: Essays in Honor of S. N. Eisenstadt* (Boulder, Colo.: Westview Press, 1985), pp. 262–283.

20. I explore this notion in greater detail in "Ritual and Ceremonial in the Reconstruction of American Judaism," in Ezra Mendelson, ed., *Studies in Contemporary Jewry VI* (New York: Oxford University Press, 1990), pp. 272–283.

21. Erik Cohen, "Citizenship, Nationality and Religion in Israel and Thailand," in Kimmerling, ed., *The Israeli State and Society* (Albany: SUNY Press, 1989), p. 70.

22. Liebman, "Jewish Ultra-Nationalism in Israel."

23. Ibid., p. 46.

24. *Yediot Aharonot,* July 6, 1989, p. 17.

25. Gideon Aran, "From Religious Zionist to a Zionist Religion: The Origin and Culture of Gush Emunim A Messianic Movement in Modern Israel." Hebrew University, Ph.D. dissertation, 1987, p. 524, in Hebrew.

26. Yosef Fund, "Agudat Israel Confronting Zionism and the State of Israel—Ideology and Policy." Bar-Ilan University, Ph.D. dissertation, 1989, in Hebrew.

27. Eliezer Don-Yehiya, "Religion and Ethnicity in Israeli Politics: The Religious Parties and the Elections to the 12th Knesset," *Medina Mimshal Veyahasim Benleumiyim* 32 (Spring 1990), pp. 11–54, in Hebrew, develops this point in some detail. See also U. O. Schmelz, Sergio DellaPergola, and Uri Avner, "Ethnic Differences Among Israeli Jews: A New Look," in David Singer, ed., *American Jewish Year Book* 90 (Philadelphia: Jewish Publication Society, 1990), pp. 3–206. The point is made in a passing reference on p. 101.

28. Ze'ev Sternhall, "The Battle for Intellectual Control," *Politika* 18 (December 1987), pp. 2–5, in Hebrew.

Selected Bibliography

Shlomo Deshen with Sigal Goldin

Abbink J. "Seged Celebration in Ethiopia and Israel: Continuity and Change of a Falasha Religious Holiday." *Anthropos 78* (1983): 789-810.

Abbink, J. "An Ethiopian Jewish 'Missionary' as Culture Broker." *Israel Social Science Research 3* (1985): 21-32.

Abramov, S.Z. *Perpetual Dilemma: Jewish Religion in the Jewish State.* Rutherford,N.J: Fairleigh Dickinson University Press, 1976.

Abramovitch, H. "An Israeli Account of a Near-Death Experience: A Case Study of Cultural Dissonance." *Journal of Near-Death Studies 6* (1988): 175-185.

Abramovitch, H. "The Jerusalem Funeral as a Microcosm of the 'Mismeeting' Between Religious and Secular Israelis." In *Jewishness and Judaism in Contemporary Israel,* 71-101, eds. Z. Sobel and B. Beit-Hallahmi. Albany: State University of N.Y Press, 1991.

Amir, Y. and Ben-Ari, R. "Enhancing Intergroup Relations in Israel: A Diferential Approach." In *Stereotyping and Prejudice,* 243-257, eds. D. Bar-Tal *et al.* N.Y.: Springer, 1989.

Aran, G. "From Religious Zionism to Zionist Religion: The Roots of Gush Emunim." *Studies in Contemporary Jewry 2* (1986): 116-143.

Aran, G. "A Mystic Messanic Interpretation of Modern Israeli History: The Six-Day War in the Religious Culture of Gush Emunim." *Studies in Contemporary Jewry 4* (1988): 263-275.

Aran, G. "Redemption as a Catastrophe: The Gospel of Gush Emunim." In *Religious Radicalism and Politics in the Middle East,* 157-177, eds. E. Sivan and M. Friedman. Albany: State University of N.Y Press, 1990.

Aronoff, M. "The Politics of Religion in a New Israeli Town." *Eastern Anthropologist 26* (1973): 145-171.

Aronoff, M. "Gush Emunim." *Political Anthropology 3* (1984): 63-84.

Aronoff, M. "The Institutionalization of Cooptation of a Charismatic, Messianic, Religious-Political Revitalization Movement." In *The Impact of Gush Emunim,* ed. D. Newman. London: Croom Helm, 1985.

Aronoff, M. "Establishing Authority: the Memorialization of Jabotinsky and the Burial of the Bar Kochba Bones in Israel Under the Likud". In *The Frailty of Authority*, 105–130, ed. M. Aronoff. New Brunswick, N.J.: Transaction Books, 1986.

Aronoff, M. "Myths, Symbols, and Rituals of the Emerging State." In *New Perspectives on Israeli History*, 175–192, ed. L.J. Silberstein. N.Y.: N.Y. University Press, 1991.

Ashkenazi, M. "'What Is This Custom?': Funeral Rites and Confusion Among Middle-Class Israelis." *Israel Social Science Research 8* (1993): 1–22.

Aviad, J. "From Protest to Return: Contemporary Tshuva." *Jerusalem Quarterly 16* (1980): 71–82.

Aviad, J. *Return To Judaism: Religious Renewal in Israel.* Chicago: University of Chicago Press, 1983.

Aviad, J. "The Contemporary Israeli Pursuit of the Millennium." *Religion 14* (1984): 199–222.

Avruch, K.A. "Gush Emunim: Religion and Ideology in Israel." *Middle East Review 11* (1979): 26–31.

Avruch, K.A. "On the 'Traditionalism' of Social Identity: American Immigrants to Israel." *Ethos 10* (1982): 95–116.

Avruch, K.A. "Gush Emunim: The 'Iceberg Model' of Extremism Reconsidered." *Middle East Review 21* (1988): 27–33.

Ayalon, H., Ben-Rafael, E. and Sharot, S. "Secularization and the Diminishing Decline of Religion." *Review of Religious Research 27* (1986): 193–207.

Ayalon, H., Ben-Rafael, E. and Sharot, S. "Religious, Ethnic and Class Divisions in Israel: Convergent or Cross Cutting?" In *Jewishness and Judaism in Contemporary Israel*, 279–305, eds. Z. Sobel and B. Beit-Hallahmi. Albany: State University of N.Y Press, 1991.

Azaryahu, M. "War Memorials and the Commemoration of the Israeli War of Independence." *Studies in Zionism 13* (1992): 57–77.

Bar-Lev M. "Cultural Characteristics and Group Image of Religious Youth." *Youth and Society 16* (1984): 153–170.

Bar-Lev, M. "Politicisation and Depoliticisation of Jewish Religious Education in Israel." *Religious Education 86* (1991): 608–618.

Bar-Lev, M. "Tradition and Inovation in Jewish Religious Education in Israel." In *Jewishness and Judaism in Contemporary Israel*, 101–135, eds. Z. Sobel and B. Beit-Hallahmi. Albany: State University of N.Y Press, 1991.

Bar-Lev, M. and Katz, Y.J. "State Religious Education in Israel: A Unique Ideological System." *Panorama 3* (1991): 93–104.

Barnea, M. and Amir, Y. "Attitudes and Attitude Change Following Intergroup

Contact of Religious and Nonreligious Students in Israel." *Journal of Social Psychology 115* (1981): 65–71.

Beit-Hallahmi, B. "Religion and Nationalism in the Arab-Israeli Conflict." *Politico 38* (1973): 232–243.

Beit-Hallahmi, B. "Judaism and the New Religions In Israel: 1970–1990." In *Jewishness and Judaism In Contemporary Israel*, 227–251, eds. Z. Sobel and B. Beit-Hallahmi. Albany: State University of N.Y Press, 1991.

Beit-Hallahmi, B. "Back to the Fold: The Return to Judaism." In *Jewishness and Judaism In Contemporary Israel*, 153–173, eds. Z. Sobel and B. Beit-Hallahmi. Albany: State University of N.Y Press, 1991.

Beit-Hallahmi, B. *Despair and Deliverance: Private Salvation in Contemporaty Israel.* Albany: State University of N.Y. Press, 1992.

Beit-Hallahmi, B. *Original Sins: Reflections on the History of Zionism and Israel.* N.Y.: Olive Branch, 1993.

Beit-Hallahmi, B. and Nevo, B. " 'Born-Again' Jews in Israel: The Dynamics of an Identity Change." *International Journal of Psychology 22* (1987): 75–81.

Ben-Ari, E. and Bilu, Y. "Saints' Sancturies in Development Towns." *Urban Anthropology 16* (1987): 243–272.

Ben-Dor, S. "The Sigd of Beta Israel: Testimony to a Community in Transition." In *Ethiopian Jews in Israel*, 140–159, eds. M.Ashkenazi and A. Weingrod. New Brunswick, N.J.: Transaction, 1987.

Ben-Rafael, E. and Sharot, S. "Ethnic Pluralism and Religious Congregations: A Comparison of Neighborhoods in Israel. *Ethnic Groups 7* (1987): 65–83.

Ben-Rafael, E. and Sharot, S. *Ethnicity, Religion, and Class in Israeli Society.* Cambridge: Cambridge University Press, 1991.

Bernstein, F. "The Socialization of Girls in an Ultra-Orthodox Institution." In *Residential Settings and the Community: Congruence and Conflict*, 13–33, eds. Y. Kashti and M. Arieli. London: Freund, 1987.

Biale, D. "The Messianic Connection: Zionism, Politics, and Settlement in Israel." *The Center Magazine* 18(1985): 35–45.

Bilu Y. "Dreams and Wishes of the Saint." In *Judaism Viewed from Within and Without*, 285–315, ed. H. Goldberg. Albany: State University of N.Y Press, 1987.

Bilu, Y. "Jewish Moroccans 'Saint Impresarios' in Israel: A Stage-Developmental Perspective." *Psychoanalytic Study of Society 15* (1990): 247–269.

Bilu, Y. "Personal Motivation and Social Meaning in the Revival of Hagiolatric Traditions Among Moroccan Jews in Israel." In *Jewishness and Judaism in Contemporary Israel*, 47–71, eds. Z. Sobel and B. Beit-Hallahmi, Albany: State University of N.Y Press, 1991.

Bilu, Y. and Abramovitch, H. "In Search of the Saddiq: Visitational Dreams Among Moroccan Jews in Israel." *Psychiatry 48* (1985): 83–92.

Bilu, Y. and Ben-Ari, E. "The Making of Modern Saints: Manufactured Charisma and the Abu-Hatseiras of Israel." *American Ethnologist 19* (1992): 672–687.

Cohen, E. "Ethnicity and Legitimation in Contemporary Israel." *Jerusalem Quarterly 28* (1983): 111–124 (also in *Politics and Society in Israel*, 320–333, ed. E. Krausz, New Brunswick, N.J.: Transaction, 1985).

Cohen, E. "Citizenship, Nationality and Religion in Israel and Thailand." In *The Israeli State and Society: Boundaries and Frontiers*, 66–93, ed. B. Kimmerling. Albany: State University of N.Y Press, 1989.

Cohen, E. "The Changing Legitimations of the State of Israel." *Studies in Contemporary Jewry 5* (1989): 148–165.

Cohen, E., Ben-Yehuda, N., and Aviad, J. "Recentering the World: The Quest for 'Elective' Centers in a Secularized Universe." *Sociological Review 35* (1987): 320–346.

Cromer, G. "Repentent Delinquents: A Religious Approach to Rehabilitation." *Jewish Journal of Sociology 23* (1981): 113–122.

Cromer, G. "The Polluted Image: The Response of Ultra-Orthodox Judaism to Israeli Television." *Sociology and Social Research 71* (1987): 198–199.

Cromer, G. "The Debate About Kahanism in Israeli Society 1984–1988." In *Occasional Papers*. N.Y.: Harry Frank Guggenheim Foundation, 1988.

Cromer, G. "'Praying With a Rifle': A Note on Religious Mofits in the Propaganda of Lehi." *Jewish Journal of Sociology 34* (1992): 121–127.

Cromer, G. "Withdrawal and Conquest: Two Aspects of the Haredi Response to Modernity." In *Jewish Fundamentalism in Comparative Perspective*, 164–180, ed. L.J. Silberstein, N.Y.: N.Y. University Press, 1993.

Deshen, S. *Immigrant Voters in Israel: Parties and Congregations in an Israeli Election Campaign*. Manchester: Manchester University Press, 1970.

Deshen, S. "Political Ethnicity and Cultural Ethnicity in Israel During the 1960s." In Urban Ethnicity, *ASA Monograph 12*, 281–309, ed. A. Cohen. London: Tavistock, 1974.

Deshen, S. "Israeli Judaism: Introduction to the Major Patterns." *International Journal of Middle East Studies 9* (1978): 141–169.

Deshen, S. "The Judaism of Middle-Eastern Immigrants." *Jerusalem Quarterly 13* (1979): 98–119.

Deshen, S. "North African Jewish Leadership and Symbolic Transformation." In *Distant Relations: Ethnicity and Politics among Arabs and North Africans Jews in Israel*, 139–153, eds. M. Shokeid and S. Deshen. N.Y.: Bergin and Praeger, 1982.

Deshen, S. "Israel: Searching for Identity." In *Religion and Society in Asia and the Middle East*, 85–118, ed. C. Caldarola. Berlin: Mouton, 1982.

Deshen, S. "Doves, Hawks, and Anthropologists: Israeli Views of Middle Eastern Settlement Proposals." In *Beyond Boundaries: Understanding, Translation, and Anthropological Discourse, 58–74*, ed. G. Palsson. Oxford: Berg, 1993.

Deshen, S. and Shokeid, M. *The Predicament of Homecoming: Cultural and Social Life of North African Immigrants in Israel.* Ithaca, N.Y.: Cornell University Press, 1974.

Diamond, J.S. *Homeland or Holy Land? The "Canaanite" Critique of Israel.* Bloomington, IN.: Indiana University Press, 1986.

Don-Yehiya, E. "The Resolution of Religious Conflict in Israel." In *Conflict and Consensus in Jewish Political Life, 203–218*, eds. S.A. Cohen and E. Don-Yehiya. Ramat-Gan: Bar-Ilan University Press, 1986.

Don-Yehiya, E. "Jewish Messianism, Religious Zionism and Israeli Politics: The Impact and Origins of Gush Emunin." *Middle Eastern Studies 23* (1987): 215–234.

Don-Yehiya, E. "Festivals and Political Culture: Independence-Day Celebrations." *Jerusalem Quarterly 45* (1988): 61–84.

Don-Yehiya, E. "Religion, Modernization and Zionism." *Modern Judaism 12* (1992): 129–155.

Don-Yehiya, E. "Hanukkah and the Myth of the Maccabees in Ideology and in Society." *Jewish Journal of Sociology 34* (1992): 5–23.

Eisenstadt, S.N. *Jewish Civilization: The Jewish Historical Experience in a Comparative Perspective.* Albany, N.Y.: State University of N.Y. Press, 1992.

Elazar, D. and Aviad, J. "Religion and Politics in Israel." In *Religion and Politics in the Middle East, 163–196*, ed. M. Curtis. Boulder, Co.: Westview, 1981.

El-Or, T. "Are They Like Their Grandmothers? A Paradox of Literacy in the Life of Ultraorthodox Jewish Women." *Anthropology and Education Quarterly 15* (1993): 61–81.

El-Or, T. "The Length of the Slits and the Spread of Luxury: Reconstructing the Subordination of Ultraorthodox Jewish Women through the Patriarchy of Men Scholars." *Sex Roles 29* (1993): 1–14.

El-Or, T. *Educated and Ignorant: Ultraorthodox Jewish Women and their World.* Boulder, Co.: Lynne Rienner, 1994.

England, I. "Law and Religion in Israel." *American Journal of Comparative Law 35* (1987): 185–208.

Etzioni-Halevy, E. and Halevy, Z. "The 'Jewish Ethic' and the 'Spirit of Achievement'." *Jewish Journal of Sociology 19* (1977): 49–66.

Fishman, A. "'Torah and Labor': The Radicalization of Religion within a National Framework." *Studies in Zionism 6* (1982): 255–271.

Fishman, A. "Religious Kibbutzim: Judaism and Modernization." *Social Forces 62* (1983): 9–31.

Fishman, A. "The Religious Kibbutz Movement: The Pursuit of a Complete Life Within an Orthodox Framework." *Studies in Contemporary Jewry 2* (1986): 97-116.

Fishman, A. "Religion and Communal Life in an Evolutionary-Functional Perspective." *Comparative Studies in Society and History 29* (1987): 763-786.

Fishman, A. "The Religious Kibbutz: A Note on the Theories of Marx, Sombart and Weber on Judaism and Economic Success." *Sociological Analysis 50* (1989): 281-290.

Florian, V. and Har-Even, D. "Fear of Personal Death: The Effects of Sex and Religious Belief." *Omega 14* (1983): 83-91.

Florian, V. and Kravetz, S. "Fear of Personal Death: Attribution, Structure and Relation to Religious Belief." *Journal of Personality and Social Psychology 44* (1983): 600-607.

Florian, V. and Kravetz, S. "Children's Concept of Death: A Cross-Cultural Comparison among Muslims, Druze, Christians and Jews in Israel." *Journal of Cross-Cultural Psychology 16* (1985): 174-189.

Florian, V., Kravetz, S. and Frankel, J. "Aspects of Fear of Personal Death: Levels of Awareness and Religious Commitment." *Journal of Research in Personality 18* (1984): 289-304.

Francis, L.J. and Katz, Y.J. "The Relationship between Personality and Religiosity in an Israeli Sample." *Journal for the Scientific Study of Religion 31* (1992): 153-162.

Friedman, M. "The NRP in Transition: Behind the Party's Electoral Decline." In *Politics and Society in Israel,* 270-297, ed. E. Krausz. New Brunswick, N.J.: Transaction, 1985.

Friedman, M. "Life Tradition and Book Tradition in the Development of Ultraorthodox Judaism." In *Judaism Viewed from Within and From Without: Anthropological Studies,* 235-255, ed. H.E. Goldberg. Albany N.Y.: State University of N.Y. Press, 1986.

Friedman, M. "Haredim Confront the Modern City." *Studies in Contemporary Jewry 2* (1986): 3-18.

Friedman, M. "The State of Israel as a Theological Dilemma." In *The Israeli State and Society: Boundaries and Frontiers,* 165-216, ed. B. Kimmerling. Albany: State University of N.Y Press, 1989.

Friedman, M. "Jewish Zealots: Conservative Versus Innovative." In *Religious Radicalism and Politics in the Middle East,* 127-143, eds. E. Sivan and M. Friedman. Albany: State University of N.Y Press, 1990.

Friedman, M. "The Haredim and the Holocaust." *Jerusalem Quarterly 53* (1990): 86-114.

Friedman, M. "The Lost *Kiddush* Cup: Changes in Ashkenazic Haredi Culture." In *The Uses of Tradition: Jewish Continuity in the Modern Era,*

175-186, ed. J. Wertheimer. Cambridge MA.: Harvard University Press, 1992.

Friedman, M. "The Market Model and Religious Radicalism." In *Fundamentalism in Comparative Perspective*, pp. 192-215, ed. L.J. Silberstein, N.Y.: N.Y. University Press, 1993.

Friedman, M. "The Ultra-Orthodox and Israeli Society." In *Whither Israel? The Domestic Challenges*, 177-201, ed. K. Kyle and J. Peters. London: Tauris, 1993.

Gilad, L. *Ginger and Salt: Yemeni Jewish Women in an Israeli Town.* Boulder, Co.: Westview, 1989.

Glanz, D. and Harrison, M. "Varieties of Identity Transformation: The Case Study of Newly Orthodox Jews." *Jewish Journal of Sociology 20* (1978): 129-141.

Goldberg, G. and Ben-Zadok, E. "Gush Emunim in the West Bank." *Middle Eastern Studies 22* (1986):52-73.

Goldberg, H. "Culture and Ethnicity in the Study of Israeli Society." *Ethnic Groups 1* (1977): 163-186.

Goldscheider, C. and Friedlander, D. "Religiosity Patterns in Israel." *American Jewish Year Book 83* (1983): 3-41.

Goshen-Gottstein, E.R. "Courtship, Marriage and Pregnancy in 'Geula': A Study of an Ultra-Orthodox Jerusalem Group." *Psychiatry 4* (1966): 1-24.

Goshen-Gottstein, E.R. "Growing Up in 'Geula': Socialization and Family Living in an Ultra-Orthodox Jewish Subculture." *Psychiatry 21* (1984): 37-55.

Goshen-Gottstein, E.R. "Mental Health Implications of Living in an Ultra-Orthodox Jewish Subculture." *Psychiatry 24* (1987): 145-166.

Gurevitch, M. and Schwartz, G. "Television and the Sabbath Culture in Israel." *Jewish Journal of Sociology 13* (1971): 65-71.

Gutmann, E. "Religion and its Role in National Integration in Israel." In *Religion and Politics in the Middle East,* 197-205, ed. M. Curtis. Boulder, Co.: Westview, 1981.

Guttmann, J. "Cognitive Morality and Cheating Behavior in Religious and Secular School Children." *Journal of Education Research 77* (1984): 249-254.

Gutwirth, J. "Réligieux et Laics en Israel: Forces Opposées ou Complémentaires?" *Archives des Sciences Sociales des Religions 49* (1980): 61-66.

Handelman, D. *Models and Mirrors: Towards an Anthropology of Public Events.* Cambridge: Cambridge University Press, 1990.

Handelman, D. and Shamgar-Handelman, L. "Shaping Time: The Choice of the National Emblem of Israel." in *Culture Through Time,* 193-226, ed. E. Ohnuki-Tierney. Stanford: Stanford University Press, 1990.

Handelman, D. and Shamgar-Handelman, L. "The Presence of the Dead: Memorials of National Death in Israel." *Suomen Antropologi 4* (1991): 3-17.

Hartman, M. "Pronatalistic Tendencies and Religiosity in Israel." *Sociology and Social Research 68* (1984): 247-258.

Haskell, G.H. *From Sofia to Jaffa: The Jews of Bulgaria and Israel.* Detroit: Wayne State University Press, 1994.

Hattis Rolef, S. (ed.). *The Dilemma of Religion and Politics: Attitudes and Positions Within the Israeli Labor Movement on Religious Pluralism.* Jerusalem: Semana, 1986.

Hazan, H. "Religion in an Old Age Home: Symbolic Adaptation as a Survival Strategy." *Aging and Society 4* (1984): 137-156.

Heilman, S.C. *The People of the Book.* Chicago: University of Chicago Press, 1983.

Heilman, S.C. "Religious Jewry in the Secular Press: Aftermath of 1988 Elections." In *Religious and Secular: Conflict and Accommodation Between Jews in Israel,* 45-67, ed. C.S. Liebman. Jerusalem: Keter, 1990.

Heilman, S.C. *Defenders of the Faith: Inside Ultra-Orthodox Jewry.* N.Y.: Schocken, 1992.

Herman, S.N. *Israelis and Jews: The Continuity of an Identity.* N.Y.: Random House, 1970.

Herman, S.N. *Jewish Identity: a Social Psychological Perspective.* Beverly Hills: Sage, 1977.

Hertzberg, A. "The Religious Right in the State of Israel." *Annals of the American Academy of Political and Social Science 483* (1986): 84-92.

Huppert, U. *Back to the Ghetto: Zionism in Retreat.* Buffalo N.Y.: Prometheus, 1988.

Kamen, C. S. "Affirmation or Enjoyment? The Commemoration of Independence in Israel." *Jewish Journal of Sociology 19* (1977): 5-20.

Kaplan, L. "The Hazon Ish: Haredi Critic of Traditional Orthodoxy." In *The Uses of Tradition: Jewish Continuity in the Modern Era,* 145-173, ed. J. Wertheimer. Cambridge, MA.: Harvard University Press, 1992 .

Kaplan, S. "The Beta Israel and the Rabbinate: Law, Ritual and Politics." *Social Science Information 27* (1988): 357-370.

Katz, E. "Culture and Communication in Israel: The Transformation of Tradition." *Jewish Journal of Sociology 15* (1973): 5-21.

Katz, E. and Gurevitch, M. *The Secularization of Leisure: Culture and Communication in Israel.* Cambridge: Harvard University Press, 1976.

Katz, Y.J. "High School Headmasters' Evaluations of Teachers Trained at Universities and Theological Colleges." *British Journal of Religious Education 19* (1988): 102-107.

Katz, Y.J. "The Connection between Religious Observance and Beliefs and

Religiosity Education." *Panorama 2* (1990): 59-63.

Katz, Y.J. and Schmida, M. "Religiosity of Students in the Israeli National-Religious Comprehensive High School." *British Journal of Religious Education 13* (1991): 109-113.

Kedem, P. "Dimensions of Jewish Religiosity." In *Tradition, Innovation, Conflict: Jewishness and Judaism in Contemporary Israel,* 251-172, eds. Z. Sobel and B. Beit-Hallahmi. Albany N.Y.: University of N.Y. Press, 1991.

Kedem, P. and Bar-Lev, M. "Is Giving up Traditional Religious Culture Part of the Price to be Paid For Acquiring Higher Education?" *Higher Education 12* (1983): 373-388.

Kimmerling, B. "Between the Primordial and the Civil Definitions of the Collective Identity: Eretz Israel or the State of Israel?" In *Comparative Social Dynamics: Essays in Honor of S.N. Eisenstadt,* 262-283, eds. E. Cohen *et al.* Boulder, CO.: Westview, 1985.

Klingman, A. and Wiener, E. "Analysis of Israeli Children's Fear: A Comparison of Religious and Secular Communities." *International Journal of Social Psychology 29* (1983): 269-274.

Kraines, O. *The Impossible Dilemma: Who is a Jew in the State of Israel.* N.Y.: Bloch, 1976.

Krausz, E. and Bar-Lev, M. "Varieties of Orthodox Religious Behavior: A Case Study of Yeshiva High School Graduates in Israel." *Jewish Journal of Sociology 20* (1978): 59-74.

Kronish, R. (ed.) *Towards the Twenty-First Century: Judaism and the Jewish People in Israel and America.* N.Y.: Ktav, 1988.

Landau, D. *Piety and Power: The World of Jewish Fundamentalism.* N.Y.: Secker & Warburg, 1993.

Lehman-Wilzig, S. and Goldberg, G. "Religious Protest and Police Reaction in a Theo-Democracy: Israel, 1950-1979." *Journal of Church and State 25* (1983):494-500.

Leslau, A., Polovin, A. and Bar-Lev, M. "Subjective Well-Being on Religious Kibbutzim: The Second Generation." *Israel Social Science Research 8* (1993): 27-46.

Levi, S., Lewinson, H. and Katz, E. *Beliefs, Observances, and Social Interaction Among Israeli Jews.* Jerusalem: Louis Guttman Israel Institute of Applied Social Research, 1993.

Lewis, H. *After the Eagles Landed: The Yemenites in Israel.* Boulder, Co.: Westwood, 1989.

Lichtenstein, A. "Ideology of Hesder." *Tradition 19* (1981): 199-217.

Liebman, C.S. "Extremism as a Religious Norm." *Journal for the Scientific Study of Religion 22* (1983): 75-86.

Liebman, C.S. "The 'Who is a Jew?' Controversy: Political and Anthropological Perspectives." In *Conflict and Consensus in Jewish Political Life,*

194-203, eds. S.A. Cohen and E. Don-Yehiya. Ramat-Gan: Bar-Ilan University Press, 1986.

Liebman,C.S. "The Religious Component in Israeli Ultra-Nationalism." *Jerusalem Quarterly* 41 (1987): 127-144.

Liebman, C.S. "The Jewish Religion and Contemporary Jewish Nationalism." In *Religious Radicalism and Politics in the Middle East*, 77-95, eds. E.Sivan and M. Friedman. Albany: State University of N.Y Press, 1990.

Liebman, C.S. "Relations Between Dati and Non-Dati Jews: Some Final Reflections." In *Religious and Secular: Conflict and Accommodation Between Jews in Israel*, 215-231, ed. C.S. Liebman. Jerusalem: Keter, 1990.

Liebman, C.S. "Religion and Democracy in Israel." In *Israeli Democracy under Stress*, 273-292, ed. E. Sprinzak and L. Diamond. Boulder, Col.: Lynne Rienner, 1993.

Liebman, C.S. and Cohen, S.M. *Two Worlds of Judaism: The Israeli and American Experiences*. New Haven: Yale University Press, 1990.

Liebman, C.S. and Don-Yehiya, E. *Civil Religion in Israel: Traditional Judaism and Political Culture in the Jewish State*. Berkeley: University of California Press, 1983.

Liebman, C.S. and Don-Yehiya, E. *Religion and Politics in Israel*. Bloomington: Indiana University Press, 1984.

Lilker, S. *Kibbutz Judaism: A New Tradition in the Making*. N.Y.: Herzl Press, 1982.

Lustick, I.S. *For the Lord and the Land: Jewish Fundementalism in Israel*. N.Y.: Council for Foreign Relations, 1988.

Lustick, I.S. "Jewish Fundamentalism and the Israeli-Palestinian Impasse." In *Jewish Fundamentalism in Comparative Perspective*, 104-116, ed. L.J. Silberstein. N.Y.: N.Y. University Press, 1993.

Neuman, S. and Zeiderman, A. "How Does Fertility Relate to Religiosity?: Survey Evidence Fron Israel." *Sociology and Social Research 70* (1986): 178-180.

Nevo, N. "Religiosity and Community: A Case Study of a Gush Emunim Settlement." In *The Impact of Gush Emunim*, 221-244, ed. D. Newman. London: Croom Helm, 1985.

Newman, D. (ed.) *The Impact of Gush Emunim*. London: Croom Helm, 1985.

Newman, D. "Gush Emunim Between Fundamentalism and Pragmatism." *Jerusalem Quarterly 39* (1986): 33-43.

Notzer, N., Levran, D. Mashiach, S. and Soffer, S. "Effects of Religiosity on Sex Attitudes, Experience and Conception among University Students." *Journal of Sex and Marital Therapy 10* (1984): 57-62.

O'Dea, J. "Gush Emunim: Roots and Ambiguities." *Forum 25* (1976): 39-50.

Oz. A. *In the Land of Israel*. London: Fontana, 1983.

Paine, R. "Israel and Totemic Time?" *RAIN 59* (1983): 19–22.

Paine, R. "Jewish Ontologies of Time and Political Legitimation in Israel." In *The Politics of Time*, 150–170, ed. H.J. Rutz. Washington D.C.: American Anthropological Association, 1992.

Peres, Y. "Religious Adherence and Political Attitudes." *Sociological Papers* (Bar-Ilan University), October 1992.

Poll, S. and Krausz, E. (eds.) *On Ethnic and Religious Diversity in Israel*. Ramat-Gan: Bar-Ilan University Press, 1975.

Ravitzky, A. "Roots of Kahanism: Consciousness and Political Reality." *Jerusalem Quarterly 39* (1986): 90–108.

Ravitzky, A. "Religious Radicalism and Political Messianism in Israel." In *Religious Radicalism and Politics in the Middle East*, 11–39, eds. E.Sivan and M. Friedman. Albany: State University of N.Y Press, 1990.

Rim, Y. and Kurzweil, Z.E. "A Note on Attitudes to Risk-Taking of Observant and Nonobservant Jews." *Jewish Journal of Sociology 7* (1965): 238–245.

Rim, Y. and Jacobsen, C. "Traditional Jewish Values, Personality and Sex." *Journal of Psychology and Judaism 11* (1987): 196–204.

Roniger, L. "From Eulogy to Announcements: Death Notices in the Jewish Press since the Late Eighteenth Century." *Omega 25* (1992): 133–168.

Rosenheim, E. and Muchnik, B. "Death Concerns in Differential Levels of Consciousness as Function of Defense Strategy and Religious Belief." *Omega 15* (1984–5): 15–24.

Rubin, N. "Death Customs in a Non-Religious Kibbutz." *Journal for the Scientific Study of Religion 25* (1986): 292–303.

Schiff, G.S. *Tradition and Politics: The Religious Parties of Israel*. Detroit: Wayne State University Press, 1977.

Schmelz, U.O. "Religiosity and Fertility Among the Jews of Jerusalem." In *Jewish Demography*. Jerusalem: Hebrew University, 1985.

Schneller, R. "Continuity and Change in Ultra-Orthodox Education." *Jewish Journal of Sociology 22* (1980): 35–46.

Schneller, R. "The Science-Religion Problem: Attitudes of Religious Israeli Youth." *Youth and Society 13* (1982): 251–282.

Schwartz, B., Zerubavel, Y. and Barnett, B. "The Recovery of Masada: A Study in Collective Memory." *Sociological Quarterly 27* (1986): 147–164.

Schwartzwald, J. and Leslau, A. "Religiosity, Subjective Norms, and Educational Attitudes in the Choice of Religious Education by Israeli Parents." *Journal for the Scientific Study of Religion 31* (1992): 261–278.

Segre, D.V. *A Crisis of Identity: Israel and Zionism*. Oxford: Oxford University Press, 1980.

Sered, S. "Ritual, Morality and Gender: The Religious Lives of Oriental Jewish Women in Jerusalem." *Israel Social Science Research 5* (1987): 87–96.

Sered, S. "The Religion of Elderly Oriental Jewish Women." *Man* 23 (1988): 506-521.

Sered, S. "Rachel's Tomb: Societal Liminality and the Revitalization of a Shrine." *Religion 19* (1989): 27-40.

Sered, S. "Women, Religion and Modernization: Tradition and Transformation Among Elderly Jews in Israel." *American Anthropologist 92* (1990): 306-318.

Sered, S. *Women as Ritual Experts: The Religious Lives of Elderly Jewish Women in Jerusalem.* Oxford: Oxford University Press, 1992.

Sered, S. "Religious Rituals and Secular Rituals: Interpenetrating Models of Childbirth in a Modern Israeli Context." *Sociology of Religion 54* (1993): 101-114.

Shaffir, W. "The Recruiment of Baalei Tshuva in a Jerusalem Yeshiva." *Jewish Journal of Sociology 25* (1983): 33-46.

Shaffir, W. "Conversion Experiences: Newcomers to and Defectors from Orthodox Judaism." In *Jewishness and Judaism in Contemporary Israel,* 173-203, eds. Z. Sobel and B. Beit-Hallahmi. Albany: State University of N.Y Press, 1991.

Shaffir, W. and Rockaway, R. "Leaving the Ultra-Orthodox Fold: Haredi Jews Who Defected." *Jewish Journal of Sociology 29* (1987): 97-115.

Sharkansky, U. "The Prophetic Tradition in Modern Israel." *Jewish Journal of Sociology 30* (1988): 85-95.

Sharot, S. "Sociological Analyses of Religion: Israel." *Sociological Analysis 51* (1990): 63-76.

Sharot, S. "Judaism and the Secularization Debate." Sociological Analysis 52 (1991): 255-275.

Shavit, Y. *The New Hebrew Nation: A Study in Israeli Heresy and Fantasy.* London: Frank Cass, 1987.

Shilhav, Y. "The Emergence of Ultra-Orthodox Neighborhoods in Israeli Urban Centers." In *Local Communities and the Israeli Polity: Conflict of Values and Interests,* 157-187, ed. E. Ben-Zadok, Albany: State University of N.Y. Press, 1993.

Shokeid, M. *The Dual Heritage: Immigrants from the Altas Mounains in an Israeli Village.* Manchester: Manchester University Press, 1971 (augmented edition, New Brunswick N.J.: Transaction, 1985).

Shokeid, M. "Conviviality Versus Strife: Peacemaking at Parties among Atlas Mountains Immigrants in Israel." In *Freedom and Constraint,* 101-121, ed. M.J. Aronoff. Amsterdam: Van Gorcum, 1976.

Shokeid, M. "The Decline of Personal Endowment of Atlas Mountains Religious Leaders in Israel." *Anthropological Quarterly 52* (1979): 186-197.

Shokeid, M. "From Personal Endowment to Bureaucratic Appointment: The

Transition in Israel of the Communal Religious Leaders of Moroccan Jews." *Journal for the Scientific Study of Religion 19* (1980): 105-13.

Shokeid, M. "Cultural Ethnicity in Israel: The Case of Middle Eastern Jews' Religiosity." *Association of Jewish Studies Review 9* (1986): 247-271.

Shokeid, M. "Contemporary Jewish Pilgrimages in Israel." In *Encyclopedia of Religion*, 346-347, ed. M. Eliade. N.Y.: Free Press, 1987.

Shokeid, M. *Children of Cicumstances: Israeli Emigrants in New York.* Ithaca, N.Y.: Cornell University Press, 1988.

Shokeid, M. and Deshen, S. *Distant Relations: Ethnicity and Politics among Arabs and North African Jews in Israel.* N.Y.: Bergin & Praeger, 1982.

Shuval, J.T. "The Structure and Dilemmas of Israeli Pluralism." In *The Israeli State and Society: Boundaries and Frontiers*, 216-237, ed. B. Kimmerling. Albany: State University of N.Y Press, 1989.

Silberstein, L.J. (ed.) *Jewish Fundamentalism in Comparative Perspective: Religion, Ideology and the Crisis of Modernity.* N.Y.: N.Y University Press, 1993.

Sivan, E. and Friedman, M. (eds.). *Religious Radicalism and Politics in the Middle East.* Albany: State University of N.Y. Press, 1990.

Smooha, S. *Israel Pluralism and Conflict.* London: Routledge & Kegan Paul, 1978.

Smooha, S. *Social Research on Jewish Ethnicity in Israel 1948-1986.* Haifa: Haifa University Press, 1987.

Sobel, Z. "Conflict and Communitas: The Interplay of Religion, Ethnicity and Community in a Galilee Village." In *Jewishness and Judaism in Contemporary Israel*, 25-47, eds. Z. Sobel and B. Beit-Hallahmi. Albany: State University of N.Y Press, 1991.

Sobel, Z. *A Small Place in Galilee: Religion and Social Conflict in an Israeli Village.* N.Y.: Holmes & Meier, 1993.

Sprinzak, E. "Gush Emunim: The Tip of the Iceberg." *The Jerusalem Quarterly 21* (1981): 28-47.

Sprinzak, E. "Kach and Rabbi Meir Kahane: The Emergence of Jewish Quasi-Fascism." In *The Elections in Israel 1984,* 169-187, eds. A. Arian and M. Shamir. Tel Aviv: Ramot, 1986.

Sprinzak, E. *The Ascendance of Israel's Radical Right.* Oxford: Oxford University Press, 1991.

Sprinzak, E. "Three Models of Religious Violence: The Case of Jewish Fundamentalism in Israel." in *Fundamentalisms and the State*, 462-490, eds. M. Marty and R. Scott Appleby. Chicago: University of Chicago Press, 1992.

Stahl, A. "Ritualistic Reading Among Oriental Jews." *Anthropological Quarterly 52* (1979): 115-120.

Stahl, A. "Parents' Attitudes Toward the Death of Infants in the Traditional Jewish-Oriental Family." *Journal of Comparative Family Studies 22* (1991): 75-83.

Strum, P. "Women and the Politics of Religion in Israel." *Human Rights Quarterly 11* (1989): 483-503.

Tabory, E. "State and Religion: Religious Conflict Among Jews in Israel." *Church and State 23* (1981): 275-283.

Tabory, E. "Reform and Conservative Judaism in Israel: A Social and Religious Profile." *American Jewish Year Book 83* (1983): 41-65.

Tabory, E. "Pluralism in the Jewish State: Reform and Conservative Judaism in Israel." In *Conflict and Consensus in Jewish Political Life*, 170-194, eds. S.A. Cohen and E. Don-Yehiya. Ramat-Gan: Bar-Ilan University Press, 1986.

Tabory, E. "Residential Integration and Religious Segregation in an Israeli Neighborhood." *International Journal of Intercultural Relations 13* (1989): 19-35.

Tabory, E. "Living in a Mixed Neighborhood." In *Religious and Secular: Conflict and Accommodation Between Jews in Israel*, 113-131, ed. C.S. Liebman. Jerusalem: Keter, 1990.

Tabory, E. "The Identity Dilemma of Non-Orthodox Religious Movements: Reform and Conservative Judaism in Israel." In *Jewishness and Judaism in Contemporary Israel*, 135-153, eds. Z. Sobel and B. Beit-Hallahmi. Albany: State University of N.Y. Press, 1991.

Tabory, E. and Lazerwitz, B. "Americans in the Israeli Reform and Conservative Denominations." *Review of Religious Research 24* (1983): 177-187.

Tal, U. "Contemporary Hermeneutics and Self-Views on the Relationship between State and Land." In *the Land of Israel: Jewish Perspectives*, ed., L. Hoffman. Notre Dame In.: University of Notre Dame Press, 1988.

Tessler, M. "Religion and Politics in the Jewish State of Israel." In *Religious Resurgence and Politics in the Contemporary World*, 263-291, ed. E. Sahliyeh. Albany, N.Y.: State University of N.Y. Press, 1990.

Trevisan Semi, E. "The Beta Israel (Falashas): From Purity to Impurity." *Jewish Journal of Sociology 27* (1985): 103-115.

Warburg, M. "Religious Renewal in Orthodox Judaism in Israel: An Interpretation." *Social Compass 38* (1991): 63-71.

Waxman, H. "Religion and State in Israel: The Perspective of American Jewry." In *Israel and Diaspora Jewry: Ideological and Political Perspectives*, 97-107, ed. E. Don-Yehiya. Ramat-Gan: Bar-Ilan University Press, 1991.

Webber, J. "Religions in the Holy Land: Conflicts of Interpretation." *Anthropology Today 1* (1985): 3-10.

Weil, S. "The Influence of Caste Ideology in Israel." In *Cultural Transition: The Case of Immigrant Youth*, 150-161, ed. M. Gottesmann. Jerusalem: Magnes, 1988.

Weil, S. "Ethiopian Jews in Israel: A Survey of Research and Documentation." *Jewish Folklore and Ethnology Review 2* (1989): 28-32.

Weiler, G. *Jewish Theocracy.* Leiden: Brill, 1988.

Weingrod, A. "Rashomon in Jerusalem." *European Journal of Sociology 22* (1981): 158-169.

Weingrod, A. *The Saint of Beersheba.* Albany, N.Y.: State University of N.Y Press, 1990.

Weingrod, A. "Saints and Shrines, Politics and Culture: A Morroco-Israel Comparison." In *Muslim Travellers,* 217-235, eds. D. Eickelman and J. Piscatori. Berkeley: University of California Press, 1990.

Weingrod, A. "Changing Israeli Landscapes: Buildings and the Uses of the Past." *Cultural Anthropology 8* (1993): 370-387.

Weissbrod, L. "Gush Emunim Ideology: From Religious Doctrine to Political Action." *Middle Eastern Studies 18* (1982): 265-275.

Weissbrod, L. "Religion as National Identity in a Secular Society." *Review of Religious Research 24* (1983): 188-205.

Weller, L. "Effects of Religiosity on Attitudes and Behavior." In *Jewishness and Judaism in Contemporary Israel,* 227-251, eds. Z. Sobel and B. Beit-Hallahmi. Albany: State University of N.Y Press, 1991.

Weller, L., Levinbok, S., Maimon, R. and Shoshan, H. "Religiosity and Authoritarianism." *Journal of Social Psychology 15* (1985): 726-734.

Weller, L. and Topper Weller, S. "Strange Bedfellows: A Study of Mixed Religious Marriages." In *Religious and Secular: Conflict and Accommodation Between Jews in Israel,* 173-193, ed. C.S. Liebman. Jerusalem: Keter, 1990.

Willner, D. "Politics and Change in Israel: The Case of Land Settlement." *Human Organization 24* (1965): 65-72.

Willis, A.P. "Shas—The Sephardic Torah Guardians: Religious 'Movement' and Political Power." In *The Elections in Israel,* 1992, eds. A. Arian and M. Shamir. Albany, N.Y.: State University of N.Y. Press, forthcoming.

Wiztum, E., Greenberg, D. and Buchbinder, J.T. "'A Very Narrow Bridge': Diagnosis and Management of Mental Illness among Bratslav Hassidim." *Psychotherapy 27* (1990): 124-131.

Yaron, Z. "Religion in Israel." *American Jewish Year Book 76* (1976): 41-90.

Yassif, E. "Storytelling of the 'Repentance Movement': Folklore and Cultural Debate in Contemporary Israel." *Jewish Folklore and Ethnology Review 14* (1992): 26-32.

Yinon, Y. and Sharon, E. "Similarity in Religiousness of Solicitor, the Potential Helper and the Recipient as Determinants of Donating Behaviour." *Journal of Applied Social Psychology 15* (1985): 726-734.

Yogev, A. and El-Dor, J. "Attitudes and Tendencies Toward Return to Judaism Among Israeli Adolescents: Seekers or Drifters?" *Jewish Journal of Sociology 29* (1987): 5-8.

Young, J. *The Texture of Memory: Holocaust Memorials and Meaning.* New Haven: Yale University Press, 1993.

Zaidman-Dvir, N. and Sharot, S. "The Response of Israeli Society to New Religious Movements: ISKCON and Teshuvah." *Journal for the Scientific Study of Religion 31* (1992): 279-295.

Zenner, W. "Saints and Piecemeal Supernaturalism Among the Jerusalem Sephardim." *Anthropological Quarterly 38* (1965): 201-217.

Zerubavel, Y. "New Beginning, Old Past: The Collective Memory of Pioneering in Israeli Culture." In *New Perspectives on Israeli History,* 193-215, ed. L.J. Silberstein. N.Y.: N.Y. University Press, 1991.

Zerubavel, Y. *Recovered Roots: Collective Memory and the Making of Israeli National Tradition.* Chicago: University of Chicago Press, 1994.

Zuckerman-Bareli, C. "The Religious Factor in Opinion Formation Among Israeli Youth." In *On Ethnic and Religious Diversity in Israel,* 53-89, eds. S. Poll and E. Krausz. Ramat-Gan: Bar-Ilan University Press, 1975.

About the Authors

GIDEON ARAN (Ph.D. Jerusalem 1987), lecturer in sociology and anthropology at the Hebrew University, works on political radicalism and religious zealotry. Among his publications are "Jewish-Zionist Fundamentalism" in *Fundamentalism Observed*, M. Marty and S. Appleby, eds. (Chicago 1991).

HANNA AYALON (Ph.D. Tel Aviv 1985) is senior lecturer in education and in sociology and anthropology at Tel Aviv University. Her main field is sociology of education and stratification, and her work on religion focuses on the link with religiosity. Among her publications are *Community in Transition* (with E. Ben-Rafael and A. Yogev, Greenwood 1993), "A Second Chance for Whom? The Social Impact of non-Regular Education in Israel" *Comparative Education Review* (34, 1990).

EYAL BEN-ARI (Ph.D. Cambridge 1984) is senior lecturer in the department of sociology and anthropology at the Hebrew University. His areas of research include modern Japan, the Israeli army, and saint veneration in Israel. Among his publications are *Changing Japanese Suburbia* (Kegan Paul, 1991) and *Unwrapping Japan* (with B. Moeran and J. Valentine, Manchester 1991).

ELIEZER BEN-RAFAEL (Ph.D. Jerusalem 1973) is professor of sociology at Tel-Aviv University. He studies ethnicity, bilingualism, and kibbutz sociology. Among his publications *Language, Identity and Social Division* (Oxford 1994), *Ethnicity, Status, Power and Conflict in the Kibbutz* (Aldershot UK 1988), *The Emergence of Ethnicity: Cultural Groups and Social Conflict in Israel* (Greenwood 1982), *Ethnicity, Religion, and Class in Israeli Society* (with S. Sharot, Cambridge 1991).

YORAM BILU (Ph.D. Jerusalem 1979) is associate professor in the departments of psychology and of sociology and anthropology at the Hebrew University. His research interests include ethnopsychiatry, folk-religion, and culture and dreaming. He has published in anthropological, psychological and psychiatric journals.

SHLOMO DESHEN (Ph.D. Manchester 1968) is professor of anthropology at Tel-Aviv University. His main research is on the cultures of Middle-Eastern

Jews, and on the anthropology of disabilities. In the area of religion Deshen focuses on the religion of Israeli Sephardim. Among his publications are *Blind People* (SUNY 1992), *The Mellah Society* (Chicago 1989), *The Predicament of Homecoming* (with M. Shokeid, Cornell 1974).

ELIEZER DON-YEHIYA (Ph.D. Jerusalem 1978) is professor of political science at Bar-Ilan University. His main research is in political culture, party politics, and religion and Israeli politics. Among his publications are *Religion and Politics in Israel* (Indiana 1984), *Civil Religion in Israel* (California 1983, both with C. Liebman).

SHMUEL N. EISENSTADT (Ph.D. London 1947) is a fellow of the Israel Academy of Sciences and professor emeritus of sociology at the Hebrew University. A recipient of many awards, he has published numerous books on social theory, comparative cultures, historical sociology, and other fields. In the area of Judaism his recent work is *Jewish Civilization* (SUNY 1993).

TAMAR EL-OR (Ph.D. Bar-Ilan 1990) is a lecturer in social anthropology at the Hebrew University. Her research interests include women and literacy. Among her publications are *Educated and Ignorant* (Rienner 1994), with G. Aran "Material Thinking: Women, Political Action and Fundamentalism on the West Bank," *Gender and Society* (1994).

ARYEI FISHMAN (Ph.D. Jerusalem 1976) is associate professor emeritus of sociology at Bar-Ilan University. His research is on Judaism as a religious culture, social movements and communal societies. Among his publications are *Judaism and Modernization on the Religious Kibbutz* (Cambridge 1992), and *Hapoel Hamizrahi 1921–1935 (Documents)* (Tel Aviv 1979, Hebrew).

MENACHEM FRIEDMAN (Ph.D. Jerusalem 1973) is in the department of sociology and anthropology at Bar-Ilan University. His main research is on ultraorthodox Jewry. Among his publications are *Society and Religion: The Non-Zionist Orthodox in Eretz-Israel, 1918–1936* (Ben-Zvi Institute 1977, Hebrew), *Haredi Society* (Jerusalem Institute for Research 1991, Hebrew), and many papers in English, Hebrew and French.

SIGAL GOLDIN (B.A. Tel-Aviv 1992) is a graduate student in sociology at Tel-Aviv University.

DON HANDELMAN (Ph.D. Manchester 1971), professor of anthropology at the Hebrew University, studies symbolism, play, mythology, and state organization, in Israel and in South India. Among his publications are *Models and Mirrors* (Cambridge 1990); with L. Shamgar-Handelman, "Shaping Time: The Choice of the National Emblem of Israel," in *Culture Through Time*, E. Ohnuki-Tierney ed. (Stanford 1990); "The Presence of the Dead: Memorials of National Death in Israel," *Journal of the Finnish Anthropological Society* (16, 1991).

ELIHU KATZ (Ph.D. Columbia 1956) is professor emeritus of sociology and communication at the Hebrew University, Scientific Director of the Guttman Institute of Applied Social Research, and Trustee Professor of communication at the University of Pennsylvania. He has recently worked on the international flow of television programs (Liebes and Katz, *The Export of Meaning*, Polity 1993), and on the broadcasting of ceremonial events (Dayan and Katz, *Media Events* (Harvard 1992).

BERNARD LAZERWITZ (Ph.D. Michigan 1959) is professor emeritus of sociology at Bar-Ilan University, and studies migration and urban housing. Among his publications are *The Israeli Condominium System and Social Integration* (with C. Schwartz, Bar-Ilan 1993); *Americans Abroad* (with A. Dashefsky, J. deAmicis, and E. Tabory, Plenum 1992); and "Metropolitan Size and Participation in Religio-Ethnic Communities," *Journal for the Scientific Study of Religion* (31, 1992).

CHARLES S. LIEBMAN (Ph.D. Illinois 1960), professor of political science at Bar-Ilan University, studies religion and politics in Israel, and American Jews. Currently he is concerned with political myths. Among his publications are "The Myth of Defeat: The Response of Israeli Society to the Yom Kippur War" *Middle Eastern Studies* (July 1993) and *Two Worlds of Judaism: The Israeli and American Experiences* (with S.M. Cohen, Yale 1990).

YOCHANAN PERES (Ph.D. Jerusalem 1968) is associate professor of sociology at Tel-Aviv University. His research interests include sociology of the family, ethnic relations, and politics. He has published *Ethnic Relations in Israel* (Ha'poalim 1977, Hebrew), and *Trends in Israeli Democracy* (with E. Ya'ar, Renner 1991), and many papers.

NISSAN RUBIN (Ph.D. Bar-Ilan 1977) is associate professor of sociology at Bar-Ilan University. His main areas of research are ritual in modern society, the sociology of Talmudic texts, and rites of passage in ancient Judaism. Among his publications are *Birth Rites in Mishnaic and Talmudic Times* (Ha-kibbutz Ha-meuchad 1993, Hebrew).

SUSAN SERED (Ph.D. Jerusalem 1986) is senior lecturer in anthropology at Bar-Ilan University. Her main area of research is the intersection of religion and gender. Among her publications are *Women as Ritual Experts* (Oxford 1992), and "Women, Religion, and Modernization: Tradition and Transformation among Elderly Jews in Israel," *American Anthropologist* (1990).

STEPHEN SHAROT (D.Phil Oxford 1969) is professor of sociology at Ben Gurion University. His main areas of research are the sociology of religion and ethnicity. Among his publications: *Judaism: A Sociology* (Holmes and Meier 1976) and *Messianism, Mysticism, and Magic* (North Carolina 1982)

MOSHE SHOKEID (Ph.D. Manchester 1968), professor of anthropology at Tel-Aviv University, has studied minorities: North African immigrants, Israeli Arabs, Israeli emigrants in New York. Recently he studied an American gay synagogue. Among his publications: *Children of Circumstances* (Cornell 1988), *Distant Relations* (with S. Deshen, Praeger 1982), *The Dual Heritage* (Manchester 1971; Transaction 1985), *A Gay Synagogue in New York* (forthcoming, Columbia).

EPHRAIM TABORY (Ph.D. Bar-Ilan 1981), senior lecturer in sociology at Bar-Ilan University, works on Reform and Conservative denominations in Israel, and relationships between religious and non-religious Jews. Among his publications: "Jewish Identity, Israeli Nationality and Soviet Jewish Migration," *Journal of Church and State* (33, 1991), "Avoidance and Conflict: Perceptions Regarding Contact Between Religious and Nonreligious Jews in Israel," *Journal for the Scientific Study of Religion* (1993).